Elusive
Equality

SECOND EDITION

Elusive Equality

Women's Rights, Public Policy, and the Law

Susan Gluck Mezey

LYNNE
RIENNER
PUBLISHERS

BOULDER
LONDON

Published in the United States of America in 2011 by
Lynne Rienner Publishers, Inc.
1800 30th Street, Boulder, Colorado 80301
www.rienner.com

and in the United Kingdom by
Lynne Rienner Publishers, Inc.
3 Henrietta Street, Covent Garden, London WC2E 8LU

Library of Congress Cataloging-in-Publication Data
Mezey, Susan Gluck, 1944–
  Elusive equality : women's rights, public policy, and the law / by Susan
Gluck Mezey. — 2nd ed.
    p. cm.
  Includes bibliographical references and index.
  ISBN 978-1-58826-770-2 (pb : alk. paper) 1. Sex discrimination against
women—Law and legislation—United States. I. Title.
  KF4758.M49 2011
  342.7308'78—dc22

                                                    2011009472

British Cataloguing in Publication Data
A Cataloguing in Publication record for this book
is available from the British Library.

Printed and bound in the United States of America

The paper used in this publication meets the requirements
of the American National Standard for Permanence of
Paper for Printed Library Materials Z39.48-1992.

5   4   3   2   1

For Michael

Contents

Acknowledgments

In fall 2010, as I was completing the last chapters of this book, I taught a class on women, law, and public policy. It was a valuable experience, as our class discussions helped me to realize which women's rights issues were important to this generation; which in turn helped me to decide the issues that should be retained in the second edition, those that should be reframed, and those that should be discarded. I thank the group collectively for this.

I want to acknowledge the work of my graduate students in the Political Science Department at Loyola University Chicago: Sarah Skowronski, Andrea Walker, and Charles Haftl. Sarah's research paper on state equal rights amendments sparked my interest in the topic and led me to pursue it in greater detail and discuss it in the book. Thanks also to Lorie Chaiten, who graciously agreed to review the section on litigation over late-term abortions to ensure that I accurately reported on the complex legal issues involved in the cases.

I also want to thank the folks at Lynne Rienner Publishers, starting with Lynne, for their help in moving this project forward. Special thanks go to Leanne Anderson, former editor at the press, whose encouragement motivated me to go forward with this edition; Jessica Gribble, my current editor, whose cooperation and calming assurances throughout the writing of the book have been invaluable; and Shena Redmond, senior project editor, who was always helpful and understanding.

Most important, I want to thank my husband, Michael—whom I greatly admire for his scholarly abilities and administrative skills—for his inspiration and encouragement of my work. He has contributed in meaningful ways to every intellectual enterprise in which I have engaged, including this book. He does this in no small way by granting me the time and space to write, and, even more significant, he joins me in keeping focused on the crucial people in our lives: Jennifer and Jonathan and their Rebecca and Benjamin; and Jason and Deirdre and their Norah, Paul, and Daniel. To all of them, thanks for being.

Introduction: Women and Equality

My aim in writing this edition of *Elusive Equality: Women's Rights, Public Policy, and the Law* is to examine the current status of gender equality in the United States, specifically to determine whether the nation has become more egalitarian since the first edition was published.

The first edition showed that a number of contentious legal issues remained to be resolved and that women's struggles for equal opportunity were far from over. This edition, recognizing that society has made significant advances in gender equality, began with a sense of optimism, for it is no longer unusual to see women holding positions of prestige and authority. Today women are, among other things, lawyers, surgeons, judges, public officials, politicians, CEOs, scientists, investment bankers, professors, astronauts, physicians, generals, and admirals. There is also evidence that women are earning higher incomes and have higher levels of education than ever before.

At the same time, there are troubling signs that a good deal of this progress is ephemeral and not evenly distributed throughout society, with lower-income women, less educated women, gay women, and women of color not receiving their share of the gains. And women, no matter what their race, education, or age, continue to lag behind men in corporate executive positions, law partnerships, high-ranking military offices, prestigious university professorships, and as high-salaried sports figures. Moreover, disturbing signs of women's continued inequality are reflected in the persistence of pay inequity, the ongoing difficulties of managing work and family, and the continuous efforts to restrict reproductive freedom. At a minimum, an egalitarian society requires that women are paid according to their worth, have control over their reproductive decisionmaking, and receive assistance in balancing the responsibilities of work and family.

1

Law as an Instrument of Social Change

This book updates the story of the continuing struggle for gender equality in the United States, focusing on public policy issues affecting women's rights. Like the first edition, it is written from the perspective of liberal feminism—the prevailing paradigm of the modern U.S. women's movement. Focusing on federal court decisionmaking, it reflects the belief that removing the legal constraints that impede women's rights and opportunities is crucial to furthering the objectives of the women's movement and advancing gender equality. An essential component of social change, legal action plays an important role in eliminating many of the constraints that society imposes on the basis of gender, and thus the courts are an integral part of the struggle for gender equality.

Waves of Feminism

The first wave of feminism grew out of the abolitionist movement in the mid-1800s and subsided with the passage of the Nineteenth Amendment in 1920. In part, the successful conclusion of the struggle for the right to vote left the leaders of the woman suffrage movement uncertain about the direction of future movement activity. The upheaval of two world wars and the Great Depression, and perhaps also an awareness of the enormity of their tasks, frustrated their efforts to mount new battles to achieve a more equal and just society.

Women's rights advocacy reasserted itself in the latter part of the twentieth century, when women began to rally under the banner of feminism, an ideology seeking to empower women in their public and private lives. In the 1960s, the feminist movement, also known as the women's rights movement or the women's liberation movement, began the slow—and as yet incomplete—task of transforming society to end women's subordination to men. This second wave of feminism sprang from women's participation in the civil rights and antiwar movements of the early 1960s. Equally committed with men to bringing about an end to racial discrimination and the war in Vietnam, women discovered that their voices were often unheard and they were expected to remain silent while the men made the important decisions and took credit for successful collective actions. Women vowed that they would no longer accept their unequal status, and while continuing to fight for racial equality and peace, they began to call attention to the imbalance of power in the workplace and in the home. During this second wave of feminism, the success of women's rights advocacy was evident in the passage of a panoply of federal laws banning pay disparity between the sexes and prohibiting discrimination on the basis of sex in employment, education, credit, and housing. Following in the steps of earlier social movements, feminists turned to the courts for assistance in enforcing their legislative gains. At the same time, women also mounted legal challenges against state and federal laws based on traditional and stereotypical notions of men and women's roles. Concomitant with these actions, women engaged in efforts to expand reproductive rights—again, largely through the courts—as part of a broader movement to enhance individual rights of privacy. Their multifaceted litigation efforts transformed most attacks on inequality into legal challenges, many of which succeeded in bringing about important societal changes.

More recently, in the early 1990s, a new type of feminism, known as third-wave feminism, emerged. Although adherents of this viewpoint do not always agree on the proper analysis of society's deficiencies, the appearance of the new wave indicated dissatisfaction with many of the premises of the 1960s brand of feminism and concern about the limits of its goals, methods, and achievements. Many of the third-wave feminists are the daughters of the second wave, seeking to forge their own images and beliefs, in part accepting the former generation's accomplishments and in part demanding a new approach that displays greater concern about inequalities based on class, race, ethnicity, cultural identity, and sexual orientation. Although some third-wave adherents acknowledge the contributions of the second-wave feminists and may even agree with many of their goals (such as reproductive freedom), third-wave feminists typically reject the significance of legal change and do not view litigation as a key feminist strategy. Rather, their strategies are based on the multiplicity of women's characteristics, concern with the role of the media and its portrayals of women, greater awareness of a global perspective, and increased acceptance of femininity and sexuality.

These waves of feminism, reflecting generational differences as well as different beliefs about the important issues of the moment, represent divergent views on the meaning of feminism and social change. Taken together, however, their supporters are all committed to the goal of greater egalitarianism and have important things to say about how to achieve it.

The Plan of the Book

In assessing the progress the women's movement has made in eliminating barriers to equal opportunity in the United States, this book bridges the gap between law and public policy. It presents women in their roles as citizens, workers, students, wives, and mothers, discussing the role of legal change in reforming social, economic, and political institutions. It does so by exploring a wide array of policy issues affecting women and men, including sex-based legal classifications, the Equal Rights Amendment (ERA), single-sex education, women's participation in sports, employment discrimination, equal pay and comparable worth, fetal protection policies, the preferential status of pregnancy in the workplace, family leave, sexual harassment at work and in school, the balance between family and work, and women's reproductive autonomy. The chapters deal with constitutional sex equality; educational equity; women and employment, including sex discrimination, pay equity, sexual harassment, and pregnancy policies; and abortion rights.

Emphasizing the effect of the role of law on societal change, the book provides a comprehensive analysis of how women's rights are closely tied to the courts and public policy decisionmaking.

1 Seeking Constitutional Equality

In 1776, with the American colonies poised to declare their independence from England, Abigail Adams wrote to her husband, John, to voice her concern about equality for women in the newly emerging nation. "Remember the ladies," she urged him, "and be more generous and favorable to them than your ancestors. Do not put such unlimited power into the hands of husbands." She reminded him that "all men would be tyrants if they could. [And] if particular care and attention is not paid to the ladies we are determined to foment a rebellion, and will not hold ourselves bound by any laws in which we have no voice or representation."

Husband John replied a few weeks later, saying, "I cannot but laugh . . . your letter was the first intimation that another tribe, more numerous and powerful than all the rest were grown discontented."[1]

Abigail renewed her criticism in a later letter, declaring, "I cannot say that I think you are very generous to the ladies; for whilst you are proclaiming peace and good-will to men, emancipating all nations, you insist on retaining an absolute power over wives."[2] Despite these admonitions, neither Adams nor the other founders shared her preoccupation with women's rights and saw no reason to constitute women as equal citizens in the new nation.

Woman Suffrage

Women's rights advocates, inspired by the experiences of Lucretia Mott and Elizabeth Cady Stanton, who had been ordered to sit in the balcony at an international antislavery conference in London in 1840, held the first women's rights convention in Seneca Falls, New York, in July 1848.

The convention was called "to discuss the social, civil, and religious rights of woman." The *Declaration of Sentiments,* the document that emerged from the convention, echoed the *Declaration of Independence* by proclaiming that "all men and women are created equal." The delegates demanded women's suffrage and other forms of civil and legal equality. Stanton and Mott, along with Henry Ward Beecher, Lucy Stone, Frederick Douglass, Susan B. Anthony, and Henry Blackwell, were also deeply committed to the antislavery struggle, and with the Civil War looming, most turned their attention to the conflict over slavery and the uncertain fate of the Union.

After the Civil War, women's rights advocates renewed their efforts to secure the right to vote, hoping that enfranchisement would lead to equality in other areas.[3] Most movement leaders supported the Reconstruction-era Fourteenth Amendment, hoping it would extend women's rights as well as those of the former slaves. However, because it only applied to men, the amendment, ratified in 1868, was a significant defeat for women. Indeed, it was the first time that the Constitution singled out men in guaranteeing rights.[4] Two years later, the Fifteenth Amendment, banning discrimination in voting on the basis of "race, color, or previous condition of servitude," was ratified. Women were ignored again, with the amendment silent about discrimination in voting on the basis of sex.

Ultimately, the failure to include women in the Fifteenth Amendment led to the collapse of the antislavery coalition. A new organization, the National Woman Suffrage Association, founded in 1869 by Stanton and Anthony, committed itself to women's rights, including a constitutional amendment to ensure suffrage. The same year, the American Woman Suffrage Association was founded by Stone to focus more narrowly on the battle over enfranchisement.[5]

The struggle for suffrage dominated the women's rights movement from the latter part of the nineteenth century into the early part of the twentieth.[6] Finally, the Nineteenth Amendment, known as the Susan B. Anthony Amendment, was ratified in 1920.[7]

Political and Social Equality

In addition to seeking political equality through the ballot, women also attempted to remove barriers to social and economic equality, such as limits on their right to choose an occupation. In *Bradwell v. Illinois*,[8] an 1873 ruling, the U.S. Supreme Court considered Myra Bradwell's challenge after she was denied admission to the Illinois Bar because of her marital status. She claimed that the privileges and immunities clause of the Fourteenth Amendment protected her right to earn a living.[9] Speaking for the high court, Justice Samuel Miller agreed that the Fourteenth

Amendment guaranteed rights of national citizenship but added that "the right to admission to practice in the courts of a State is not one of them. This right," he continued, "in no sense depends on citizenship of the United States."[10]

Bradwell relied on the Court's constrained interpretation of the privileges and immunities clause in the *Slaughterhouse Cases,*[11] decided the previous day. In the *Slaughterhouse Cases,* the Court had held that this clause protected only a narrow range of federal constitutional rights, such as the right to sail on navigable waters. Thus, the *Bradwell* Court concluded that the privileges and immunities clause did not guarantee a woman's right to become a lawyer and dismissed Bradwell's demand for equality.

Justice Joseph Bradley's concurring opinion reflected society's prevailing view that a woman did not have the same right as a man to pursue an occupation.[12] "Nature herself," he insisted, "has always recognized a wide difference in the respective spheres and destinies of man and woman. . . . The natural and proper timidity and delicacy which belongs to the female sex evidently unfits it for many of the occupations of civil life." He concluded that "the paramount destiny and mission of woman are to fulfil the noble and benign offices of wife and mother. This is the law of the Creator."[13]

In 1875, the Court decided *Minor v. Happersett,*[14] a voting rights case. The case arose when Virginia Minor challenged a Missouri law, claiming that the right to vote was a privilege of national citizenship protected by the Fourteenth Amendment.

Speaking for the Court, Justice Morrison Waite explained that the Fourteenth Amendment did not confer suffrage and that Minor could only prevail if women had a right to vote at the time the Constitution was adopted.[15] And because suffrage had been restricted to men at that time, he denied her claim. As in *Bradwell,* the Court adopted a narrow view of the privileges and immunities clause, saying that it did not add to a citizen's rights but "simply furnished an additional guaranty for the protection of such as he already had."[16]

Around the turn of the century, a number of states attempted to ameliorate the harsh working conditions of the time by enacting regulations to limit the working day; businesses argued that such laws exceeded the state's lawmaking authority. In 1905, in *Lochner v. New York,*[17] the Court struck a New York law prohibiting bakers from working more than sixty hours a week or ten hours a day; it held that the "right to make a contract . . . is part of the liberty of the individual protected by the Fourteenth Amendment of the Federal Constitution."[18] The Court reasoned that baking is not dangerous work and that the quality of the baked goods would not improve if bakers worked fewer hours. Moreover, as adults, bakers could decide for themselves how many hours to work, and the Court believed there was no need to restrict their choice.

Lochner marked the beginning of an era of judicial support for laissez-faire economics that lasted until the 1930s.[19] However, three years later, in *Muller v. Oregon,*[20] the Court departed from this position by upholding an Oregon statute limiting female laundry workers to a maximum ten-hour workday. Arguing for the state, future Supreme Court justice Louis D. Brandeis presented a 113-page brief to the Court, contending that, unlike the male bakers, female laundry workers needed the state's protection. Known as the "Brandeis Brief," the document proclaimed that women were physically incapable of working more than ten hours a day.

The Court departed from its commitment to laissez-faire principles, allowing the government to interfere with the laundry workers' contracts because of women's limited physical capacity and societal roles. It believed that a woman's "physical structure and a proper discharge of her maternal functions . . . justify legislation to protect her from the greed as well as the passion of man."[21]

Some labor reformers welcomed *Muller,* but others believed the Court's ruling harmed women by justifying restrictions aimed only at them. They argued that by withholding job opportunities under the guise of protection, these laws limited women's availability for work and also made them more expensive to employ. Criticizing the Court's approach, Frances Olsen notes that "although the case might have seemed to exalt women, it effectively degraded them by treating the asserted differences as evidence of [their] inferiority."[22] And in her book on women's employment rights, Barbara Brown argues that most of these laws "were based on stereotypes about women's transient and secondary role in the labor market and their weak physical condition as well as on the desire of male workers to reduce competition for higher paying jobs."[23]

In 1924, the Court also upheld a New York law prohibiting women from working in restaurants between 10:00 P.M. and 6:00 A.M. In *Radice v. New York,* the Court accepted the state's argument that "night work . . . so injuriously affects the physical condition of women, and so threatens to impair their peculiar and natural functions, and so exposes them to the dangers and menaces incident to night life in large cities."[24] It did not question the logic of barring women from nighttime restaurant work while allowing them to work nights as performers, ladies' cloakroom attendants, or hotel kitchen help (all exempted from the law). It also did not inquire whether the statute was intended to preserve men's monopoly in the more lucrative nighttime restaurant jobs.

Forty years after *Muller,* in *Goesaert v. Cleary,*[25] a 1948 decision, the Supreme Court again considered the constitutionality of excluding women from certain occupations.

Under Michigan law, only women related to male bar owners could be licensed as bartenders. Speaking for the Court, Justice Felix Frankfurter derisively commented that as "beguiling as this subject is, it need not detain us long."[26] Perhaps because he did not consider the issue important, Frankfurter also did not question why the state allowed women to work as waitresses in the taverns. He was persuaded, he said, that it was reasonable to believe that women related to tavern owners would be protected from the dangers of bartending. Rejecting the insinuation that the law reflected the legislature's attempt to preserve the higher-paying bartending jobs for returning World War II veterans, Frankfurter concluded that there was no constitutional violation.

The Modern Equal Protection Clause

The equal protection clause of the Fourteenth Amendment puts states on notice that they must justify their decisions to treat persons as legally different. Under equal protection doctrine, differential treatment is constitutionally permissible only when it is based on relevant differences among individuals.[27] Because immutable characteristics such as race or national origin bear no relationship to ability and are considered irrelevant to valid legislative goals, the Court views laws based on such classifications as inherently suspect and scrutinizes them carefully, placing the government under a heavy burden to justify distinctions in law based on those criteria.

The Supreme Court first articulated the concept of a suspect classification based on race in *Korematsu v. United States,*[28] a case challenging the government's policy of interning persons of Japanese ancestry—citizens and noncitizens alike—during World War II. The Court warned that "all legal restrictions which curtail the civil rights of a single racial group are immediately suspect."[29] However, despite the indications that racial discrimination was the primary reason for the internment camps and exclusion orders, the Court ruled that the policy was not based on race and accepted the government's defense that it was justified by military necessity and national security.

In the years following *Korematsu,* the Court established a new approach to laws based on race and national origin. Because the legislature's motives for enacting such laws are often suspect, the Court subjects them to a more careful analysis, applying "strict" scrutiny and placing the burden of proof on the state to show that there is a "compelling" reason for the law. It also requires the government to demonstrate that the classifications (the means) are "necessarily" related to the goals (the ends) that the statute seeks to achieve and are the "least restrictive" means to achieve those goals.

When a law involves a nonsuspect classification, the Court applies a lesser form of scrutiny and merely seeks to determine if there is a "legitimate" reason for it and if the classification "rationally" relates to that reason. Called minimal scrutiny, this is the more common approach that is used to judge the constitutionality of economic and social regulations, as well as laws based on classifications with mutable characteristics (such as wealth or income) or those related to ability (such as age).

Thus, determining the proper level of scrutiny is crucial for the outcome of the case: laws reviewed under minimal scrutiny almost always receive the Court's approval. Conversely, because it strongly disfavors classifications based on racial or ethnic classifications, the Court almost always strikes such laws.[30]

During Earl Warren's tenure as chief justice from 1953 to 1969, the high court took a leading role in promoting racial equality in the nation. However, it did not extend this commitment to equality to women, as its 1961 decision, *Hoyt v. Florida,*[31] demonstrated.

Hoyt revolved around a Florida law creating a voluntary jury registration system for women. The defendant was convicted of second-degree murder by a jury of men for killing her husband with a baseball bat. She appealed her conviction on equal protection grounds, arguing that the law discriminated against her because female jurors would have been more sympathetic to her defense that she killed him because he was unfaithful. Speaking for the Court, Justice John Marshall Harlan pointed out that defendants are not entitled to juries of their choice but to juries "indiscriminately drawn from among those eligible in the community for jury service."[32] Florida did not exclude women from juries, Harlan noted; it merely exempted them from jury service at their option.

The Court reasoned that "despite the enlightened emancipation of women from the restrictions and protections of bygone years, and their entry into many parts of community life formerly considered to be reserved to men, woman is still regarded as the center of home and family life." And because she plays a unique role in the family, a woman should be allowed to "determine [for herself] that such service is consistent with her own special responsibilities."[33] Acknowledging that the state could have achieved its goal by limiting the exemptions to women with child care responsibilities, Harlan refused to declare the law "irrational."[34]

Equal Protection and Scrutiny

By the end of the 1960s, Warren Burger had become chief justice, and women's rights advocates became more vocal, their rising consciousness fueled in part by the struggle to ratify the ERA.[35] They turned to the courts to fight for equal rights in employment, education, and reproduction.

During Burger's years as chief justice from 1969 to 1986, the Court furthered sex equality by striking laws predicated on assumptions about women's and men's roles in society.[36] Just as important as the rulings in the individual *cases,* however, the Burger Court developed a new approach to assessing the constitutionality of sex-based classifications by incorporating another level of scrutiny into its equal protection jurisprudence.

The Court first addressed the appropriate limits of sex-based classifications in 1971 in *Reed v. Reed.*[37] Sally Reed's attorney was Ruth Bader Ginsburg, the head of the Women's Rights Project at the American Civil Liberties Union (ACLU) and a future Supreme Court justice.[38] *Reed* ushered in the Court's new approach to constitutional sex equality under the Fourteenth Amendment's equal protection clause.[39]

Reed challenged an Idaho law preferring a man over a woman to serve as administrator of an estate when both were equally qualified, that is, equally related to the deceased. The state argued that the statute was designed to prevent conflict within the family and reduce the workload of probate courts in determining the status of estate administrators. Conceding that the state's objectives were legitimate, the Supreme Court found the statute unconstitutional because the preference for the man did not have a "fair and substantial relation to the object of the legislation." Speaking for a unanimous Court, Burger characterized the law as "mak[ing] the very kind of arbitrary legislative choice forbidden by the Equal Protection Clause of the Fourteenth Amendment; and whatever may be said as to the positive values of avoiding intra-family controversy, the choice in this context may not lawfully be mandated solely on the basis of sex."[40]

Without openly acknowledging it, the Court appeared to have moved toward a stricter standard of scrutiny for sex-based classifications. The Idaho law was based on the likely accurate—for the time—assumption that men were more experienced in matters of business and finance than women. And although it was more rational and defensible than other laws that had survived judicial scrutiny in the past, the high court invalidated it.

Frontiero v. Richardson,[41] decided in 1973, involved a military regulation requiring married women to prove they provided over one-half of their family's support before obtaining certain benefits; married men automatically received the benefits. A plurality of four justices declared sex a suspect classification and held that the regulation violated Lieutenant Sharon Frontiero's constitutional rights. Justice William Brennan explained that by rejecting the state's "apparently rational" explanation for its probate scheme in *Reed,* the Court departed from its traditional use of minimal scrutiny in sex-based classifications. He justified the use of strict scrutiny because of the nation's "long and unfortunate history of sex discrimination . . . which, in practical effect, put women, not on a pedestal, but in a cage."[42]

Moreover, Brennan said, like race and national origin, sex is immutable and is "frequently" unrelated to ability; therefore, sex deserved the same searching scrutiny that those two classifications received. He rejected the government's assertion that the Air Force regulation was administratively convenient and cost-efficient, noting that, as the Court stated in *Reed,* such line-drawing between the sexes for the sake of administrative convenience was constitutionally forbidden.[43]

Together *Reed* and *Frontiero* indicate that the Court was moving away from the equal protection decisionmaking associated with minimal scrutiny. In declining to accept the government's argument of administrative convenience, typically considered a reasonable basis for a law, the *Reed* Court signaled that it was holding the government to a stricter standard. *Frontiero* represented a milestone in the development of the Court's sex equality doctrine, with four justices agreeing to apply strict scrutiny to laws based on sex. But the concurring justices, who also rejected the government's justification, nevertheless refused to adopt strict scrutiny. And because a majority of the Court did not approve the use of strict scrutiny, the level of scrutiny applied to sex-based classifications was left unresolved.

Then in 1976, in *Craig v. Boren,*[44] the Court formally adopted a third level of scrutiny, called heightened or intermediate scrutiny, for laws involving sex-based classifications. *Craig* arose over an Oklahoma law allowing eighteen-year-old women—but not men—to buy 3.2 or "near" beer. Brennan delivered the 7 to 2 opinion for the Court and, without explicitly acknowledging the shift toward stricter scrutiny, asserted that "previous cases establish that classifications by gender must serve important governmental objectives and must be substantially related to achievement of those objectives."[45] He firmly stated that the Court would not tolerate laws grounded in "archaic and overbroad generalizations," on "'old notions' of role typing," or on "outdated misconceptions concerning the role of females in the home rather than in the 'marketplace and world of ideas.'"[46]

The Court accepted Oklahoma's assertion that the law was intended to reduce incidents of driving under the influence of alcohol yet held that it did not pass a higher level of scrutiny. In declaring it unconstitutional, the Court indicated that the new standard applied to laws disadvantaging men as well as women.

Justice William Rehnquist (who served as chief justice from 1986 until his death in 2003) dissented, objecting to the stricter standard of review because he believed that it was inappropriate to apply it to laws challenged by men. He stressed that the Court had justified its departure from minimal scrutiny for sex-based classifications because of historical discrimination against women. But because there was no history of discrimination against men, Rehnquist said he would only apply minimal scrutiny to the Oklahoma law and would find it constitutional.[47]

After *Craig,* the Court reached a consensus on the proper level of scrutiny for sex-based laws. Unwilling to equate them with racial classifications, it resisted Brennan's approach of declaring sex a suspect category; yet mindful of the nation's history of sex discrimination against women, the Court also refused to apply minimal scrutiny to such laws.[48] Table 1.1 shows the three levels of scrutiny.

The Court later elaborated on the "intermediate scrutiny" test by requiring the government to provide an "exceedingly persuasive justification" for a sex-based law challenged under equal protection.[49] In *Mississippi University for Women v. Hogan,*[50] Justice Sandra Day O'Connor, the newest member of the Court, formally subsumed the "exceedingly persuasive justification" language into the intermediate scrutiny test. Speaking for a 5 to 4 majority in striking the university's women-only nursing program, O'Connor declared that the party seeking to uphold a statute classifying individuals on the basis of sex must

Table 1.1 Levels of Scrutiny

Classification	Scrutiny	Ends	Means
Suspect (e.g., race)	Strict	Compelling	Necessarily related
Semisuspect (e.g., sex)	Intermediate[a]	Important	Substantially related
Nonsuspect (e.g., age)	Minimal	Legitimate	Rationally related

Note: a. Also known as heightened scrutiny.

demonstrate an "exceedingly persuasive justification" for the classification. She continued, saying that the burden is met only by showing at least that the classification serves "important governmental objectives and that the discriminatory means employed" are "substantially related to the achievement of those objectives."[51] She also proclaimed that the Court would apply this heightened form of scrutiny to all cases involving sex-based classifications, regardless of the challenger's sex.[52]

The Supreme Court and Sex-Based Laws

Since 1971, when the Supreme Court first held that a law discriminated on the basis of sex, there have been thirty rulings in cases based on challenges to state or federal laws on constitutional grounds.[53] Table 1.2 presents these cases.

As Table 1.2 shows, the Court expanded sex equality by striking the challenged laws in fifteen of the thirty cases. Ironically, even though most of the lawsuits were spurred by the feminist movement, twenty-two of the thirty cases were brought by men, only eight by women. The men won in nine of the twenty-two cases, for a 41 percent success rate. In contrast, women prevailed in six of the eight cases, for a success rate of 75 percent. The difference between men's and women's success rates suggests that the Court was more amenable to striking laws disadvantaging women than laws disadvantaging men. However, although the rulings represent a victory for women's rights, they also demonstrate the Court's reluctance to abandon its belief in the legitimacy of biological constraints on equality.

The Burger Court ruled on myriad laws based on outmoded stereotypical notions of proper roles for men and women.[54] *Reed, Frontiero,* and *Craig* provide striking examples of these laws. The Court also deliberated on such laws in *Stanley v. Illinois,*[55] a 1972 decision in which it held that unwed fathers were entitled to individualized custody hearings to determine their fitness for custody; *Stanton v. Stanton,*[56] in 1975, in which the Court invalidated a Utah law setting twenty-one as the age of majority for men and eighteen for women; *Orr v. Orr,*[57] decided in 1979, in which it struck an Alabama law that based alimony awards on sex; *Kirchberg v. Feenstra,*[58] a 1981 case invalidating a sex-based provision of Louisiana's community property law; and *Hogan,* in which the Court rejected a state nursing school's single-sex admissions policy.

Table 1.2 Supreme Court Constitutional Sex Equality Rulings, 1971–2011

Case	Date	Issue[b]	Ruling[c]
Reed	1971	Estate administration	Expands equality
Stanley[a]	1972	Child custody	Expands equality
Frontiero	1973	Dependency benefits	Expands equality
Kahn[a]	1974	Tax exemptions	Limits equality
Geduldig	1974	Pregnancy benefits	Limits equality
Ballard[a]	1975	Promotions/discharges	Limits equality
Wiesenfeld[a]	1975	Survivor benefits	Expands equality
Stanton	1975	Age of majority	Expands equality
Craig[a]	1976	Age to purchase alcohol	Expands equality
Goldfarb[a]	1977	Dependency benefits	Expands equality
Webster[a]	1977	Retirement benefits	Limits equality
Vorchheimer	1977	Single-sex education	Limits equality
Fiallo[a]	1977	Immigration	Limits equality
Quilloin[a]	1978	Adoption	Limits equality
Orr[a]	1979	Alimony	Expands equality
Parham[a]	1979	Wrongful death	Limits equality
Caban[a]	1979	Adoption	Expands equality
Westcott	1979	Unemployment benefits	Expands equality
Wengler[a]	1980	Workers' compensation	Expands equality
Kirchberg	1981	Community property	Expands equality
Michael M.[a]	1981	Statutory rape	Limits equality
Rostker[a]	1981	Military registration	Limits equality
Hogan[a]	1982	Single-sex education	Expands equality
Lehr[a]	1983	Adoption	Limits equality
Mathews[a]	1984	Pension benefits	Limits equality
J. E. B.[a]	1994	Jury selection	Expands equality
VMI	1996	Single-sex education	Expands equality
Miller[a]	1998	Immigration	Limits equality
Nguyen[a]	2001	Immigration	Limits equality
Flores-Villar[a]	2011	Immigration	Limits equality

Notes: a. Case brought to challenge a law disadvantaging men.

b. Based on the major issue in the case.

c. Based on the overall outcome of the case.

The Court also invalidated laws stemming from traditional notions of women's dependency that were incorporated into the Social Security Act and numerous state workers' compensation laws: *Weinberger v. Wiesenfeld,*[59] decided in 1975, in which the Court struck a provision of the Social Security law allowing widows only to receive child care benefits; *Califano v. Goldfarb,*[60] a 1977 case reminiscent of *Frontiero,* which invalidated a provision of the Social Security Act restricting survivors' benefits to widowers who received at least one-half their support from their deceased wives; *Califano v. Westcott,*[61] in 1979, in which the Court held that the Aid to Families with Dependent Children Unemployed Father program must provide benefits to families if either parent were unemployed; and *Wengler v. Druggists Mutual Insurance Company*,[62] decided in 1980, in which the Court held that a Missouri law requiring widowers to prove their dependency on their deceased wives before receiving death benefits under a workers' compensation plan was unconstitutional.

In these cases, the Court served notice that laws reflecting stereotypical generalizations of women's and men's roles were inconsistent with equal protection. In striking the laws, the justices indicated awareness of the discriminatory assumptions behind them and acknowledged women's roles as citizens and wage earners.

Contrary to the egalitarian spirit behind these rulings, *Geduldig v. Aiello*,[63] decided in 1974, upheld a California disability insurance program that excluded pregnancy benefits for women workers. Ruling that the policy was based on pregnancy, not sex, and therefore applying minimal scrutiny, the Court found it a reasonable cost-saving measure. By simply declaring that the policy did not differentiate on the basis of sex, the Court was able to avoid ruling on the obvious discriminatory implications for women, a seeming contradiction with the cases in which it struck laws that conflicted with the role of women at work.

The Court upheld laws in which it believed the government properly sought to compensate women for past or present inequalities as well as laws that implicated physical differences between the sexes. In these types of cases, the Court seemed untroubled about the fact that many of the challenged laws unfairly discriminated against men.

Cases such as *Kahn v. Shevin*,[64] decided in 1974; *Schlesinger v. Ballard*,[65] a 1975 decision; *Califano v. Webster*,[66] a 1977 case; and *Heckler v. Mathews*,[67] decided in 1984, were based on measures designed to redress inconsistencies or minor inequalities in the law. The decisions suggest that the Court was not fully committed to applying a higher form of scrutiny in sex-based classifications. *Webster* and *Mathews* concerned relatively minor provisions of the Social Security Act that were no longer in place by the time the case reached the Court. *Kahn* revolved around the constitutionality of a law entitling widows to claim a $500 property tax exemption, an amount equaling $15 a year. Despite its stereotypical notion of a family with a dependent wife and breadwinner husband, the Court upheld the law because it agreed with the state that it was a reasonable way to compensate widows for the prevailing economic disparity between men and women.[68] Ironically, *Kahn* was handed down a year after *Frontiero,* the case in which the Court appeared to be on the verge of adopting strict scrutiny for sex-based laws.

Ballard involved a navy policy permitting men to serve as officers for nine years before being discharged for lack of promotion, while women were allowed thirteen years.[69] Rejecting the challenge from the male navy lieutenant, the Court ignored the navy's restrictions on women in combat or sea duty, simply accepting the government's argument that the extra time in rank was justified because women's opportunities for professional advancement were limited. Because the restrictions on women serving on ships have eased over time, such a policy would make little sense today.

Perhaps it was reasonable to uphold these laws and policies intended to compensate women for traces of past discrimination, but the Court never questioned whether the benefits provided were worth the cost of allowing society to continue to draw legal distinctions between the sexes.

The next set of cases, revolving around laws based on physical sex differences, demonstrates the contradictions within the Court's sex equality doctrine. In *Rostker v. Goldberg,*[70] the Court addressed a law, enacted after the 1979 Soviet invasion of Afghanistan, that required only nineteen- and twenty-year-old men to register for the military. President Jimmy Carter's authority allowed him to order men to register without congressional approval, but he proposed legislation that would require both men and women to register. Because the administration was not prepared to send women into combat, the policy would have established two draft pools: one for men in combat roles and the other for men and women in noncombat positions. In defending the proposal before a House Armed Services Personnel subcommittee, Bernard Rostker, head of the Selective Service, called it "a question of equity." He continued, "it is a question of whether women should bear an equal risk of being called." A subcommittee member responded, "We're talking about national security; we're not talking about sociological things."[71]

A majority in Congress supported the idea of registering men but opposed registering women. Moreover, in addition to opposition from Congress and the military, anti-ERA groups also lined up against the plan to register women. Shortly after introducing it, the administration withdrew the proposal.

The male plaintiffs in the suit argued that the male-only registration policy was an unconstitutional sex-based classification. The Court, however, minimized the concern about sex equality and instead framed the issue within the context of national defense, accepting the government's argument that women's ineligibility for combat justified the policy.

Because the majority believed that its opinion did not stem from stereo-typical notions about women's roles in society, it felt no need to question the government's assumption about the relationship between excluding women and military effectiveness, ignoring the fact that some registered men would also be ineligible for combat.[72]

Applying little scrutiny to the challenged policy, the Court deferred to the government's authority over national security, and, in a 6 to 3 ruling, accepted the government's position equating registration with combat. As in *Ballard,* the Court did not question whether the military's restrictions on women in combat reflected unequal treatment of men and women service members.[73] Even the dissent offered no objection to the constraints on women in the armed forces; it simply argued that women could be registered and drafted as needed.[74]

In *Michael M. v. Superior Court,*[75] the Court assessed the constitutionality of a California statutory rape law that punished men over seventeen for engaging in sex with women under seventeen.[76] The state argued that the law aimed at lowering rates of teen pregnancy, and because women faced the risk of pregnancy, they did not need the threat of a criminal prosecution to refrain from engaging in sex. The law was intended to deter men, who did not face the same consequences from their sexual acts. The Court agreed that it reasonably served the state's purpose of preventing men from engaging in sexual acts with underage women.[77]

Instead of applying intermediate scrutiny, Rehnquist (then an associate justice), treated the law with "great deference" and upheld it on the grounds that men and women were not similarly situated with respect to the statute's intent of deterring teenage pregnancy. However, as Brennan pointed out in dissent, despite the state's claim, the legislative history of this 1800s law indicated that it was primarily based on concern for women's virtue.[78]

Once again, the Court failed to explore the stereotypical assumptions behind the statute. Although women are more likely than men to be rape victims, a sex-neutral statutory rape law would have accomplished the same purpose. Indeed, by the late 1970s, many states had revised their statutory rape laws to punish older individuals of either sex who engaged in inappropriate sexual conduct with minors. Such laws help promote sexual equality while still accomplishing the state's aim of protecting young victims from sexual predators. Many of these laws are premised on the age differences between the two parties—the greater the age difference, the higher the penalty.

Other Burger Court rulings addressed the constitutionality of laws distinguishing between unwed mothers and unwed fathers; here too, the

Court was forced to decide whether these laws were based on real physical sex differences or primarily on assumptions about women's and men's societal roles. The challenge for the Court was to disentangle the relationship between physical sex differences and society's norms about culturally derived roles.

In *Fiallo v. Bell*,[79] decided in 1977, the Court rejected a challenge to a provision of the Immigration and Nationality Act of 1952 that granted automatic preferential immigrant status to children born abroad of unwed citizen mothers but not to children born abroad of unwed citizen fathers. In this and other cases revolving around sex-based differences in immigration law, the Court applied a lower level of scrutiny, "roughly equivalent to a rational basis test," deferring to Congress's broad power over immigration and naturalization matters.[80] *Quilloin v. Walcott*,[81] a 1978 decision, upheld a Georgia law permitting unwed mothers, but not fathers, to veto their children's adoption. And in *Parham v. Hughes*,[82] a 1979 ruling, the Court approved a Georgia statute permitting all unwed mothers— but only fathers who had legitimated their children under applicable state law—to sue for wrongful death. Finally, in *Lehr v. Robertson*,[83] decided in 1983, the Court upheld a New York law denying an unwed father the right to receive prior notice of an adoption proceeding involving his child unless he had formalized his claim to paternity. Announcing the majority opinion in *Lehr*, Justice John Paul Stevens justified the differential treatment on the grounds that mothers were more committed to their children, as seen by their decision to give birth to them.

The Court upheld these laws, accepting the state's position that it had a legitimate interest in ensuring that fathers have relationships with their children and avoiding fraudulent lawsuits brought by men claiming to be fathers of children born out of wedlock.[84] In *Caban v. Mohammed*,[85] the Court took a contrary position, striking a New York law that permitted an unwed mother, but not a father, to block an adoption simply by withholding consent. The Court believed the law unjustified because this father had established a relationship with his child. However, in accepting the other laws involving unwed fathers, the Court once again neglected to probe the assumption that women are naturally more willing to assume primary responsibility for their children and that men seek to avoid responsibility.

These rulings indicate that the Burger Court struck laws that it believed were based on traditional notions of proper societal roles for women and men; at the same time, it largely rejected challenges to laws that the justices felt were grounded in real (that is, physical) differences between women and men. In permitting such policies to stand, as Ann

Freedman argues, "the paradoxical—although hardly surprising—result . . . has been to uphold those views about sex differences that are most entrenched in cultural beliefs and legislation, which in turn pose the greatest dangers of stereotyping."[86]

These Burger Court rulings on laws implicating physical sex differences marred its record of championing women's rights. But despite its reluctance to put aside its cultural beliefs in such cases, the Burger court handed women's rights litigators an impressive number of victories in the 1970s and 1980s.[87]

A new era of Supreme Court decisionmaking emerged during the Rehnquist Court, beginning with its first ruling on a sex-based classification in 1994. Two years later, in *United States v. Virginia (VMI)*,[88] speculation arose over whether the Court had adopted a new, higher level of scrutiny in equal protection jurisprudence.[89]

In *J. E. B. v. Alabama*,[90] the Rehnquist Court was asked to decide whether a peremptory challenge may be used to exclude jurors on the basis of sex.[91] The defendant in a paternity and child support action argued that the state violated the equal protection clause by using its peremptory challenges to exclude all men from the jury. Announcing the decision for a 6 to 3 majority, Justice Harry Blackmun strongly reaffirmed that intentional discrimination based on sex "violates the Equal Protection Clause, particularly where, as here, the discrimination serves to ratify and perpetuate invidious, archaic, and overbroad stereotypes about the relative abilities of men and women."[92] The Court rejected the state's argument that it was more important to eliminate racial challenges than sex-based challenges in the jury selection process, refusing to engage in a debate over which group suffered more discrimination. Reiterating that the "long and unfortunate history of sex discrimination" in the nation requires the use of heightened scrutiny, the Court sought to determine whether allowing sex-based peremptory challenges was substantially related to the state's goal of ensuring a fair trial.

Concluding that they were not, the Court added in a footnote that it "need not decide whether classifications based on gender are inherently suspect."[93] It rejected the state's argument that sex could be used as a proxy to eliminate potential juror bias because studies showed that attitudes differed by sex. Characterizing the state's evidence largely as gender stereotyping, Blackmun noted that the equal protection clause does not allow states to base laws on a stereotypical generalization about the sexes, "even when some statistical support can be conjured up for the generalization."[94]

Rehnquist dissented, arguing that the Court must distinguish between the level of scrutiny applied to race- and sex-based classifications. In his view, racially based peremptory strikes were clearly unconstitutional; however, he believed that the principle did not apply to sex-based strikes and he would permit jurors to be excluded on the basis of their sex.

The *VMI* case, perhaps the most widely discussed equal protection ruling of the 1990s, was initiated by a complaint from a female high school student to the Department of Justice (DOJ) in 1990. Filed by the U.S. attorney general, the suit charged that the state violated the equal protection clause by refusing to admit women. Guided by the high court's ruling in *Hogan,* the district court judge applied intermediate scrutiny and found that schools with single-sex environments, such as VMI, furthered the goal of a diverse educational system throughout the state.[95] Moreover, he held that VMI's adversative education system, upon which much of its reputation was based, would be appreciably altered if women were admitted.

A three-judge panel of the Fourth Circuit Court of Appeals agreed that VMI's uniqueness justified the single-sex admissions policy and that admitting women would change the nature of the education offered at VMI.[96] In effect, the court declared that the institution would be transformed if women were admitted and it would no longer be the school to which they sought admission. Nevertheless, the appeals court vacated the lower court's judgment, ruling that the state had not satisfactorily explained why it should be permitted to offer this type of educational benefit only to men. It refused to order that women be admitted to VMI, however, instead offering the state three choices: stop funding VMI, offer a "parallel" program for women elsewhere, or admit them to VMI.

The state chose the second option, establishing a military-style training program for women at neighboring Mary Baldwin College, a private liberal arts school 30 miles from VMI. Called Virginia Women's Institute for Leadership (VWIL), this program allowed women to attend VMI for reserve officer training while taking leadership courses and a liberal arts curriculum at Mary Baldwin.

On remand, the district court judge acknowledged substantial differences between VMI and VWIL but found that they were "justified pedagogically and . . . not based on stereotyping." He added that VWIL need not be "a mirror image" of VMI and that the equal protection clause is satisfied if the two programs "achieve substantially similar outcomes."[97]

On appeal again, the circuit court upheld the lower court, agreeing that the state had cured its equal protection violation by creating VWIL.

Anxious to avoid overstepping its judicial role, the appellate court explained that a reviewing court must defer to the legislative will and approve legislation as long as its purpose was not "pernicious." According to the court, the intermediate scrutiny analysis "begins with the limited inquiry into whether the state objective is both consistent with a legitimate governmental role and important in serving that role. Thereafter it shifts to an inquiry of heightened scrutiny into whether the classification 'substantially and directly furthers' that objective."[98]

In assessing the equal protection violation, the court weighed the benefits of the arrangement to each sex. The state's objective in providing a single-sex education was clearly not "pernicious," the court said, nor was it insidious to exclude women from VMI because admitting them would sabotage the adversative system by forcing the academy to accommodate their needs for privacy and such. Because it considered the state's purpose legitimate, the court determined that the separate institutions played a key role in fulfilling the state's purpose of providing single-sex education. But the court did not evaluate whether the two programs were equal; it merely inquired whether they were "sufficiently comparable" to withstand the equal protection challenge. It concluded that they were.

Ginsburg's opinion for the 7 to 1 Supreme Court decision began by discussing VMI's notable achievements and its excellent reputation, which, she said, not surprisingly, made it attractive to women as well as men. After reviewing the lower court rulings, she summarized the two issues before the Court: First, does VMI's single-sex admissions policy deny equal protection to eligible women? Second, if so, what is the proper remedy?

Ginsburg explained that the nation's long history of sex discrimination required courts to view sex-based classifications, such as VMI's, with skepticism. Quoting from *Hogan,* she said that "the state must show 'at least that the [challenged] classification serves important governmental objectives and that the discriminatory means employed' are 'substantially related to the achievement of those objectives.'" Moreover, "the justification must be genuine, not hypothesized or invented post hoc in response to litigation; nor can it rely on overbroad generalizations about the different talents, capacities, or preferences of males and females."[99]

She noted that the Court reserved strict scrutiny for racial classifications but emphasized that although "physical differences between men and women are . . . enduring," they may not be used to denigrate "members of either sex or for artificial constraints on an individual's opportunity."[100]

The state had argued that VMI's single-sex educational policy provides important benefits that contribute to the diversity of the state's educational system. Ginsburg agreed that a diverse educational system was a legitimate goal, but questioned the state's claim that it maintained VMI as a single-sex school to promote such diversity.[101] She also made short shrift of the state's claim that opening VMI's adversative education system to women would require such radical modifications that it would destroy the school.

Conceding that most women would not wish to enter such a program, she insisted that the real issue was whether the state may deny the opportunity to those who seek it and are qualified. Because a state may not base its policies on generalizations about the "tendencies" of the sexes, the Court found no evidence that women would destroy the school's adversative system. In the past, Ginsburg exclaimed, such predictions, which proved erroneous, were made to exclude women from other men-only educational institutions, including the national military academies. Barring women from its "premier citizen-soldier corps" will not advance VMI's goal of creating "citizen-soldiers." Echoing *Hogan,* she concluded that the state "has fallen far short of establishing the 'exceedingly persuasive justification' . . . that must be the solid base for any gender-based classification."[102]

The next step was to determine whether VWIL cured the constitutional violation. Pointing to the numerous differences between the two programs, including VWIL's lack of the rigorous adversative method of education, Ginsburg dismissed the lower court's view that the two programs were "sufficiently comparable" to satisfy equal protection and ruled that VMI must open its doors to qualified women who seek admission.

The chief justice, concurring in the opinion, took exception to what he believed was the majority's revision of the intermediate scrutiny test.[103] He believed the "exceedingly persuasive justification" language was merely part of the heightened scrutiny standard, rather than a separate layer of analysis. In his view, the majority opinion had raised the level of scrutiny applied to sex-based laws.

Justice Antonin Scalia was the lone dissenter. He also accused the majority of elevating the level of scrutiny in applying the "exceedingly persuasive justification" test and argued that the exclusionary admissions policy would have been constitutionally permissible had the majority applied the traditional intermediate scrutiny test. Lamenting the loss of chivalry if the VMI experience were extended to women on an equal basis, he protested that the Court should have allowed VMI to retain its traditions.

Despite Ginsburg's condemnation of VMI's exclusion of women, she had left the door open for laws implicating physiological sex differences by referring to physical differences between the sexes as "enduring" and declared that "inherent differences" between the sexes are cause for "celebration."[104] And notwithstanding the speculation about the Court's reformulation of the heightened scrutiny test that arose after *VMI*, two subsequent decisions indicate the Court's reluctance to abandon its approach to laws based on physical differences.

The issue of physical sex differences that had occupied much of the Burger Court's attention returned to the Court in 1998, when the Rehnquist Court ruled on the constitutionality of a law at the intersection of immigration policy and equal protection jurisprudence.[105] Specifically, the Court was asked to determine whether immigration laws could favor children born to unwed mothers over children born to unwed fathers. Under the law, a child born out of wedlock on foreign soil to a citizen mother and noncitizen father is automatically considered a citizen, whereas a child born to a citizen father and noncitizen mother is not granted automatic citizenship but must comply with certain procedures. Moreover, there is no time limit on the mother's ability to claim citizenship for her child.

Lonera Penero was born in the Philippines in 1970 to a noncitizen Filipino mother and a U.S. citizen father serving in the military. Her parents did not marry, and her father left the country before her birth and never returned; he finally acknowledged her as his daughter after she turned eighteen. In 1992, Penero applied for U.S. citizenship and was rejected because of her father's failure to establish paternity as specified in immigration law. After a Texas court issued a declaration of paternity, she reapplied for citizenship. This time she was refused because, according to § 309 of the Immigration and Nationality Act, a child born abroad to an unmarried citizen father and foreign national mother must be properly legitimated before age eighteen—either through a voluntary acknowledgment of paternity or court adjudication—to acquire citizenship. Once the age limit passes, citizenship cannot be established through the father.

Both father and daughter sued the secretary of state in federal court, seeking to have the daughter declared a citizen. They argued that because the law treated citizen fathers and citizen mothers differently, it violated his right to equal protection under the Fifth Amendment.

The Texas district court transferred the case to the District Court for the District of Columbia.[106] In turn, that court dismissed her suit, ruling that it could not redress her injury because federal courts do not have the power to grant citizenship.[107] On appeal, the circuit court affirmed the lower court.[108] It ruled that the law distinguishing between unwed mothers and unwed fathers was justified because of the differences between mothers and fathers in establishing relationships with their children. Thus, the court believed that the law furthered the government's interest in fostering early ties between foreign-born children and the United States as well as with their citizen parents.

During oral arguments before the U.S. Supreme Court, the deputy solicitor general reminded the Court that it must defer to Congress when reviewing immigration policy. The law, he said, is grounded in the reality that mothers are always present at birth and Congress may require additional evidence from fathers to ensure they have a relationship with the child so the child does not become dependent on society. The burden of the law is minimal, he added, because it allows paternity to be easily established.[109]

In a fractured 6 to 3 ruling, in *Miller v. Albright*[110] in 1998, the high court affirmed the lower court. But although six justices agreed the law was constitutional, their opinions were split three different ways. Stevens, who wrote the opinion, found the law constitutional because of the differences in the nature of the parents' relationship to the child. Echoing the appellate court, he held that the government may rightfully conclude that men and women are not similarly situated with respect to establishing proof of a biological relationship between a parent and a child. The law simply requires the father to do (and gives him eighteen years in which to do it) what the mother accomplishes by giving birth. Moreover, he noted, the statute advanced the government's interest in encouraging relationships among foreign-born children, their citizen parents, and the nation. Anxious to refute charges that the law reflected stereotypical views that women are better parents than men, Stevens insisted that it reflected Congress's "solid" assumption that unwed mothers are likelier to establish relationships with their children because they are present at birth and can attend to the paperwork that establishes parentage.

O'Connor and Justice Anthony Kennedy concurred because they believed that Penero did not have standing (was legally barred) to raise her father's equal protection challenge; they thought his claim might have succeeded because, in their view, the law did not pass the heightened scrutiny test. Scalia and Justice Clarence Thomas also concurred in the judgment, reasoning that even if there were an equal protection violation, the Court could not confer citizenship. Dissents by Justices Stephen Breyer, David Souter, and Ginsburg argued that the law did not satisfy heightened scrutiny.[111]

Three years later, in *Nguyen v. INS*,[112] the Court addressed the issue left unresolved in *Miller*. Tuan Anh Nguyen was born in Saigon to an unmarried Vietnamese-citizen mother and U.S.-citizen father. His mother abandoned him at birth, and he lived with the family of his father's new girlfriend in Vietnam until he was almost six. Then after Saigon fell in

1975, Nguyen joined his father in Texas, where he was granted permanent resident status.[113] When he was twenty-two, he pleaded guilty to two counts of sexual assault on a child and was sentenced to eight years in prison on each count. After he had served three years, the Immigration and Naturalization Service (INS) began proceedings to deport him. He was deemed "deportable" by an immigration judge, and in 1998, while his appeal was pending before the Board of Immigration Appeals, his father used the results of a DNA test to obtain an order of parentage from a Texas state court. The board, however, rejected his citizenship claim because he had not met the requirements of the law for a child born out of wedlock to a citizen father and noncitizen mother. On appeal of the board's ruling, the circuit court found the law constitutional and rejected their equal protection challenge.[114]

Announcing the majority opinion for himself, Rehnquist, Stevens, Scalia, and Thomas, Kennedy found that the government had an important interest in obtaining reliable proof of a biological relationship between the citizen and the child. Because the mother's blood relationship is evident, Congress can require men to provide proof of fatherhood. Rejecting the argument that fathers should be able to satisfy the law with DNA evidence, the Court held that it was not going to dictate to Congress how it should achieve its goal.

A second objective, Kennedy noted, was to ensure that the child and parent have an opportunity to form "real everyday ties" while the child is a minor, that, in turn, allow the child to develop ties to the nation. Because the father may not be present at the birth—indeed, may not know of the pregnancy—Congress could require the father to establish paternity before the child was eighteen to ensure that he and his child have the opportunity to develop these ties. Acknowledging that a positive DNA test could establish paternity, the majority noted that it would not ensure that a relationship between father and child could develop. Reacting to the dissent's criticism that the law simply reflects the stereotypical notion that women are more likely to bond with their children, the Court asserted that Congress intended to create the circumstances in which the tie could develop, not to guarantee that it would, and that the distinction between the parents reflects "a basic biological difference."[115] Citing its rulings in *VMI* and *Hogan,* the Court found that the law easily passed the intermediate scrutiny test.

O'Connor's dissent sharply criticized the majority's application of intermediate scrutiny. In her view, the sex-based classification was not "substantially related" to the government's objective of establishing a relationship between the parent and the child and a sex-neutral alternative, such as the amount of time they spent together, could achieve the government's objective. She accused the majority of applying a heightened scrutiny that was "a stranger to our precedents."[116] O'Connor stressed that intermediate scrutiny requires a substantial "fit" between the legislation's means and ends, not merely a reasonable one. The Court would not have to question whether alternative means exist to achieve the government's purpose under minimal scrutiny, but, she said, heightened scrutiny requires it to determine the availability of sex-neutral alternatives.

O'Connor also pointed to internal inconsistencies in the majority opinion. Most important, she declared that the government's interest in proving the existence of a biological relationship between a parent and child is met by another section of the statute that requires "clear and convincing evidence" of a blood relationship between the person seeking citizenship and the father. She questioned why Congress should also require proof of legitimation when the law already ensured the relationship. In her view, the law does not substantially further the government's aim, especially when, as here, a sex-neutral alternative was readily available. Last, O'Connor questioned the government's claim that it merely wanted proof that a relationship could develop because it was not clear that proving it before the child turned eighteen furthered that interest, especially when other forms of proof that did not depend on sex—such as requiring the parent's presence at birth or at least knowledge of it—were available to satisfy it. Citing Breyer's dissent in *Miller,* she asserted that the law was based on an impermissible stereotype.

Almost a decade after *Nguyen* was decided, the Ninth Circuit ruled on another challenge to a U.S. immigration law with a sex-based classification. The appeals court relied on *Nguyen* in determining the constitutionality of two sections of the Immigration and Nationality Act. The law at issue required citizen fathers to be physically present in the United States for ten years (five of which had to be after they were fourteen) "before they may transmit citizenship to a child born out of wedlock abroad to a non-citizen."[117] A citizen mother whose child was born outside the United States was able to confer citizenship on her child if she were physically present in the United States for one year before the child's birth.

In 1986, the law was amended to allow a citizen father to confer citizenship on a child "born out of wedlock" after being in the country for five years, with the requirement that two of those five years had to be after the age of fourteen. In any event, the 1986 amendment did not apply to Ruben Flores-Villar because he was born in 1974.

Ruben was born in Tijuana, Mexico, and moved to San Diego to live with his father and grandmother when he was two months old. His mother was a Mexican citizen; his father, a U.S. citizen, was sixteen years old when Ruben was born.

In 1997, Ruben was convicted of importing marijuana into the United States and was removed from the country; this scenario was repeated several times between 1997 and 2005. He entered the country illegally again in 2006 and was ordered deported. He challenged the deportation, claiming he was a U.S. citizen because of his father's citizenship status.

The court found, however, that although Ruben's father was a U.S. citizen, he could not confer citizenship on his son because he (the father) had only been physically present in the country for two years after he became fourteen.

Weighing Ruben's argument that the age and sex classifications violated the Fifth Amendment's due process clause, the appeals court used intermediate scrutiny to determine the constitutionality of the sex-based classification in the law. It determined that Congress's interests in avoiding a child's statelessness and ensuring that a biological relationship exists between a father and his child are important and found that the sex-based classification was substantially related to those ends. The court stressed that it was loath to interfere with Congress's authority over matters related to immigration and citizenship.

On March 22, 2010, the high court agreed to review the Ninth Circuit opinion.[118] On June 13, 2011, "an equally divided Court," let stand the lower court ruling in a 4 to 4 vote. Justice Elena Kagan recused herself from the case because of her previous position as the solicitor general of the United States. Thus, without explanation, the high court affirmed the Ninth Circuit judgment that upheld the federal law and denied Ruben Flores-Villar's right to citizenship based on his father's status as a citizen when Ruben was born.[119]

Although many hoped that the Court would use the case as an opportunity to declare a new approach to sex-based laws, perhaps even raising the level of scrutiny, the decision left unanswered the myriad questions about the continued use of intermediate scrutiny in sex-based laws, about the extent of the Court's continued adherence to its belief that physical differences between the sexes play a legitimate role in structuring the laws of the nation, and about the Court's deference to Congress in matters related to immigration and naturalization.

Some believed that Ginsburg's majority opinion in the *VMI* decision indicated that the Court might be amenable to raising the level of scrutiny when reviewing laws based on sex. Taken together, however, the three physical differences cases (*Miller, Nguyen,* and, to some extent, *Flores-Villar*) suggest that the Court remains unwilling to abandon its belief in the legitimacy of laws stemming from physical difference between the sexes. Because of the ambiguity of the *Flores-Villar* decision, the Court will again be asked to rule on a law reflecting physical sex differences and will have to indicate whether it is simply acknowledging the reality of sex-based differences with respect to pregnancy and childbirth or relying on stereotypes and overbroad generalizations arising from beliefs about culturally determined sex roles.

The Equal Rights Amendment

The ERA prompted a nationwide debate over the role of sex-based classifications in the nation's laws.[120] First proposed by suffragist Alice Paul in 1923, the amendment was introduced in every congressional session thereafter; its key phrase simply stated, "Equality of rights under the law shall not be denied or abridged by the United States or by any State on account of sex."[121]

The amendment eventually received the necessary two-thirds vote in each House of Congress forty-nine years later in 1972 and was sent to the states on March 22, 1972, where the long and ill-fated ratification process began in earnest. Its key sponsors were Senator Birch Bayh, Indiana Democrat, and Representative Martha Griffiths, Democrat from Michigan. The outcome initially appeared promising when more than half the thirty-eight states required to ratify did so in the first year. Moreover, a majority of the American public consistently indicated its approval of the amendment.[122]

The ratification process was soon characterized by excessive claims from opponents, such as that the ERA would require all public bathrooms to become unisex (ignoring the fact that its framers explicitly talked about the privacy exception in the amendment and that state ERAs have not been interpreted to achieve this result).[123] They also warned that the ERA would require women to be drafted into the armed forces (an unlikely scenario given that the involuntary draft had already ended and was unlikely to be reinstated); would require abortion on demand (largely irrelevant because the Supreme Court had already ruled on abortion rights); and would end married women's special protections (to the extent that such protections existed, they were being eroded by emerging economic and social forces in the nation).[124]

A key opponent of the amendment, Senator Sam Ervin, Democrat from North Carolina, who had used his position as chair of the Judiciary Committee to keep the amendment bottled up in committee, now issued dire warnings about its effect on women if it were passed. He was soon joined by Phyllis Schlafly, a Republican Party activist, who became the public face of ERA opposition.[125] The seven-year time limit for ratification established by Congress expired in 1979. By 1978, the amendment had secured the votes of only thirty-five states, three short of the requisite thirty-eight. A year later, with no more states ratifying, Congress extended the time for ratification by three years.[126] The amendment finally went down to defeat, still missing three votes, in 1982. The southern states—the least comfortable with women's demands for equal rights—were the primary obstacle to ratification; Illinois was the only northern state to refuse to ratify, largely as a result of turf wars among local politicians.

During the stormy ratification process, five state legislatures (South Dakota, Nebraska, Tennessee, Idaho, Kentucky, all of which had ratified in the first year) sought to withdraw their prior approval of the amendment.[127] But because the U.S. Supreme Court did not rule on the issue, the legality of their attempted rescission remains an open question. The issue eventually became moot because the amendment's supporters were unable to secure the votes of thirty-eight states.

For more than a decade, the two sides had engaged in rhetorical battle over the significance of the proposed amendment; when it finally went down to defeat in 1982, there were still many unanswered questions about its potential impact on the nation's laws. A version of the ERA has continued to be introduced in each session of Congress since 1982. Its supporters had renewed hope in 2007 when the Democrats again claimed the majority in the House of Representatives as a result of the 2006 election. Twenty-five years after its demise in 1982, on March 27, 2007, it was reintroduced, this time as the Women's Equality Amendment, in the House of Representatives by Carolyn Maloney, Democrat from New York, and in the Senate by Edward (Ted) Kennedy, Democrat from Massachusetts. The discussion surrounding the bill centered on whether the courts' interpretation of the equal protection doctrine as well as the changing role of women in society made an equal rights amendment irrelevant. No action was taken on the measure, and it was reintroduced on July 21, 2009, again by Maloney, with eighty-one co-sponsors. Titled "House Joint Resolution 61," it was referred to the House Judiciary Committee and sent to the Subcommittee on the Constitution, Civil Rights, and Civil Liberties, where it languished.

Some argue that there is still a need for a federal ERA because it would ensure strict scrutiny for sex-based classifications, which is preferable to the loosely structured intermediate scrutiny. The longtime ERA opponent Schlafly, the primary obstacle to its passage in the 1970s, warns that the amendment would require courts to allow same-sex marriage.[128]

Meanwhile state legislatures persisted in their efforts to enact state ERAs.[129] By 2004, a total of twenty states guaranteed equal rights on the basis of sex as a matter of state constitutional law. The variation in the wording—some mirrored the federal ERA, some included sex within a general equal rights provision, and some, such as California's, limited its protections more narrowly to employment—has led to differing interpretations among the state courts.[130]

Conclusion

For most of its history, the nation's laws reflected society's view that sex-based classifications are permissible. Women and men were treated differently; ironically, in many cases, the laws disadvantaged men more than women. Few such laws were challenged on constitutional grounds, and when they were, the courts were often reluctant to abandon their views of the proper roles of women and men in society. Then in 1971, spurred by the activities of the feminist movement, women's rights advocates mounted a campaign against such laws. The federal courts began to assess sex-based laws more carefully, subjecting them to a higher form of scrutiny and requiring the government to justify the differential treatment of women and men. Over the next twenty-five years, the Court became increasingly unwilling to accept the government's arguments that such laws were constitutional.

In the late 1990s, it appeared that the Court was becoming more willing to adopt a higher level of scrutiny for laws involving sex-based classifications, perhaps even to the point of equating them with laws based on racial classifications. However, largely because of its view of laws based on physical sex differences, the Court has retreated from this position.

Notes

1. David McCullough, *John Adams* (New York: Simon and Schuster, 2001), pp. 104–105. According to McCullough, Abigail was partially teasing John.

2. *Familiar Letters of John Adams and His Wife, Abigail Adams During the Revolution* (New York, 1876), reprinted in Eve Cary and Kathleen Willert Peratis, eds., *Woman and the Law* (Skokie: National Textbook Company, 1977), p. 2.

3. See Suzanne M. Marilley, *Woman Suffrage and the Origins of Liberal Feminism in the United States, 1820–1920* (Cambridge: Harvard University Press, 1996).

4. W. William Hodes, "Women and the Constitution: Some Legal History and a New Approach to the Nineteenth Amendment," *Rutgers Law Review* 25 (1970): 35–37, reprinted in Kermit L. Hall, ed., *Women, the Law, and the Constitution* (New York: Garland Publishing, 1987). In *The Ideas of the Woman Suffrage Movement, 1890–1920* (Garden City: Anchor, 1971), chaps. 1 and 7, Aileen S. Kraditor discusses the dispute over ratification of the Fourteenth Amendment that led to a split in the women's rights movement in 1869. Anthony and Stanton argued against ratification, but Stone, speaking for a majority of women's rights advocates, supported it despite its neglect of women's rights.

5. Nancy E. McGlen, Karen O'Connor, Laura Van Assendelft, and Wendy Gunther-Canada, *Women, Politics, and American Society*, 4th ed. (New York: Pearson Longman Publishing, 2005), chap. 1. In 1890, the two groups merged to form the National American Woman Suffrage Association under Anthony.

6. Jo Freeman, *A Room at a Time: How Women Entered Party Politics* (Lanham, Md.: Rowman and Littlefield, 2002), chap. 3, discusses state suffrage movements and the battle over the Nineteenth Amendment.

7. Martha Craig Daughtrey, "Women and the Constitution: Where We Are at the End of the Century," *New York University Law Review* 75 (2000): 1–25.

8. 83 U.S. (16 Wall) 130 (1873).

9. For a discussion of the privileges and immunities clause, see John Denvir, *Democracy's Constitution: Claiming the Privileges of American Citizenship* (Urbana: University of Illinois Press, 2001).

10. *Bradwell*, 83 U.S. at 139.

11. 83 U.S. (16 Wall) 36 (1873).

12. There was a widely held belief that society was (and should be) divided into separate spheres, in which the "public sphere of work was considered men's and the private world of family was women's." Ava Baron, "Feminist Legal Strategies: The Powers of Difference," in Beth B. Hess and Myra Marx Ferree, eds., *Analyzing Gender* (Beverly Hills: Sage Publications, 1987), p. 477. See Frances Olsen, "The Family and the Market: A Study of Ideology and Legal Reform," *Harvard Law Review* 96 (1983): 1497–1578; Nadine Taub and Elizabeth M. Schneider, "Perspectives on Women's Subordination and the Role of Law," in David Kairys, ed., *The Politics of Law: A Progressive Critique* (New York: Pantheon, 1982). During the 1800s, states began to lessen the constraints on women and allow them a measure of equality with men by enacting Married Women's Property Acts. These laws removed some of the legal restrictions on married women by giving them the right to contract, to sue and be sued, and to sell property. See Liane Kosaki and Susan Gluck Mezey, "Judicial Intervention in the Family: Interspousal Immunity and Civil Litigation," *Women and Politics* 8 (1988): 69–85.

13. *Bradwell*, 83 U.S. at 141. Twenty years later in *In re Lockwood*, 154 U.S. 116 (1894), the Supreme Court also rejected Belva Lockwood's attempt to seek admission to the Virginia bar.

14. 88 U.S. (21 Wall) 627 (1875).

15. The Court's decision was reminiscent of *Dred Scott*, 60 U.S. (19 How.) 393 (1857), in which it denied citizenship to an African American man. Why the Court chose to base *Minor* on the thoroughly discredited *Dred Scott* is not known, but his-

torian W. William Hodes suggests that it viewed women as "second-class citizens—citizens with less legal rights than other citizens." Hodes, "Women and the Constitution," pp. 45–46; see also Joan Hoff Wilson, "The Legal Status of Women in the Late Nineteenth and Early Twentieth Centuries," *Human Rights* 6 (1977), reprinted in Kermit L. Hall, ed., *Women, the Law, and the Constitution* (New York: Garland Publishing, 1987).

16. *Minor*, 88 U.S. at 629.

17. 198 U.S. 45 (1905).

18. *Lochner*, 198 U.S. at 53.

19. Under the "substantive due process doctrine" adopted in *Lochner*, the Court looked at the substance of the law to determine if it was "reasonable"; its assessment of reasonableness was largely influenced by the current laissez-faire attitude that viewed regulation of working conditions as undue interference with the prerogatives of industry. The era ended in the late 1930s, when the Court began to uphold New Deal legislation.

20. 208 U.S. 412 (1908).

21. *Muller*, 208 U.S. at 422.

22. Olsen, "The Family and the Market," p. 1557. See also Thomas H. Barnard and Adrienne L. Rapp, "Pregnant Employees, Working Mothers, and the Workplace: Legislation, Social Change, and Where We Are Today," *Cleveland State Journal of Law and Health* 32 (2009): 197–239.

23. Barbara Brown, Ann Freedman, Harriet Katz, and Alice Price, *Women's Rights and the Law* (New York: Praeger Publishers, 1977), p. 209.

24. 264 U.S. 292, 294 (1924).

25. 335 U.S. 464 (1948).

26. *Goesaert*, 335 U.S. at 465.

27. Some classic discussions of equal protection analysis can be found in Owen Fiss, "Groups and the Equal Protection Clause," *Philosophy and Public Affairs* 5 (1976): 107–177; Gerald Gunther, "Foreword: In Search of Evolving Doctrine on a Changing Court: A Model for a Newer Equal Protection," *Harvard Law Review* 86 (1972): 1–48; Joseph Tussman and Jacobus tenBroek, "The Equal Protection of the Laws," *California Law Review* 37 (1949): 341–381.

28. 323 U.S. 214 (1944).

29. *Korematsu*, 323 U.S. at 216.

30. In the 1970s, the Court was forced to grapple with the question of whether to treat laws that benefited racial minority groups, such as "affirmative action" laws, differently from laws that had a negative impact on such groups. In the 1990s, the Court began its current approach of applying strict scrutiny to all racial classifications, including those intended to advantage racial minority groups; see *Parents Involved in Community Schools v. Seattle School District*, 551 U.S. 701 (2007).

31. 368 U.S. 57 (1961).

32. *Hoyt*, 368 U.S. at 59.

33. *Hoyt*, 368 U.S. at 61–62.

34. More than a decade after *Hoyt*, in *Taylor v. Louisiana*, 419 U.S. 522 (1975), the Court held that a Louisiana law requiring women to register for jury duty violated the Sixth Amendment; ironically, that case was brought by a man convicted of rape.

35. The ill-fated ERA would likely have transformed sex into a suspect category, although it is likely that the Court would have allowed exceptions for laws that infringed on the right of privacy or laws implicating unique physical differences between the sexes.

36. This analysis is limited to equal protection cases, omitting other Burger Court decisions affecting women.

37. 404 U.S. 71 (1971). *Reed* was the first case in which the high court upheld a challenge to a sex-based classification; see Vicki Lens, "Supreme Court Narratives on Equality and Gender Discrimination in Employment: 1971–2002," *Cardozo Women's Law Journal* 10 (2004): 501–567.

38. Ginsburg argued six sex discrimination cases before the Court in the early years, succeeding in five, but despite her successes, she failed to persuade the Court to adopt strict scrutiny in sex-based classifications.

39. The equal protection clause of the Fourteenth Amendment applies to states and local governmental units, not the federal government. In *Bolling v. Sharpe,* 347 U.S. 497 (1954), a case involving segregated schools in the District of Columbia, the Supreme Court held that there was an equal protection component of the due process clause of the Fifth Amendment that applied to the federal government. Thus, equal protection challenges to federal laws fall within the due process clause of the Fifth Amendment.

40. *Reed,* 404 U.S. at 76–77.

41. 411 U.S. 677 (1973).

42. *Frontiero,* 411 U.S. at 684.

43. Stephanie M. Wildman, "The Legitimation of Sex Discrimination: A Critical Response to Supreme Court Jurisprudence," *Oregon Law Review* 63 (1984): 278–279. Wildman claims that despite the plurality's assertion that it was using the strict scrutiny doctrine, the justices did not really follow a strict scrutiny approach. In her view, the Court would have accepted the dependency rule if the government had shown that it saved money.

44. 429 U.S. 190 (1976).

45. *Craig,* 429 U.S. at 197.

46. *Craig,* 429 U.S. at 198–199.

47. Leo Kanowitz, "'Benign' Sex Discrimination: Its Troubles and Their Cure," *Hastings Law Journal* 31 (1980): 1394, argues that "sex discrimination against males in statutes and judicial decisions has been widespread and severe."

48. As a 2004 study demonstrates, intermediate scrutiny leads to a higher degree of unpredictability about the outcome of the case and courts are more likely to uphold plaintiffs' complaints of sex discrimination when using strict scrutiny rather than intermediate scrutiny. Lee Epstein, Andrew D. Martin, Lisa Baldez, and Tasina Nitzschke Nihiser, "Constitutional Sex Discrimination," *Tennessee Journal of Law and Policy* 1 (2004): 11–68.

49. See *Personnel Administrator of Massachusetts v. Feeney,* 442 U.S. 256 (1979) in which the Court upheld the veteran's preference for state jobs even though women had fewer opportunities to become veterans than men. The Court followed *Washington v. Davis,* 426 U.S. 229 (1976) in ruling that the Fourteenth Amendment's equal protection clause only applies to laws that are discriminatory on their face, rather than facially neutral laws making no mention of race or sex or other protected category.

50. 458 U.S. 718 (1982).

51. *Hogan,* 458 U.S. at 724.

52. *Hogan,* 458 U.S. at 723.

53. Constitutional equal protection cases comprise only one type of sex-based claim; other cases involving women revolve around the right to privacy and the right to equal opportunity in the workplace and in education.

54. Wendy Williams, "The Equality Crisis: Some Reflections on Culture, Courts, and Feminism," *Women's Rights Law Reporter* 7 (1982): 175–200, calls these "easy cases." She contrasts them with "hard cases" in which the challenged laws are traceable to physiological sex differences that force the Court to reassess its commitment to equality between the sexes.

55. 405 U.S. 645 (1972).

56. 421 U.S. 7 (1975).

57. 440 U.S 268 (1979).

58. 450 U.S. 455 (1981).

59. 420 U.S. 636 (1975).

60. 430 U.S. 199 (1977).

61. 443 U.S. 76 (1979).

62. 446 U.S. 142 (1980).

63. 417 U.S. 484 (1974).

64. 416 U.S. 351 (1974).

65. 419 U.S. 498 (1975).

66. 430 U.S. 313 (1977).

67. 465 U.S. 728 (1984).

68. The Florida law was repealed in 1988.

69. The navy policy was revised in 1981.

70. 453 U.S. 57 (1981).

71. *New York Times,* February 20, 1980.

72. See Lens, "Supreme Court Narratives on Equality," p. 535.

73. For a historical view of women in the military, see Linda Grant De Pauw, *Battle Cries and Lullabies: Women in War from Prehistory to the Present* (Norman: University of Oklahoma Press, 1998); see also Cynthia Enloe, *Does Khaki Become You?* (Boston: South End Press, 1983); Lorry M. Fenner and Marie E. DeYoung, *Women in Combat: Civic Duty or Military Liability?* (Washington, D.C.: Georgetown University Press, 2001).

74. See Judith Hicks Stiehm, *Arms and the Enlisted Woman* (Philadelphia: Temple University Press, 1989), chap. 5, for a discussion of litigation against the military on sex discrimination grounds.

75. 450 U.S. 464 (1981).

76. Prosecutors sometimes include statutory rape charges when, as appeared to be the case in *Michael M.,* they believe the woman was forcibly raped but lack sufficient evidence to prove it.

77. California's statutory rape law was amended in the early 1990s to allow prosecution of either men or women. Most prosecutions, however, are aimed at men as defendants and women as victims; see Kay L. Levine, "The Intimacy Discount: Prosecutorial Discretion, Privacy, and Equality in the Statutory Rape Caseload," *Emory Law Journal* 55 (2006): 720.

78. Williams, "The Equality Crisis," p. 181, n. 47.

79. 430 U.S. 787 (1977).

80. Katharine B. Silbaugh, "*Miller v. Albright:* Problems of Constitutionalization in Family Law," *Boston University Law Review* 79 (1999): 1144.

81. 434 U.S. 246 (1978).

82. 441 U.S. 347 (1979).

83. 463 U.S. 248 (1983).

84. In a later decision involving an unwed father and his child, *Michael H. v. Gerald D.,* 491 U.S. 110 (1989), the Court ruled on a California law that presumed

that a child born to a woman living with her husband was the husband's child. The Court decided the case on due process grounds and upheld the law, despite evidence that there was a 98.07 percent probability that the plaintiff, who wanted the opportunity to prove his paternity, was the child's father.

85. 441 U.S. 380 (1979).

86. Ann E. Freedman, "Sex Equality, Sex Differences, and the Supreme Court," *Yale Law Journal* 92 (1983): 944–945; Williams, "The Equality Crisis," pp. 182–183, n. 50.

87. See Ruth Bader Ginsburg, "The Burger Court's Grapplings with Sex Discrimination," in Vincent Blasi, ed., *The Burger Court: The Counter-Revolution That Wasn't* (New Haven: Yale University Press, 1983).

88. 518 U.S. 515 (1996).

89. There was speculation that O'Connor had elevated the level of scrutiny in *Hogan* by inserting the "exceedingly persuasive justification" language into the intermediate scrutiny test. *VMI* led to renewed speculation that the Court created a new form of scrutiny for sex-based classifications. See Kathryn A. Lee, "Intermediate Review 'with Teeth' in Gender Discrimination Cases: The New Standard in *United States v. Virginia*," *Temple Political and Civil Rights Law Review* 7 (1997): 221–244; David K. Bowsher, "Cracking the Code of *United States v. Virginia*," *Duke Law Journal* 48 (1998): 305–339; Elizabeth A. Douglas, "*United States v. Virginia:* Gender Scrutiny Under an 'Exceedingly Persuasive Justification Standard,'" *Capital University Law Review* 26 (1997): 173–199; Jeffrey A. Barnes, "The Supreme Court's 'Exceedingly [Un]persuasive' Application of Intermediate Scrutiny in *United States v. Virginia*," *University of Richmond Law Review* 31 (1997): 523–548.

90. 511 U.S. 127 (1994).

91. *J. E. B.* was part of a series of cases in which the Court determined the limits of peremptory challenges. The Court held in *Batson v. Kentucky,* 476 U.S. 79 (1986), that a prosecutor's use of peremptory challenges in a racially discriminatory manner violated the equal protection clause. In *Powers v. Ohio,* 499 U.S. 400 (1991); *Edmonson v. Leesville Concrete Company,* 500 U.S. 614 (1991); *Georgia v. McCollum,* 505 U.S. 42 (1992), the Court extended *Batson* to cases involving white defendants, cases involving the use of peremptory challenges by defendants, and civil cases.

92. *J. E. B.,* 511 U.S. at 130–131.

93. *J. E. B.,* 511 U.S. at 137 n. 6.

94. *J. E. B.,* 511 U.S. at 140 n. 11.

95. *United States v. Virginia (VMI),* 766 F. Supp. 1407 (W.D. Va. 1991).

96. *United States v. Virginia (VMI),* 976 F.2d 890 (4th Cir. 1992).

97. *United States v. Virginia (VMI),* 852 F. Supp. 471, 481 (W.D. Va. 1994).

98. *United States v. Virginia (VMI),* 44 F.3d 1229, 1237 (4th Cir. 1995).

99. *VMI,* 518 U.S. at 532–533.

100. *VMI,* 518 U.S. at 533.

101. Ginsburg stopped short of accusing the state of manufacturing this goal for purposes of the litigation.

102. *VMI,* 518 U.S. at 546, quoting *Hogan,* 458 U.S. at 731. In "*United States v. Virginia* and Our Evolving 'Constitution': Playing Peek-a-boo with the Standard of Scrutiny for Sex-Based Classifications," *Case Western Reserve Law Review* 47 (1997): 1121–1155, Steven A. Delchin argues that Ginsburg's use of this language instead of the traditional intermediate scrutiny language signifies a change in the Court's position on sex-based classifications.

103. According to Philippa Strum, Ginsburg herself later acknowledged that "the line between strict scrutiny and intermediate scrutiny was now blurred" as a result of

VMI. See Strum, *Women in the Barracks: The VMI Case and Equal Rights* (Lawrence: University of Kansas Press, 2002), p. 287.

104. In "A Postscript on *VMI*," *American University Journal of Gender and the Law* 6 (1997): 59–64, Elizabeth M. Schneider notes that the Court's meaning is very obscure.

105. Debra L. Satinoff discusses the contradiction between the Court's review of immigration laws, which receive almost no scrutiny, and its review of sex-based laws, which are supposed to be analyzed with heightened scrutiny. The Court seems to have resolved this conflict by relying on one standard or the other and not attempting to reconcile the two. See Satinoff, "Sex-Based Discrimination in U.S. Immigration Law: The High Court's Lost Opportunity to Bridge the Gap Between What We Say and What We Do," *American University Law Review* 47 (1998): 1353–1392.

106. *Miller,* C.A. No. 6: 93 CV 39 (E.D. Tex. June 2, 1993).

107. *Miller,* 870 F. Supp. 1 (D.D.C. 1994).

108. *Miller v. Christopher,* 96 F.3d 1467 (D.C. Cir. 1996).

109. *Washington Post,* November 5, 1997.

110. 523 U.S. 420 (1998).

111. None of the justices believed that the daughter's rights were violated. O'Connor and Kennedy rejected her argument for standing because the statute distinguished on the basis of the parents' sex, not the children's. Rehnquist, Stevens, and the three dissenters, however, believed she had standing to bring a third-party claim on her father's behalf; Silbaugh, "*Miller v. Albright,*" p. 1148.

112. 533 U.S. 53 (2001).

113. *Houston Chronicle,* June 12, 2001.

114. *Nguyen v. INS,* 208 F.3d 528 (5th Cir. 2000). Because the father joined his son in this suit, standing was not an issue here, as in *Miller.* The presence of the father as a plaintiff in the case determined that the sex-based classification in the statute would be subjected to heightened scrutiny. See Clay M. West, "*Nguyen v. INS:* Is Sex Really More Important Now?" *Yale Law and Policy Review* 19 (2001): 525–537.

115. *Nguyen,* 533 U.S. at 73.

116. *Nguyen,* 533 U.S. at 74.

117. *United States v. Flores-Villar,* 536 F.3d 990, 993 (9th Cir. 2008).

118. *Flores-Villar v. United States,* 130 S.Ct. 1878 (2010). During oral arguments on November 10, 2010, some of the justices expressed concern about interfering with Congress's authority to determine immigration policy; *Washington Post,* November 11, 2010.

119. *Flores-Villar v. United States,* 2011 U.S. LEXIS 4378. The tie vote on the high court resulted in an affirmance of the lower court ruling. Obama had nominated Kagan to be solicitor general of the United States (the federal government's top lawyer) in January 2009; she was approved by the Senate in March. He nominated her for the high court in May 2010. After winning Senate approval and being sworn in a few months later, she took her place on the Court at the opening of the 2010–2011 term in October 2010. See *New York Times,* May 10, 2010; *Boston.com,* August 5, 2010. Because the solicitor general's office represents the United States in cases before the Court, she has had to recuse herself from participating in numerous cases that have come before the Court. The Court does not indicate how each justice voted in such tied rulings so it is open to speculation on which justices voted to uphold the Ninth Circuit and which justices wished to reverse it; one must also speculate on whether the justices took the opportunity to discuss the scrutiny issue and their views of laws based on physical sex differences. See Jeffrey Hochstetler, "A Father's Presence: *Flores-Villar v. United States,*" *Duke Journal of Constitutional Law & Public Policy Sidebar* 6 (2011): 142–159 for a prediction of the Court's likely vote in the case.

120. Jo Freeman, "How 'Sex' Got into Title VII: Persistent Opportunism as a Maker of Public Policy," *Law and Inequality: A Journal of Theory and Practice* 9 (1991): 163–184. She discusses the role of women's groups and political parties in the struggle over the ERA.

121. The proposed Equal Rights Amendment read: "Section 1: Equality of rights under the law shall not be denied or abridged by the United States or by any State on account of sex; Section 2: The Congress shall have the power to enforce, by appropriate legislation, the provisions of this article; Section 3: This amendment shall take effect two years after the date of ratification."

122. There is a plethora of books explaining the defeat of the ERA; see, for example, Jane Mansbridge, *Why We Lost the ERA* (Chicago: University of Chicago Press, 1986); Janet K. Boles, *The Politics of the Equal Rights Amendment: Conflict and the Decision Process* (New York: Longman, 1979); Mary Frances Berry, *Why ERA Failed: Politics, Women's Rights, and the Amending Process of the Constitution* (Bloomington: Indiana University Press, 1986).

123. Perhaps the most authoritative analysis of the likely interpretation of the ERA is Barbara Brown, Thomas Emerson, Gail Falk, and Ann E. Freedman, "The Equal Rights Amendment: A Constitutional Basis for Equal Rights for Women," *Yale Law Journal* 80 (1971): 871–985; for a more recent analysis, see Martha F. Davis, "The Equal Rights Amendment: Then and Now," *Columbia Journal of Gender and Law* 17 (2008): 419–459.

124. Gail Collins, *When Everything Changed: The Amazing Journey of American Women from 1960 to the Present* (New York: Little, Brown, 2009).

125. See David E. Kyvig, "Historical Misunderstandings and the Defeat of the Equal Rights Amendment," *Public Historian* 18 (1996): 45–63, for analysis of errors made by ERA proponents. Schlafly first attracted attention in 1964 with the publication of her book supporting Arizona senator Barry Goldwater's candidacy for the presidency; she founded the Eagle Forum in 1972 and was chief organizer of the "Stop the ERA" movement; see *St. Louis Post-Dispatch,* July 31, 2005; PhyllisShlafly.com, 2009, available at http://www.phyllisschlafly.com/.

126. See Brannon P. Denning and John R. Vile, "Necromancing the Equal Rights Amendment," *Constitutional Commentary* 17 (2000): 593–602.

127. In *Idaho v. Freeman,* 529 F. Supp. 1107 (D. Idaho 1981), the district court held that the matter was to be determined by the courts and that a state could validly rescind a prior ratification if it did so before the amendment was ratified by three-fourths of the states; see also *Dyer v. Blair,* 390 F. Supp. 1287 (N.D. Ill. 1974).

128. See Davis, "The Equal Rights Amendment"; *Washington Post,* March 28, 2007; *Missouri Lawyers Weekly,* October 8, 2007.

129. State constitutional provisions are interpreted by state supreme courts; the U.S. Supreme Court is precluded from reviewing these decisions.

130. See Leslie W. Gladstone, *Equal Rights Amendments: State Provisions* (Washington, D.C.: Congressional Research Service, 2004), for wording of state equal rights amendments; see also Inessa Baram-Blackwell, "Separating Dick and Jane: Single-Sex Public Education Under the Washington State Equal Rights Amendment," *Washington Law Review* 81 (2006): 337–362; Linda J. Wharton, "State Equal Rights Amendments Revisited: Evaluating Their Effectiveness in Advancing Protection Against Sex Discrimination," *Rutgers Law Journal* 36 (2005): 1201–1293. In "Does the U.S. Constitution Need an Equal Rights Amendment?" *Journal of Legal Studies* 35 (2006): 243–281, Lisa Baldez, Lee Epstein, and Andrew D. Martin compare sex discrimination rulings in states with ERAs and states without ERAs. They found that courts in ERA states used a higher level of scrutiny than those in non-ERA states.

2 Eliminating Gender Bias in Education

In 1992, the American Association of University Women (AAUW) presented unwelcome news about gender equity in U.S. classrooms. After surveying the results of numerous studies, the AAUW concluded that "the educational system is not meeting girls' needs." It noted that although public schools were failing both boys and girls in substantial ways, "in many respects girls are put at a disadvantage simply because they are girls."[1] And, it added, these "disadvantages" are intensified for minority and low-income girls.

The report, entitled *How Schools Shortchange Girls,* pointed to examples of gender bias in schools, such as girls receiving less attention in the classroom and being increasingly victimized by sexual harassment as well as stereotypical curricular content. As a result, it warned, their confidence and self-esteem suffered, and, among other things, they were discouraged from pursuing nontraditional careers such as science and math. The report ended by calling for greater awareness of gender inequities in the classroom and an end to discrimination against girls.

A follow-up AAUW report, based on research published between 1990 and 1998, discussed the extent to which girls were still being "shortchanged" by the educational system. This report, issued in 1998, recognized advances in equality during the preceding six years but emphasized that "for girls, an equitable education is in many respects still an elusive goal, in sight yet out of reach."[2] Stressing that boys are also disadvantaged by inequality, the study made clear that gender equity benefits all students, not just girls.

Demonstrating its ongoing concern about gender inequality in schools, the AAUW convened a conference in 2000 to assess whether progress had been made in the nation's education system. Participants from a number of disciplines and differing ideological perspectives discussed the necessity of continuing research on achievement. They urged researchers to focus attention on the interdependence of boys and girls in schools and to stop viewing gender equity as a zero-sum game between boys and girls.[3]

The AAUW's most recent effort to date to appraise the status of gender equity—a report released in 2008—revealed that a gender gap still existed in some areas (such as math, where boys continued to outperform girls). But these results were more mixed: the report also showed that there were no gender differences in the rate of entry into college and that girls had a higher percentage of bachelors' degrees and higher high school grade point averages than boys. Overall, the report concluded that contrary to popular rhetoric, boys were not negatively affected by advances made by girls.[4]

Single-Sex Education

Advocates of single-sex education argue that educational disparities between girls and boys diminish when they are separately educated. Thus, ironically, as the Supreme Court deliberated the future of VMI's single-sex admissions policy, public schools in Maryland, Pennsylvania, California, New York, and Illinois were experimenting with single-sex educational programs.[5]

In part as a result of the growing awareness of gender inequality in schools, as evidenced in the 1992 AAUW report, researchers began to focus attention on the delivery of educational services in single-sex schools and programs. After assembling a group of scholars on November 12, 1997, the AAUW issued another report in 1998, assessing the benefits offered by single-sex schooling. The scholars who contributed to it believed that single-sex education was advantageous for some students but was not a magic cure for gender inequity in education.[6] The consensus among them was that "there is no evidence that single-sex education in general 'works' or is 'better' than coeducation."[7]

The scholars acknowledged that many girls seemed to prefer the single-sex environment, but they also pointed out that single-sex classes may reinforce gender stereotypes and promote sexism. Additionally, some believed that a single-sex school or program improved their self-confidence and generated greater interest in math and science but seemed to have little effect on girls' achievement levels, including in these subjects. In part because of the variety of educational experiences offered in a single-sex environment, ranging from a single class to an entire school day, the researchers concluded that there were insufficient data to determine the long-range effectiveness of single-sex education.[8]

By the end of the twentieth century there were only about a dozen public school systems with single-sex programs. The debate continues, however, with opponents and proponents of single-sex education arguing about the benefits of their approach but citing little scientific evidence to support their views. Given the scarcity of data, probably the most significant argument against single-sex education is that it diverts attention from the problems facing both boys and girls in the classroom, especially in inner-city schools. Many civil rights groups, including feminist organizations, oppose single-sex education on these grounds, citing federal law and the U.S. Supreme Court's ruling in *VMI* to bolster their argument.

Two well-known efforts at single-sex schooling, an African American boys' school in Detroit and an African American girls' school in New York City, drew opposition from civil liberties and civil rights groups, such as the National Organization for Women (NOW), the National Association for the Advancement of Colored People (NAACP), and the ACLU. A Michigan federal court judge ordered Detroit to abandon its plan, and the school never opened. Similarly, Milwaukee reversed itself before opening a school for African American boys and admitted girls as well.

Perhaps the best-known single-sex public school, New York City's Young Women's Leadership School—concentrating on math and science programs—opened its doors in East Harlem in 1996. Opposition arose here as well from local civil rights groups such as the New York City Civil Liberties Union and the New York chapter of NOW. They filed a complaint with the Office for Civil Rights (OCR) of the Department of Education (DOE), charging that federal law required the school district to provide similar facilities for boys. However, OCR failed to act on the complaint, and more than ten years after its founding, the school remained open.[9]

Despite the uncertainties about the advantages of single-sex education, the passage of the 2001 No Child Left Behind Act (NCLB) spurred a number of female senators from both parties to urge the Bush White House to propose new rules to allow schools to offer same-sex classes and schools. As a result of their interest, NCLB included funding for demonstration projects; Secretary of Education Rod Paige expressed enthusiasm for the idea and announced that DOE would promulgate rules to allow schools to explore the option of creating some single-sex education environments—for boys as well as girls, while promising to ensure equal opportunity for both sexes.

By the beginning of 2006, the National Association for Single Sex Public Education reported that nearly fifty single-sex public schools and

150 single-sex programs within schools had been established.[10] And in October 2006, Paige's successor, Margaret Spellings, announced that final regulations easing restrictions on single-sex education would go into effect the next month.[11] Whatever the purported benefits of single-sex education, however, most public school systems eschewed it because of its questionable legal status and potential political and social costs.

In the 1970s, the U.S. courts began to address single-sex admissions policies, common in many states throughout most of the twentieth century. In *Kirstein v. Rector and Visitors of the University of Virginia*,[12] the federal district court rejected the plaintiffs' demand to order the University of Virginia to admit women to the Charlottesville campus, the most prestigious in the state system, immediately. Nevertheless, the school agreed to allow the gradual admission of women to the campus. In part, the judge feared that an order to admit women would affect the all-male Virginia Military Institute.

Soon after *Kirstein,* in *Williams v. McNair,*[13] a South Carolina district court refused to grant a man's request to attend the all-female Winthrop College. The district court reasoned that "the Constitution does not require that a classification 'keep abreast of the latest' in educational opinion, it only demands that the discrimination not be wholly wanting in reason."[14] Applying minimal scrutiny, the court saw nothing arbitrary or irrational in a single-sex school and no Fourteenth Amendment violation in denying admission to men.[15]

In the first circuit court ruling on single-sex education, *Vorchheimer v. School District of Philadelphia,*[16] a teenage girl who was rejected by Central High, the city's all-boys high school, filed suit against the city. In a 2 to 1 vote, the appeals court upheld the city policy, explaining that differences between the sexes "may, in limited circumstances, justify disparity in law."[17] The court believed that both sexes were equally affected by the sex-segregated school system, and because evidence showed that adolescents benefited from single-sex high schools, both sexes were also possibly advantaged. Using minimal scrutiny, the court found the city policy rational and held that Vorchheimer's desire to attend Central High was an insufficient reason to alter it.[18]

A strong dissent by Judge John Gibbons drew comparisons between the majority opinion and *Plessy v. Ferguson,*[19] in which the Supreme Court formulated the "separate but equal" doctrine for racial classifications. Outraged at the court's ruling, Gibbons said he "was under the distinct impression [that] separate but equal" was no longer acceptable—especially in public education.[20]

In a divided vote, the Supreme Court affirmed the circuit court, allowing Central High to remain a boys-only school.[21] Thus, two decades after *Brown v. Board of Education*,[22] in which the high court declared that public schools may not separate children on the basis of race, the Court refused to repudiate the separate but equal doctrine for boys and girls.[23] After *Vorchheimer,* the Supreme Court issued two rulings on single-sex schooling in public education; Table 2.1 presents these cases.

The Court addressed a single-sex admissions policy in *Mississippi University for Women v. Hogan* in 1982.[24] Mississippi University for Women (MUW), the oldest public women's college in the United States, established its School of Nursing in 1971, admitting only women but allowing men to audit classes. The school's charter defined its purpose, essentially unchanged since its founding in 1884, as

> the moral and intellectual achievement of the girls of the state by the maintenance of a first-class institution for their education in the arts and sciences, for their training in normal school methods and kindergarten, for their instruction in bookkeeping, photography, stenography, telegraphy, and typewriting, and in designing, drawing, engraving, and painting, and their industrial application, and for their instruction in fancy, general and practical needlework, and in such other industrial branches as experience, from time to time, shall suggest as necessary or proper to fit them for the practical affairs of life.[25]

When registered nurse Joe Hogan sought admission to MUW's nursing program, he was rejected despite his qualifications. Because MUW was the only single-sex school in the state, the Court explained in a footnote that the case did not raise the "question of whether States can provide 'separate but equal' undergraduate institutions for males and females."[26]

The state argued that the school's single-sex policy was intended to compensate women for past discrimination. But speaking for a 5 to 4

Table 2.1 Supreme Court Single-Sex Education Rulings, 1977–1996

Case	Date	Issue[a]	Ruling[b]
Vorchheimer	1977	Public high school	Limits educational equality
Hogan	1982	State nursing program	Expands educational equality
VMI	1996	Military academy	Expands educational equality

Notes: a. Based on the major issue in the case.
b. Based on the overall outcome of the case.

majority, O'Connor stressed that an exclusionary admissions policy may only be justified by showing that "the members of the gender benefitted by the classification actually suffer a disadvantage related to the classification."[27] There was insufficient evidence that women in nursing suffered compared to men; indeed, O'Connor noted, the school's policy served the opposite end of maintaining the stereotypical image of nursing as a woman's occupation. Finally, she pointed out that the state failed to show that its policy was substantially related to its compensatory goal; because men were accepted as classroom auditors, MUW could not realistically claim that it was offering female nursing students a single-sex environment.

Because the decision was narrowly focused, it failed to resolve the legality of MUW's admissions policy for the rest of the school. Moreover, some argue that the Court should have addressed the "separate but equal" doctrine because the ruling left open the possibility that the Court would uphold a true compensatory policy as long as the state offered an "exceedingly persuasive justification" for it.[28] Others believe that because single-sex schools are said to empower women and encourage them to assume nontraditional leadership roles, the Court should have allowed the state to maintain its single-sex policy.[29]

Echoing this view in dissent, Justice Lewis Powell protested that this was the first time the equal protection clause had been invoked to restrict women's opportunities. In his view, the Court should allow the state to take women's differing educational needs into account rather than insisting on a formalistic equal treatment approach.

With two exceptions, single-sex education in the nation's military colleges ended when West Point and the Naval Academy began admitting women in 1976.[30] These schools, VMI and the Citadel, claimed that women would interfere with their purpose of training men for the military.[31] As one observer noted, however, "what really mattered to VMI was its cult of masculinity in a world sealed from the presence of women who might either meet or undermine the masculine standard, in each case threatening male privilege."[32]

The six-year legal battle against VMI began in 1990. Responding to the federal government's suit, the state argued that admitting women to VMI would destroy the school's educational mission. Following a six-day trial, in June 1991, federal court judge Jackson L. Kiser ruled that allowing women into VMI would significantly impair the educational environment. He concluded by stating that "VMI truly marches to the beat of a different drummer, and I will permit it to continue to do so."[33]

After the Fourth Circuit remanded the case to Kiser to determine whether the hastily established VWIL at Mary Baldwin College cured the constitutional violation, he ruled in May 1994 that despite the fact that the two programs were substantially different, they satisfied equal protection requirements. He wrote, "If VMI marches to the beat of a drum, then Mary Baldwin marches to the melody of a fife, and when the march is over, both will have arrived at the same destination."[34] On appeal, the circuit court agreed that the state's remedy was adequate.

In June 1996, the Supreme Court found that VMI's admissions policy violated the equal protection clause of the U.S. Constitution.[35] In comparing the two programs, the majority noted that the women's program was "different in kind from VMI and unequal in both tangible and intangible facilities."[36] VWIL was based on cooperation and self-esteem and lacked the rigors of VMI's military training, including barracks life, uniforms, communal eating arrangements, and leadership development. Moreover, its academic standards, curriculum, and financial resources were inferior to VMI's. Looking to the past, the Court compared VWIL to the University of Texas's allegedly "separate but equal" African American law school, an arrangement it found unacceptable in its 1950 ruling in *Sweatt v. Painter*.[37]

By insisting on "substantial equality" in both tangible and intangible factors, the Court seemed to move closer to repudiating the concept of "separate but equal" on the basis of sex. However, by stressing the inequality of the two programs, the Court did not foreclose the possibility that separate schools might be constitutional if the state were able to present evidence that the facilities were equal.

The Citadel case arose when Shannon Faulkner challenged the college's male-only admissions policy. In August 1993, a federal judge ordered her admission to the school but not to the corps of cadets. Following numerous legal delays, she was finally permitted to enroll in January 1994—the first woman ever to sit in regular day classes at the Citadel. After a trial in July 1994, the judge ordered Faulkner into the corps of cadets, but because of appeals and other legal challenges, during which time the state made a half-hearted attempt at creating an alternative program such as VWIL, Faulkner did not enter the corps until August 1995.

About a week after she became the first woman cadet at the Citadel, Faulkner unexpectedly resigned—along with about thirty other new male cadets. Citing ill health and emotional stress, she explained that the lengthy battle with its two and a half years of stress had "all crashed in" on her during the week.[38] Another plaintiff was substituted in the suit against the Citadel, but the action was placed on hold to allow the high court to rule in *VMI*.

On the day the Supreme Court announced its decision in *VMI*, the Citadel declared it would immediately begin to accept women, and four were admitted into the corps of cadets in August 1996. In contrast, VMI alumni began to explore the possibility of amassing the millions of dollars necessary to maintain it as a private institution. Three months after the Court's ruling, in a 9 to 8 vote, VMI's Board of Visitors finally abandoned its efforts and decided to admit women in the upcoming semester.[39] Ironically, despite VMI's insistence throughout the litigation that it would have to undergo massive changes to accommodate the presence of women, it was forced to make only slight alterations. It allowed women to have slightly longer hair (about the same as upperclass men), added a skirt to the official uniform, and modified the bathrooms to afford each sex some measure of privacy. In contrast, the Citadel substantially changed the environment for its students, adapting its regulations as well as its physical structure to accommodate women.[40]

Title IX of the Education Amendments of 1972

The federal government assumed an important role in shaping educational policy affecting women when it enacted Title IX of the Education Amendments of 1972. This path-breaking law states, "No person in the United States shall, on the basis of sex, be excluded from participation in, be denied the benefits of, or be subjected to discrimination under any education program or activity receiving Federal financial assistance." It was included in an omnibus higher education bill largely through the efforts of Democrats Edith Green of Oregon, chair of the Special Education Subcommittee in the House, and Bayh of Indiana in the Senate.[41] It was signed by President Richard Nixon on June 23, 1972.

Title IX bans discriminatory admissions in vocational, professional, and graduate programs as well as most public undergraduate schools. According to Caspar Weinberger, secretary of the Department of Health, Education, and Welfare (HEW)—the agency charged with formulating Title IX regulations—the statute covered 16,000 public school systems and nearly 2,700 postsecondary institutions. However, although the law was a major achievement for educational equality, it fell short of a comprehensive attack on sex discrimination, leaving major gaps in a number of areas, including admissions, curriculum, and athletics.

Single-sex admissions policies remained legal in most elementary and secondary schools, private undergraduate schools, and public undergraduate institutions "that traditionally and continually" from their inception only admitted students of one sex. However, the law barred these institutions from discriminating against students already enrolled. It also exempted military academies, that is, schools with a "primary purpose" of training students for the military services or merchant marine, as well as religious schools if the law conflicted with their basic principles. Two years later, Congress amended the law to exempt sororities and fraternities; the Young Men and Young Women's Christian Associations; and the Boy Scouts, Girl Scouts, and Campfire Girls. In 1976, further amendments restored father-son and mother-daughter activities as well as scholarships awarded to beauty contest winners.

Despite its importance, Title IX received little attention from most members of Congress during its passage. And because of its scant legislative history, the courts have had minimal guidance in interpreting Congress's intent. However, the discussion on the Senate floor and Bayh's remarks give a few clues to Congress's design.[42]

Title IX is modeled after the almost identically worded section of Title VI of the 1964 Civil Rights Act, and to the extent that they discussed it, members of Congress indicated that they intended the laws to be interpreted similarly.[43] Moreover, there had been extensive debate on an earlier version of Title IX the year before when Green and Bayh had initially sought to include sex discrimination provisions in the 1971 Education Amendments.[44]

Because legislation is written in broad strokes, administrative agencies are charged with promulgating the regulations that reflect the intent of Congress. When regulations are challenged, courts often defer to the agency's interpretation of the statute but are not bound to do so; they may strike regulations they believe are inconsistent with the intent of Congress or the text of the law. The federal agency in charge of issuing Title IX regulations—HEW, or more specifically, OCR—released the proposed regulations in June 1974. Not surprisingly, once HEW indicated that the regulations applied to athletics, there was an avalanche of comments during the four-month public comment period.

The final regulations, signed by President Gerald Ford on July 2, 1975, and made effective a few weeks later, encompassed physical education classes; course offerings, such as shop and home economics; extracurricular activities; financial aid; and counseling. Despite concern about sex stereotyping in textbooks, the regulations did not impose restrictions on books and other curricular materials because of the possible conflict with First Amendment guarantees of freedom of expression.

Title IX and Athletics

Commemorating National Girls and Women in Sports Day on February 3, 2010, President Barack Obama proudly noted that "women compete at all levels today, in large part due to the foundation laid by Title IX, which has done much to advance the number of women taking part in collegiate athletic programs and has increased access to the classroom. Today, as we celebrate, we must also recognize that more needs to be done and we should recommit ourselves to achieving true equality for all."[45]

Title IX's vision of equality in the nation's school systems soon spread to the thousands of girls involved in high school and college sports, as well as the thousands more who wanted to become involved but were discouraged from doing so. This promise of greater equality in athletic programs was sorely needed in the 1970s, for it was commonplace in many states to bar girls from participating in high school sports activities. In states such as Pennsylvania, Nebraska, Indiana, Michigan, Minnesota, and Illinois, to name a few, rules often prevented women from playing on the same teams as men (even when no women's team was provided) and excluded them from playing on teams against men (even in noncontact sports like swimming, golf, and track). To contest these restrictions, women filed lawsuits—typically against state athletic associations—challenging such rules, usually on the grounds that they violated constitutional equal protection principles. Such suits highlighted the inequality inherent in numerous high school and intercollegiate athletic programs and the need for effective enforcement of Title IX.[46]

A coalition of women's groups, known as the Education Task Force, led the charge to expand the scope of the statute through regulations.[47] The primary opposition came from the National Collegiate Athletic Association (NCAA) and the American Football Coaches Association (AFCA).[48] The nearly 10,000 comments received from June to October 1974 indicate the intensity surrounding the debate. Moreover, because Congress had the authority to reject the proposed regulations, lobbying efforts were directed at it as well.[49]

Ironically, the subject of athletics was only mentioned twice during the floor debate over Title IX and was not addressed in any congressional reports. Yet soon after its passage, the nation's attention began to focus on athletics as groups such as the AFCA and the NCAA attempted to block regulations that would compel greater equality in high school and college athletic programs.[50]

Before the final regulations were promulgated, Congress enacted the Education Amendments of 1974 to amend Title IX to clarify congressional intent about the effect of the law on athletics.[51] In the Senate's consideration of this bill, Republican senator John Tower of Texas attempted to prevent Title IX from applying to sex discrimination in intercollegiate sports, arguing that Congress had not intended Title IX to cover athletics. His proposed bill incorporated an NCAA proposal, seeking to exempt revenue-producing intercollegiate sports (such as football and basketball) from the law; he maintained that to do otherwise would diminish funds for the institution's entire athletic program, and that, ultimately, the loss of these funds would harm women's sports activities.

The Senate approved the Tower Amendment, but it was deleted during the Senate-House conference. Instead, the conference committee adopted the Javits Amendment (proposed by Senator Jacob Javits, Republican from New York), which authorized HEW to promulgate Title IX regulations "relating to the prohibition of sex discrimination in federally assisted education programs which shall include, with respect to intercollegiate athletic activities, reasonable provisions considering the nature of particular sports."[52] Ford signed the bill into law in August 1974.

The final regulations, issued in 1975, divided sports activities into two categories: physical education classes and team activities.[53] All physical education classes, except those involving ability grouping and contact sports, were required to be coeducational. Elementary schools were given one year to comply with the regulations; high schools and colleges were given three years.[54]

Not long after the regulations went into effect, the NCAA sued HEW secretary Joseph Califano in a Kansas federal district court, arguing, among other things, that the Title IX regulations did not apply to athletic programs because they did not receive federal aid.[55] The court dismissed the case, ruling that because the NCAA received no federal funds, the regulations did not affect it, and therefore it had no standing to sue.

The Title IX regulations barred schools from fielding separate teams in the same sport but exempted sports involving body contact, such as wrestling, boxing, football, basketball, ice hockey, and rugby, as well as sports in which selection was based on competitive skill. Although they required that schools provide "equal athletic opportunity for members of both sexes," the competitive skill exception broadly allowed for separate teams in most sports (because most athletic teams are based on competitive skills). More important, the contact sport exception allowed separate teams for the more popular contact sports and barred women from trying out for the men's teams. However, the regulations required an institution to allow the excluded sex to compete for a place on teams in noncontact sports if there was only one team.[56]

When women's groups criticized the proposed regulations, HEW suggested a new policy interpretation requiring equal per capita spending in the areas of scholarships, recruitment, and equipment.[57] The final regulations called for equal per capita funding in scholarships but only equivalency in the other areas.[58] In an effort to further define "equal opportunity" in sports, HEW issued a policy interpretation in 1979, a document that sought to clarify an institution's duty to comply with Title IX. After receiving nearly 1,000 comments, the agency promulgated the 1979 policy interpretation, focusing on intercollegiate sports.[59]

The document addressed three issues: scholarship aid, access to opportunities and benefits, and effective accommodation of students' abilities and interests. The interpretation stated that scholarship aid must be available on a substantially proportional basis to the number of men and women participating in the school's athletic programs, that there must be equivalency in benefits and opportunities, and that the athletic interests of male and female students must be equally accommodated.[60]

The policy interpretation established a three-part test to determine whether the institution has accommodated the interests of its underrepresented students. The first prong, known as the "substantial proportionality" factor, requires the institution to provide athletic opportunities for students in intercollegiate sports in numbers "substantially proportionate" to their respective undergraduate enrollments. When one sex is underrepresented among intercollegiate athletes, the second prong allows the school to "show a history and continuing practice of program expansion which is demonstrably responsive to the developing interest and abilities of the members of that sex." And when there is an underrepresented sex and the institution has not expanded such programs, it can satisfy the third prong by showing "that the interests and abilities of the members of that sex have been fully and effectively accommodated by the present program."[61] Institutions must comply with at least one of the prongs of the three-part test to be considered in compliance with Title IX.[62]

The majority of Title IX athletics cases have, in one way or another, revolved around the validity of the three-part test, with the primary issue being whether a school's failure to satisfy the test is enough to prove that it is violating Title IX.[63]

Despite the indicators that many universities were out of compliance with Title IX, especially in distributing benefits in athletic programs, the enforcement mechanisms were cumbersome and generally ineffective, requiring individuals to file complaints with OCR and wait for the agency to act on their behalf. This problem was partially alleviated when, shortly after HEW issued the 1979 policy interpretation, the Supreme Court ruled that Title IX allows individuals to sue schools directly, holding that the law implies a private right of action.[64] The ruling was momentous, permitting victims of discrimination to seek judicial intervention rather than forcing them to lodge complaints with the federal government and await results.

Title IX, like a number of federal statutes, does not explicitly authorize individuals to seek relief in the courts when their rights are violated; instead, it specifies that the federal government can terminate federal funding to institutions found guilty of discrimination. Therefore, when Geraldine Cannon sued the University of Chicago's medical school for sex discrimination, the Seventh Circuit dismissed her case, holding that Title IX does not allow suits by private individuals.[65]

In *Cannon v. University of Chicago*,[66] decided in 1979, the Supreme Court reversed that decision, basing its ruling primarily on the similarity between Title VI and Title IX. Speaking for a 6 to 3 majority, Stevens devoted most of the opinion to discussing the two purposes of Title IX: to prevent institutions from using federal funds for discriminatory practices and to protect individuals from discrimination. He noted that cutting off federal funds to a guilty institution would prevent the federal government from subsidizing discrimination but would be of little use to the victim. A private suit, he declared, would serve the victim better and fulfill the second aim of the statute.

A study of Title IX litigation published in 2008 found that there have been almost 200 claims of discrimination in athletic programs since 1972, with almost half filed between 2000 and 2007; the cases arose in thirty-five states and the District of Columbia, with most decided by the federal courts.[67]

The first major test of Title IX's promise of equality in athletic programs (specifically, of the 1979 policy interpretation) arose in a federal suit against Brown University. In this case, as in most others, the courts were primarily concerned with the policy interpretation's formulation of the three-part test. The lawsuit against Brown arose when members of the women's volleyball and gymnastic teams filed suit against university officials for downgrading their sports to the status of clubs. The school also demoted men's golf and men's water polo to club status. The key question for the courts was whether Brown's actions satisfied the "effective accommodation" prong (prong 3) of the three-part test.[68] The university denied that it discriminated and argued that any disparity in athletic participation indicated that women were less interested in sports than men.

In the first ruling in the lawsuit in 1992, the district court judge found the school out of compliance with the first prong of the test because of the large gap between the percentage of women enrolled at Brown and the athletic opportunities available to them.[69] On appeal, the circuit court upheld the lower court's reliance on the 1979 policy interpretation and the three-part test. The First Circuit rejected the university's argument that the test essentially required an institution to impose an affirmative action program for female athletes; it also held that eliminating men's teams was an acceptable strategy to satisfy Title IX. In 1996, the district court's 1992 opinion was affirmed.[70]

The First Circuit reiterated the district court's first ruling that institutions would only be found liable under the act if they failed all three parts of the test. It noted that if a school wished to ensure compliance with Title IX, it should consider the proportionality prong (prong 1) of the three-part test a "safe harbor," meaning that it will be found in compliance if it can show "parity" between its overall enrollment of men and women and participation by men and women in athletics.

> The first benchmark furnishes a safe harbor for those institutions that have distributed athletic opportunities in numbers substantially proportionate to the gender composition of their student bodies. Thus, a university which does not wish to engage in extensive compliance analysis may stay on the sunny side of Title IX simply by maintaining gender parity between its student body and its athletic lineup.[71]

The court concluded that Brown University was out of compliance with Title IX because it had not "fully and effectively" accommodated the interests and abilities of its female athletes.

Critics have argued that *Cohen* paved the way for institutions to privilege female athletes at the expense of men's sports teams because schools are barred from cutting women's sports programs even in the face of budgetary constraints. However, Title IX supporters say that the problem lies with the institution's reluctance to disturb funding for revenue-producing sports, thus leaving men's non-revenue-producing sports without the legal protection offered by Title IX.[72] The federal appellate courts (eight in all) have followed *Cohen* in accepting the three-part test.[73]

Sensing a receptive ear when the Republicans took control of Congress in 1994, the Board of Trustees of the AFCA asked Congress to hold hearings on Title IX and its effect on athletic programs. Accordingly, on

May 9, 1995, the Subcommittee on Postsecondary Education, Training, and Lifelong Learning of the House Economic and Educational Opportunities Committee held a hearing on Title IX and the three-part test. On June 7, 1995, 142 members of Congress wrote to DOE, expressing concern that the three-part test caused educational institutions to eliminate men's athletic opportunities.

On January 16, 1996, DOE attempted to clarify the 1979 policy interpretation by releasing a policy guidance document, explaining that proportionality would likely become the preferred approach for colleges and universities. But it also noted that institutions could satisfy any of the three prongs of the three-part test to show they were in compliance with Title IX. Additionally, it stressed that participation opportunities would be based on the number of athletes and not on the number of available spots and that a university could, but was not required to, satisfy the proportionality requirement by eliminating or reducing the size of existing teams.[74]

To commemorate the twenty-fifth anniversary of Title IX in June 1997, President Bill Clinton signed a document called "Memorandum on Strengthening Title IX Enforcement and Addressing Discrimination on the Basis of Sex, Race, Color, and National Origin." His remarks at the signing charged federal agencies with enhancing Title IX enforcement to eliminate discrimination on the basis of sex.[75] Three years later, in June 2000, Clinton issued Executive Order 13160, extending Title IX coverage to the federal government, that is, to "programs and activities conducted, operated, or undertaken by an executive department or agency."[76]

Title IX greatly expanded women's opportunities, but because universities and colleges are often reluctant to cut funding for their revenue-producing sports, the burden often falls on men's non-revenue-producing sports such as golf, wrestling, and tennis, thus pitting the men on such teams against the female athletes.[77]

Arguing that Title IX was responsible for depriving men's sports teams of funding, in January 2002 the National Wrestling Coaches Association (NWCA), the National Coalition for Athletics Equity, and three private universities (Bucknell, Marquette, and Yale) filed a federal lawsuit against DOE. Citing constitutional and statutory violations, they contended that the 1979 policy interpretation and the 1996 guidance were discriminatory and had failed to go through the formal rule-making process. Specifically, the suit claimed that the 1996 guidance prompted colleges and universities to eliminate men's athletic programs, such as wrestling, to meet the Title IX proportionality requirement.[78] They asked the court to require DOE to promulgate new regulations that measured opportunities for women based on the number of women interested in athletics rather than on the number enrolled at the school. The Bush Justice Department filed papers with the court, seeking to dismiss the suit, yet according to the National Women's Law Center (NWLC) in Washington, D.C., the documents did not sufficiently emphasize the importance of Title IX.[79]

The district court dismissed the lawsuit in June 2003, ruling that the associations lacked standing to sue DOE.[80] In May 2004, the court of appeals affirmed the lower court. The appeals court agreed that it was only speculative that voiding the Title IX regulations would lead to restoring the wrestling programs; it held that associations must sue the individual colleges that cut the programs.[81] After a long, tortuous path through the federal courts, the Supreme Court denied review in the NWCA suit in 2005.[82]

On June 18, 2002, the NWLC issued a press release to commemorate the upcoming thirtieth anniversary of Title IX. Rather than celebrating its victories, however, the statement charged that as many as thirty colleges and universities in twenty-four states still failed to give women a fair share of the athletic scholarships offered at these institutions. Based on data reported to the federal government, the NWLC stressed that women were being shortchanged by a total of at least $6.5 million, with female athletes receiving an average of $2,131 less a year than the male athletes.[83]

In 2002, the Bush administration reacted to the controversy surrounding Title IX by creating a federal commission to assess the law. The commission's report, released in February 2003, stressed the importance of Title IX in securing equal opportunity for women and urged DOE to continue its "strong commitment" to the principles of the statute.[84] However, despite this ringing endorsement of Title IX, in March 2005, the administration announced that schools would be permitted to use a web-based survey to determine the extent to which their female students wished to participate in athletics. Critics argued that such surveys typically have low response rates and would not accurately measure student interest in sports. A year later, the administration reaffirmed that surveys were an acceptable means to gauge students' interest in athletics.[85]

In November 2010, the NWLC filed a civil rights complaint with OCR, citing inequity in high school sports programs in twelve school districts around the country, including Chicago, Houston, and New York. The organization based its complaint on 2004 and 2006 DOE data showing that girls' participation in athletics lagged behind boys. In response to concerns that districts would respond by cutting boys' sports programs, the head of the NWLC said that it did not seek to reduce boys' participation as a result of the complaint.[86]

The Supreme Court and Title IX Litigation

After *Cannon* paved the way for private individuals to sue under Title IX, the Supreme Court continued to expand the scope of the statute by protecting employees in federally funded institutions from sex discrimination, allowing suits for sexual harassment, and permitting plaintiffs to collect money damages. Table 2.2 presents these cases.

The first major test of Title IX came in 1982, when the Supreme Court upheld the law's prohibition on employment discrimination in federally funded educational institutions in *North Haven Board of Education v. Bell*.[87] Although most federal courts had ruled that the law did not cover employment discrimination, the Supreme Court disagreed.[88]

In a 6 to 3 vote, the high court affirmed the Second Circuit opinion that employment policies in federally funded educational institutions were within the scope of Title IX. Speaking for the Court, Blackmun observed that it was more plausible to interpret the ban on discrimination against any "person" to include rather than exclude employees. In the absence of committee reports to explain legislative intent, he looked to the Senate floor debate and concluded that it revealed Congress's expectation that employment practices fell under Title IX. Additionally, Blackmun quoted Bayh's statement that the bill would "cover such crucial aspects as admissions, procedures, scholarships, and faculty employment."[89]

Table 2.2 Supreme Court Title IX Rulings, 1979–2009

Case	Date	Issue[a]	Ruling[b]
Cannon	1979	Private right of action	Expands educational equality
North Haven	1982	Employment	Expands educational equality
Grove City	1984	Program specificity	Limits educational equality
Franklin	1992	Availability of damages	Expands educational equality
Gebser	1998	School liability	Expands educational equality
Davis	1999	School liability	Expands educational equality
Jackson	2005	Retaliation claims	Expands educational equality
Fitzgerald	2009	Exclusive remedy	Expands educational equality

Notes: a. Based on the major issue in the case.
b. Based on the overall outcome of the case.

The next major test of Title IX was in 1984, in *Grove City College v. Bell*.[90] The Court addressed two issues: first, whether Title IX applied to the institution when the federal aid was indirect, that is, given to the students; second, whether it applied to the entire institution or only to the program receiving the federal aid.

Grove City was a private, coeducational, liberal arts college in western Pennsylvania with approximately 2,200 students. Almost one-quarter of its students received federal financial aid through the Basic Education Opportunity Grant (BEOG) and the Guaranteed Student Loan (GSL) programs. According to Title IX regulations, educational institutions in which students received BEOG funds were considered recipients of federal financial assistance and therefore within the reach of the law.[91]

When Grove City College refused to file the requisite assurance of compliance, DOE announced its intention to terminate its funding. The college argued that since it did not receive federal funds, it was not a program or activity within the meaning of the law.

With Justice Byron White speaking for the majority, the Court held that indirect student aid subjected an institution to Title IX. He said there was no evidence in Title IX's language, legislative intent, or post-enactment history to suggest that Congress intended to distinguish between direct and indirect aid. "We have little trouble concluding," he said, "that Title IX coverage is not foreclosed because federal funds are granted to Grove City's students rather than directly to one of the College's educational programs."[92]

Grove City also argued that if Title IX applied to it, it was limited to the program receiving the aid—its financial aid office. It urged the Supreme Court to reverse the lower court's ruling that the law extended to all programs in the college.

The majority agreed that Congress had intended the "program or activity" language of Title IX to be narrowly interpreted, saying it "found no persuasive evidence" that Congress meant to have HEW's "regulatory authority follow federally aided students from classroom to classroom, building to building, or activity to activity."[93] Thus, it concluded that Title IX only banned discrimination by Grove City's financial aid office, not by other sectors of the institution.

The implications of the Court's decision were soon apparent as collegiate athletic programs around the nation claimed to be exempt from Title IX's ban on sex discrimination, arguing they were not programs or activities receiving federal funds. Moreover, the Supreme Court's constrained interpretation of Title IX threatened to set back the major civil rights advances of the 1960s and 1970s more generally. Members of the civil rights community reacted with dismay to the ruling, fearing that it would lead to narrow interpretations of other civil rights laws, such as Title VI and Section 504 of the 1973 Rehabilitation Act, which had the same "program" or "activity" language as Title IX.[94] The decision had a drastic effect on pending civil rights litigation: "According to the Leadership Conference on Civil Rights, the Department of Education had 'closed, limited or suspended hundreds of [discrimination] cases' because of the *Grove City* ruling."[95]

Shortly after the opinion was announced, a bill was introduced in the House to propose three changes in the civil rights statutes affected by the Court's ruling: replace the words "program" and "activity" with "recipient"; define a "recipient" as an institution receiving assistance "directly or through another"; and specify that the entire institution or system would lose funding if one of its units violated the ban on discrimination.[96]

After hearings in the Education and Labor and Judiciary Committees, the House voted 375 to 32 to reverse *Grove City* on June 26, 1984. But opposition from the Reagan administration and the Republican-controlled Senate, despite the support of sixty-three bipartisan cosponsors, stalled the Senate version of the bill in the 98th Congress.

Two House committees in the 99th Congress approved versions of a similar bill, but neither reached the House floor. Congress adjourned with the bills in limbo, as well as two other bills pending in the Senate Labor and Human Resources Committee. A Senate version of the bill was later approved in committee in May 1987, but no further action was taken on it during that year either.[97]

Neither Title IX nor the proposed bill referred to abortion, yet Senate debate, often bitter, primarily revolved around the implications of the bill for abortion rights. The U.S. Catholic Conference and the National Right to Life Committee lobbied against it, insisting that it would expand abortion rights. Current administrative regulations specified that federal aid recipients were required to treat pregnancy and the termination of pregnancy "in the same manner and under the same policies as any other temporary disability." The regulations also barred discrimination against students or employees who received abortions. Opponents of the bill argued that it would force hospitals with religious ties that received federal aid to perform abortions or be subject to suits for discrimination.[98] Proponents insisted that such hospitals could claim an exemption and that the bill only addressed coverage of the civil rights laws, not definitions of discrimination.

The controversy over abortion continued to stymie any attempts to reverse *Grove City*. The Senate finally passed a bill, S. 557, on January 28, 1988, by a 75 to 14 vote; the price for its passage was the Danforth Amendment, proposed by John Danforth, Republican from Missouri. Supported by the Catholic Conference and other anti-abortion groups, the amendment contained a "conscience" clause that permitted federally funded hospitals (and their medical personnel) to refuse to perform abortions and allowed educational institutions to exclude abortion from health and disability plans. Although it was characterized by its supporters as abortion-neutral because it also prohibited discrimination against women who had abortions, opponents charged that there was "a certain anti-woman animus in the proponents of this amendment." Nevertheless, the Senate approved the amendment in a 56 to 39 vote.

In the House, civil rights advocates were torn over whether to support the Senate version of the bill with the Danforth Amendment. Despite their desire to see the *Grove City* decision overturned, women's groups were upset with the abortion language and did not lobby for the bill. Nevertheless, the Senate-passed bill was approved in the House on March 2, 1988, in a 315 to 98 vote.[99]

Entitled the Civil Rights Restoration Act, the bill extended Title IX to state and local governments, including public school systems; schools receiving federal aid; and private organizations if aid is given to the enterprise as a whole or if the enterprise is "principally engaged" in providing education, housing, health care, parks, or social services.[100]

On March 16, 1988, President Ronald Reagan vetoed S. 557, saying it "would vastly and unjustifiably expand the power of the Federal government over the decisions and affairs of private organizations, such as churches and synagogues, farms, businesses, and State and local governments. In the process," he said, "it would place at risk such cherished values as religious liberties." The administration offered a weaker substitute bill, entitled the Civil Rights Protection Act, that proposed to extend the religious exemption to institutions that are "closely identified" with but not "controlled by" a religious organization. By limiting coverage to the entity receiving federal aid, the administration substitute would have substantially undercut the government's ban on discrimination in private businesses, religious school systems, and state and local government units.[101]

Less than a week later, on March 22, 1988, Congress overrode the president's veto on a 73 to 24 vote in the Senate and a 292 to 133 vote in the House.[102] With this action, the Supreme Court's narrow interpretation of the program-specific language of the nation's federal civil rights laws was reversed, and according to its congressional sponsors, Congress had now ensured that the laws would be interpreted consistent with their original intent.

Title IX Remedies

For the most part, plaintiffs seek two types of compensation in civil lawsuits: money damages or injunctive relief (in which the court orders the defendant to cease illegal conduct or provide the sought-after remedy). Although *Cannon* opened the courthouse doors to Title IX plaintiffs, it did not address the issue of the type of compensation (or remedies) available to successful plaintiffs. Most lower courts ruled that because the statute failed to specify the availability of money damages, plaintiffs were limited to injunctive relief.

Injunctive relief was irrelevant to plaintiffs such as Judith Lieberman who, like Cannon, sued the University of Chicago medical school for sex discrimination under Title IX. Unlike Cannon, however, because Lieberman attended another medical school while her suit was pending, she sought monetary compensation rather than injunctive relief.[103] In 1981, in *Lieberman v. University of Chicago*,[104] the Seventh Circuit dismissed her suit, ruling that the statute did not authorize courts to award money damages. The appeals court relied on an earlier 1981 ruling, *Pennhurst State School and Hospital v. Halderman*,[105] in which the Supreme Court declared that recipients of federal aid enter into a contract with the federal government in which they agree to certain conditions in exchange for the funds. But, the high court ruled in *Pennhurst*, because contracts must clearly specify the terms of the agreement, Congress must provide adequate notice to recipients that they may incur financial obligations when accepting the aid. The *Lieberman* court concluded that Title IX failed to warn institutions that the receipt of federal funds put them at risk for damage suits.

The dissenting judge questioned the majority's logic in requiring Congress to specify money damages in a statute that had not expressly created a right to sue. He warned that the majority opinion will cut back enforcement of Title IX because the best qualified applicants, like Lieberman, who are admitted to other schools will have no incentive to sue for discrimination, leaving only less qualified applicants, who will have greater difficulty proving their claims to file suit.[106]

Sexual Harassment in Schools

Title IX also played an important role in the effort to curb sexual harassment in schools. According to two surveys commissioned by the AAUW in 1993 and 2001, sexual harassment is common in schools. In the 1993 survey—the first systematic study of sexual harassment in schools—researchers asked 1,632 students in grades eight through eleven whether they ever experienced sexual harassment; an astonishing 85 percent of the girls and 76 percent of the boys said "yes."[107] Girls also reported greater fear in school and less self-confidence than boys. Similarly, the 2001 survey of 2,064 students in the same grades found that 83 percent of girls and 79 percent of boys reported experiencing harassment; the study also showed that the practice begins in elementary school and that teachers often witness the harassing behavior.[108] Most students reported being subject to verbal harassment, with over half also indicating they had been physically harassed, most often by their schoolmates. Ironically, most students in the survey reported being aware of their school's policy against sexual harassment.

In 1992, the Supreme Court addressed the issue of the availability of money damages under Title IX in a suit for sexual harassment as a form of sex discrimination. Christine Franklin, a Georgia high school student, claimed that a teacher verbally and physically harassed her for more than two years, including forcing her to have sexual intercourse with him on school grounds three times.[109] According to Franklin, school officials knew of the harassment but took no action to stop it and even discouraged her from filing charges against him. Eventually, the school compelled his resignation, agreeing to his condition to drop the case against him. Franklin filed a complaint with DOE, which found that the school had violated Title IX. However, the agency decided that since the teacher resigned and the school had instituted a grievance procedure, it was now in compliance with the law. The lower court also rejected her claim.

In *Franklin v. Gwinnett County Public Schools,*[110] a unanimous Supreme Court decision announced by White, the Court noted that the question of damages was "analytically distinct" from the question of whether an individual could sue under the act, citing a long-held presumption that federal courts have the authority to order appropriate relief, absent a contrary indication from Congress.

Echoing the dissenting judge in *Lieberman,* the Court said it was not surprising that Congress had not indicated its intent to allow money damages in Title IX since it had not explicitly authorized suit under the statute. In determining whether Congress intended to alter the fundamental rule of the availability of damage remedies, the Court cited two laws, enacted after *Cannon* was decided, that had expanded the right to sue under Title IX: the Civil Rights Remedies Equalization Act of 1986 and the 1988 Civil Rights Restoration Act. It found no evidence in either statute that Congress had intended to limit damages.[111]

The Court also rejected other arguments against awarding damages in Title IX suits, the most important revolving around the question of whether such remedies were appropriate in statutes enacted under Congress's spending power. Agreeing that recipients of federal funds could not be held accountable for acts of unintentional discrimination because they lacked notice of their liability, the Court believed there was no bar against holding them accountable for acts of intentional discrimination. Title IX, White pointed out, put federally funded school districts on notice that they must not discriminate on the basis of sex. Because other remedies for students such as Franklin, who had already graduated, were inadequate, it was appropriate to award money damages to victims of intentional sex discrimination. He also reiterated the long-standing principle that federal courts are authorized to award appropriate relief in enforcing federally protected rights.[112]

Franklin established that monetary damages may be awarded in Title IX suits but was silent on the appropriate standard to determine the school's liability for sexual harassment. Federal guidelines issued in March 1997 state that Title IX covers harassing behavior by school employees, such as teachers, as well as other students.[113] As with workplace harassment, the guidelines indicate that the conduct must be sufficiently severe and pervasive to adversely affect the student's educational experience or create a hostile environment.

The precise nature of the school's liability for harassment by a teacher came squarely before the Court in 1998, when a fifteen-year-old eighth grader filed suit against her school. She had engaged in sex with her teacher but had not reported it, and school authorities had no knowledge of it, only learning about it when the two were discovered having sex. The teacher was arrested and fired from his position. Defending against her Title IX suit, the school argued it should not be held responsible because it had no direct knowledge of the sexual behavior. There had been other complaints against the same teacher, but following an investigation in which he denied any responsibility, the matter was dropped. The school had never issued a formal antiharassment policy, nor had it created and publicized a grievance procedure.

After the lower federal courts dismissed her suit for damages, the high court reversed in a 5 to 4 decision in *Gebser v. Lago Vista Independent*

School District.[114] O'Connor narrowly framed the issue as one of how Congress would have handled the question of a Title IX defendant's liability had it expressly included a right to sue in Title IX. Principally because the statute stated that an offending school must be given an opportunity to comply with the law, the Court inferred that Congress had not intended to impose liability on an institution if it were unaware of its employee's illegal conduct.

O'Connor reasoned that Congress would not have wanted the school to be strictly liable for its employees' actions without being given notice of the illegal acts, and it would be inappropriate for the Court to attach such a penalty in a statute with a judicially implied remedy. Citing the *Pennhurst* requirement that a recipient of federal funding must have notice of its potential financial liability when accepting funding, the Court was unwilling to make the school responsible for conduct of which it was unaware. It concluded that a school may only be liable for damages when it displayed "deliberate indifference," that is, when a school official with responsibility to correct the behavior knew of it and deliberately failed to act.[115]

In restricting the school's liability for Title IX violations, the Court adopted a standard that differed from the one it established in workplace sexual harassment cases, namely, that an employer is held liable when a supervisor who has immediate control over an employee creates a hostile work environment.[116] The Court refused to apply these principles to school situations, notwithstanding the fact that children require even greater protection from those in authority than adults in the workplace and that its ruling would encourage schools to remain ignorant of Title IX violations such as sexual harassment by teachers.

The Supreme Court addressed the question of the school's liability for students harassing each other in *Davis v. Monroe County Board of Education,*[117] a 1999 ruling involving a Georgia fifth grader who claimed she was physically and verbally harassed for five months by the boy who sat next to her in class. The problem in such cases typically arises because when schools are notified that students are being harassed by other students, they often dismiss such incidents as childish teasing or name-calling, sexual banter, or harmless flirting; they also argue that they cannot be held legally responsible for their students' bad behavior.

According to the girl's complaint, the boy grabbed her breasts, rubbed against her, and made lewd comments. Although she and her mother complained to school officials numerous times, they were unresponsive; it was three months before a teacher finally allowed her to change her seat in the classroom. The Board of Education in her district had no sexual harassment policy, nor had it trained school personnel to respond to complaints about harassment.

The child's grades began to suffer, and she threatened suicide. The abuse finally ended when the Davis family pressed criminal charges against the boy, and he pleaded guilty to sexual battery in juvenile court. The family then filed suit in federal court, claiming that the harassment created a hostile, intimidating, and offensive environment in violation of Title IX. They sought damages and a court order that the school establish a sexual harassment policy.

With the support of the Clinton administration, the lawyers for the family argued that the school was legally responsible for the boy's behavior, especially once it was told about the harassment and failed to stop it. They insisted that the school was liable because a responsible school official knew of the behavior and was "deliberately indifferent" to it. In their view, it was insignificant that, unlike *Gebser,* this harassment was caused by a classmate.

The lower courts dismissed her claim, ruling that schools were not liable for peer harassment. During oral arguments before the Supreme Court, the justices expressed concern about the difficulty of distinguishing between ordinary teasing and the kind of harassment that was alleged here and the consequences that might ensue if suits for student-on-student harassment were permitted. "Little boys tease little girls through their years in school," O'Connor noted; "is every incident going to lead to a lawsuit?"[118] In her opinion for a 5 to 4 Court, O'Connor adopted an intermediate approach by allowing suits for peer harassment under Title IX, but only under narrow circumstances.

The school had argued that it was not responsible for harassment by students because school officials were unable to control such behavior. And the Court also expressed concern about the conditions under which a school district could be sued for damages, asking whether the district had sufficient notice of its liability for third parties when accepting federal funds.[119] The key question, stated O'Connor, was whether deliberate indifference to acts of harassment by a student or teacher constitutes intentional discrimination under Title IX. She cited federal law and state common law, as well as a publication released by the National School Board Association showing that schools are aware of their responsibility for the conduct of such individuals who are under their control.

O'Connor concluded that a school that was aware of and deliberately indifferent to one student harassing another was accountable under Title IX. Spelling out the exact nature of the school's liability, she stated that

funding recipients are properly held liable in damages . . . where they are
deliberately indifferent to sexual harassment, of which they have actual
knowledge, that is so severe, pervasive, and objectively offensive that it
can be said to deprive the victims of access to the educational opportunities or benefits provided by the school.[120]

Acknowledging that children's behavior is often manifested in gender-
specific name-calling and teasing, she stressed that the Court was not
subjecting schools to liability for every antisocial act that occurs there.

Kennedy dissented, fearing the implications of the majority's opinion. He warned of increasing federal control over the day-to-day disciplinary actions in the nation's schools, fearing that it would turn Title IX
into a "Federal Student Civility Code."[121] Moreover, he questioned the
Court's characterization of the child's inappropriate behavior as sex discrimination because, in his view, it was not necessarily sexual harassment, much less sex discrimination. He predicted there would be a flood
of litigation in the wake of the ruling. Citing the AAUW survey on the
frequency of sexual harassment incidents in schools, he cautioned that
"the number of potential lawsuits against our schools is staggering."[122]
Additionally, he feared that even first and second graders who did not
understand the consequences of their behavior would be targeted by
overzealous administrators who wanted to insulate themselves from liability by overreacting to innocent acts.

Ironically, however, school officials seemed less concerned, undoubt-
edly pleased with the high standard of proof required in such lawsuits.[123]
"We can live with this standard," said the general counsel for the
National School Board Association. "I think it will be the rare occasion
when a school board is found liable in the future."[124] Other school
administrators echoed these views. "The days of boys will be boys and
girls will be girls are long gone," another said. "The school needs to
address all elements of the school environment, . . . [and] there won't be
liability if you are proactive and out there teaching kids about appropriate behavior."[125]

In 2001, DOE released a revised guidance on sexual harassment that
reflected the Court's rulings in *Gebser* and *Davis*. More recently, Title
IX has also been the basis of lawsuits for sexual harassment and sexual
assault on women on university campuses.[126] In *Simpson v. University of
Colorado Boulder*,[127] two women sued the university, claiming they
were sexually assaulted during an on-campus party. They argued that the
university was liable because it knew of the risks entailed by such
recruitment visits and failed to act.

The district court ruled in favor of the university, finding that despite the incidents on campus, the school did not have requisite notice of the danger. The Tenth Circuit Court reversed, noting that the university's policy of ensuring potential recruits "a good time" on these visits and its "failure to provide adequate supervision and guidance to player-hosts" assigned to the recruits created a "likelihood . . . [that] was so obvious" that its failure to act constituted "deliberate indifference."[128]

In *McGrath v. Dominican College of Blauvelt,*[129] a New York district court had reached the opposite conclusion from the lower court in *Simpson. McGrath* involved a woman student who claimed she was raped by three other students and charged the college with deliberate indifference for failing to investigate and act after she reported the sexual assault to officials.

Dominican moved to dismiss the suit, maintaining that the deliberate indifference standard for liability under Title IX required a plaintiff to prove that the school had "deliberately attempted to sabotage . . . [her] complaint or its orderly resolution."[130] The court disagreed and refused to dismiss her Title IX action.

The Supreme Court subsequently resolved another unsettled Title IX issue in *Jackson v. Birmingham Board of Education.*[131] In this 2005 ruling, the Court was asked to decide whether the law extends to victims of retaliation and to individuals who complain of discrimination against others.[132]

Roderick Jackson, a physical education teacher and coach of the girls' basketball team at an Alabama public high school, complained of discrimination against his team. He charged that the girls' team received less funding than the boys' team and was denied equal access to equipment and facilities. His complaints were ignored, and a few months later, Jackson began receiving poor performance evaluations and was soon removed from his position as coach; the removal cost him an extra stipend and retirement benefits. He filed suit under Title IX, claiming that he was fired as coach because he had raised his voice against the unequal treatment of the girls' team. He asked for money damages and a decree ordering the school to comply with Title IX.

The lower courts dismissed his suit, ruling that Title IX does not protect individuals against retaliation by their employers, in effect, determining that there was no private right of action to sue for retaliation under Title IX.

O'Connor announced the opinion in the Court's 5 to 4 decision. She began by noting that the Court had steadily expanded the definition of discrimination in Title IX in *North Haven, Cannon, Franklin, Gebser,* and *Davis,* subsuming claims of equal employment opportunity and sexual harassment by teachers as well as a student's peers.[133] Acknowledging that the statute does not explicitly allow claims for retaliation, she pointed out that the Court had broadly interpreted Title IX to prohibit any federally funded educational institution from intentionally discriminating on the basis of sex. Retaliation is clearly intentional, she stressed, and when it follows an individual's complaint of sex discrimination, it must be considered a "form of intentional sex discrimination encompassed by Title IX's private cause of action."[134]

Turning to the second question, the Court also rejected the board's argument that Title IX did not apply to Jackson because he had not been discriminated against on the basis of sex. O'Connor explained that the statute is broadly written and does not require that the individual subjected to retaliation also be the victim of the discriminatory act. Congress's purpose in enacting Title IX was to end discrimination on the basis of sex; its enforcement depends on individuals reporting violations of the law—against themselves and others. If they can be punished for speaking out, very few will be willing to do so, and the enforcement mechanism of the law would be drastically weakened. She added that it is especially appropriate that adults such as Jackson complain of the discrimination because, as a teacher, he will be more likely to be aware of it and able to call the administration's attention to it.

Finally, the Court addressed the board's contention that because Title IX was enacted under Congress's spending clause authority, the law had to state that recipients of federal funding were liable for retaliation claims. Without such an explicit statement of liability, the board insisted, schools would be unaware that they could be sued on those grounds when accepting federal dollars. The Court disagreed. Since 1979, when *Cannon* was decided, O'Connor said, recipients of federal aid were made aware that they could be sued for committing intentional acts of sex discrimination, such as retaliation.

The Court remanded the case to allow Jackson the opportunity to prove that he was removed from his coaching position in retaliation for his complaints.[135]

Speaking for the dissent, Thomas refused to equate claims of retaliation with claims of sex discrimination and argued that Congress intended that Title IX only apply to actual victims of sex discrimination, not to third parties such as Jackson. He stressed the unfairness of the majority decision because a claim for retaliation does not even require proof of the underlying claim of discrimination. Finally, he protested the majority's interpretation of Congress's spending clause power. In his view, the statute must clearly indicate the legislature's intent to hold recipients liable for claims of retaliation, and Title IX does not.

In 2009, the Supreme Court decided *Fitzgerald v. Barnstable School Committee*,[136] another case stemming from sexual harassment of a child in school. With facts similar to those in *Davis,* the Fitzgerald family filed suit against the school board and the superintendent of the school their daughter attended. They claimed that school officials failed to take appropriate action when they complained that their kindergarten-aged daughter was being sexually harassed by an eight-year-old third grader. The child told her parents that when she wore a dress to school, the boy forced her to raise the skirt, causing the children on the bus to laugh at her. Her mother immediately called the school and made an appointment with the principal. School officials met with the family and then questioned the boy, who denied the charges. Nobody who rode the bus with them, including the bus driver, substantiated her account. When the little girl told her mother that he also forced her to act sexually, she called for another meeting at the school, with the same result. The police investigated and concluded there was insufficient evidence to charge the boy with criminal conduct; the school also decided not to pursue disciplinary action against him.

When the principal suggested transferring their daughter to a different bus, they refused, proposing instead that they transfer the boy. No action was taken the rest of that year, despite the child's reports of further incidents at school.

At the beginning of the next year, the Fitzgeralds filed a Title IX suit, claiming that the school's response had been inadequate and led to increased harassment against their daughter. However, because Title IX does not allow suits against individuals (such as teachers and principals), the family also claimed that the defendants violated the equal protection clause of the Fourteenth Amendment.[137]

Following the *Davis* formula for determining liability, the First Circuit Court concluded that school officials had acted reasonably and had not displayed deliberate indifference to the harassment complaints and dismissed the Title IX action. It also rejected the Fitzgeralds' constitutional claim after determining that Congress had intended Title IX to be the sole remedy for claims of sex discrimination in schools.[138]

Because this was an issue upon which the circuit courts were divided, the Supreme Court accepted the case for review.[139] Justice Samuel Alito, appointed by President George W. Bush to replace the retiring O'Connor, announced the Court's unanimous opinion, reversing the appellate court's dismissal of the constitutional claim. Alito explained that in contrast to laws with elaborate enforcement mechanisms, Title IX as written merely authorized the withdrawal of federal funds from offending institutions and was silent on the availability of private suits. He noted that in implying private remedies for damages in *Franklin,* the Court had stressed that Congress had not intended to limit relief under Title IX. Thus, he concluded that nothing prevented the Fitzgeralds from adding an equal protection claim to their Title IX lawsuit against the school district. Because the lower courts had dismissed the suit without a hearing on its merits, the Court remanded the case to give the family an opportunity to determine whether the school had discriminated against the child.[140]

Conclusion

Over the last several decades, the nation moved toward greater sex equality in its public school systems, with the federal courts taking a dim view of separate schools and separate admission policies. By the 1990s, the only remaining single-sex institutions were men-only military academies, which argued that tradition and the physical inferiority of the female applicants justified the maintenance of their single-sex environment. By the end of the decade, even those schools were forced to abandon single-sex education.

The nation took a significant step forward in realizing sex equality in schools by enacting Title IX in 1972. It has allowed victims of discrimination and harassment to hold school districts accountable for the acts of their employees as well as their students. The law also played an important role in bringing about change in athletic programs.

Title IX has substantially increased women's participation in sports activity. But there is evidence that inequities between men's and women's athletics programs persist as well as substantial opposition to Title IX from those who view increased opportunities for female athletes coming at the expense of opportunities for men.

Notes

1. American Association of University Women, *How Schools Shortchange Girls: A Study of Findings on Girls and Education,* Executive Summary (Washington, D.C.: American Association of University Women Educational Foundation, 1992), p. 1, available at http://www.aauw.org/research/upload/hssg.pdf.

2. American Association of University Women, *Gender Gaps: Where Schools Still Fail Our Children.* Executive Summary (Washington, D.C.: American Association of University Women Educational Foundation, 1998), p. 1, available at http://www.aauw.org/research/upload/GGES.pdf.

3. American Association of University Women, *Beyond the "Gender Wars": A Conversation About Girls, Boys, and Education* (Washington, D.C.: American Association of University Women Educational Foundation, 2001), available at http://www.aauw.org/research/upload/BeyondGenderWar.pdf.

4. Christianne Corbett, Catherine Hill, and Andresse St. Rose, *Where the Girls Are: The Facts About Gender Equity in Education.* Executive Summary (Washington, D.C.: American Association of University Women Educational Foundation, 2008), available at http://www.aauw.org/research/upload/WhereGirlsAre_execSummary.pdf.

5. See Kenneth Jost, "Single-Sex Education," *CQ Researcher Online* 12, no. 25 (July 12, 2002): 569–592, available at http://library.cqpress.com/cqresearcher/cqresrre2002071200.

6. American Association of University Women, *Separated by Sex: A Critical Look at Single-Sex Education for Girls* (Washington, D.C.: American Association of University Women Educational Foundation, 1998), available at http://www.aauw.org/research/upload/SeparatedBySex.pdf.

7. American Association of University Women, *Separated by Sex,* p. 2.

8. Because of legal constraints, only a small number of single-sex schools in the United States were public schools. Because most of the single-sex schools in the United States are private and affiliated with a particular religion, the researchers' data were largely based on single-sex educational programs and schools in other nations.

9. *New York Sun,* September 13, 2006.

10. *Daily News* (New York), January 1, 2006.

11. *New York Sun,* October 26, 2006; see Rebecca A. Kiselewich, "In Defense of the 2006 Title IX Regulations for Single-Sex Public Education: How Separate Can Be Equal," *Boston College Law Review* 49 (2008): 217–261.

12. 309 F. Supp. 184 (E.D. Va. 1970).

13. 316 F. Supp. 134 (D.S.C. 1970).

14. *McNair,* 316 F. Supp. at 137.

15. In "Sex Discrimination by Law: A Study in Judicial Perspective," *New York University Law Review* 46 (1971): 675–747, John D. Johnston Jr. and Charles L. Knapp criticize the court's ruling in *McNair.*

16. 532 F.2d 880 (3d Cir. 1976).

17. *Vorchheimer,* 532 F.2d at 886.

18. Although the circuit court decided *Vorchheimer* nine months before the Supreme Court adopted heightened scrutiny for sex-based classifications in *Craig,* the court held that the city policy would have survived even under a more rigorous scrutiny.

19. 163 U.S. 537 (1896).

20. *Vorchheimer,* 532 F.2d at 888.

21. *Vorchheimer v. School District of Philadelphia,* 430 U.S. 703 (1977). A tie vote on the high court affirms the lower court decision. See also Rosemary Salomone, *Equal Education Under Law* (New York: St. Martin's Press, 1986).

22. 347 U.S. 483 (1954).

23. In *Newberg v. Philadelphia,* 478 A.2d 1352 (Pa. Super. 1984), a Pennsylvania superior court judge affirmed a lower court ruling ordering the Philadelphia school district to admit women to Central High. The court held that excluding women violated state and federal constitutional equal protection guarantees.

24. 458 U.S. 718 (1982).

25. Mississippi Code Annotated § 37-117-3 (1972), cited in *Hogan,* 458 U.S. at 720.

26. *Hogan,* 458 U.S. at 720, n. 1.

27. *Hogan,* 458 U.S. at 728.

28. See Heather Larkin Eason, "Gender Equality and Single-Sex Education: *United States v. Virginia,* 116 S.Ct. 2264 (1996)," *University of Arkansas at Little Rock Law Journal* 20 (1997): 191–211.

29. See Janella Miller, "The Future of Private Women's Colleges," *Harvard Women's Law Journal* 7 (1984): 153–187.

30. Two earlier cases were *Edwards v. Schlesinger,* 377 F. Supp. 1091 (D.D.C. 1974), and *Waldie v. Schlesinger,* 509 F.2d 508 (D.C. Cir. 1974); see also Alfred Blumrosen, "Single-Sex Public Schools: The Last Bastion of 'Separate but Equal?'" *Duke Law Journal* (1977): 259–276.

31. See Susan Gluck Mezey, "The Persistence of Sex-Segregated Education in the South," *Southeastern Political Review* 22 (1994): 371–395.

32. Mary Anne Case, "Discrimination and Inequality Emerging Issues 'The Very Stereotype the Law Condemns': Constitutional Sex Discrimination Law as a Quest for Perfect Proxies," *Cornell Law Review* 85 (2000): 1455.

33. *VMI,* 766 F. Supp. at 1415.

34. *VMI,* 852 F. Supp. at 484.

35. *VMI,* 518 U.S. at 515.

36. *VMI,* 518 U.S. at 547.

37. 339 U.S. 629 (1950).

38. Newspaper accounts revealed that Faulkner had received death threats for her attempts to integrate the Citadel. When she announced her departure, Citadel students yelled and cheered. *Houston Chronicle,* August 19, 1995.

39. Kathryn A. Lee, "Intermediate Review 'with Teeth' in Gender Discrimination Cases: The New Standard in *United States v. Virginia,*" *Temple Political and Civil Rights Law Review* 7 (1997): 243.

40. Case, in "Discrimination and Inequality," p. 1484, describes the changes at each institution and raises the interesting question of whether the Citadel's accommodations may be more susceptible to legal challenge than VMI's response of virtually ignoring the presence of women.

41. In *National Politics and Sex Discrimination in Education* (Lexington: Lexington Books, 1977), Andrew Fishel and Janice Pottker discuss the passage of Title IX.

42. See Birch Bayh, "Personal Insights and Experiences Regarding the Passage of Title IX," *Cleveland State Law Review* 55 (2007): 463–471; Bernice Resnick Sandler, "Title IX: How We Got It and What a Difference It Made," *Cleveland State Law Review* 55 (2007): 473–489.

43. Title VI has a broader reach, barring racial discrimination in federally assisted programs or activities such as public elementary and high schools, hospitals, highway departments, and housing authorities.

44. See Ross A. Jurewitz, "Playing at Even Strength: Reforming Title IX Enforcement in Intercollegiate Athletics," *American University Journal of Gender, Social Policy, and the Law* 8 (2000): 283–351.

45. The White House, Office of the Press Secretary, "Statement of the President on National Girls and Women in Sports Day," February 3, 2010, available at http://www.whitehouse.gov/the-press-office/statement-president-national-girls-women-sports-day. A 2010 study found that participation in high school sports

activities is associated with a range of positive effects on women in later life, including increases in their education and employment levels. Another study that year found that women who participated in athletic activities as girls had long-term health benefits as adults (*New York Times*, February 16, 2010).

46. See *Reed v. Nebraska School Activities Association*, 341 F. Supp. 258 (D. Neb. 1972); *Haas v. South Bend Community School Corp.*, 289 N.E.2d 495 (Ind. 1972); *Bucha v. Illinois High School Association*, 351 F. Supp. 69 (N.D. Ill. 1972); *Brendan v. Independent School District*, 477 F.2d 1292 (8th Cir. 1973).

47. See Joyce Gelb and Marian Lief Palley, *Women and Public Policies*, 2d ed. (Princeton: Princeton University Press, 1987); Salomone, *Equal Education Under Law*.

48. Anne Costain, "Eliminating Sex Discrimination in Education: Lobbying for Implementation of Title IX," in Marian Lief Palley and Michael Preston, eds., *Race, Sex, and Policy Problems* (Lexington: Lexington Books, 1979), p. 11.

49. The regulations were subject to a newly enacted provision of the 1974 Education Amendments that allowed Congress to issue a concurrent resolution within forty-five days if it disapproved of any administrative regulations dealing with education because they were inconsistent with legislative intent.

50. Note, "Sex Discrimination and Intercollegiate Athletics: Putting Some Muscle on Title IX," *Yale Law Journal* 88 (1979): 1254–1279; June E. Jensen, "Title IX and Intercollegiate Athletics: HEW Gets Serious About Equality in Sports," *New England Law Review* 15 (1980): 573–596.

51. The Education Amendments of 1974 were passed as the Elementary and Secondary Education Act of 1965 was about to expire. The legislation included the Javits Amendment and the Women's Educational Equity Act, which created an Advisory Council on Women's Educational Programs.

52. Jurewitz, "Playing at Even Strength," notes that Title IX supporters believe that in rejecting the Tower Amendment, Congress rejected distinguishing revenue-producing sports from other intercollegiate sports.

53. 40 Fed. Reg. 24,128 (June 4, 1975).

54. 40 Fed. Reg. 24,137 (June 4, 1975).

55. *National Collegiate Athletic Association v. Califano*, 444 F. Supp. 425 (D. Kan. 1978).

56. Equal opportunity was measured by ten factors, including expenditures in equipment and supplies, travel, coaching, and facilities. However, the regulations also noted that "unequal aggregate expenditures" did not signify lack of compliance. See Jensen, "Title IX and Intercollegiate Athletics"; Joan Ruth Kutner, "Sex Discrimination in Athletics," *Villanova Law Review* 21 (1976): 876–936.

57. HEW also tried to address the effects of past discrimination against women by asking institutions to encourage women to participate in sports, to increase the number of sports offered to women, and to raise the level of awareness of women's sports. These provisions were eliminated in the final regulations; see Jurewitz, "Playing at Even Strength."

58. See Jensen, "Title IX and Intercollegiate Athletics."

59. 44 Fed. Reg. 71,413 (December 11, 1979).

60. See Jensen, "Title IX and Intercollegiate Athletics."

61. Jurewitz, in "Playing at Even Strength," p. 301, discusses the complexities of the three-part test. In his view, the policy interpretation "failed miserably" in clearing up the uncertainties about compliance.

62. Christopher Paul Reuscher, "Giving the Bat Back to Casey: Suggestions to Reform Title IX's Inequitable Application to Intercollegiate Athletics," *Akron Law*

Review 35 (2001): 117–158. He suggests that if an institution is unable to comply with the first prong, it will be unlikely to satisfy the second prong.

63. See Paul Anderson and Barbara Osborne, "A Historical Review of Title IX Litigation," *Journal of Legal Aspects of Sport* (2008): 127–164.

64. In deciding whether to imply a private right (or cause) of action from a statute that does not specify the right to litigate, the Court is largely guided by a four-part test derived from *Cort v. Ash,* 422 U.S. 66 (1975). The test, to determine if a private suit is compatible with the purpose of the statute, requires consideration of four questions: First, is the person bringing the suit someone for whose "especial benefit" the statute was designed? Second, is there evidence of congressional intent, either explicit or implicit, to create or deny a private remedy or suit? Third, is a private suit consistent with the legislative purpose of the statute? Fourth, is it inappropriate to infer a cause of action in federal law because the suit is in an area that traditionally concerns state law? See Susan Gluck Mezey, "Judicial Interpretation of Legislative Intent: The Role of the Supreme Court in the Implication of Private Rights of Action," *Rutgers Law Review* 36 (1983): 53–89.

65. *Cannon v. University of Chicago,* 559 F.2d 1063, 1072 (7th Cir. 1976). The court's refusal to allow a private cause of action was not unique. Similar rulings were handed down in *Jones v. Oklahoma Secondary School Association,* 453 F. Supp. 150 (W.D. Okla. 1977), and *Cape v. Tennessee Secondary School Athletic Association,* 424 F. Supp. 732 (E.D. Tenn. 1977).

66. 441 U.S. 677 (1979).

67. Anderson and Osborne, "A Historical Review of Title IX Litigation."

68. The federal courts issued four rulings on the merits in the litigation: *Cohen v. Brown University,* 809 F. Supp 978 (D.R.I. 1992); *Cohen v. Brown University,* 991 F.2d 888 (1st Cir. 1993); *Cohen v. Brown University,* 879 F. Supp. 185 (D.R.I. 1995); *Cohen v. Brown University,* 101 F.3d 155 (1st Cir. 1996). The U.S. Supreme Court denied review in *Cohen v. Brown University,* 520 U.S. 1186 (1997).

69. *Cohen,* 809 F. Supp at 978–979.

70. *Cohen,* 879 F. Supp. at 185; *Cohen,* 101 F.3d at 155.

71. *Cohen,* 991 F.2d at 897–898.

72. Jurewitz, in "Playing at Even Strength," criticizes *Cohen* and the way in which later courts relied on the substantial proportionality prong.

73. See, for example, *Roberts v. Colorado State University,* 814 F. Supp. 1507 (D. Colo. 1993); *Favia v. Indiana University of Pennsylvania,* 812 F. Supp. 578 (N.D. Pa. 1993).

74. U.S. Department of Education, Office for Civil Rights, "Clarification of Intercollegiate Athletic Policy Guidance: The Three-Part Test," January 16, 1996, available at http://www2.ed.gov/about/offices/list/ocr/docs/clarific.html#two. The document was released by DOE because in 1980, when HEW was split into the Department of Health and Human Services (HHS) and DOE, the latter was given responsibility for implementing Title IX. The original Title IX regulations, which were published by HEW, were codified at 45 C.F.R. Part 86. When HEW was divided, the regulations were recodified by DOE at 34 C.F.R. Part 106. The former HEW regulations remain in effect, under the oversight of HHS, at 45 C.F.R. § 86.41.

75. Bill Clinton, 1997, "Remarks on Signing a Memorandum Strengthening Enforcement of Title IX," *Weekly Compilation of Presidential Documents* (June 17, 1997).

76. Bill Clinton, 2000. "Executive Order 13160—Nondiscrimination on the Basis of Race, Sex, Color, National Origin, Disability, Religion, Age, Sexual

Orientation, and Status as a Parent in Federally Conducted Education and Training Programs," *Weekly Compilation of Presidential Documents* (June 27, 2000).

77. See Jurewitz, "Playing at Even Strength"; Brian L. Porto, "Halfway Home: An Update on Title IX and College Sports," *Vermont Bar Journal and Law Digest* 34 (2008): 28–34.

78. The associations asked DOE to write new regulations that would allow schools to create athletic programs that reflected the number of interested women rather than overall enrollment; see *Legal Issues in College Athletics,* February 2002; *Higher Education Legal Alert,* April 2002.

79. The NWLC submitted a "friend of the court" brief on behalf of a number of women's organizations. News Release, National Women's Law Center, May 29, 2002; June 5, 2002.

80. *National Wrestling Coaches Association v. United States Department of Education,* 263 F. Supp. 2d 82 (D.D.C. 2003).

81. *National Wrestling Coaches Association v. United States Department of Education,* 366 F.3d 930 (D.C. Cir. 2004).

82. *National Wrestling Coaches Association v. United States Department of Education,* 545 U.S. 1104 (2005).

83. National Women's Law Center, "Investigation by NWLC Finds $6.5 Million Athletic Scholarship Gap for Women at 30 Colleges and Universities" (Washington, D.C.: National Women's Law Center, June 18, 2002).

84. U.S. Department of Education, *Open to All: Title IX at Thirty,* available at http://www.ed.gov/about/bdscomm/list/athletics/report.html.

85. See Katherine B. Woliver, "Title IX and the 'E-mail Survey' Exception: Missing the Goal," *Southern California Interdisciplinary Law Journal* 18 (2009): 463–483.

86. *New York Times,* November 10, 2010; *Chicago Tribune,* November 10, 2010; *Christian Science Monitor,* November 10, 2010.

87. 456 U.S. 512 (1982).

88. *Romeo Community Schools v. HEW,* 600 F.2d 581 (6th Cir. 1979); *Islesboro School Committee v. Califano,* 593 F.2d 424 (1st Cir. 1979); *Junior College District of St. Louis v. Califano,* 597 F.2d 119 (8th Cir. 1979). The Second Circuit ruled in favor of the plaintiffs in *North Haven Board of Education v. Hufstedler,* 629 F.2d 773 (2d Cir. 1980). See Rosemary Salomone, "Title IX and Employment Discrimination: A Wrong in Search of a Remedy," *Journal of Law and Education* 9 (1980): 433–447; Susan Gluck Mezey, "Gender Equality in Education: A Study of Policymaking by the Burger Court," *Wake Forest Law Review* 20 (1984): 793–817.

89. Rosemary Salomone, "*North Haven* and *Dougherty:* Narrowing the Scope of Title IX," *Journal of Law and Education* 10 (1981): 195.

90. 465 U.S. 555 (1984).

91. DOE regulations describing a "recipient" of federal aid, cited in *Grove City,* are at 34 C.F.R. § 106.2. These regulations accorded with HEW regulations enforcing Title VI. See Barrie L. Brejcha, "*Grove City College v. Bell:* Restricting the Remedial Reach of Title IX," *Loyola University Law Journal* 16 (1985): 319–358.

92. *Grove City,* 465 U.S. at 569–570. All nine justices agreed that indirect aid triggered Title IX coverage.

93. *Grove City,* 465 U.S. at 573–574.

94. In *Department of Transportation v. Paralyzed Veterans of America,* 477 U.S. 597 (1986), the Supreme Court held that federal aid to airports and the air traffic

control system did not bring commercial airlines within the reach of the 1973 Rehabilitation Act prohibiting discrimination against people with disabilities.

95. *Congressional Quarterly Almanac,* 1987, p. 281.

96. Civil Rights Act of 1984, H.R. 5490, 98th Cong., 2d sess. (1984); S. 2568, 98th Cong., 2d sess. (1984). See Brejcha, *"Grove City College v. Bell,"* for a discussion of Congress's attempts to reverse *Grove City.*

97. Civil Rights Restoration Act of 1987, S. 557, 100th Cong., 1st sess. (1987).

98. *Congressional Quarterly Almanac,* 1985, p. 24.

99. *Congressional Quarterly Almanac,* 1988, pp. 65–66. The Danforth Amendment provided that "nothing in this title shall be construed to require or prohibit any person or public or private entity to provide or pay for any benefit or service, including use of facilities, related to abortion. Nothing in this section shall be construed to permit a penalty to be imposed on any person because such person has received any benefit or service related to legal abortion." The amendment superseded Title IX regulations that barred educational institutions from treating health insurance, leave policies, and other services related to abortion differently from services provided for pregnancy and childbirth and prohibited discrimination against students who had abortions.

100. *Congressional Quarterly Almanac,* 1988, pp. 63–64.

101. *Congressional Quarterly Weekly,* March 19, 1988, pp. 752–753.

102. *Congressional Quarterly Weekly,* March 26, 1988, pp. 774–776.

103. Nancy Peterson, *"Lieberman v. University of Chicago:* Refusal to Imply a Damages Remedy Under Title IX of the Education Amendments of 1972," *Wisconsin Law Review* (1983): 181–210.

104. 660 F.2d 1185 (7th Cir. 1981).

105. 451 U.S. 1 (1981).

106. In *Pfeiffer v. Marion Center Area School District,* 917 F.2d 779 (3d Cir. 1990), the Third Circuit ruled in the opposite direction. Acknowledging that other circuits expressed contrary positions, the appellate court held that if plaintiffs, such as Pfeiffer, were able to prove their claims of intentional discrimination, they were entitled to money damages. The circuit court was guided by the high court's ruling in *Guardians Association v. Civil Service Commission of New York,* 463 U.S. 582 (1983), in which a majority of the Court suggested that plaintiffs were entitled to money damages if they proved their claims of intentional discrimination under Title VI of the 1964 Civil Rights Act, the statute upon which Title IX was modeled.

107. American Association of University Women, *Hostile Hallways: The AAUW Survey on Sexual Harassment in America's Schools* (Washington, D.C.: American Association of University Women Educational Foundation, 1993).

108. American Association of University Women, *Hostile Hallways: Bullying, Teasing, and Sexual Harassment in School* (Washington, D.C.: American Association of University Women Educational Foundation, 2001), available at http://www.aauw.org/research/upload/hostilehallways.pdf.

109. The first case to rule that sexual harassment claims could be brought under Title IX was *Alexander v. Yale University,* 631 F.2d 178 (2d Cir. 1980). For the results of a recent survey of sexual harassment on college campuses, indicating that nearly two-thirds of students reported experiencing sexual harassment, see Catherine Hill and Elena Silva, *Drawing the Line: Sexual Harassment on Campus* (Washington, D.C.: American Association of University Women Educational Foundation, 2005), available at http://www.aauw.org/research/upload/DTLFinal.pdf.

110. 503 U.S. 60 (1992).

111. The 1986 act revoked the state's immunity in suits brought to enforce Title VI, Title IX, and § 504 of the 1973 Rehabilitation Act.

112. Susan Wright, "*Franklin v. Gwinnett County Public Schools:* The Supreme Court Implies a Damage Remedy for Title IX Sex Discrimination," *Vanderbilt Law Review* 45 (1992): 1367–1386.

113. See Kathy Lee Collins, "Student-to-Student Sexual Harassment Under Title IX: The Legal and Practical Issues," *Drake Law Review* 46 (1998): 789–834, for a survey of lower court cases in the context of the 1997 OCR guidelines.

114. 524 U.S. 274 (1998).

115. The *Gebser* Court imposed an actual knowledge standard, rejecting a negligence standard in which the school would be liable if it knew or should have known of the harassment.

116. Montre Underwood, "*Gebser v. Lago Vista Independent School District:* The Supreme Court Adopts Actual Knowledge Standard as Basis for School District's Liability Under Title IX," *Tulane Law Review* 73 (1999): 2181–2193.

117. 526 U.S. 629 (1999).

118. *New York Times,* January 13, 1999.

119. To sue a recipient of federal funds for violating a program enacted under Congress's spending clause authority, it is necessary to show that the recipient was aware of the restrictions imposed by Congress.

120. *Davis,* 526 U.S. at 650. The majority opinion places a burden on students to come forward with complaints, notwithstanding the school's failure to promulgate or publicize a sexual harassment policy or a procedure for filing complaints; see Kristen Safier, "A Request for Congressional Action: Deconstructing the Supreme Court's (In)Activism in *Gebser v. Lago Vista Independent School District,* 118 S.Ct. 1989 (1988) and *Davis v. Monroe County Board of Education,* 119 S.Ct. 1661 (1991)," *University of Cincinnati Law Review* 68 (2000): 1309–1329.

121. *Davis,* 526 U.S. at 684.

122. *Davis,* 526 U.S. at 680.

123. In "Students as Targets and Perpetrators of Sexual Harassment: Title IX and Beyond," *Hastings Women's Law Journal* 12 (2001): 177–214, Martha McCarthy argues that the Court's standard is too high for Title IX plaintiffs and that the proper standard should be "constructive notice," that is, whether the school knew or should have known of the harassment. Carrie Urrutia Sponseller takes the opposite view in "Peer Sexual Harassment in Light of *Davis v. Monroe County Board of Education:* A Successful Balance or Tipping the Scales?" *University of Toledo Law Review* 32 (2001): 271–291, arguing that the standard adopted by the Court fairly balances the child's rights under Title IX and the school's concern with the threat of litigation.

124. David Savage, "Look the Other Way and Pay," *American Bar Association Journal* (July 1999): 34.

125. *New York Times,* May 25, 1999.

126. In *United States v. Morrison,* 529 U.S. 598 (2000), the Supreme Court struck a portion of the Violence Against Women Act that allowed federal lawsuits by victims of violence. In this case, the student, Christy Brzonkala, sued the university after she claimed she had been raped by two football players at Virginia Polytechnic University. The Court said Congress exceeded its authority under the Commerce Clause in enacting this law.

127. 372 F. Supp. 2d 1229 (D. Colo. 2005).

128. *Simpson v. University of Colorado Boulder,* 500 F.3d 1170, 1173 (10th Cir. 2007). See Porto, "Halfway Home"; Ann Scales, "Student Gladiators and Sexual

Assault: A New Analysis of Liability for Injuries Inflicted by College Athletes," *Michigan Journal of Gender and Law* 15 (2009): 205–289; Abigail Frank, "Education Law Chapter: Athletics and Title IX of the 1972 Education Amendments," *Georgetown Journal of Gender and the Law* 9 (2008): 769–794.

129. 672 F. Supp. 2d 477 (S.D.N.Y. 2009). The rapes allegedly occurred during the 2005–2006 academic year; in December 2006, the plaintiff took her own life, and her mother filed suit as administrator of the estate. The suit was brought under Title IX, § 1983 (on equal protection grounds), fraud, and intentional infliction of emotional distress. The court did not rule on the merits of the case, but on whether the plaintiff had alleged sufficient facts to overcome the defendant's motion to dismiss for failure to state a claim.

130. *McGrath,* 672 F. Supp. 2d at 487. In *J.K. v. Arizona Board of Regents,* 2008 U.S. Dist. LEXIS 83855 (D. Ariz.), a case involving a student who claimed she was raped by a football player, the court rejected the university's interpretation of the deliberate indifference standard. The district court made it clear in *J.K.* that the key to deliberate indifference was whether the defendant had knowledge of the harasser's bad behavior in general and had the means to control it, not whether it knew of the harasser's conduct toward the particular plaintiff. The court indicated this was the prevailing view among courts and cited numerous rulings interpreting deliberate indifference in a similar manner: *Williams v. Board of Regents of the University System of Georgia,* 477 F.3d 1282 (11th Cir. 2007); *Escue v. Northern Oklahoma College,* 450 F.3d 1146 (10th Cir. 2006); *Delgado v. Stegall,* 367 F.3d 668 (7th Cir. 2004); *Michelle M. v. Dunsmuir Joints Union School District,* 2006 U.S. Dist. LEXIS 77328 (E.D. Cal.); *Doe A. v. Green,* 298 F. Supp. 2d 1025 (D. Nev. 2004); *Johnson v. Galen Health Institutes, Inc.,* 267 F. Supp. 2d 679 (W.D. Ky. 2003).

131. 544 U.S. 167 (2005).

132. See Elisa M. Butler, "Civil Rights—No Hitting Back: Schools Have to Play by the Title IX Rules; *Jackson v. Birmingham Board of Education,* 544 U.S. 167 (2005)," *Wyoming Law Review* 7 (2007): 577–603.

133. The Court was influenced by a 1969 decision, *Sullivan v. Little Hunting Park,* 396 U.S. 229 (1969), in which it had allowed a claim for retaliation under another civil rights statute. The Court reasoned there that the law intended to prevent racial discrimination was broad enough to cover those who suffered retaliation for complaining of discrimination.

134. *Jackson,* 544 U.S. at 173.

135. According to Porto, "Halfway Home," *Jackson* has had the greatest effect on colleges, with women coaches suing on the basis of retaliation after being terminated following their complaints of unequal treatment for their teams, with some even winning multimillion dollar settlement or jury verdicts.

136. 555 U.S. 246 (2009).

137. The Fitzgerald family filed suit under the Civil Rights Act of 1871, 42 U.S.C. § 1983, the post–Civil War statute that provides a federal remedy for the violation of a federal constitutional or statutory right by a state actor; § 1983 opens the doors of the federal courts to individuals who have been deprived of a "right, privilege or immunity secured by the Constitution and laws" of the United States by persons acting for, or on behalf of, the state. Thus, public school officials may be sued for damages in a § 1983 suit.

138. In a series of cases beginning in 1981, the Supreme Court established a rule for determining whether Congress intended to preclude § 1983 lawsuits in certain laws. The issue in all cases is to discern congressional intent; see Mezey, "Judicial Interpretation of Legislative Intent." If a statute contains specific procedures and

limitations, the Court believes that Congress would not have wanted plaintiffs to bypass these restrictions with a § 1983 suit, that is, that it intended the statute in question—in this case, Title IX—to serve as the exclusive remedy. The circuit court found that Congress intended Title IX to be the sole remedy available to victims of sex discrimination in federally funded educational institutions.

139. See Leigh E. Ferrin, "Pencil Me In: The Use of Title IX and § 1983 to Obtain Equal Treatment in High School Athletics Scheduling." *American University Modern American* 3 (2007): 15–22; Lindsay Niehaus, "The Title IX Problem: Is It Sufficiently Comprehensive to Preclude § 1983 Actions?" *Quinnipiac Law Review* 27 (2009): 499–529.

140. At least one circuit had ruled that § 1983 plaintiffs must also demonstrate that school officials are deliberately indifferent to sexual harassment complaints; see *Murrell v. School District No. 1,* 186 F.3d 1238 (10th Cir. 1999). During oral arguments in *Fitzgerald* in December 2008, some of the justices indicated that they believed that the plaintiffs would have little chance of success in their equal protection claim because the lower court had determined that the school's actions were reasonable. See the *New York Times,* December 3, 2008.

3 Securing Workplace Equality

In 2009, 66 million women were employed in the United States; 74 percent worked in full-time jobs and 26 percent worked part-time. Of the 122 million women in the nation who were sixteen years and older, 59.2 percent (72 million) were considered labor force participants— either working or looking for work. The comparable figure for men in the labor force was 72 percent (82 million). Overall, in 2009, women comprised 46.8 percent of the total U.S. labor force.[1]

Women in the United States have been working outside their homes for wages since the 1800s. The onset of World War II spurred them to enter the workforce in record numbers as the government encouraged them to replace men serving in the armed forces and fill jobs in the wartime production industries. They became factory workers, welders, and truck drivers, with the iconic "Rosie the Riveter" typifying their new image. The number of working women rose to 18 million in 1944, an increase of almost 8 million from 1941. Although they were not relieved of their responsibility for their families, their tasks were made easier by government-subsidized child care and household assistance. By the end of the war, many women had grown to appreciate the pay and autonomy of their new roles; three-quarters of the respondents in a survey said they intended to stay on the job.[2]

But that was not to be, for when the men returned home and the nation returned to a peacetime economy, most women were involuntarily removed from their wartime jobs. Their departure was propelled by common societal beliefs about men's proper role in the workplace and women's traditional place in the home. The postwar policy of granting legal preferences to returning veterans was another significant factor in moving women out of the workforce and into the home.

Many women withdrew (either voluntarily or involuntarily) from the labor market entirely, yet a good number stayed. By 1950, there were 18.4 million working women (comprising almost 30 percent of the workforce).[3] Over the next several decades, increasing numbers of women entered the workforce. Spurred by the women's movement and increased educational opportunities, as well as the economic necessity of two-earner incomes, by 1980 there were more women in the workforce than out of it.[4]

The movement of women into the labor force has been called "revolutionary, perhaps the greatest social transformation of our time."[5] By the early 1960s, the inequities between men and women workers in pay, working conditions, and opportunities for advancement finally captured the attention of the nation's public officials. Spurred in part by the efforts of the President's Commission on the Status of Women and the Women's Bureau in the Department of Labor (DOL), Congress enacted the 1963 Equal Pay Act (EPA) and the 1964 Civil Rights Act to address pervasive workplace inequalities. But as women discovered, these laws were only the starting point for achieving their goal of equality in the workforce.

Title VII of the 1964 Civil Rights Act

Passage of the epochal 1964 Civil Rights Act, signed into law on July 2, was a pivotal moment on the path toward equal employment opportunity. As originally proposed, Title VII, the provision banning employment discrimination, had made no mention of equality for women. Then on February 8, 1964, in the final days of House debate over the bill, Representative Howard Smith, Democrat from Virginia, offered an amendment to add sex as a protected class within Title VII (the others were race, color, national origin, and religion). Smith declared that his "amendment is offered to the fair employment practices title of this bill to include within our desire to prevent discrimination against another minority, the women." Insisting that he was "very serious" about it, he explained that the amendment "has been offered several times before, but it was offered at inappropriate places in the bill. Now this is the appropriate place for this amendment to come in."[6]

The commonly accepted explanation is that Smith proposed the amendment in an attempt to derail the civil rights bill. He was said to believe that it would pass because a majority of the House would not want to antagonize women by voting against it, and, once included, it would turn sentiment away from Title VII and, indeed, the entire bill.

A number of scholars reject this view. They argue that the impetus for including sex as a protected class within Title VII originated with the

National Women's Party (NWP), a group that had supported the ERA since 1923 and lobbied to include sex in all civil rights bills, including this one. Citing Smith's long-standing support for the ERA, his personal friendship with the leader of the NWP, and his position as powerful chair of the House Rules Committee, they believe that the NWP leadership had asked him to introduce the amendment. Smith never revealed his true motive; at times, he insisted he was serious about extending the ban on employment discrimination to women, and, at other times, he admitted that it was intended as a joke.[7]

There was immediate resistance from a number of Democratic House leaders who feared for the future of the civil rights measure if the Smith Amendment were approved. Representative Emmanuel Celler, Democrat from New York, chair of the House Judiciary Committee and floor manager of the civil rights bill, spoke next and warned that the amendment would jeopardize passage of the entire bill. In an attempt at humor, Celler proclaimed that women are certainly not a minority in his house and that one of the reasons for the survival of his forty-nine-year marriage is that "I usually have the last two words, and those words are 'yes dear.'"[8]

Celler opposed the Smith Amendment in part because he feared it would conflict with existing state laws that protected working women from dangers on the job, a type of protection he believed they needed because they were the weaker sex. He said he dreaded "the upheaval that would result from adoption of blanket language requiring total equality. This is the entering wedge . . . [and] the list of foreseeable consequences . . . is unlimited."[9] Celler also worried that the amendment would be an "entering wedge" for the ERA, which he also opposed because it would spell the end of protective legislation.

Despite the laughter from many of the male representatives, the women in the House took the amendment seriously, with eleven out of twelve rising to speak in favor of it. A fervent supporter of the proposed civil rights bill, only Green from Oregon, perhaps under pressure from President Lyndon Johnson (who was also concerned about its effect on the historic civil rights measure), was opposed. She insisted that she condemned sex discrimination yet believed that racial discrimination was more invidious and felt that Smith's purpose in adding sex to Title VII was to doom passage of the entire bill. When he regained the floor, Smith spoke in favor of his amendment, arguing that it was needed to protect white women from employment discrimination since African American women would be protected by the ban on racial discrimination in Title VII.

Support for the amendment quickly came from women on both sides of the aisle. Griffiths, longtime supporter of the ERA, strongly endorsed it, warning the male members of the House that "a vote against [Smith's] amendment today . . . is a vote against his wife, or his widow, or his daughter, or his sister."[10] Katherine St. George, Republican from New York, also urged Congress to support the amendment, saying "we are entitled to this little crumb of equality."[11]

In the end, the amendment passed the House in a 168 to 133 vote; two days later, the entire bill cleared the House in a vote of 290 to 130. Senate Democrats were no longer concerned that the amendment would doom the entire bill, and with the outspoken support of Margaret Chase Smith, Republican from Maine, the upper body approved the House bill, with the Smith Amendment intact, in a 73 to 27 vote on June 17, 1964. On July 2, the House agreed to the final Senate version, and Johnson signed the Civil Rights Act of 1964.[12]

Title VII, applying to employers and labor unions with fifteen or more employees, provides that

it shall be an unlawful employment practice for an employer:
(1) to fail or refuse to hire or to discharge any individual, or otherwise to discriminate against any individual with respect to his compensation, terms, conditions, or privileges of employment, because of such individual's race, color, religion, sex, or national origin.
(2) to limit, segregate, or classify his employees or applicants for employment in any way which would deprive or tend to deprive any individual of employment opportunities or otherwise adversely affect his status as an employee, because of such individual's race, color, religion, sex, or national origin.

Fearing that Title VII would prevent employers from hiring on the basis of sex—even when sex was relevant to job performance—Congress permitted exceptions to the ban on discrimination "where religion, sex, or national origin is a bona fide occupational qualification (BFOQ) reasonably necessary to the normal operation of that particular business or enterprise." Employers charged with discrimination may defend themselves by showing that sex, religion, or national origin is a legitimate requirement of the job.

The law established the Equal Employment Opportunity Commission (EEOC), which opened its doors on July 2, 1965, a year after the act was passed. Under the direction of five commissioners (including the chair), the agency devoted little energy to enforcing the ban on sex discrimination in employment. Indeed, its first public document, "Guidelines on Discrimination Because of Sex," appeared to undermine Title VII by justifying state laws that restricted women's job opportunities and defending sex-segregated help-wanted advertisements.[13]

The EEOC was given authority to enforce Title VII's ban on employment discrimination on the basis of race, color, sex, national origin, and religion. Because Congress sought to deflect litigation by allowing the agency to settle disputes between the parties before a suit was filed, a complainant must file an administrative charge with the EEOC (or a designated state or local Fair Employment Practices Agency).[14] The agency received more than four times the number of complaints it had expected during its first year and faced immediate staff shortages.[15]

Complaints steadily grew: in FY 1966, the agency received almost 9,000 complaints; five years later (in FY 1970), the number of complaints had risen to just over 20,000.[16] And although the agency had not expected sex discrimination to play a major role in its work, one-third (33.5 percent) of the complaints filed during its first year pertained to sex discrimination.[17]

The proportion of charges based on sex has remained relatively constant. From FY 1997 to FY 2009, sex-based charges (not counting claims of retaliation) continued to be at about 30 percent of the total number of charges filed with the EEOC. In the decade from FY 1997 to FY 2007, the number of sex-based charges filed with the EEOC ranged from 23,000 to 25,000. In FY 2008, the number jumped to 28,372 and then dropped slightly in FY 2009 to 28,028. These figures continued to represent about a third of the total number of charges the agency received: 95,402 in FY 2008 and 93,277 in FY 2009.[18]

In 1972, the Equal Employment Opportunity Act expanded Title VII protection to the millions of federal, state, and local government workers as well as employees at educational institutions. The act gave the EEOC litigating authority, allowing it to file suit against employers, unions, and employment agencies.[19] Over the next two decades, the EEOC was gradually given responsibility over other antidiscrimination laws; today it serves as the lead federal agency in enforcing Title VII, the EPA, the Pregnancy Discrimination Act of 1978 (PDA), the Age Discrimination in Employment Act of 1967 (ADEA), the 1973 Rehabilitation Act, and the 1990 Americans with Disabilities Act (ADA).

The EEOC's primary task is to investigate charges and, if it finds discrimination, attempt to settle the complaint. Like other federal agencies, the agency issues guidelines and regulations that the courts consider but do not have to follow.

One of the first legal issues arising under Title VII revolved around state laws enacted during the late nineteenth and early twentieth centuries that regulated women's work, ostensibly to protect them. Most states had laws limiting women's working hours, but a number of them were repealed in response to Title VII; court challenges were required in others.[20]

In *Weeks v. Southern Bell Telephone and Telegraph,*[21] a Fifth Circuit case decided in 1969, the circuit court held that Southern Bell did not prove that sex was a bona fide occupational qualification for the job of switchman. To rely on a BFOQ defense, the court said, an employer has to prove it has "reasonable cause to believe, that is, a factual basis for believing, that all or substantially all women would be unable to perform safely and efficiently the duties of the job involved."[22] Two years later, in *Rosenfeld v. Southern Pacific,*[23] the Ninth Circuit ruled that Title VII does not permit assumptions about the physical characteristics of a group to serve as the basis for employment decisions.

Diaz v. Pan American World Airways[24] also restricted the interpretation of the BFOQ defense. The Fifth Circuit held that the passengers' preferences for women flight attendants did not constitute a BFOQ since Title VII only allows employers to use sex as a BFOQ when it is "reasonably necessary" to the operation of a business. The test, held the court, is "business *necessity,*" not "business *convenience.*" The court ruled that employers may only hire on the basis of sex "when the *essence* of the business operation would be undermined by not hiring members of one sex exclusively."[25] Together, the decisions underscored the limitations of the BFOQ defense, the courts ruling that such restrictions on women's work opportunities were inconsistent with the aim of Title VII.

The Supreme Court and Title VII Litigation

The Supreme Court's first ruling in a Title VII discrimination case affecting women was in 1971, the same year as *Reed,* the case in which it appeared to raise the level of scrutiny in sexual equality cases. Table 3.1 presents the Court's decisions in employment discrimination cases.

Phillips v. Martin Marietta Corporation,[26] the first Title VII suit to reach the Supreme Court, arose when Martin Marietta rejected Ida Phillips's application as a trainee on the assembly line at its Florida plant because she had preschool children. She filed a Title VII suit, arguing that the company's policy of accepting men with preschool children for these positions discriminated against her on the basis of sex. The company asserted that she was not rejected because of sex but because of her status as a mother and that other women were hired for the position.

The lower courts ruled in the company's favor. In a brief per curiam (unsigned) opinion, the Supreme Court held that they were wrong to believe that Title VII allows separate hiring policies for men and women. However, the high court refused to categorically rule out separate hiring policies, adding that if the company had evidence that caring for small children was "demonstrably more relevant to job performance for a woman than for a man," it could raise an affirmative defense that sex was a BFOQ for the position. Moreover, as the transcripts of the oral argument reveal, the justices displayed a cavalier attitude toward women, asking whether railroads would be required to hire "porteresses" and whether women would demand to be employed as ditch diggers.[27]

In 1977, the Supreme Court returned to the BFOQ defense in *Dothard v. Rawlinson*.[28] Dianne Rawlinson applied for the job of "correctional counselor" in an Alabama prison and was initially rejected because she failed to meet the height and weight requirements. While her suit was pending in federal court, the prison authorities adopted Regulation 204. The new regulation restricted "contact" positions in the prison wards to guards of the prisoners' sex because such positions required "continual close physical proximity to [the] inmates."[29] When Rawlinson amended her complaint to include Regulation 204, the prison claimed that sex was a bona fide occupational qualification for the job of prison guard.

Announcing the opinion for a 6 to 3 Court, Justice Potter Stewart upheld Regulation 204. Although he acknowledged that women should ordinarily be permitted to decide how much risk to undertake in their

Table 3.1 Supreme Court Employment Discrimination Rulings, 1971–2007

Case	Date	Issue[a]	Ruling[b]
Phillips	1971	Sex-plus hiring	Expands employee rights
Pittsburgh	1973	Sex-segregated advertisements	Expands employee rights
Dothard	1977	BFOQ/height and weight	Expands employee rights
Hopkins	1989	Mixed motives	Expands employee rights
Costa	2003	Mixed motives	Expands employee rights
Ledbetter	2007	Wage discrimination	Limits employee rights

Notes: a. Based on the major issue in the case.
b. Based on the overall outcome of the case.

jobs, he believed the state's interest in prison security outweighed this right. Because of the dangers stemming from overcrowded conditions, he felt female guards would be susceptible to attacks from male prisoners. Stewart denied that the Court was motivated by a "romantic paternalism" toward women, insisting that a woman's ability to keep order in a maximum-security prison could be directly "reduced by her womanhood."[30]

In August 1965, an EEOC guideline condemned discrimination in newspaper advertising on the basis of race, religion, or national origin but was silent on the question of sex. After protests by women's groups, the EEOC created an ad hoc committee to study sex-segregated ads. Dominated by advertising agencies and newspapers, the committee determined that Title VII did not bar such ads. The EEOC subsequently voted 3 to 2 in favor of allowing sex-segregated ads but required newspapers to insert disclaimers that they were not intended to deter job applicants of the other sex. In August 1968, the EEOC reversed itself and issued a guideline against such advertising.[31]

Some newspapers had voluntarily abandoned the practice of running separate help wanted ads, but many did not. Following the model of Title VII, Pittsburgh adopted an ordinance prohibiting sex discrimination in employment, except where sex was a bona fide occupational qualification.[32] In October 1969, NOW filed a complaint with the Pittsburgh Commission on Human Relations, charging the Pittsburgh Press Company with violating the ordinance by allowing advertisers to advertise jobs by sex.[33] The press argued that the First Amendment protected its right to advertise sex-segregated positions. In a 5 to 4 decision, in *Pittsburgh Press v. Pittsburgh Commission on Human Relations*,[34] the Court upheld the city ordinance, ruling that it did not violate the First Amendment.

Title VII litigation revolves around two types of discrimination: disparate treatment, in which plaintiffs must prove intentional discrimination, and disparate impact, in which plaintiffs challenge employment policies that are facially neutral but have disproportionate impacts on them.[35] Disparate treatment claims are more numerous; disparate impact claims affect larger numbers of people at one time. Most of the charges filed with the EEOC during its early years involved disparate impact claims over height and weight requirements, testing procedures, and seniority systems. The agency's 1966 Guidelines on Employment Testing Procedures formalized disparate impact theory by stating that it applied to neutral employment practices that have a disproportionate effect on persons covered by Title VII unless the practice is necessary for the operation of the business.[36]

One of the key distinctions between disparate treatment and disparate impact cases lies in the type of evidence the plaintiff must present to prove the employer guilty of violating Title VII.[37] The Supreme Court set forth the procedure for proving disparate treatment claims in *McDonnell Douglas v. Green*.[38] Subsequent rulings clarified and refined the *McDonnell Douglas* formula.[39]

There are three phases of a disparate treatment case. Plaintiffs must establish a prima facie case (create a presumption) of discrimination by showing that (1) they are members of a class protected by Title VII, (2) they are qualified for the job or promotion they sought, (3) they applied for the job and were rejected or denied the promotion, and (4) the employer continued to seek employees with their qualifications. Once plaintiffs establish a prima facie case, the second phase begins, and employers must offer a "legitimate, nondiscriminatory reason" for the decision not to hire or promote. Because plaintiffs retain the burden of proof throughout the trial, employers do not have to prove that the proffered reason actually motivated the decision. In the last phase, plaintiffs must prove that the employers' reasons were a pretext for discriminatory motives.

Employment decisions often reflect legitimate and illegitimate reasons. The Supreme Court first wrestled with the thorny issue of a mixed-motive employment decision in a lawsuit brought by Ann Hopkins against the giant public accounting firm, Price Waterhouse.[40] Hopkins, a senior manager in the Office of Government Services in the District of Columbia for four years, was first considered for partnership in 1982. She was the only female candidate.[41] At the time the firm was deliberating over whether to offer her a partnership, there were seven female partners at Price Waterhouse, out of a total of 662.[42] Partnership decisions at the firm were based on evaluations by the existing partners. Written evaluations were submitted to a committee that made recommendations to a policy board, which could either forward the application to the entire partnership for a vote, reject it, or place it on hold.

There were eighty-eight candidates for partner that year; Price Waterhouse promoted forty-seven, rejected twenty-one, and deferred twenty, including Hopkins. The firm primarily attributed its decision to concerns about her interpersonal skills. Acknowledging her competence and intelligence, the partners felt that she lacked "femininity" and had an abrasive personality. They characterized her in stereotypical sex-based terms, a common experience for women in professional fields. Their evaluations revealed that they "reacted negatively" to her "because she was a woman"; they described her as "macho" and suggested she take a "course at charm school." In explaining to her why her candidacy was placed on hold, a partner counseled her that her professional problems would be solved if she would "walk more femininely, talk more femininely, dress more femininely, wear make-up, have her hair styled, and wear jewelry."[43]

A year later, after being passed over for partner a second time, Hopkins resigned and filed suit, claiming that the firm violated Title VII by basing its decision on sexual stereotyping. The primary question for the courts was whether a decision based on a mixture of permissible and impermissible factors was made "because of sex," the crucial element in a Title VII suit. Unlike most plaintiffs, though, Hopkins had written evidence that sex bias played a role in the firm's decisionmaking process.[44] Price Waterhouse argued that plaintiffs such as Hopkins should be required to prove that they would have been promoted in the absence of discrimination. She contended that firms are guilty of violating Title VII if they allow an impermissible motive to play any role in an employment decision. The District of Columbia Circuit Court took the middle ground and held that once a plaintiff shows that sex is a motivating factor in an employment action, the employer can avoid liability if it can show it would have taken the same action if discrimination had not played a role.

Seeking to balance the employer's autonomy in personnel decisions with the employee's right not to be discriminated against, a divided Court substantially affirmed the appeals court. Speaking for himself, Blackmun, Stevens, and Justice Thurgood Marshall, Brennan described the burden-shifting scheme as an affirmative defense:

> When a plaintiff in a Title VII case proves that her gender played a *motivating* factor in an employment decision, the defendant may avoid a finding of liability only by proving . . . that it would have made the same decision even if it had not taken the plaintiff's gender into account.[45]

Thus, he concluded, the purpose of the statute is served by preventing employers from relying on sex-based considerations while allowing them to ground their decisions in legitimate employment factors.

The four-justice plurality agreed with the district court that the firm had based its decision on both legitimate and illegitimate factors. "It takes no special training," Brennan said,

> to discern sex stereotyping in a description of an aggressive female employee as requiring "a course in charm school." Nor . . . does it require expertise in psychology to know that, if an employee's flawed "interpersonal skills" can be corrected by a soft-hued suit or a new shade of lipstick, perhaps it is the employee's sex and not her interpersonal skills that has drawn the criticism.[46]

He explained that the partners may have been justified in disliking her personality, but Title VII bars them from reacting "negatively to her personality because she is a woman."[47] The Court remanded the case to allow the lower court to determine whether the firm would have rejected her application in the absence of discrimination.[48]

White and O'Connor concurred, agreeing with the plurality that the burden of proof should shift to the employer, but disagreeing about when the shift should take place. White believed it should shift after a plaintiff "show[ed] that the unlawful motive was a *substantial* factor in the adverse employment action."[49] O'Connor expressed concern that courts would shift the burden to the employer too easily, perhaps on the basis of stray remarks in the workplace or discriminatory comments from nondecisionmakers. Seeking to avoid such precipitous action by a court, she stated, "in my view, in order to justify shifting the burden on the issue of causation on the defendant, a disparate treatment plaintiff must show by *direct evidence* that an illegitimate criterion was a substantial factor in the decision."[50] Her threshold was high: the employee must do more than simply present evidence of stray remarks or derogatory comments. In her view, because Hopkins had supplied "direct evidence that decisionmakers placed substantial negative reliance on an illegitimate criterion in reaching their decision," she had crossed the threshold.[51]

On May 14, 1990, Judge Gerhard Gesell of the District of Columbia District Court ruled "that the firm maintained a partnership evaluation system that 'permitted negative sexually stereotyped comments to influence partnership selection.'" He ordered Price Waterhouse to pay her $371,175 in back pay and award her the partnership it had denied her eight years ago. Explaining his ruling, Gesell said, "Price Waterhouse plainly does not want her and would not voluntarily admit her. Partnership, not simply a new vote, is the logical remedy, given the finding that Ms. Hopkins was likely to have been made a partner if not for unlawful discrimination."[52] On December 4, 1990, a three-judge panel of the Court of Appeals for the District of Columbia affirmed Gesell's decision, ruling that the firm had failed to prove there were nondiscriminatory reasons for rejecting her partnership bid.[53]

Companies often rely on seemingly neutral criteria for job selection, and although they may not be openly discriminatory, such facially neutral policies may have the *effect* of restricting job opportunities for women and minorities.[54]

The Court first considered whether Title VII applied to company policies that disproportionately affected minority employees in the 1971 landmark decision *Griggs v. Duke Power Company*.[55] The plaintiffs,

African Americans working in Duke Power Company's Dan River Steam Station, complained that the company used criteria for obtaining higher-status jobs in the plant that disqualified them at a "substantially" greater rate than whites.[56]

Speaking for a unanimous Court, Burger held that the statute "proscribes not only overt discrimination but also practices that are fair in form, but discriminatory in operation. The touchstone is business necessity. If an employment practice which operates to exclude Negroes cannot be shown to be related to job performance, the practice is prohibited."[57] Because Duke Power was unable to show that its criteria were related to job performance, the Court found it violated Title VII.

The importance of *Griggs* cannot be overstated. Former chief of the EEOC Office of Conciliations Alfred Blumrosen believes that "few decisions in our time—perhaps only *Brown v. Board of Education*—have had such momentous social consequences" as *Griggs*.[58] Similarly, past EEOC chair Eleanor Holmes Norton agrees, proclaiming that "the *Griggs* Court, in announcing the disparate impact theory, defined the most important concept in modern employment discrimination work."[59]

The Supreme Court's three-part test in disparate impact suits arose from its rulings in *Griggs* and *Albemarle Paper Company v. Moody*,[60] a 1975 opinion. Under the *Griggs-Albermarle* formula, after plaintiffs identify a neutral (nondiscriminatory on its face) employment policy with a disproportionate effect on them, the burden of proof shifts to the employer to show that the criteria have "a manifest relationship" to the job. If the employer proves the criteria are job-related, the plaintiffs must demonstrate there is a less discriminatory alternative available.[61]

Following *Griggs* and *Albemarle,* most lower courts shifted the burden of proof to the employer after the plaintiffs demonstrated that the standards had an adverse impact on them. But the courts did not agree on the nature of the employer's proof; the high court added to the confusion by variously identifying the employer's burden as "business necessity," "related to job performance," and "manifest relationship to the employment in question" in discussing the employer's burden.[62]

Disparate impact cases often arise from challenges to an employer's minimum height and weight requirements. In *Dothard,* in addition to deciding whether Regulation 204 was a legitimate BFOQ, the Court also addressed the Alabama prison system's 120-pound minimum weight requirement and 5-foot, 2-inch minimum height requirement. The plaintiff, arguing that the specifications disproportionately affected women, presented evidence that women fourteen years and over constituted 52.75 percent of the Alabama population and 36.89 percent of its total labor force, yet they held only 12.9 percent of the correctional counselor positions.

The state contended that the statistics represented national figures, not actual job applicants. Speaking for the Court, Stewart noted that the statistics need not reflect the applicant pool because applicants below the minimum height or weight would have been discouraged from applying. Moreover, he said, the nationwide statistics are acceptable because there is no reason to assume that the physical characteristics of Alabama men and women differ from those in the national population.

Alabama also maintained that height and weight were related to strength, essential to the job of prison guard. But it offered no evidence that they were correlated to "the requisite amount of strength thought essential to good job performance."[63] Reiterating an earlier theme, the Court held that the state violated Title VII because it was unable to prove "that the challenged requirements are job related."[64]

The Court dramatically changed the procedure in disparate impact suits in *Wards Cove Packing Company v. Atonio*.[65] In 1974, minority workers, primarily Filipinos and Alaska natives, filed a Title VII suit against the Alaska fishing company. They charged they were relegated to the unskilled, lower-paying cannery positions, with white workers occupying most of the higher-paying, skilled, noncannery positions. Additionally, they claimed the company maintained segregated housing and dining facilities.

Cannery workers were hired locally in Alaska, whereas the noncannery workers were hired during the winter off-months from the company's Washington and Oregon offices. Identifying these and other hiring and promotion policies, the workers filed suit under both disparate treatment and disparate impact theories. The Ninth Circuit ruled that the plaintiffs' statistics showing that a higher percentage of minority workers held cannery jobs had established a prima facie case of disparate impact; it remanded the case to the lower court, instructing it to require the employer to prove the business necessity defense.[66]

In a 5 to 4 vote, with White delivering the majority opinion, the high court rejected the plaintiffs' statistical proof, saying the proper comparison is between the number of persons in the jobs at issue and the number of qualified persons in the labor market, for employers did not violate Title VII if there were no qualified nonwhite applicants available for the better-paying jobs. Under the appellate court's approach, he emphasized, employers could be sued simply because there were few minorities in the superior jobs. The Court held that the plaintiffs had not established a prima facie case of disparate impact and reversed the court below. The Court also modified the *Griggs* requirement that employment practices with a discriminatory effect must be justified by showing they have "a manifest relationship to the employment in question" to the more lenient (for the employer) principle of allowing such practices if they "serve, in a significant way, the legitimate employment goals of the employer." And perhaps most significantly, *Wards Cove* established that plaintiffs in disparate impact suits retain the burden of proof at all times—just like disparate treatment plaintiffs. Thus, plaintiffs must prove that the challenged practice is unrelated to the job. Because employees are unlikely to have access to such information, the ruling diminished the likelihood of a plaintiff's success in a disparate impact suit.

Blackmun's dissent accused the Court of "tak[ing] three major strides backwards in the battle against race discrimination," asking whether the majority "still believes that race discrimination—or, more accurately, race discrimination against nonwhites—is a problem in our society, or even remembers that it ever was."[67] In strong language, he charged the industry with "a kind of overt and institutionalized discrimination [that] we have not dealt with in years: a total residential and work environment organized on principles of racial stratification and segregation which . . . resembles a plantation economy."[68]

In his own bitterly worded dissent, Stevens accused the majority of "retreat[ing]" from its long-established commitment to furthering the principles of equality and "turning a blind eye to the meaning and purpose of Title VII."[69] Claiming that the majority's cavalier treatment of "settled law" required a "primer" on Title VII, he reviewed the eighteen-year history of disparate impact and disparate treatment analysis and explained the reason for distinguishing between the two. In disparate treatment cases, he stressed, the plaintiff only offers indirect evidence of the employer's intent to discriminate by making a prima facie case, and a court uses the *McDonnell Douglas* formulation to explore the employer's motive. It is appropriate that the burden of proof remain with the plaintiff throughout the trial because there is no Title VII violation until the discriminatory motive is established during the third stage of the trial.

Because intent is irrelevant in disparate impact cases, however, plaintiffs demonstrate the Title VII violation when they present evidence that they are disproportionately affected by an employment policy. With the Title VII violation established, he said, the employer can only "justify the practice by explaining why it is necessary to the operation of business." Drawing on established legal principles, Stevens characterized the employer's burden in this second phase of a disparate impact case as "a classic example of an affirmative defense."[70] He argued that the Court had always placed the burden of proof on the employer in disparate impact cases. Protesting the majority's "casual—almost summary—rejection of the statutory construction that developed in the wake of *Griggs*," he emphasized that he "always believed that the *Griggs* opinion correctly reflected the intent of the Congress that enacted Title VII. [And] even if I were not so persuaded," he continued, "I could not join a rejection of a consistent interpretation of a federal statute."[71]

Title VII and the 1991 Civil Rights Act

By changing the long-standing procedure in disparate impact lawsuits, the Court had undermined *Griggs* and sharply reduced Title VII's effectiveness in battling employment discrimination.[72] In February 1990, Senator Kennedy and Representative Augustus Hawkins, Democrat from California, introduced a bill, S. 2104 and H.R. 4000, in their respective chambers. Known as the Kennedy-Hawkins bill, the legislation began the long journey to restore the civil rights protections that the Court had restricted. Attempting to counter the proposed legislation, the White House and congressional Republicans objected to reversing the Supreme Court rulings. "We've got a piece of machinery that basically works well," an administration official warned; "it's designed to get people to settle differences and get back to work. I don't know if we want to create a system that is more strongly adversary."[73]

Among other provisions, the bill would have reversed *Wards Cove* and restored the *Griggs* formula for allocating the burden of proof in disparate impact cases. President George H. W. Bush said he agreed with the reallocation of the burden of proof but still objected to the proposed law, arguing that it went beyond *Griggs* and would force employers to establish racial and sexual hiring and promotion quotas to avoid suits for discrimination. Bill supporters countered that *Griggs* had not led to companies adopting quotas to protect themselves against discrimination suits. In a White House Rose Garden ceremony on May 17, 1990, Bush warned: "I will not sign a quota bill."[74]

On July 18, 1990, the Senate approved S. 2104 in a 65 to 34 vote, with ten Republicans joining the fifty-five Democrats.[75] A few weeks later, on August 3, 1990, the House approved H.R. 4000 in a 272 to 154 vote, twelve short of the votes needed to override the promised presidential veto.[76] Bush objected to the bill, reiterating that it would "forc[e] businesses to adopt quotas in hiring and promotion" as well as "foster divisiveness and litigation rather than conciliation and do more to promote legal fees than civil rights."[77] On October 22, 1990, he became the second president (Reagan was the first) in the twentieth century to veto a civil rights measure. Bush charged that the bill would "introduce the destructive force of quotas into our nation's employment system" and "will lead to years—perhaps decades—of uncertainty and expensive litigation."[78]

Two days later, the Senate failed to override the veto by just one vote short of the necessary two-thirds. The presidential veto was a stunning defeat for the civil rights community, especially women, who would have been one of the bill's primary beneficiaries. Justifying the president's opposition to the bill, an official stated that "we fought a Civil War for blacks, we didn't fight a Civil War for women."[79]

A new version of the civil rights bill was introduced in the 102d Congress as H.R. 1 on January 3, 1991. Among other things, it would have amended Title VII to allow women to sue for money damages in cases of intentional discrimination. It also proposed to establish a commission to study the "glass ceiling" effect on women.[80] House Republicans objected to the new bill, again raising the specter of quotas. Henry Hyde, Republican from Illinois, caustically commented, "I can envision signs that read: 'Help Wanted: four women, two African-American males and one Hispanic.'"[81]

H.R. 1 passed the House on June 5, 1991, in a 273 to 158 vote, still short of the number needed to override the expected veto. The House effort represented a last-ditch attempt to avoid a veto by explicitly banning quotas and limiting damages in suits brought by women, religious minorities, and people with disabilities.[82] A few months later, the Senate and White House agreed on a compromise bill, S. 1745, put together by administration officials, Danforth, and Kennedy. It was overwhelmingly approved by the Senate on October 30, 1991, in a 93 to 5 vote and in the House by a wide margin of 381 to 38 on November 7, 1991; two weeks later, on November 21, 1991, Bush signed the Civil Rights Act of 1991.[83]

The new law reversed or modified nine Supreme Court decisions, five decided during the 1988–1989 term, that had limited the rights of women and minorities in employment discrimination suits.[84] Perhaps most important, the 1991 act reversed *Wards Cove* by reverting to the *Griggs-Albemarle* procedure in two ways: first, it specified that to survive a Title VII challenge, a practice must be "job-related for the position in question and consistent with business necessity"; second, it shifted the burden of proof back to the employer in the second stage of a disparate impact suit. Although it would leave their definitions to the courts to determine, a memo inserted into the *Congressional Record* on October 25, 1991, declared that the terms "business necessity" and "job-related" should be interpreted according to *Griggs* and other pre–*Wards Cove* rulings. However, in an apparent attempt to negate this principle, Bush's written signing statement approvingly referred to a contrary interpretative memo by Senator Bob Dole, Republican from Kansas (and the 1996 Republican candidate for president). Dole characterized the act as "an affirmation of existing law," an obvious contradiction of congressional intent and the text of the act and indeed, Bush's own more conciliatory remarks at the signing ceremony.[85]

The 1991 act reversed *Hopkins* by amending Title VII to state that "an unlawful employment practice is established when the complaining party demonstrates that race, color, religion, sex, or national origin was a motivating factor for any employment practice, even though other factors also motivated the practice." Thus, under the 1991 act, an employer is liable if a plaintiff establishes that discrimination plays any role in a negative employment decision. If the employer is able to demonstrate that its decision would have been the same in the absence of discrimination, it is entitled to "a limited affirmative defense that does not absolve it of liability, but restricts the remedies available to a plaintiff" to declaratory and injunctive relief (such as a court order that the company cease the discriminatory practice), attorney's fees, and costs.[86]

The law also allows plaintiffs in sex and disability discrimination cases to request jury trials and receive compensatory and punitive damages if they succeed in proving intentional discrimination.[87] To collect punitive damages, workers must show the employer acted with "malice or reckless indifference to [their] federally-protected rights."[88] If they succeed, the damages are available according to the size of the business: $50,000 for employers with 15 to 100 workers, $100,000 for employers with 101 to 200 employees, $200,000 for employers with 201 to 500 employees, and $300,000 for employers with more than 500 employees.[89] The law also extends protection under Title VII and the ADA to U.S. workers on foreign soil, reversing the Court's 1991 ruling in *Equal Employment Opportunity Commission v. Arabian American Oil Company*.[90]

The Court again attempted to clarify the issue of proof in disparate treatment cases in *St. Mary's Honors Center v. Hicks*,[91] the first major Title VII decision after passage of the 1991 act. Although the plaintiff argued that the act entitled him to a jury trial in his Title VII case, the 5 to 4 ruling, announced by Scalia, rejected his interpretation of the act. The Court dismissed his claim, reiterating that plaintiffs bear the burden of proof throughout the case. Reversing the appeals court, the majority held that plaintiffs cannot prevail in Title VII cases simply by showing that the employer's proffered explanation for the employment action is untrue.[92]

In addition to the confusion generated by the president's statement at the signing ceremony over the interpretation of the 1991 act, there was also controversy about how the law affected actions filed before it was passed. About a month after the bill was signed, the EEOC issued a policy statement, saying that because Congress had not specified whether the law was retroactive, it did not apply to persons whose suits were pending on November 21 or if the discrimination they complained of occurred before November 21.[93] In 1994, in two companion cases, *Rivers v. Roadway Express, Inc.*,[94] involving a claim of racial discrimination under § 1981, and *Landgraf v. USI Film Products*,[95] involving a suit for sexual harassment under Title VII, the Court agreed with the EEOC, ruling 8 to 1 that the 1991 act did not apply to conduct that occurred before it was passed. The majority was in part persuaded that because the president had vetoed the 1990 bill that had established retroactivity, Congress omitted the language of retroactivity in the later bill to avoid a presidential veto. Blackmun dissented in both cases, saying it was not "unjust" to hold employers accountable for laws that had been on the books for decades.

The Court returned to the question of proof raised in *St. Mary's Honors Center* in *Reeves v. Sanderson Plumbing Products, Inc.*,[96] an age discrimination case decided in 2000. In a ruling that also applies to suits brought under Title VII and the ADA, the Court unanimously held that courts may consider any evidence in the record to find for plaintiffs, including the evidence showing the employer's stated reason was a pretext for discrimination.

The Court revisited the thorny issue of mixed-motive decisionmaking in 2003 in *Desert Palace, Inc. v. Costa*.[97] *Costa* addressed a crucial question that was left open in *Hopkins* and was not resolved by the passage of the 1991 Civil Rights Act: whether a plaintiff must offer direct evidence that sex is a motivating factor in an employment decision before receiving a mixed-motive jury instruction. In the absence of such an instruction, the plaintiff retains the burden of proof throughout the trial and must prove that the employer's stated reason for dismissal is a pretext for discrimination.[98]

Catherine Costa worked in the warehouse of the famous Caesars Palace Hotel and Casino in Las Vegas as a truck driver and heavy equipment operator from 1987 until 1994, the only woman employed in this capacity. She had frequent disputes with her fellow employees and supervisors, including a fight with a male coworker for which she was disciplined and finally terminated. The man she fought with was disciplined but not fired. She sued on the grounds of sexual harassment and sex discrimination; the court dismissed her sexual harassment claim. Costa presented evidence at trial that she was treated more harshly and received less favorable assignments than the men with whom she worked and was the frequent target of "sex-based slurs." Despite the fact that Costa had not presented direct evidence of the discrimination, the trial judge instructed the jury on the standard of proof necessary for a mixed-motive case; it awarded her $364,000 in back pay and damages.[99] A three-judge Ninth Circuit panel reversed the jury award, but upon rehearing, the en banc (entire) court of eleven judges reinstated it. The full circuit held that O'Connor's direct evidence standard in *Hopkins* was obviated by the 1991 act. With the exception of the Ninth Circuit, all circuits had relied on O'Connor's concurring opinion in *Hopkins* to require plaintiffs to produce direct evidence, such as personal observation or knowledge, of discrimination in mixed-motive cases.

The Supreme Court accepted the case to clarify whether the 1991 act required the plaintiff in a mixed-motive case to present direct evidence of the employer's discriminatory motive. The defendant had argued on appeal that unless plaintiffs present direct evidence of discrimination, they are not entitled to a special mixed-motive jury instruction as specified in the 1991 act.

Thomas announced the decision for a unanimous Court, explaining that the act resolved the question. Simply put, he said, if Congress intended to require direct evidence in a mixed-motive case, it would have explicitly stated it in the act, and its failure to do so is dispositive.[100] He concluded that Title VII plaintiffs are entitled to mixed-motive jury instructions once they convince the judge that their employer was motivated by an impermissible factor in making an employment decision.[101] O'Connor concurred, agreeing that the 1991 act nullified the direct evidence requirement.

Title VII and Wage Discrimination

Lilly Ledbetter, an Alabama factory worker, symbolized a Supreme Court ruling that undercut women's efforts to redress wage discrimination under Title VII. Ledbetter was a supervisor at a Goodyear tire plant in Gadsden, Alabama, from 1979 until November 1998, when she took early retirement. Her pay was roughly commensurate with a man's at the beginning of her employment, yet over time the disparity increased, and by 1997, when she was the only female area manager, her pay was $3,727 a month.

The salary range for the fifteen male area managers was from $4,286 to $5,236 a month. In 1998, she received an anonymous letter, informing her that she was being underpaid compared to male area supervisors.[102]

Shortly thereafter, in March 1998, she submitted a questionnaire about sex discrimination to the EEOC and, in July 1998, filed a formal charge of discrimination with the agency, stating that Goodyear had discriminated against her on the basis of sex by giving her poor performance evaluations in the past and that these acts of discrimination led to the current wage disparity.[103] In August 1998, she signed an agreement to retire in November; after leaving the company, she filed a Title VII suit in federal court early in 1999.[104]

At trial, Ledbetter testified that her poor performance evaluations resulted from her rejection of her supervisor's sexual advances during the early 1980s.[105] Because Goodyear based most of its salaried employees' pay on performance evaluations, these evaluations led to a pay gap between her and her fellow male employees. She also presented evidence of pervasive sex discrimination at the plant.

The company argued that the evaluations were not based on sex discrimination but on her poor job performance. The federal court jury found in her favor, persuaded that she was discriminated against by receiving lower salary raises, which had a cumulative effect of depressing her salary over time. It found that Goodyear had intentionally discriminated against her in pay and awarded her $3.8 million in back pay and damages; the amount was reduced to $360,000 because of the caps on Title VII damages.

On appeal, the Eleventh Circuit reversed the lower court, ruling that Title VII barred her from suing for wage decisions made before September 26, 1997—the six months before she filed the EEOC questionnaire.[106] Departing from the position taken by the majority of circuits as well as the EEOC, the Eleventh Circuit dismissed her case, ruling that Title VII required discrimination claims to be filed within 180 days (6 months) after the date each discriminatory act occurred. Any acts of discrimination by Goodyear prior to 1997, even if she were able to prove them, the court said, were irrelevant to her Title VII claim.[107]

The question presented to the Supreme Court was

> whether and under what circumstances a plaintiff may bring an action under Title VII of the Civil Rights Act of 1964 alleging illegal pay discrimination when the disparate pay is received during the statutory limitations period, but is the result of intentionally discriminatory pay decisions that occurred outside the limitations period.[108]

With Alito speaking for the 5 to 4 majority, consisting of himself, Scalia, Kennedy, Thomas, and Chief Justice John Roberts, the Supreme Court upheld the circuit court in *Ledbetter v. Goodyear Tire and Rubber Co., Inc.*[109] Signaling sympathy for the employer, the high court agreed with the circuit court's restrictive view of Title VII that she must file her EEOC claim within six months after the company's first act of discrimination against her. Thus, according to the high court's interpretation of the law, if Goodyear made its first discriminatory decision in 1980, she had six months from that date to bring a charge with the EEOC. Ledbetter argued that a new charging period, that is, a new six-month window, began with each paycheck. Not so, said Alito: "the EEOC charging period is triggered when a discrete unlawful practice takes place. A new violation does not occur, and a new charging period does not commence, upon the occurrence of subsequent nondiscriminatory acts that entail adverse effects resulting from the past discrimination."[110]

Acknowledging that six months was a short time, the majority stressed that it indicated Congress's concern about employers having to defend themselves against charges of discrimination long after the alleged discriminatory act occurred. The major problem, Alito explained, is the difficulty of determining whether there was discriminatory intent (required for a successful Title VII wage discrimination claim) so far after the fact. "This short deadline," Alito continued, "reflects Congress' strong preference for the prompt resolution of employment discrimination allegations through voluntary conciliation and cooperation."[111] He concluded that her Title VII suit must be dismissed because she failed to bring a timely charge to the EEOC at the time the discrimination occurred.

In dissent for herself, Stevens, Breyer, and Souter, Ginsburg strongly criticized the majority for its constricted approach to Title VII, saying that the only way Ledbetter could have satisfied the Court's interpretation of Title VII was to file an EEOC complaint each year her salary was below her male coworkers' salaries. "Any annual pay decision not contested immediately (within 180 days), the Court affirms, becomes grandfathered, a fait accompli beyond the province of Title VII ever to repair."[112] She accused the majority of failing to understand the nature of wage discrimination; salary inequities typically accumulate in small amounts over time and are largely invisible to the employees.[113]

A single action may be insufficient for a lawsuit, she said, especially for employees such as Ledbetter, working in a male-dominated atmosphere and unwilling to draw adverse attention to themselves. She disagreed that each salary decision is a discrete event; rather, Ledbetter's paychecks were part of an ongoing process of illegal discrimination, consisting of the initial discriminatory act and the paychecks that followed. Painting a bleak picture of Goodyear's treatment of women, Ginsburg summarized by pointing out that "Ledbetter's evidence demonstrated that her current pay was discriminatorily low due to a long series of decisions reflecting Goodyear's pervasive discrimination against women managers in general and Ledbetter in particular."[114]

Finally, she disputed the majority's contention that claims such as Ledbetter's would require the company to defend itself on discriminatory actions "long past"; Ledbetter, she insisted, was a victim of discrimination at the start of her employment from poor evaluations and was victimized each time she received a paycheck.

There was a swift reaction to the Court's ruling in the 110th Congress, with House Democrats promising to reverse it. A month later, the Lilly Ledbetter Fair Pay Act of 2007 was introduced by Representative George Miller, Democrat from California, with dozens of cosponsors and made its way quickly through the House. The act would have amended the ADEA, the ADA, the Rehabilitation Act of 1973, and Title VII of the 1964 Civil Rights Act "to clarify that a discriminatory compensation decision or other practice that is unlawful under such Acts occurs each time compensation is paid pursuant to the discriminatory compensation decision or other practice, and for other purposes" (H.R. 2831). On July 31, 2007, the House approved the bill in a vote of 225 to 199 (six Democrats voted no, and only two Republicans voted yes).

The Senate version of the Ledbetter bill, the Fair Pay Restoration Act (S. 1843), was blocked by Republicans when it came up for a vote on April 23, 2008. With fifty-six votes in favor, it still fell four short of the sixty votes needed to invoke cloture, that is, cut off the threatened Republican filibuster. Democratic candidates Hillary Rodham Clinton and Obama returned to cast their votes in favor of the bill, while John McCain, the likely Republican candidate, continued his campaign and missed the vote. Opponents charged that the bill was bad for business and would lead to frivolous lawsuits, characterizing it "as a windfall for trial lawyers"; McCain said that had he been there, he would have voted against it.[115]

With the new 111th Congress in place, on January 22, 2009, the Senate finally approved the measure in a 61 to 36 vote; the House followed suit on January 27, 2009, in a vote of 250 to 177.[116] When the bill named after her had cleared the Senate, Ledbetter declared, "I'm so excited, I can hardly stand it." On January 29, 2009, a week after he took office, one of Obama's first official acts was to sign the Lilly Ledbetter Fair Pay Restoration Act of 2009 into law; a proud Ledbetter was at the signing ceremony.[117]

The law reversed the Court's ruling by specifying that a Title VII violation occurs each time a worker receives a paycheck that reflects past discrimination.[118] Thus, workers may now file a charge within 180 days of receiving any paycheck that they believe is based on discrimination.[119]

Wage Inequity and the EPA

The earnings gap—measured by comparing the average earnings of full-time female workers to the average earnings of full-time male workers—between men and women in the United States has always existed, even when they worked for the same employer and performed the same or similar jobs.[120]

In 1963, when the EPA was enacted, full-time women workers earned only 59 cents (59 percent) for every dollar men earned.[121] By 1979, with the act in place for more than a decade, women had only succeeded in closing the gap an additional 3 cents, earning 62 cents as much as men. The gap slowly but steadily narrowed during the 1980s and 1990s, and by 2006, women's earnings had risen to an all-time high of 81 percent of men's earnings. However, in 2009, notwithstanding almost fifty years of equal pay legislation, the median weekly earnings for full-time female wage and salary workers were $657, about 80 percent of the $819 earned by full-time male wage and salary workers.

Ironically, the earnings gap persists despite the fact that women are better educated than men. Beginning in 2003, the percentage of women in the labor force with college degrees exceeded the percentage of men in the workforce with college degrees. By 2007, 34.9 percent of women in the labor force were college graduates, compared to 32.9 percent of men.[122]

The wage gap between women and men varies with education, race, age, and state of residence. When comparing the wage gap between men and women by level of education, the figures show that the gap widens as the level of education rises. Among men and women with less than a high school diploma, women earned an average of $382 in 2009, whereas men with less than a high school diploma earned an average of $500, for a pay gap of 76.4 percent. Comparing the weekly earnings of men and women with a bachelor's degree or higher, women earned an average of $970 a week; men earned an average of $1,327 a week. Thus, the most educated women in the workforce earn only 73.1 percent of what men at their level of education earn. Paradoxically, wage inequality between men and women worsens as women achieve more education.

Comparing the average weekly earnings of women and men within each racial group in 2009 shows that the gap persists within and across racial groups. The earnings gap between white women and white men was the largest, with white women earning only 79 percent of what white men earned ($669 for women to $845 for men). The next largest gap was between Asian women and men, with Asian women earning 82 percent of what Asian men earn ($779 for women and $952 for men). The earnings of Hispanic and African American women and men are closer. Hispanic women earn almost 90 percent of what Hispanic men earn ($509 for women and $569 for men), and African American women earn almost 94 percent of what African American men workers earn ($582 for women to $621 for men). The smaller gap between Hispanic and African American women and men is likely explained by the fact that the wages of both sexes in these racial groups are depressed compared to whites and Asians of both sexes.

Focusing on age differences among full-time women workers in 2009 shows that the average weekly earnings of women ages sixteen to twenty-four was 92.6 percent of the average weekly earnings of full-time male workers in the same age group ($424 for women to $458 for men). However, contrary to conventional wisdom, the earnings gap did not decrease as women's earnings rose; on the contrary, it widened. In 2009, women ages fifty-five to sixty-four earned only 75 percent of what men earned; women's weekly average was $727 a week (making them the highest-earning age group among women) while the average weekly earnings for men in this age group was $965.

Women in all states earned less than men; in 2009, the wage gap between their average weekly earnings ranged from 67 percent to 97 percent. The earnings gap between men and women was highest in Wyoming, with women earning only 67 percent of what men earned. The gap was smallest in the District of Columbia, with women there earning almost 97 percent of what men earned. Washington, D.C., is the only place in the country with almost no differences between women's and men's average weekly earnings.[123]

Equal Pay Legislation

Esther Peterson, head of the Women's Bureau, spearheaded the drive for pay equity legislation that eventually resulted in the passage of the 1963 EPA.[124] Signed by President John F. Kennedy on June 10, 1963, the law went into effect a year later. An amendment to the Fair Labor Standards

Act (FLSA), the EPA originally applied only to workers covered by the FLSA. In 1972, Congress extended it to executive, administrative, and professional employees. Two years later, the 1974 FLSA Amendments expanded equal pay protection to federal, state, and municipal workers.[125]

The EPA, giving rise to the popular slogan "equal pay for equal work," prohibits employers from paying members of one sex (but it is usually women) less than the other if their work is essentially the same.[126] To win an EPA suit, the plaintiff must prove that an employer has a different wage scale for men and women who work in the same establishment and perform substantially equal work.[127] If that is shown, the defendant has an opportunity to prove that the difference in wages is based on one of the following: seniority, merit, production, or a factor other than sex.[128] If the plaintiff ultimately prevails, the law requires employers to raise the wages of the lower-paid sex, which, in almost all cases, are women.

Although women won millions of dollars in increased wages in EPA suits, the act's equal work requirement has meant that it "contribute[d] only modestly to closing the salary gap."[129] Criticism of the EPA arises from two directions: one view, embodied in the writings of Seventh Circuit judges Richard Epstein and Richard Posner, argues that the EPA interferes with the free market, causing business inefficiencies and ultimately hurting the women it purports to benefit.[130] However, the primary criticism leveled at the EPA is that it has not eliminated the earnings disparity between the sexes because it only applies to employment settings where men and women work in the same establishment and perform substantially equal jobs. It is of limited use, therefore, in a workforce consisting of sex-segregated occupations, that is, occupations predominantly (defined at about 70 percent) held by members of one sex.

Occupational Segregation and Comparable Worth

The pervasiveness of sex segregation is illustrated by the fact that, in the early 1980s, over half of employed women held clerical or service jobs.[131] This oversupply of workers in the so-called pink-collar jobs—a term assigned to work dominated by women—depresses the wages of workers in those occupations.[132] In 2009, more than 96 percent of all secretaries were women, as were more than 90 percent of bookkeepers, receptionists, typists and word processors, medical and dental assistants, and teachers' assistants.[133] There were almost 100 occupations, including computer programmers, computer software engineers, industrial

engineers, broadcast and sound engineering technicians and radio opera-
tors, aerospace engineers, chief executives, chefs and head cooks, air-
craft pilots, flight engineers, and chemical engineers, to name just a few,
in which women constituted less than 25 percent of the workforce.[134]
Moreover, of the twenty top occupations dominated by women, only
registered nurses and managers earned more than $1,000 a week.[135]

Occupational segregation is one of the chief causes of the gap
between women's and men's earnings. According to a 2006 DOL report,
women comprised 43.6 percent of the workforce, yet they were only 31
percent of workers in the highest earnings category and 53.2 percent of
workers in the lowest earnings category. Women were greatly underrepresented in the construction and manufacturing industries, two fields in
which the workers were among the highest earners. More than 25 percent of the highest-earning men were in these two areas, compared with
10 percent of women. In contrast, there were nearly four times as many
women as men in the education and health services fields, two occupations in the lowest earning category.[136]

Seeking to overcome the EPA's equal work requirement, women
attempted to redress pay inequity through Title VII suits; they cited the
law's ban on discrimination in compensation as well as other terms and
conditions of employment. The rallying cry among women's rights advocates changed from "equal pay for equal work" to "equal pay for jobs of
comparable worth." Comparable worth theory is based on the premise that
men and women who work for the same employer in jobs of comparable
skill, effort, and responsibility merit comparable pay. Relying on the
assumption that the value of a job can be objectively measured, pay equity
policy begins with a job evaluation scheme.[137] Every job classification
receives a score based on factors such as responsibilities, skills, and working conditions. Comparable worth advocates argue that jobs such as secretary, truck driver, nurse, or physical plant worker can be evaluated by their
worth to the employer and that jobs with equal value should receive equal
wages, assuming no differences in seniority or merit. They contend that
because the jobs performed predominantly by women pay less than the
jobs performed by men, comparable worth policy is necessary to reduce
pay inequities between the sexes.[138]

Opponents of comparable worth theory maintain that employers do
not base salary decisions solely on job classification scores. They argue
that salaries are largely determined by neutral and nondiscriminatory market conditions, such as the supply of available workers, the demand for
the work, and the rate of unionization.[139] And because these factors are
outside their control, employers cannot be held responsible for disparities
in wage rates.[140]

Comparable worth proponents counter that sex segregation in the workforce is one of the primary reasons for the salary gap between men and women, and hence the law of supply and demand is not a neutral force.[141] They contend that women are channeled into low-paying and low-prestige job categories that, according to economist Ruth Blumrosen, are undervalued because they are predominantly held by women. She asserts that "the same forces which determine that certain jobs or job categories will be reserved for women or minorities also and simultaneously determine that the economic value of those jobs is less than if they were 'white' or 'male' jobs."[142]

Part of the debate over comparable worth policy revolves around whether the labor market should be considered a neutral factor in determining wages or is a reflection of wage discrimination against women. In their study of comparable worth, Joseph and Timothy Loudon argue that "the higher wages paid to tree trimmers (a male-dominated job category) as compared to nurses (a female-dominated job category) is the result of a discriminatory compensation system that simply perpetuates historical discrimination."[143]

Women's rights advocates who sought to bring pay discrimination suits under Title VII were soon confronted by the substantial roadblock of the Bennett Amendment. During debate over the 1964 Civil Rights Act, Republican senator Wallace Bennett of Utah offered an amendment to Title VII. Described as a "technical correction" and hastily accepted by the Senate without prior discussion in any committee, it allows pay differentials based on sex under Title VII if they are "authorized" by the EPA. The uncertainty about which pay differentials are allowed under the EPA led to varying interpretations by the courts. Some courts insisted that the amendment required plaintiffs to meet the equal work requirement in a Title VII wage discrimination claim. Others held that it merely incorporated the four affirmative defenses into the Title VII wage claim, allowing employers to prevail if they could show that a wage difference was based on seniority or merit, for example.

A year later, Bennett futilely attempted to clarify his meaning by inserting a statement into the *Congressional Record* that the Senate had understood that the amendment was intended to ensure "that discrimination in compensation on account of sex does not violate Title VII unless it also violates the Equal Pay Act."[144] According to Anne Draper, head of the National Committee for Equal Pay, this interpretation would have nullified Title VII for claims of wage discrimination and would have left "the Equal Pay Act as the only applicable Federal statute in the field."[145]

Exemplifying the narrow approach to the Bennett Amendment that equated the EPA with Title VII, in *Christensen v. Iowa*,[146] the Eighth

Circuit dismissed a Title VII suit brought by women clerical workers at the University of Northern Iowa. The plaintiffs complained that they were being paid less than physical plant workers even though they were equal in the university's wage scheme. The university argued that its wages were based on neutral market forces, not discrimination. The circuit court agreed, saying it did not believe "Congress intended to abrogate the laws of supply and demand or other economic principles that determine wage rates for various kinds of work."[147]

Taking the broad approach, the Third Circuit ruled in *International Union of Electrical, Radio, and Machine Workers v. Westinghouse Electric Company*[148] that Westinghouse's point system violated Title VII; with just one exception, all workers in the four lowest grades were women, and no women were in the highest four grades. The court held that the amendment merely incorporated the four affirmative defenses of the EPA into Title VII, stressing that placing an equal work requirement on a Title VII sex discrimination claim allowed employers to discriminate on the basis of sex where they could not do so on the basis of race, religion, or national origin. It questioned why sex-based wage claims should be treated differently from other Title VII wage claims. Commenting on the "turbidity" of the amendment, the court believed that its interpretation was the one Congress had intended.[149]

The Supreme Court resolved the conflict among the circuits in *County of Washington v. Gunther*,[150] a Title VII suit brought by female prison guards in Washington County, Oregon, who were paid less than male guards. Although they worked at the same facility, the female guards could not claim that they performed work that was "substantially equal" to that of the male guards, and thus the narrow interpretation of the Bennett Amendment would have doomed their case. The high court adopted the broad interpretation, ruling that a Title VII wage claim need not satisfy the EPA's equal work requirement. In remanding to the lower court, the Supreme Court suggested that Title VII plaintiffs relying on comparable worth theory must prove that their employer's wage policy was the result of intentional discrimination against them.

Spaulding v. University of Washington,[151] brought by nursing faculty at the University of Washington, showed the judiciary's discomfort with comparable worth. The nurses charged the university with sex-based wage discrimination under Title VII and the EPA. The Ninth Circuit rejected the EPA claim, ruling that the jobs were not substantially equal. Turning to the Title VII disparate treatment claim, the court refused to "infer intent merely from the existence of wage differences between jobs that are only similar."[152] It concluded that the plaintiffs' evidence of discriminatory intent—statistical evidence as well as reported attitudes among university administrators—failed to establish that discrimination motivated the university's wage system.

The nurses premised their disparate impact claim on the university's market-based wage policy, thus requiring the court to decide whether disparate impact theory could be adapted to a claim of sex-based wage discrimination based on comparable jobs.[153] Stressing that *Gunther* was a disparate treatment case, the court refused to accept disparate impact theory in a wage discrimination claim, emphasizing that no other court had done so either. It added in a footnote that "courts are not competent to engage in a sweeping revision of market wage rates."[154]

Another suit, brought by the American Federation of State, County, and Municipal Employees Union on behalf of 15,500 women employees in the state of Washington, also showed the judiciary's reluctance to accept comparable worth claims. Suing under disparate impact and disparate treatment theories, the plaintiffs claimed that relying on a market-based wage system disproportionately affected women and that the court could infer discriminatory intent from the state's failure to correct the pay disparities, especially because the state's own studies showed that women earned about 20 percent less than men for performing comparable work.

Announcing his decision in *American Federation of State, County, and Municipal Employees v. Washington (AFSCME),*[155] Judge Jack Tanner agreed on both counts. Echoing *Griggs,* he held that the market system had a disparate impact on women in job classes predominantly held by women and was not justified by business necessity. He inferred intentional discrimination from the state's continued use of its compensation scheme in the face of studies showing it was unfair to women. Tanner's acceptance of disparate impact theory represents the only time in which a court allowed plaintiffs to apply the theory to a Title VII wage claim based on comparable worth.[156]

On appeal, the three-judge panel of the Ninth Circuit unanimously reversed Tanner.[157] The appeals court rejected the plaintiffs' attempt to use disparate impact theory, holding that a valid disparate impact claim requires a "challenge [to] a specific, clearly delineated employment practice applied at a single point in the job selection process."[158] Here, because the workers' salaries were based on a multiplicity of complex factors, there was no unique element to challenge. Moreover, the appellate court added, a wage system that mirrors market supply and demand is not sufficiently narrow to fall within disparate impact theory.

Turning to the disparate treatment charge, the circuit court rejected the union's argument that discriminatory intent could be inferred from the state's reliance on a market-based wage system shown by its own studies to be discriminatory. Nor, said the court, would it infer the intent to discriminate from the state's failure to implement the recommendations of the commission that conducted the study.[159] The link between the state's wage policy and the economic realities of the market is insufficient to prove intentional discrimination, said the court, and although the state may elect to implement a comparable worth pay scheme, "Title VII does not obligate it to eliminate an economic inequality that it did not create."[160] Conceding that discriminatory intent may be inferred from statistical evidence, the circuit court held that the job evaluation studies and comparable worth statistics the *AFSCME* plaintiffs offered did not prove intent in this case because they were not corroborated by specific testimony.[161]

American Nurses' Association v. Illinois,[162] decided in 1986, also illustrates the difficulties of proving disparate treatment in a wage discrimination suit. The nurses claimed that men in jobs predominantly held by men were paid higher wages that were not justified by the relative worth of the jobs. Moreover, they argued that the state had not implemented its own job evaluation study that showed women were underpaid.

The Seventh Circuit held that proof of intentional wage discrimination cannot be inferred merely from the state's inaction in raising women's wages in accordance with the results of the job evaluation study. Citing *AFSCME,* it pointed out that a state's failure to implement a job evaluation study and to eliminate existing wage disparities does not violate Title VII. "The critical thing lacking in *AFSCME,*" the court explained, "was evidence that the State decided not to raise the wages of particular workers *because* most of those workers were female."[163]

The court remanded the case to allow the lower court to assess the plaintiffs' evidence of discrimination, suggesting that they needed to show that the state deliberately kept women out of jobs predominantly held by men or that it departed from market rates only for those jobs because they were held by men. It ended by cautioning that it did "not want to arouse false hopes; the plaintiffs have a tough row to hoe."[164] The court's pessimism about comparable worth theory was well-founded; *American Nurses* is considered "the final blow to the endeavor to incorporate comparable worth into Title VII."[165]

With the discouraging responses of the courts, women's rights advocates abandoned their efforts to redress pay inequities through litigation in the late 1980s. Writing in 1987, one scholar gloomily noted that "the judiciary has been and, apparently, will continue to be unreceptive to the doctrine of comparable worth as a viable legal theory under Title VII."[166]

In opening the door to Title VII wage discrimination suits in *Gunther,* the high court had cautioned that it was not deciding "the precise contours of lawsuits challenging sex discrimination in compensation under Title VII."[167] Indeed, *Gunther* proved to be an ephemeral victory for women's rights advocates, who had hoped it would lead to judicial acceptance of comparable worth theory in Title VII suits. Instead, fearing they would be inundated with comparable worth suits that would require them to impose sweeping economic changes in the public and private sectors, the judiciary refused to apply comparable worth theory to Title VII wage discrimination claims, negating efforts to close the wage gap through litigation.[168]

Comparable Worth Legislation

Discouraged by the outcome of pay equity suits in the courts, women's rights advocates turned their attention to legislatures, focusing on wage inequities in state and municipal governments. Their activities ranged from research and data collection to creating task forces, performing job evaluation studies, and implementing pay equity plans. Within the states, the demands for pay equity were often initiated by commissions on the status of women, with unions adding their voices as well. As a result of pay equity legislation and collective bargaining agreements with state employee unions, a number of states enacted laws prescribing pay equity for jobs of "comparable character" or "comparable value"; predominantly affecting public employees, some extended to private sector workers as well.[169] Comparable worth bills were introduced in thirteen state legislatures between 1981 and 1983.[170]

Minnesota, the first state to enact pay equity legislation, provided a model for the nation. In 1982, the Minnesota legislature approved a law affecting 9,000 state employees; it called for a job evaluation study for civil service positions every two years and appropriated more than $20 million for pay adjustments over the next two years. In 1984, the state mandated pay equity at the municipal level.[171]

The city of San Jose, California, ordered a job evaluation study that showed women working in "women's jobs" were paid less than men working in "equal" job classifications that were dominated by men. But despite the evidence of pay inequity, the city council turned down a union demand for $3.2 million in comparable worth adjustments over a four-year period. The union voted to strike. After a job action lasting nine days, the city agreed to spend approximately $1.45 million over two years to correct the pay inequities.[172]

By 1990, twenty states had implemented pay equity plans to reduce inequities in jobs in which women predominated. Of the twenty states, however, only six—Iowa, Minnesota, New York, Oregon, Washington, and Wisconsin—enacted comprehensive reforms covering a wide range of job classifications with corresponding pay increases. Reforms in the remaining fourteen states were more narrowly applied.[173] In assessing the effect of pay equity in the sixteen states for which they could collect data, Heidi Hartmann and Stephanie Aaronson found that state governments spent more than $527,000,000 for this purpose through 1992, raising the pay of approximately 335,000 workers.[174] Despite the warnings of pay equity opponents, they found no increases in public sector unemployment and no declines in women's wages in the private sector. Moreover, there were positive results: women in states that had implemented pay equity plans had attained "significant absolute wage gains relative to their male co-workers, and relative to the national experience for all women."[175]

The issue of pay inequity returned to the federal arena during the Clinton administration, with the struggle revolving around attempts to strengthen the EPA and Title VII to combat sex-based wage differentials more effectively. The efforts revolved around two measures: the Paycheck Fairness Act and the broader, more controversial, Fair Pay Act, which attempted to incorporate comparable worth theory into wage discrimination lawsuits.

In 1994, Norton, former chair of the EEOC and a nonvoting delegate in the House representing the District of Columbia, introduced the Fair Pay Act to amend the EPA. Aimed at workers in sex-segregated occupations, it proposed to measure jobs on the basis of "skill, effort, responsibility, and working conditions" and bar employment discrimination on the basis of race, sex, or national origin for "work in equivalent jobs." Despite its three dozen sponsors and support from labor unions, the bill died before any action was taken on it.[176] Norton reintroduced the bill in several consecutive sessions, but it never passed out of the chamber.

In 1997, her colleague, Representative Rosa DeLauro, Democrat from Connecticut, introduced the Paycheck Fairness Act to amend the EPA and Title VII by enhancing remedies available to victims of wage discrimination, adding an antiretaliation provision, and directing the EEOC to require employers to report payroll data analyzed on the basis of race, sex, and national origin.[177] In the Senate, Tom Daschle,

Democrat from South Dakota and Senate minority leader, introduced his version of the Paycheck Fairness Act in 1999. Similar to DeLauro's bill, it included an antiretaliation measure and expanded remedies to allow successful plaintiffs to recover compensatory and punitive damages. The same year, Senator Tom Harkin, an Iowa Democrat, introduced the Fair Pay Act; similar to Norton's bill, it also incorporated comparable worth principles. It proposed to amend the FLSA to reduce or eliminate wage disparities on the basis of sex, race, and national origin. Like its counterpart, the Paycheck Fairness Act, it enhanced penalties and barred retaliation against workers. Although both Senate bills were referred to committee, they died in the Senate without coming up for a vote.[178]

Bills to fight wage discrimination were introduced year after year with no success until the House passed the Paycheck Fairness Act (H.R. 1338) on July 31, 2008. In August 2008, the bill moved to the Senate, but after it was referred to the Committee on Health, Education, Labor, and Pensions, no further action was taken.

A year later, in a vote of 256 to 163 (with support from ten Republicans), the House again approved the Paycheck Fairness Act (H.R. 12) on January 10, 2009. Its chief sponsor, DeLauro, said it closes "numerous loopholes that have enabled employers to evade liability." And again, it never came up in the Senate for a vote.[179] A Senate version of the bill (S. 182), introduced by Senator Clinton of New York, was never voted on.

In the proposed bill, Congress recognized that "pay disparities exist in both the private and governmental sectors. In many instances, the pay disparities can only be due to continued intentional discrimination or the lingering effects of past discrimination." The bill replaced the affirmative defense "any other factor other than sex" with "a bona fide factor other than sex, such as education, training, or experience." The employer would only be able to offer the affirmative defense if it could show that the "bona fide factor other than sex" is unrelated to a sex-based wage difference, is "job-related," and is "consistent with business necessity." The defense would be unavailable if employees could point to an alternative sex-neutral policy that the employer had failed to implement.

The bill would have broadened the definition of the employer's establishment to include different workplaces within the same state or county. It included an antiretaliation provision to protect workers who file complaints against the employer or, in most cases, inquire about or discuss the wages of other workers. The penalties for successful plaintiffs in pay equity suits would have included compensatory damages and, if the employer acted with "malice or reckless indifference," punitive damages as well. Finally, it made grant funds available for projects to train girls and women to negotiate for better wages; directed DOL to conduct research on methods of eliminating pay disparities; and required the EEOC to collect information on differences in workers' pay on the basis of race, sex, and national origin. Despite the evident need for this legislation, the Senate was unwilling to go along with the House and address the problem of pay inequity, one of the most pervasive sources of discrimination against working women.

Conclusion

Women workers secured employment rights in the 1960s with the passage of the EPA and Title VII. Their efforts to enforce Title VII in the courts have led to protracted litigation as they battled over legal concepts such as disparate treatment, disparate impact, and mixed-motive discrimination. Women's rights advocates achieved a number of important victories during the early 1970s, but as the judiciary became dominated by Reagan-Bush appointees, the courts became less sympathetic to Title VII plaintiffs.

By the end of the 1980s, the Supreme Court seemed to be ruling against Title VII plaintiffs in case after case. *Hopkins* and *Wards Cove*, the two most important cases, tilted Title VII toward employers and were reversed by the 1991 Civil Rights Act. The scenario repeated itself with the Court ruling in *Ledbetter*, reversed by Congress two years later.

The wage gap between female and male wage earners in the United States persists, in part because comparable worth litigation proved ineffective in remedying wage disparities based on occupational segregation. Some subnational governments implemented wage equity programs for public employees, yet the policies were not widely instituted. At the national level, the House twice approved bills intended to redress some of the problems of pay inequity between men and women, but those bills never cleared the Senate to reach the president's desk.

Notes

1. U.S. Department of Labor, Women's Bureau, "Quick Stats on Women Workers, 2009," available at http://www.dol.gov/wb/stats/main.htm; U.S. Department of Labor, Bureau of Labor Statistics, "Table 2: Employment Status of the Civilian Noninstitutional Population 16 Years and over by Sex, 1973 to Date," available at http://www.bls.gov/cps/cpswom2009.pdf.

2. Barnard and Rapp, "Pregnant Employees," pp. 202–203.

3. American Federation of Labor–Congress of Industrial Organizations, "Working Women: Equal Pay—Facts About Working Women," 1998, available at http://www.afl-cio.org/women/wwfacts.htm.

4. Vicki Lens, "Supreme Court Narratives on Equality and Gender Discrimination in Employment: 1971–2002," *Cardozo Women's Law Journal* 10 (2004): 501–567; Diane L. Bridge, "The Glass Ceiling and Sexual Stereotyping: Historical and Legal Perspectives of Women in the Workplace," *Virginia Journal of Social Policy and the Law* 4 (1997): 581–643; Barbara R. Bergmann, *The Economic Emergence of Women* (New York: Basic Books, 1986).

5. Heather Boushey, *The New Breadwinners* (Center for American Progress, October 16, 2009), available at http://www.americanprogress.org/issues/2009/10/pdf/awn/chapters/economy.pdf.

6. *Congressional Record,* 88th Cong., 2d sess., Vol. 110 (1964): H2577.

7. U.S. Equal Employment Opportunity Commission, "Celebrating the 40th Anniversary of Title VII," available at http://www.eeoc.gov/eeoc/history/40th/panel/expanding.html; see Jo Freeman, "How 'Sex' Got into Title VII: Persistent Opportunism as a Maker of Public Policy," *Law and Inequality: A Journal of Theory and Practice* 9 (1991): 163–184; Rachel Osterman, "Origins of a Myth: Why Courts, Scholars, and the Public Think Title VII's Ban on Sex Discrimination Was an Accident," *Yale Journal of Law and Feminism* 20 (2009): 409–439; Carl M. Brauer, "Women Activists, Southern Conservatives, and the Prohibition of Sex Discrimination in Title VII of the 1964 Civil Rights Act," *Journal of Southern History* 49 (1983): 37–56; Cynthia Harrison, *On Account of Sex: The Politics of Women's Issues, 1945–1968* (Berkeley: University of California Press, 1988); Celia Wolf-Devine, *Diversity and Community in the Academy: Affirmative Action in Faculty Appointments* (Lanham, Md.: Rowman and Littlefield, 1977).

8. *Congressional Record,* 88th Cong., 2d sess., Vol. 110 (1964): H2577.

9. Katie J. Colopy, Sandra K. Dielman, and Michelle A. Morgan, "Women and the Law: Gender Discrimination in the Workplace: 'We've Come a Long Way, Baby,'" *The Advocate* 49 (2009): 11.

10. Colopy, Dielman, and Morgan, "Women and the Law," p. 11.

11. U.S. Equal Employment Opportunity Commission, "Shaping Employment Discrimination Law," available at http://www.eeoc.gov/eeoc/history/35th/1965-71/shaping.html.

12. See Charles Whalen and Barbara Whalen, *The Longest Debate: A Legislative History of the 1964 Civil Rights Act* (New York: Mentor Books, 1985); Francis J. Vaas, "Title VII: Legislative History," *Boston College Industrial and Commercial Law Review* (1966): 441–442.

13. The account of Smith's effort to derail the civil rights bill is a familiar one, yet Osterman, "Origins of a Myth," rejects the conventional view that Smith offered the amendment as a weapon against the civil rights bill. She traces the origins of the tale to the year after the bill became effective, when the EEOC began operations. She criticizes the agency's officials, including the chair, Franklin D. Roosevelt, Jr., and executive director Herman Edelsberg, for perpetuating the story in an effort to delegitimize the ban on sex discrimination. She argues the agency attempted to justify its lax enforcement of sex discrimination by characterizing the provision as a joke, a "fluke," that lacked a credible legislative history and slipped through the cracks without real support or understanding of its implications.

14. See Kymberly K. Evanson, "Employment Law Chapter: Title VII of the Civil Rights Act of 1964," *Georgetown Journal of Gender and the Law* 7 (2006): 981–998.

15. Instead of the anticipated 2,000 complaints, the EEOC received 8,852. U.S. Equal Employment Opportunity Commission, "1965–1971: A Toothless Tiger Helps Shape the Law and Educate the Public," available at http://www.eeoc .gov/eeoc/history/35th/1965-71/index.html.

16. U.S. Equal Employment Opportunity Commission, "Early Enforcement Efforts," available at http://www.eeoc.gov/eeoc/history/35th/1965-71/early_ enforcement.html.

17. See U.S. Equal Employment Opportunity Commission, "Shaping Employment Discrimination Law."

18. See U.S. Equal Employment Opportunity Commission, "Sex-Based Charges FY 1997–FY 2009, available at http://www1.eeoc.gov//eeoc/statistics/ enforcement/sex.cfm?; U.S. Equal Employment Opportunity Commission, "Charge Statistics FY 1997 Through FY 2009, available at http://www1.eeoc.gov// eeoc/statistics/enforcement/charges.cfm?.

19. Prior to 1972, the agency had no authority to litigate on its own and could only ask DOJ to file suit.

20. Karen Maschke, *Litigation, Courts, and Women Workers* (New York: Praeger Publishers, 1989), p. 13.

21. 408 F.2d 228 (5th Cir. 1969).

22. *Weeks,* 408 F.2d at 235.

23. 444 F.2d 1219 (9th Cir. 1971).

24. 442 F.2d 385 (5th Cir. 1971).

25. *Diaz,* 442 F.2d at 388 (emphasis in the original).

26. 400 U.S. 542 (1971).

27. Martha Chamallas, "Mothers and Disparate Treatment: The Ghost of *Martin Marietta,*" *Villanova Law Review* 44 (1999): 346.

28. 433 U.S. 321 (1977).

29. *Dothard,* 433 U.S. at 325.

30. *Dothard,* 433 U.S. at 335.

31. See Carolyn Bird, *Born Female* (New York: Pocket Books, 1970), pp. 13–15; Donald Robinson, "Two Movements in Pursuit of Equal Employment Opportunity," *Signs* 4 (1979): 423–424.

32. Sex was added to the list of classifications in 1969.

33. The legal case against the press was supported by research conducted by Dr. Gerald Gardner, a mathematician who calculated the wages lost to women by being barred from jobs advertised for men only (*Washington Post,* July 31, 2009).

34. 413 U.S. 376 (1973).

35. The Court explains the difference between disparate treatment and disparate impact violations in *International Brotherhood of Teamsters v. United States,* 431 U.S. 324, 335 n. 15 (1977). In disparate treatment cases, "the employer simply treats some people less favorably than others because of their race, color, religion, sex, or national origin. Proof of discriminatory motive is critical, although it can in some situations be inferred from the mere fact of differences in treatment. . . . Claims of disparate treatment may be distinguished from claims that stress 'disparate impact.' The latter involve employment practices that are facially neutral in their treatment of different groups but that in fact fall more harshly on one group than another and cannot be justified by business necessity. Proof of discriminatory motive, we have held, is not required under a disparate-impact theory."

36. U.S. Equal Employment Opportunity Commission, "Shaping Employment Discrimination Law."

37. The nation's potentially largest employment discrimination action involved a suit against the giant Wal-Mart company. In June 2001, current and former employees sued Wal-Mart, the largest private employer in the world, citing discrimination in pay and promotion. The plaintiffs asked the court to certify that they represented a nationwide class of all women employees, more than one million, who claimed they were discriminated against by Wal-Mart since 1998. Wal-Mart objected to the motion for class certification, saying that the plaintiffs did not meet the standard for a class action suit. In June 2004, the district court judge granted the plaintiffs' motion for class certification, and Wal-Mart appealed. In 2007, a three-judge panel of the Ninth Circuit upheld the lower court, and upon reconsideration, the en banc court agreed. These lower court rulings were limited to the validity of the class certification; no decisions were made on the merits of the claim.

On June 20, 2011, the Supreme Court reversed the courts below, ruling in favor of Wal-Mart and denying the plaintiffs' request to be certified as a class (*Wal-Mart Stores, Inc. v. Dukes,* 2011 U.S. LEXIS 4567). The high court held that the plaintiffs had not shown there were common issues in their suit, a requirement for class certification. The opinion will have a significant impact on the ability of all plaintiffs hereafter to receive class certification, thus hindering their efforts to sue their employers for employment discrimination.

38. 411 U.S. 792 (1973). The *McDonnell Douglas* formula is applied to suits based on race, sex, age, and disability discrimination. With some variation, the formula applies to suits alleging discrimination in hiring, promotion, and firing.

39. See *Furnco Construction Company v. Waters,* 438 U.S. 567 (1978); *Board of Trustees of Keene State College v. Sweeney,* 439 U.S. 24 (1978); *Texas Department of Community Affairs v. Burdine,* 450 U.S. 248 (1981); *United States Postal Service Board of Governors v. Aikens,* 460 U.S. 711 (1983).

40. *Price Waterhouse v. Hopkins,* 490 U.S. 228 (1989).

41. In *Hishon v. King and Spalding,* 467 U.S. 69 (1984), the Supreme Court allowed a Title VII suit against a law firm that was accused of discrimination against a woman associate. The Court rejected the firm's argument that partnerships were immune from suit under Title VII.

42. During the 1950s and 1960s, most public accounting firms refused to hire women, saying they "were unsuited for out-of-town travel, weren't career-minded and had high turnover." Glenda E. Reid, Brenda T. Acken, and Elise G. Jancura, "An Historical Perspective on Women in Accounting," *Journal of Accountancy* 163 (1987): 344.

43. *Price Waterhouse v. Hopkins,* 490 U.S. at 235.

44. William L. Kandel, "Current Developments in Employment Litigation," *Employee Relations Law Journal* 15 (1989): 103.

45. *Price Waterhouse v. Hopkins,* 490 U.S. at 258 (emphasis added). The District of Columbia District Court and Circuit Court had held that the defendant's proof must be shown by "clear and convincing evidence"; the Supreme Court reversed on this ground and held the defendant only had to satisfy the lower "preponderance of evidence" standard.

46. *Price Waterhouse v. Hopkins,* 490 U.S. at 256.

47. *Price Waterhouse v. Hopkins,* 490 U.S. at 258.

48. Transgender plaintiffs cite *Hopkins* to argue that Title VII bars discrimination on the basis of gender identity as well as sex. They note the Court's finding that the employer's refusal to promote Hopkins because she did not conform to societal gender norms of femininity violated Title VII. In contrast to plaintiffs who claim

discrimination on the basis of sexual orientation, some transgender plaintiffs have succeeded in their Title VII suits. For a discussion of transgender plaintiffs and Title VII, see Tanya A. De Vos, "Sexuality and Transgender Issues in Employment Law," *Georgetown Journal of Gender and the Law* 10 (2009): 599–624; Shawn D. Twing and Timothy C. Williams, "Title VII's Transgender Trajectory: An Analysis of Whether Transgender People Are a Protected Class Under the Term 'Sex' and Practical Implications of Inclusion," *Texas Journal on Civil Liberties and Civil Rights* 15 (2010): 173–203; Amanda Raflo, "Evolving Protection for Transgender Employees Under Title VII's Sex Discrimination Prohibition: A New Era Where Gender Is More Than Chromosomes," *Charlotte Law Review* 2 (2010): 217–250; Kevin Schwin, "Toward a Plain Meaning Approach to Analyzing Title VII: Employment Discrimination Protection of Transsexuals," *Cleveland State Law Review* 57 (2009): 645–670.

49. *Price Waterhouse v. Hopkins,* U.S. 490 at 259 (emphasis in the original).

50. *Price Waterhouse v. Hopkins,* U.S. 490 at 276 (emphasis added). O'Connor contrasted direct evidence, such as Hopkins had produced, with indirect evidence of discrimination, such as statistical evidence about the workforce.

51. *Price Waterhouse v. Hopkins,* U.S. 490 at 277.

52. *Hopkins v. Price Waterhouse,* 737 F. Supp. 1202, 1210–1211 (D.D.C. 1990).

53. *Hopkins v. Price Waterhouse,* 287 U.S. App. D.C. 173 (D.C. Cir. 1990).

54. Alfred Blumrosen, "Strangers in Paradise: *Griggs v. Duke Power Co.* and the Concept of Employment Discrimination," *Michigan Law Review* 71 (1972): 59.

55. 401 U.S. 424 (1971).

56. Before Title VII, Duke Power had openly discriminated against its African American employees by restricting them to the lowest-paying department, the labor department. Other departments were exclusively white. In 1955, the company started requiring high school diplomas from all white employees hired after that year. When the 1964 Civil Rights Act went into effect and all employees became legally eligible to work in previously all-white departments, the company created new hiring and transfer rules. Beginning employees in all departments other than labor had to pass two aptitude tests in addition to producing a high school diploma. Current employees wishing to transfer between departments were also required to show a high school diploma. White employees protested the new transfer rule because it kept many of them out of the more desirable jobs. In response, the company changed the rule to permit employees to substitute a passing grade on two standardized intelligence tests for a high school diploma. Satisfactory scores on these tests were based upon a national median grade of high school graduates. Neither test was shown to be related to ability to perform on the job.

57. *Griggs,* 401 U.S. at 431.

58. Alfred Blumrosen, "The Legacy of *Griggs:* Social Progress and Subjective Judgments," *Chicago-Kent Law Review* 63 (1987): 1–2.

59. Eleanor Holmes Norton, "Equal Employment Law: Crisis in Interpretation—Survival Against the Odds," *Tulane Law Review* 62 (1988): 691 n. 41.

60. 422 U.S. 405 (1975). The *Albermarle* Court specified that once the defendant rebuts the prima facie case, the plaintiff has an opportunity to demonstrate that other tests, which would not have a disparate impact, would also serve the employer's needs. A year later, in *Washington v. Davis,* 426 U.S. 229 (1976), African American plaintiffs filed suit against the District of Columbia police department, claiming they were rejected on the basis of a verbal skills test that had a disproportionate impact on them. The Supreme Court held that the *Griggs-Albermarle* dis-

parate impact analysis was inapplicable to equal protection claims and that the plaintiffs had to prove intentional discrimination against them.

61. In *Smith v. City of Jackson,* 544 U.S. 228 (2005), the Supreme Court announced that ADEA plaintiffs may use disparate impact theory in age discrimination cases. The Court dismissed the case because the plaintiffs had not singled out a specific employment practice that disproportionately affected them.

62. George Rutherglen, "Disparate Impact Under Title VII: An Objective Theory of Discrimination," *Virginia Law Review* 73 (1987): 1312–1313; see Linda Lye, "Title VII's Tangled Tale: The Erosion and Confusion of Disparate Impact and the Business Necessity Defense," *Berkeley Journal of Employment and Labor Law* 19 (1998): 315–361.

63. *Dothard,* 433 U.S. at 331.

64. *Dothard,* 433 U.S. at 329.

65. 490 U.S. 642 (1989). A year earlier, in *Watson v. Fort Worth Bank and Trust,* 487 U.S. 977 (1988), O'Connor spoke for a plurality of four, urging that plaintiffs in disparate impact cases be required to carry the burden of proof throughout the trial, as they do in disparate treatment cases. *Wards Cove* presented an opportunity for the Court to resolve this question.

66. *Wards Cove Packing Company v. Atonio,* 827 F.2d 439 (9th Cir. 1987).

67. *Wards Cove,* 490 U.S. at 661–662.

68. *Wards Cove,* 490 U.S. at 662.

69. *Wards Cove,* 490 U.S. at 663.

70. *Wards Cove,* 490 U.S. at 670.

71. *Wards Cove,* 490 U.S. at 671–672.

72. See Anita Allessandra, "When Doctrines Collide: Disparate Treatment, Disparate Impact, and *Watson v. Fort Worth Bank and Trust,*" *University of Pennsylvania Law Review* 137 (1989); Merrill D. Feldstein, "*Watson v. Fort Worth Bank and Trust:* Reallocating the Burdens of Proof in Employment Discrimination Litigation," *American University Law Review* 38 (1989): 919–951.

73. *Congressional Quarterly Weekly,* February 10, 1990, pp. 392–393.

74. *Congressional Quarterly Weekly,* May 19, 1990, p. 1563.

75. *Congressional Quarterly Weekly,* July 21, 1990, p. 2312.

76. *Congressional Quarterly Weekly,* August 4, 1990, p. 2517.

77. *New York Times,* October 17, 1990.

78. *Congressional Quarterly Weekly,* October 27, 1990, p. 3654.

79. *New York Times,* October 26, 1990.

80. *Congressional Quarterly Weekly,* February 9, 1991, pp. 366–373.

81. *Congressional Quarterly Weekly,* March 23, 1991, p. 745.

82. *Congressional Quarterly Weekly,* May 25, 1991, pp. 1378–1380; *Congressional Quarterly Weekly,* June 8, 1991, pp. 1498–1503.

83. See *Congressional Quarterly Weekly,* October 26, 1991, pp. 3124–3126; *New York Times,* October 26, 1991; *Congressional Quarterly Weekly,* November 2, 1991, pp. 3200–3204; *New York Times,* November 22, 1991; *Congressional Quarterly Weekly,* November 23, 1991, p. 3463.

84. The most important rulings affected by the 1991 law were *Price Waterhouse v. Hopkins,* 490 U.S. at 228; *Wards Cove,* 490 U.S. at 642; *Martin v. Wilks,* 490 U.S. 755 (1989); *Lorance v. AT&T Technologies,* 490 U.S. 900 (1989); *Patterson v. McLean Credit Union,* 491 U.S. 164 (1989); *Independent Federation of Flight Attendants v. Zipes,* 491 U.S. 754 (1989).

85. *New York Times,* November 22, 1991; *Congressional Quarterly Weekly,* December 7, 1991, pp. 3620–3622.

86. 42 U.S.C. § 2000e-5(g)(2)(B).

87. Plaintiffs suing under the EPA and the ADEA had the right to request jury trials before 1991. The 1991 act allowed jury trials in claims of discrimination on the basis of sex, religion, and disabilities. The Bush administration had objected to the jury trial provision in the 1991 act and sought to cap damages at $150,000 and allow them only in harassment cases. *New York Times,* October 26, 1991.

88. See Ann M. Anderson, "Whose Malice Counts? *Kolstad* and the Limits of Vicarious Liability for Title VII Punitive Damages," *North Carolina Law Review* 78 (2000): 799–830, for a discussion of *Kolstad v. American Dental Association,* 527 U.S. 526 (1999), in which the Supreme Court addressed the issue of the defendant's liability for punitive damages under Title VII.

89. The damage limitations apply only to suits brought by women, religious minorities, and people with disabilities. Racial minorities are entitled to unlimited punitive damages if they sue under § 1981 of the Civil Rights Act of 1866. The 1991 act broadened the protection of § 1981 to racial minorities by extending the ban on racial discrimination in hiring to the entire employment career.

90. 499 U.S. 244 (1991).

91. 509 U.S. 502 (1993).

92. See Terri L. Dill, "*St. Mary's Honors Center v. Hicks:* Refining the Burden of Proof in Employment Discrimination Litigation," *Arkansas Law Review* 48 (1995): 617–637, for a discussion of proof in Title VII cases.

93. *New York Times,* December 31, 1991.

94. 511 U.S. 298 (1994).

95. 511 U.S. 244 (1994).

96. 530 U.S. 133 (2000).

97. 539 U.S. 90 (2003).

98. The Bush administration urged the Court to retain the direct evidence requirement in mixed-motive cases, arguing that the 1991 act did not affect it. *New York Times,* June 10, 2003.

99. *New York Times,* June 10, 2003.

100. Thomas differentiated between direct evidence and circumstantial evidence; the latter, he said, is accepted even in criminal cases, which require the highest standard of proof.

101. Most lower courts have not applied *Costa* to discrimination suits brought under the ADA or the ADEA, retaining the direct evidence rule in such cases. In "Stray Remarks and Mixed-Motive Cases After *Desert Palace v. Costa:* A Proximity Test for Determining Minimal Causation," *Cardozo Law Review* 29 (2008): 1795–1836, Ezra S. Greenberg argues that *Costa* left many questions about mixed-motive cases unanswered and that the courts have ruled inconsistently in trying to answer these questions.

102. From her testimony before the House Committee on Education and Labor, as reported in Amalia Goldvaser, "Inflating Goodyear's Bottom Line: Paying Women Less and Getting Away with It," *Cardozo Journal of Law and Gender* 15 (2008): 99–116.

103. Under Title VII, the plaintiff must file a complaint with the EEOC prior to filing a federal court claim; the complaint must be filed within 180 days (six months) "after the alleged unlawful employment practice occurred."

104. Ledbetter also sued under the Equal Pay Act, but the district court awarded Goodyear summary judgment on that claim.

105. Ledbetter had a number of unpleasant incidents related to sex in the plant. She filed a charge of sexual harassment with the EEOC in the early 1980s, which was settled when the company moved her to a different part of the plant. During the

1990s, her supervisor retaliated against her for refusing to go out with him by filing false reports about her. Her next supervisor relied on these false reports in determining her raises. See Tristin K. Green, "Insular Individualism: Employment Discrimination Law After *Ledbetter v. Goodyear,*" *Harvard Civil Rights–Civil Liberties Law Review* 43 (2008): 353–383.

106. The appeals court also held that she could not prove that Goodyear intentionally discriminated against her in the two salary decisions made prior to the charging period—in 1997 and 1998; she did not appeal this part of the ruling to the Supreme Court. *Ledbetter v. Goodyear Tire and Rubber Co.,* 421 F.3d 1169 (11th Cir. 2005).

107. *Ledbetter,* 421 F.3d at 1169.

108. Appellate Brief, *Ledbetter v. Goodyear Tire and Rubber Company, Inc.,* 2006 WL 2610990, Supreme Court of the United States.

109. 550 U.S. 618 (2007).

110. *Ledbetter,* 550 U.S. at 628.

111. *Ledbetter,* 550 U.S. at 630–631.

112. *Ledbetter,* 550 U.S. at 644.

113. Indeed, company policy prohibited employees from discussing salary information with each other; see Goldvaser, "Inflating Goodyear's Bottom Line." Green, in "Insular Individualism," notes that workers in the United States are typically unaware of their coworkers' salaries.

114. *Ledbetter,* 550 U.S. at 659. Ginsburg analogized Ledbetter's claim to a situation of a hostile work environment in which the cumulative effect of individual acts constitutes discrimination. In "Pay-Setting Decisions as Discrete Acts: The Court Sharpens Its Focus on Intent in Title VII Actions in *Ledbetter v. Goodyear Tire and Rubber Co.,* 127 S. Ct. 2162 (2007)," *Nebraska Law Review* 86 (2008): 955–986, Joseph M. Aldridge suggests, however, that the Court's approach to Title VII in *Ledbetter* may pose problems for plaintiffs who bring hostile environment sexual harassment suits; see also Green, "Insular Individualism," who fears that all Title VII plaintiffs may be disadvantaged by the Court's interpretation of the law, which may allow employers to disclaim responsibility for discriminatory acts of individual employees.

115. *New York Times,* April 24, 2008; *Washington Post,* April 24, 2008; *Congressional Quarterly Weekly,* February 2, 2009, p. 259.

116. *Congressional Quarterly Weekly,* February 2, 2009, p. 259; *Congressional Quarterly Weekly,* January 22, 2009, p. 195.

117. *New York Times,* January 29, 2009.

118. In "*Ledbetter* in Congress: The Limits of a Narrow Legislative Override," *Yale Law Journal* 117 (2008): 971–979, Kathryn A. Eidman argues that the law is too narrow because it only excuses the six-month limit for actions involving discrimination in pay, holding employees to the six-month limit for a wide range of discriminatory actions.

119. The law amended Title VII, 42 U.S.C. § 2000e5(e), by adding "(3)(A) For purposes of this section, an unlawful employment practice occurs, with respect to discrimination in compensation in violation of this title, when a discriminatory compensation decision or other practice is adopted, when an individual becomes subject to a discriminatory compensation decision or other practice, or when an individual is affected by application of a discriminatory compensation decision or other practice, including each time wages, benefits, or other compensation is paid, resulting in whole or in part from such a decision or other practice. In addition to Title VII, the statute applies to the ADEA and the employment sections of the ADA and the 1973 Rehabilitation Act."

120. Bridge, "The Glass Ceiling and Sexual Stereotyping," p. 587, reports that wages of pre-industrial women were 20 to 50 percent less than men for doing the same work.

121. U.S. Bureau of the Census, "Historical Income Tables—People, Table P-40: Women's Earnings as a Percentage of Men's Earnings by Race and Hispanic Origin: 1960 to 2008," available at http://www.census.gov/hhes/www/income/data/historical/people/p40.xls.

122. U.S. Department of Labor, Bureau of Labor Statistics, "Table 9: Percent Distribution of the Civilian Labor Force 25 to 64 Years of Age by Educational Attainment and Sex, 1970–2007 Annual Averages," available at http://www.bls.gov/cps/wlftable9-2008.pdf.

123. The following tables appear in U.S. Department of Labor, Bureau of Labor Statistics, "Highlights of Women's Earnings in 2009," available at http://www.bls.gov/cps/cpswom2009.pdf. "Table 1: Median Usual Weekly Earnings of Full-Time Wage and Salary Workers, by Selected Characteristics, 2009 Annual Averages"; "Table 3: Median Usual Weekly Earnings of Full-Time Wage and Salary Workers, by State and Sex, 2009 Annual Averages"; "Table 12: Median Usual Weekly Earnings of Full-Time Wage and Salary Workers, in Current Dollars, by Sex and Age, 1979–2009 Annual Averages"; "Table 16: Median Usual Weekly Earnings of Full-Time Wage and Salary Workers, 25 Years and Older, in Current Dollars, by Sex and Educational Attainment, 1979–2009 Annual Averages." When measured in annual wages, the ratio between men's and women's wages decreases (that is, the wage gap is wider). For example, in 2008, the annual earnings gap between men and women was 77.1 percent; see Institute for Women's Policy Research, "The Gender Wage Ratio: Women's and Men's Earnings" (February 2008), available at http://www.iwpr.org/pdf/c350.pdf.

124. Congress's initial effort to enact pay equity legislation was based on the principle of "equal pay for comparable work" because supporters feared that "equal work" would be interpreted as "identical work" and minor differences between jobs would be used to justify differentials in pay. However, in the end, the phrase "equal pay for equal work" was substituted for "equal pay for comparable work." See Cynthia Harrison, *On Account of Sex: The Politics of Women's Issues, 1945–1968* (Berkeley: University of California Press, 1988), pp. 96–97; see also Virginia Dean, "Pay Equity/Comparable Worth," in Carol Lefcourt, ed., *Women and the Law* (New York: Clark Boardman, 1987).

125. In *National League of Cities v. Usery,* 426 U.S. 833 (1976), the Supreme Court struck down the extension of the FLSA's provision on wages and hours to state and local employees. In 1985, in *Garcia v. San Antonio Metropolitan Transit Authority,* 469 U.S. 528 (1985), the Supreme Court overruled *National League of Cities* on the issue of state and local government workers. Even before *Garcia,* however, most lower courts had limited *National League of Cities* to wages and hours provisions and allowed EPA claims against state and local governments. More recently, states have argued that the Eleventh Amendment to the U.S. Constitution bars public employees from suing them for wage disparities under the EPA.

126. 29 U.S.C. § 206(d)(1) provides, "No employer having employees subject to any provisions of this section shall discriminate, within any establishment in which such employees are employed, between employees on the basis of sex by paying wages to employees in such establishment at a rate less than the rate at which he pays wages to employees of the opposite sex in such establishment for equal work on jobs the performance of which requires equal skill, effort, and responsibility, and which are performed under similar working conditions, except where such payment is made pursuant to (i) a seniority system; (ii) a merit system; (iii) a system which

measures earnings by quantity or quality of production; or (iv) a differential based on any other factor other than sex: Provided, That an employer who is paying a wage rate differential in violation of this subsection shall not, in order to comply with the provisions of this subsection, reduce the wage rate of any employee."

127. In *Schultz v. Wheaton Glass Company,* 421 F.2d 259, 265 (3d Cir. 1970), the Third Circuit held that the act only required the jobs to be "substantially equal"; they need not be "identical." The court declared that Congress intended the law to "overcome the age-old belief in women's inferiority and to eliminate the depressing effects on living standards of reduced wages for female workers and the economic and social consequences which flow from it." See also *Hodgson v. Brookhaven General Hospital,* 436 F.2d 719 (5th Cir. 1970); *Schultz v. American Can Company–Dixie Products,* 424 F.2d 356 (8th Cir. 1970).

128. In *Corning Glass Works v. Brennan,* 417 U.S. 188 (1974), its first EPA case, the Supreme Court held that the difference between day and night work did not justify the company's wage differential between men and women as a "factor other than sex." The company's own job evaluation scheme indicated that working conditions differed by "surroundings" and "hazards," not by time of day. See Nina Joan Kimball, "Not Just Any 'Factor Other Than Sex': An Analysis of the Fourth Affirmative Defense of the Equal Pay Act," *George Washington Law Review* 52 (1984): 318–336; L. Tracee Whitley, "'Any Other Factor Other Than Sex': Forbidden Market Defenses and the Subversion of the Equal Pay Act of 1963," *Northeastern University Forum* 2 (1997): 51–81.

129. Bergmann, *The Economic Emergence of Women,* p. 186. See Deborah Thompson Eisenberg, "Shattering the Equal Pay Act's Glass Ceiling," *Southern Methodist University Law Review* 63 (2010): 17–69, for a discussion of the limitations of the Equal Pay Act in redressing wage discrimination. Eisenberg's data demonstrate the limited success of EPA plaintiffs in the federal courts, especially from 2000 to 2009. She notes that professional and executive women seem to have benefited least from the act because of the difficulty they have in proving that their jobs are substantially equal to those held by men.

130. See Whitley, "'Any Other Factor Other Than Sex,'" for analysis of the "neoclassical" criticism of the EPA.

131. See Francine D. Blau and Marianne A. Ferber, "Occupations and Earnings of Women Workers," and Ray Marshall and Beth Paulin, "Employment and Earnings of Women: Historical Perspective," both in Karen Shallcross Koziara, Michael H. Moskow, and Lucretia Dewey Tanner, eds., *Working Women: Past, Present, Future* (Washington, D.C.: Bureau of National Affairs, 1987).

132. Lucy Bednarek, "The Gender Wage Gap: Searching for Equality in a Global Economy," *Indiana Journal of Global Legal Studies* 6 (1998): 223–224.

133. U.S. Department of Labor, Bureau of Labor Statistics, "Table 11: Employed Persons by Detailed Occupation, Sex, Race, and Hispanic or Latino Ethnicity," available at http://www.bls.gov/cps/cpsaat11.pdf.

134. U.S. Department of Labor, Women's Bureau, "Nontraditional Occupations for Women in 2009," April 2010, available at http://www.dol.gov/wb/factsheets/nontra2009.htm; U.S. Department of Labor, Bureau of Labor Statistics, "Table 11."

135. U.S. Department of Labor, Women's Bureau, "20 Leading Occupations of Employed Women, 2009 Annual Averages," available at http://www.dol.gov/wb/factsheets/20lead2009.htm.

136. U.S. Department of Labor, Bureau of Labor Statistics, "Women Still Underrepresented Among Highest Earners," March 2006, available at http://www.bls.gov/opub/ils/pdf/opbils55.pdf.

137. See discussions of job evaluation studies in Judith Brown, Phyllis Tropper Baumann, and Elaine Millar Melnick, "Equal Pay for Jobs of Comparable Worth: An Analysis of the Rhetoric," *Harvard Civil Rights–Civil Liberties Law Review* 21 (1986): 127–170; Henry Aaron and Cameran M. Lougy, *The Comparable Worth Controversy* (Washington, D.C.: Brookings Institution, 1986).

138. See Sara Evans and Barbara Nelson, "Comparable Worth: The Paradox of Technocratic Reform," *Feminist Studies* 15 (1989): 171–190; Jane Bayes, "Women, Labor Markets, and Comparable Worth," *Policy Studies Review* 5 (1986): 776–799.

139. Sharon Rabin-Margalioth, in "The Market Defense," *University of Pennsylvania Journal of Business Law* 12 (2010): 807–847, argues that market theory should usually not be considered a valid defense in EPA suits where workers perform the same jobs.

140. A primary difference between an equal pay action and a comparable worth action lies in the employer's ability to use market wages as a defense in the latter. In an EPA suit, employers are not permitted to use prevailing market rates to justify less pay for their workers.

141. Donald Treiman and Heidi Hartmann, eds., *Women, Work, and Wages: Equal Pay for Jobs of Equal Value* (Washington, D.C.: National Academy Press, 1981). See also Roslyn Feldberg, "Comparable Worth: Toward Theory and Practice in the United States," *Signs* 10 (1984): 311–328; Bayes, "Women, Labor Markets, and Comparable Worth." The U.S. labor force is also segregated by race, a fact that helps explain wage gaps between the races. See National Committee on Pay Equity, *Pay Equity: An Issue of Race, Ethnicity, and Sex* (Washington, D.C.: National Committee on Pay Equity, 1987); Mary Corcoran and Greg Duncan, "Work History, Labor Force Attachment, and Earnings Differences Between the Races and Sexes," *Journal of Human Resources* 14 (1979): 3–20.

142. Ruth Blumrosen, "Wage Discrimination, Job Segregation, and Title VII of the Civil Rights Act of 1964," *University of Michigan Journal of Law Reform* 12 (1979): 401.

143. Joseph P. Loudon and Timothy D. Loudon, "Applying Disparate Impact to Title VII Comparable Worth Claims: An Incomparable Task," *Indiana Law Journal* 61 (1986): 165.

144. *Congressional Record*, 89th Cong., 1st sess., Vol. 111 (1965): S13359.

145. *Congressional Record*, 89th Cong., 1st sess., Vol. 111 (1965): S18263.

146. 563 F.2d 353 (8th Cir.1977). In *Lemons v. City and County of Denver*, 620 F.2d 228 (10th Cir. 1980), the court dismissed a Title VII suit brought by Denver nurses. It accepted the city's argument that its wage structure was comparable to the private sector's and expressed concern about the propriety of courts interfering in market relationships. In *Briggs v. City of Madison*, 536 F. Supp. 435 (W.D. Wis. 1982), the district court dismissed the Title VII complaint brought by women public health nurses in Madison, Wisconsin, accepting the employer's argument that it based its wages for the predominantly male sanitarian jobs on market forces.

147. *Christensen*, 563 F.2d at 356. See Rabin-Margalioth, "The Market Defense," for a discussion of the market defense in comparable worth cases.

148. 631 F.2d 1094 (3d Cir. 1980).

149. *Westinghouse*, 631 F.2d at 1101–1102.

150. 452 U.S. 161 (1981).

151. 740 F.2d 686 (9th Cir. 1984).

152. *Spaulding*, 740 F.2d at 700.

153. *Spaulding*, 740 F.2d at 705.

154. *Spaulding*, 740 F.2d at 706 n.11.

155. 578 F. Supp. 846 (W.D. Wash. 1983).

156. Loudon and Loudon, "Applying Disparate Impact to Title VII Comparable Worth Claims," p. 174.

157. *American Federation of State, County, and Municipal Employees v. Washington (AFSCME)*, 770 F.2d 1401 (9th Cir. 1985).

158. *AFSCME*, 770 F.2d at 1405.

159. Ruth Blumrosen, in "Wage Discrimination, Job Segregation, and Title VII," p. 465, argues that plaintiffs should merely have to show sex segregation to raise a prima facie case of discrimination because "evidence of segregated jobs justifies an inference of discrimination in compensation." *Briggs*, 536 F. Supp. at 435 explicitly rejected this theory. See also Loudon and Loudon, "Applying Disparate Impact to Title VII Comparable Worth Claims," pp. 171–172.

160. *AFSCME*, 770 F.2d at 1407.

161. See George Rutherglen, "The Gender Gap in Compensation: The Theory of Comparable Worth as a Remedy for Discrimination," *Georgetown Law Journal* 82 (1993): 135–146, for a discussion of the use of statistical evidence in comparable worth suits.

162. 783 F.2d 716 (7th Cir. 1986).

163. *American Nurses*, 783 F.2d at 722 (emphasis in the original).

164. *American Nurses*, 783 F.2d at 730.

165. Rabin-Margalioth, "The Market Defense," p. 818 n. 54.

166. Tina L. Speiser, "The Future of Comparable Worth: Looking in New Directions," *Syracuse Law Review* 37 (1987): 1207.

167. *Gunther*, 452 U.S. at 181.

168. Brown, Baumann, and Melnick, "Equal Pay for Jobs of Comparable Worth," p. 143.

169. Rich Arthurs discusses activity at the state level in "State Legislatures See Flood of Comparable Worth Proposals," *Legal Times*, October 15, 1984.

170. See Keon Chi, "Comparable Worth in State Government: Trends and Issues," *Policy Studies Review* 5 (1986): 800–814, for discussion of the adoption of state comparable worth policies.

171. Aaron and Lougy, *The Comparable Worth Controversy*, pp. 37–38.

172. Robert H. Cohen, "Pay Equity: A Child of the 80s Grows Up," *Fordham Law Review* 63 (1995): 1485–1486.

173. Heidi I. Hartmann and Stephanie Aaronson, "Pay Equity and Women's Wage Increases in the States: A Model for the Nation," *Duke Journal of Gender Law and Policy* 1 (1994): 72–73.

174. Hartmann and Aaronson, "Pay Equity and Women's Wage Increases in the States," p. 76; the figures are in 1990 dollars; see Arthurs, "State Legislatures See Flood of Comparable Worth Proposals," for a discussion of pay equity actions at the state level.

175. Hartmann and Aaronson, "Pay Equity and Women's Wage Increases in the States," pp. 85–86.

176. Thomas, Legislative Information on the Internet, *Bill Summary and Status for the 103rd Congress,* available at thomas.loc.gov/bss/; for an analysis of the proposed Fair Pay Act, see Cohen, "Pay Equity"; Bednarek, "The Gender Wage Gap"; Sandra J. Libeson, "Reviving the Comparable Worth Debate in the United States: A Look Toward the European Community," *Comparative Labor Law Journal* 16 (1995): 358–398; B. Tobias Isbell, "Gender Inequality and Wage Differentials Between the Sexes: Is It Inevitable or Is There an Answer?" *Washington University Journal of Urban and Contemporary Law* 50 (1996): 369–400.

177. See various editions, Thomas, Legislative Information on the Internet, *Bill Summary and Status for the 103d–106th Congresses,* available at thomas.loc.gov/bss/.

178. Thomas, Legislative Information on the Internet, *Bill Summary and Status for the 106th Congresses,* available at thomas.loc.gov/bss/; see Janice Goodman, "Comparable Worth: Time May Be Now," *New York Law Journal* (June 28, 1999); *Legal Times,* August 23, 1999, for a discussion of the two Senate bills.

179. *New York Times,* January 10, 2009. In April 2011, versions of the legislation were reintroduced in each chamber by Democrats, but passage appears unlikely with the Republican majority in the House and the reduced number of Democrats in the Senate. *New York Times,* April 21, 2011.

4 Battling Sexual Harassment at Work

The EEOC received almost 13,000 complaints of workplace sexual harassment in FY 2009 (from October 1, 2008, until September 30, 2009); 16 percent were filed by men. Not including damages won through litigation, the monetary awards resulting from these charges amounted to more than $50 million.[1]

During the 1970s, as women began to come forward to describe their common experiences of sexual misconduct at work, awareness of the problem developed, and the search for legal recourse followed.[2] One of the first open discussions of sexual harassment appeared in a survey published in *Redbook* Magazine in 1976 in an article entitled, "What Men Do to Women on the Job: A Shocking Look at Sexual Harassment." The survey revealed that 85 percent of the women responding to it had been subject to sexual harassment on the job.[3]

The federal government polled its employees about their experiences with sexual harassment in a series of surveys conducted in 1980, 1987, and 1994; the results for both women and men did not vary greatly over time. Asked whether they had been sexually harassed over the last two years, 42 percent of female employees said yes in the 1980 and 1987 surveys; there was a slight increase to 44 percent in 1994. When men were asked the same question, 15 percent said yes in 1980, 14 percent in 1987, and 19 percent in 1994. Across all three surveys, both men and women were most frequently harassed by coworkers or other employees; the respondents reported that their supervisors were much less often the source of the harassment.

Looking at the 1994 data alone, the three most common forms of harassment of women were sexual remarks, sexual gestures, and intentional touching. The survey also showed that the most common response of most victims (44 percent) was to do nothing, with only 12 percent reporting the behavior to a supervisor or other official.[4]

Men may also be victims, but sexual harassment on the job most commonly involves an "assertion of power by men over women, perceived to be in a vulnerable position with respect to male authority."[5] In her pathbreaking 1979 book on sexual harassment, Catharine MacKinnon identifies two types of sexual harassment in employment. The first, called quid pro quo, occurs when a supervisor (or other person in authority) requires sexual favors from an employee in exchange for employment benefits. MacKinnon labels the other "condition of work" harassment to describe a situation in which sexuality pervades the workplace environment.[6] This type of harassment, based on words, gestures, pictures, or other displays of a sexual nature from supervisors or coworkers, later became known as "hostile environment" harassment.[7]

The Lower Courts and Sexual Harassment

Sexual harassment lawsuits began to appear in the early 1970s, with women charging their employers with violating Title VII's ban on sex discrimination in employment. As these cases illustrate, the courts dismissed the actions, refusing to acknowledge that harassment had employment consequences. Off-color jokes, sexual paraphernalia, and invitations to engage in sexual relations were considered irrelevant to the terms and conditions of employment—even when there were negative consequences for the women's jobs. In dismissing the suits, the courts denied the legitimacy of the complaints, ruling that even if the charges were true, there was no Title VII violation.

The courts were also reluctant to rule in the plaintiffs' favor because they were uncertain about whether to hold employers legally responsible for the misbehavior of their employees, especially when there was a company policy against harassment and the victim bypassed internal grievance procedures. Judges also believed they would be inundated with sexual harassment suits if they allowed plaintiffs to prevail.[8]

In *Barnes v. Train*,[9] decided in 1974, Paulette Barnes claimed that shortly after she began working at the Environmental Protection Agency, the director asked her to join him in after-hours social activities, during which he made sexual remarks to her and promised her extra privileges if she began a sexual relationship with him. When she refused, he decreased her job duties and eventually abolished her position. The District Court for the District of Columbia dismissed the suit, ruling that the director's actions were not motivated by sex but stemmed from her refusal to engage in sexual relations—not a Title VII matter.

A year later, in *Corne v. Bausch and Lomb*,[10] the plaintiffs claimed that their supervisor's verbal and physical harassment created intolerable working conditions and that the company was responsible for his conduct. An Arizona federal district court dismissed the suit, holding that the supervisor's behavior was not company policy but "appeared to be nothing more than a personal proclivity, peculiarity, or mannerism."[11] The court concluded that the plaintiff had not proved sex discrimination because her supervisor could have harassed male employees as well.

Tomkins v. Public Service Electric and Gas,[12] a 1976 case, was brought by Adrienne Tomkins, whose supervisor invited her for lunch, ostensibly to discuss his evaluation of her work and the possibility of a future promotion. He propositioned her, making it clear that her compliance was a condition of her continued employment. The New Jersey federal court refused to apply Title VII to her claim, despite her charge that he physically attacked her. The judge dismissed her case, expressing no concern about whether the supervisor's behavior affected her employment status, describing his acts merely as an "abuse of authority . . . for personal purposes."[13]

In *Miller v. Bank of America*,[14] another 1976 ruling, Margaret Miller filed a Title VII suit against the bank, claiming that her supervisor promised her a better job if she agreed to engage in sexual activity with him and fired her when she refused. A California federal court judge dismissed her suit, saying she had not presented evidence of a systematic policy of harassing women. Indicating his reluctance to interfere in a personnel decision involving sexual attraction, the judge asked "whether Title VII was intended to hold an employer liable for what is essentially the isolated and unauthorized sex misconduct of one employee to another."[15] He noted the bank's policy against immoral behavior and stressed that Miller had not complained about his conduct. While not ruling out the possibility of a Title VII suit against an employer for allowing sex to be a condition of employment, the judge felt it was premature at this time. He warned of the potential flood of litigation, stating "it would not be difficult to foresee a federal challenge based on alleged sex motivated considerations of the complainant's superior in every case of a lost promotion, transfer, demotion or dismissal."[16]

The outcome was different for Diane Williams, an information officer at DOJ, who was fired less than two weeks after she refused her supervisor's sexual advances. *Williams v. Saxbe*,[17] decided in 1976, was the first sexual harassment suit to succeed in federal court. The district court judge recognized that the supervisor's conduct was linked to Williams's employment status and that she had a legitimate claim of sex discrimination. Rejecting the defendant's argument that sexual demands could be made to both sexes, the district court found that the actions of her supervisors "created an artificial barrier to employment which was placed before one gender and not the other."[18]

Barnes v. Costle[19] (*Barnes v. Train* in the district court) was the first sexual harassment lawsuit to succeed at the appellate level. In 1977, the District of Columbia Circuit Court ruled that Paulette Barnes's complaint of sexual harassment stated a valid claim of sex discrimination under Title VII.[20] The court was most concerned with whether the harassment was "based on sex," as Title VII required, and found that Barnes was treated differently from other employees because of her sex. Citing examples of her supervisor's attempts to persuade her to have sex with him, the court agreed that she had successfully shown that "retention of her job was conditioned upon submission to sexual relations—an exaction which the supervisor would not have sought from any male."[21]

In adjudicating these suits for sexual harassment, the courts were forced to grapple with the thorny question of the extent to which employers should be held accountable for acts of sexual harassment by their employees. In *Munford v. James T. Barnes and Company,*[22] a 1977 decision, a Michigan federal court held that companies could be held liable for the acts of supervisory employees under some circumstances. The judge ruled that the employer had an affirmative duty to investigate complaints and take appropriate action against the offender. By failing to investigate, the court declared, it appeared that the company consented to the harassing behavior. A year later, in *Heelan v. Johns-Manville,*[23] a Colorado federal court ruled that because the plaintiff's complaints to management were either ignored or summarily dismissed, the company could be held liable for the supervisor's harassment.

At the appellate level, the Third Circuit was the first to expand employer liability when it reversed the lower court in *Tomkins v. Public Service Electric and Gas.*[24] The appeals court ruled that her supervisor's sexual demands were linked to her employment status and that a Title VII violation occurs when a supervisory employee "makes sexual advances or demands towards a subordinate employee, . . . and the employer does not take prompt and appropriate remedial action" after learning of it.[25]

When Margaret Miller appealed the district court ruling against her to the Ninth Circuit, the bank could no longer contend that the harassment had no implications for her employment status. Instead it defended itself by pointing to its policy against harassment, including an internal grievance procedure that she did not utilize.

The Ninth Circuit analogized the bank's position to that of a taxi company which would be held liable if its drivers caused harm.[26]

> It would be shocking to most of us if a court should hold, for example, that a taxi company is not liable for injuries to a pedestrian caused by the negligence of one of its drivers because the company has a safety training program and strictly forbids negligent driving. Nor would the taxi company be exonerated even if the taxi driver, in the course of his employment, became enraged at a jaywalking pedestrian and intentionally ran him down.[27]

Citing *Barnes* and *Tomkins,* the *Miller* court determined that Congress did not intend to exempt employers from the customary rules of liability. It held that the bank was responsible because the supervisor, with the authority to "hire, fire, discipline or promote," was guilty of harassment.[28] The court rejected the bank's argument that Miller forfeited her right to sue because she had bypassed the personnel office. There was no indication, it said, that Congress required Title VII plaintiffs to exhaust company grievance procedures before filing suit in federal court.

On November 10, 1980, the EEOC issued guidelines on sexual harassment, for the first time recognizing it as a form of sex discrimination.[29] The document, entitled "Final Amendment to Guidelines on Discrimination Because of Sex," formally incorporated sexual harassment within the prohibition of sex discrimination in Title VII.[30] According to the guidelines,

> (a) Unwelcome sexual advances, requests for sexual favors, and other verbal or physical conduct of a sexual nature constitute sexual harassment when (1) submission to such conduct is made either explicitly or implicitly a term or condition of an individual's employment, (2) submission to or rejection of such conduct by an individual is used as a basis for employment decisions affecting such individual, or (3) such conduct has the purpose or effect of unreasonably interfering with an individual's work performance or creating an intimidating, hostile, or offensive working environment.[31]

The EEOC broadly assigned employer liability in both hostile environment and quid pro quo harassment situations when supervisors were guilty of the sexual misconduct. According to the guidelines, the employer was

> responsible for its acts and those of its agents and supervisory employees with respect to sexual harassment regardless of whether the specific acts complained of were authorized or even forbidden by the employer and regardless of whether the employer knew or should have known of their occurrence.[32]

The guidelines also stated an employer should be accountable when coworkers created a hostile environment, if "it (or its agents or supervisory employees) knows or should have known of the conduct, unless it can show it took immediate and appropriate corrective action."[33]

The courts accepted quid pro quo harassment suits more readily because their effect on the terms and conditions of employment were more evident. Employees complaining of a hostile sexual environment were less likely to prevail because the courts were reluctant to believe that such situations had adverse job consequences.

Sandra Bundy reported numerous instances of sexually charged statements directed at her, including the one by a high-level supervisor who, when she complained to him of his subordinates' actions, told her that "any man in his right mind would want to rape you."[34] When she filed suit against the District of Columbia Department of Corrections for sexual harassment, the district court held that she did not have a valid Title VII claim because the law did not forbid the conduct she had experienced. The judge dismissed her complaint, saying that she was not denied employment benefits because there were no job-related consequences when she refused her superiors' sexual advances. Instead, he found that "the making of improper sexual advances to female employees [was] standard operating procedure, a fact of life, a normal condition of employment in the office."[35] The court viewed the sexual attention toward women employees as a "game" played without retaliation against anyone who refused to play.

The circuit court disagreed, recognizing that Bundy's complaint was within the bounds of Title VII. It cited Title VII case law in which employers were held liable for discriminatory working conditions, whether or not employees suffered any tangible job effects because of the discrimination. Ruling otherwise, said the court, would subject a woman to

> a "cruel trilemma" [in which] she can endure the harassment. [Or] she can attempt to oppose it, with little hope of success, either legal or practical, but with every prospect of making the job even less tolerable for her. Or she can leave her job, with little hope of legal relief and the likely prospect of another job where she will face harassment anew.[36]

The Supreme Court and Sexual Harassment

Table 4.1, presenting the Supreme Court's rulings on sexual harassment in the workplace, indicates the Court's responsiveness to victims of sexual misconduct at work. After a decade of litigation in the lower courts, the high court formally recognized in *Meritor Savings Bank v. Vinson*,[37] a 1986 decision, that Title VII's ban on sex discrimination applies to incidents of harassment at work.

When she was fired from her job as assistant branch manager, Mechelle Vinson filed suit against her supervisor, Sidney Taylor, and her employer, the Capital City Federal Savings and Loan Association. After working at the branch for four years, she took an indefinite sick leave and was discharged for excessive time on leave.

Vinson testified at trial that Taylor propositioned her, saying that she initially refused him but ultimately capitulated because she was afraid to report him and afraid of losing her job. She claimed that she was forced to submit to him during the day as well as after work, that he touched her in front of other employees, that he followed her into the restroom where he exposed himself to her, and that he assaulted and raped her. She testified that she had sexual intercourse with him forty or fifty times during the three-year period in which the harassment took place.

Taylor denied her story, and the bank declined responsibility, arguing that even if he committed these acts, he did so without its knowledge or authorization. Following the trial, the district court judge ruled that Vinson had failed to establish a Title VII claim of sex discrimination. Even though this ruling disposed of her suit, the lower court nevertheless assessed the bank's liability. Because it had a policy against discrimination and because Vinson had never complained about Taylor, the district court judge concluded that even if Vinson's charges were true, the bank was not responsible.[38]

The District of Columbia Circuit Court reversed on appeal, ruling that victims of sexual harassment have two alternative legal theories

Table 4.1 Supreme Court Workplace Sexual Harassment Rulings, 1986–2009

Case	Date	Issue[a]	Ruling[b]
Vinson	1986	Hostile environment	Expands employee protection
Harris	1993	Psychological injury	Expands employee protection
Oncale	1998	Same-sex harassment	Expands employee protection
Ellerth	1998	Employer liability	Expands employee protection
Faragher	1998	Employer liability	Expands employee protection
Suders	2004	Constructive discharge	Expands employee protection
White	2006	Retaliation	Expands employee protection
Crawford	2009	Retaliation	Expands employee protection

Notes: a. Based on the major issue in the case.
b. Based on the overall outcome of the case.

available to them.[39] Citing *Barnes,* the court stated that it was now settled that quid pro quo harassment was illegal under Title VII. It added
that following *Bundy,* an employee could also bring a sexual harassment
suit when forced to endure a hostile or offensive environment in the
workplace. Referring to the EEOC guidelines, the court held that Title
VII applied to both types of harassment and remanded the case to the
district court to determine whether Taylor's actions had created a hostile
work environment for Vinson.

The district court had held that even if Vinson and Taylor had a sexual
relationship, it was voluntary, basing its judgment in part on evidence presented on her manner of dressing. The appellate court rejected the view
that Vinson's "voluntary" acquiescence to Taylor's sexual demands defeat-
ed her claim. Quoting the EEOC definition of sexual harassment as
"unwelcome sexual advances . . . [that have] the purpose or effect of unreasonably interfering with an individual's work performance or creating an
intimidating, hostile or offensive working environment," the appellate
court stressed that her "voluntariness" was immaterial.[40] Because victims
do not forfeit their rights when they are forced to capitulate to sexual
demands to keep their jobs, evidence of her clothing was irrelevant. The
appeals court also ruled that Vinson could introduce evidence to show that
Taylor had sexually harassed other employees to bolster her claim that
there was a sex-based hostile environment in the workplace.

Finally, and perhaps most important, the appellate court rejected the
lower court's view of the employer's responsibility. Although the
Barnes and *Bundy* courts had not directly ruled on the issue of employer
liability, the employers were held accountable for the acts of their supervisory personnel in both cases. The *Vinson* court pointed out that Title
VII forbids discrimination by employers and their agents and held that
Taylor's violation of Title VII was attributable to his employer, regardless of its knowledge of his behavior, because he was an agent of the
bank. Justifying its broad view of employer liability for the acts of its
employees, the circuit court pointed to the legislative debate on Title
VII. Although there was no direct evidence that Congress intended to
impose such liability on the employer, the court considered it significant
that the legislature discussed the matter and had not ruled it out.[41]

Finding the EEOC guidelines "persuasive," the circuit court accepted
its view of employer responsibility, holding that an employer is accountable for sexual harassment committed by its supervisory personnel,
"regardless of whether the specific acts complained of were authorized or
even forbidden by the employer and regardless of whether the employer
knew or should have known of their occurrence." Moreover, the court

added, Title VII case law generally considers supervisory personnel agents of their employers and holds employers accountable for their actions. The court defined an agent as a supervisor or any employee with authority to hire and fire. Employees with power over subordinates can threaten and coerce and thereby harass.[42] Taylor lacked the authority to hire or fire workers but was able to recommend salaries and promotions.

By holding the company accountable, the court sought to create a disincentive to escape responsibility simply by disclaiming knowledge of the harassment. "Much of the promise of Title VII will become empty," it declared, "if victims of unlawful discrimination cannot secure redress from the only source capable of providing it."[43]

Vinson's employer, now known as Meritor Savings Bank, appealed to the Supreme Court, and in 1986, the Court unanimously affirmed the circuit court's holding that a hostile work environment created by sexual harassment violates Title VII. The bank maintained Title VII was limited to sexual discrimination that erects "tangible, economic barriers."[44] Not true, Rehnquist said; the injury caused by the discrimination need not be economic. Title VII was intended to reach an array of employment disparities between the sexes. He also pointed out that the EEOC guidelines clearly state that Title VII extends to complaints of a hostile environment. Cautioning that not all offensive or annoying behavior at work can be considered harassment, he agreed that the conduct Vinson described was sufficiently severe to constitute harassment. On these grounds, the Court affirmed the circuit court's order to remand.

The high court disagreed with the circuit court's expansive interpretation of employer liability, however, as well as its ruling that the defendant could not present evidence that the employee provoked the harassing conduct by her manner or her clothing. Rehnquist said it was irrelevant whether Vinson voluntarily participated in the sexual relationship. The crucial question, he stressed, was whether the sexual advances were "unwelcome." The circuit court had flatly stated that Vinson's dress or speech "had no place in this litigation," but the Supreme Court disagreed, finding them relevant in determining whether the sex was unwelcome to her.

The Court took a middle ground on the issue of employer liability for hostile environment harassment. By this time, the EEOC had shifted its position on employer liability. The agency's 1980 guidelines stated that employers should be held strictly (that is, always) liable whenever supervisory personnel are involved; the EEOC now argued that employers should only be held strictly liable for the acts of supervisors in quid pro quo cases, but not in hostile environment situations. Rather, employer liability should rest on two factors: first, whether the employer had an express policy against harassment and a grievance procedure to resolve complaints, and second, whether the employer knew of the harassment and failed to take action to remedy it.

The Supreme Court agreed with the revised EEOC position, ruling that employers must have notice to be held responsible in hostile environment situations, even for acts of supervisors. But it also held that "absence of notice to an employer does not necessarily insulate that employer from liability."[45] The Court adopted a case-by-case approach, ruling that trial courts must examine the facts of each case to determine whether to hold employers accountable for acts committed by their supervisors. It criticized the bank's grievance policy because it merely prohibited sex discrimination without specifically forbidding sexual harassment. Moreover, it required employees to direct their complaints to their supervisors, a questionable procedure when, as in Vinson's case, the supervisor was the harasser.

Despite the victory for victims of sexual harassment in *Vinson,* the ruling had two major shortcomings. First, the Court permitted evidence of the employee's dress, manner, and speech to be introduced at trial, allowing the employer to argue that the woman had invited the sexual attention. Second, it departed from the original EEOC position on strict employer liability for supervisor harassment. Objecting to this part of the opinion, Marshall wrote separately, pointing out that under Title VII law, as expressed in the 1980 EEOC guidelines, the employer is always liable for harassment by supervisors—in both quid pro quo and workplace harassment cases—and that lack of notice to the employer is not a defense. He saw no "justification for a special rule, to be applied *only* in 'hostile environment' cases, that sexual harassment does not create employer liability until the employee suffering the discrimination notifies other supervisors."[46]

The Lower Courts and Hostile Environment Claims

In January 1991, two lower court decisions, *Robinson v. Jacksonville Shipyards,*[47] a Florida district court ruling, and *Ellison v. Brady,*[48] a Ninth Circuit opinion, broadened the scope of the employer's liability and established a new standard of proof for determining harassment. Jacksonville Shipyards, where Lois Robinson worked, was characterized by a sexually explicit atmosphere dominated by men. She charged that her work environment was hostile, pointing to drawings and photographs of nude and partially clothed women on the walls and in locker rooms. In particular, she described a picture circulating among her coworkers of a nude woman with long blonde hair and a whip, which she said was especially threatening to her because of her long blonde hair and her work with a welding tool known as a whip. She and her coworkers also complained of numerous lewd remarks and vulgarities written on walls in their work areas. Their repeated protests were essentially ignored; in one instance, the response was to move an offensive calendar from one wall to another.

The district court cited five elements of a sexual harassment claim based on a hostile environment: (1) the plaintiff belongs to a protected group, (2) the plaintiff is subjected to unwelcome verbal or physical sexual behavior, (3) the harassment is based on sex, (4) the harassment is sufficiently severe or pervasive to affect a term or condition of employment, and (5) the employer knows or should know of the harassment and fails to take prompt remedial action.[49]

The key element was the fourth. The court explained that to satisfy it, the plaintiff must show her work is affected by the harassment, and the court must determine that a reasonable person of her sex, that is, a reasonable woman, would believe the working environment was abusive.

The district court easily concluded that Robinson satisfied both parts of the test. Turning to the issue of the employer's liability, the court explained that employers may be directly or indirectly liable for hostile work environments. They are directly liable when supervisors are responsible for the harassment. They are indirectly liable when employees create a hostile environment and they know about it and make no effort to correct it.

The court found Robinson's employer liable for both kinds of harassment, and because it demonstrated little concern for the conduct of its employees, the court believed that she was entitled to a broad decree, ordering the employer to stop the harassing conduct, adopt an employee training and education program, and establish a reporting procedure for future complaints.

Robinson presaged a new approach to pornography in the workplace and its effect on female employees; it also demonstrated a heightened sensitivity for the predicament of women employed in a male-dominated workplace. Rejecting the company's defenses that it attempted to deal with the women's complaints and ordering it to devise a sexual harassment policy, the court paved the way for greater judicial involvement in remedying workplace sexual harassment.[50]

Shortly thereafter, the Ninth Circuit added another dimension to sexual harassment law.[51] Kerry Ellison worked in the San Mateo, California, office of the Internal Revenue Service. Her coworker, Sterling Gray, began to lavish her with unwelcome attention, including asking her out and writing her increasingly intrusive and disturbing notes and letters expressing his attraction to her. When she filed a grievance against him, he was transferred to another office. His grievance, in which he asked to return to the San Mateo office, was also granted, however. Learning of this, Ellison filed a complaint, which was rejected by the Treasury Department and the EEOC; she eventually filed a Title VII suit against the government in federal court. The district court ruled against her, labeling his conduct "isolated and genuinely trivial."[52]

On appeal, the Ninth Circuit announced that the major point of contention in the suit was whether his behavior was sufficiently "severe or pervasive" to alter the condition of her employment by creating an abusive working environment. The circuit court emphasized that "in evaluating the severity and pervasiveness of sexual harassment, we should focus on the perspective of the victim."[53] Women have a different view of offensive or abusive conduct, and judging the harassment by a "reasonable person" standard, the customary approach, would only perpetuate sexual harassment if it were based on common practices in the workplace. The traditional sex-neutral reasonable person approach, the court explained, "tends to be male-biased and tends to systematically ignore the experiences of women."[54]

Under the Ninth Circuit approach, the victim, assuming she is a woman, would be required to show that a reasonable woman would consider the behavior sufficiently "severe or pervasive." She would not have to offer proof of unwelcomeness, nor would she have to show that the person guilty of the harassment intended to discriminate against her.[55] Therefore, compliments or ostensibly well-meaning remarks may be considered sexual harassment if the victim believes they altered the terms or conditions of her employment.

The Thomas Nomination

In 1991, the nation got a glimpse into the problem of sexual harassment at work when Professor Anita Hill of the University of Oklahoma Law School testified before the Senate Judiciary Committee on national television that she had been sexually harassed by Supreme Court nominee Clarence Thomas when she worked for him at the Equal Employment Opportunity Commission in the early 1980s.[56]

Even before Hill's charges were aired, women's and civil rights groups had opposed Thomas because of his positions on abortion and affirmative action; they also questioned his qualifications for the post and were skeptical of the president's statement that Thomas was "the best person for this position."[57] They warned that he would not follow in the footsteps of the retiring Marshall, the first African American Supreme Court justice. Marshall, who had successfully argued school desegregation cases before the high court, including *Brown v. Board of Education,* was a hero of the civil rights and women's rights movements.

In a vote on September 27, the all-male Judiciary Committee split 7 to 7 on whether to send Thomas's name to the full Senate with a favorable recommendation. All Democrats but one voted no, citing Thomas's propensity to evade many of their questions. The committee then voted 13 to 1 to send Thomas's name to the Senate floor without a recommendation.[58]

Shortly thereafter, on October 5, Hill's claims, of which members of the committee had been aware for some time, became known; committee members were forced to defend themselves against charges that they had not viewed Hill's allegations as sufficiently grave to delay the committee vote or bring them to the attention of the full Senate before voting.[59] To underscore this point, on October 8, seven Democratic female members of the House of Representatives marched across the Capitol and attempted to interrupt the Senate Democratic Caucus luncheon to protest the nomination; they were not allowed to enter the room. The Senate, scheduled to vote on Thomas's confirmation on October 11, delayed the vote, in part to demonstrate they took Hill's charges seriously. Televised hearings began on October 11 and continued throughout the weekend.

Although many senators expressed concern about the effect of harassment on working women, their treatment of Hill illustrated the dilemma that women confront when complaining of sexual harassment at work. Senators—mostly Republican—either obliquely or openly accused her of perjury and attacked her motivation in coming forward; Senator Arlen Specter, Republican from Pennsylvania, flatly declared that she had committed perjury. The committee, and indeed the entire Senate, ultimately dismissed Hill's testimony.[60] In part, they were cowed by Thomas's charges of racism (even though Hill was also African American) and his claim that he was being subjected to what he characterized as "a high-tech lynching."[61] In the end, Thomas was narrowly confirmed by the Senate in a 52 to 48 vote on October 16, 1991, and soon took his seat on the high court.[62]

The much-publicized controversy over Thomas's nomination had the unanticipated consequence of creating a greater awareness of the problem of harassment on the job. At the time of the hearings, just before the Senate voted to confirm Thomas, a *New York Times/CBS News* poll reported that four out of ten women said they had been on the receiving end of unwelcome physical advances and verbal harassment from male supervisors or others with the ability to affect their working environment; most said they had not reported the incident at the time. Slightly more than half the men surveyed admitted to engaging in behavior that could be construed as harassment.[63]

As a result of the Thomas hearings, the nation paid increasing attention to sexual harassment, amid a widespread belief that had more women been in the Senate—there were only two at the time—Hill's allegations would have been taken more seriously.[64] In partial response to the furor over the Senate's reaction to Hill, female candidates gained an unprecedented number of seats in Congress in the 1992 election, labeled the "Year of the Woman."[65] When the dust settled and the results of the election were tabulated, there were record numbers of women in the House and Senate: four new women joined the two in the Senate, including the first African American woman senator, Carol Moseley Braun, Democrat from Illinois, and a pair of Democrats from California, Barbara Boxer and Dianne Feinstein.[66] Determined not to show an exclusively male Judiciary Committee to the nation again, Senate leadership appointed two of the new women, Moseley Braun and Feinstein, to the committee.

Proof of Injury

The Supreme Court again addressed sexual harassment in 1993 in *Harris v. Forklift Systems, Inc.,*[67] in which it considered whether victims must prove they suffered psychological injuries to prevail in sexual harassment suits.

Teresa Harris worked as the rental manager at Forklift Systems, a company selling, leasing, and repairing forklift machines, from 1985 to 1997. Of the six managers in the firm, two were women, the other the president's daughter. During her years at Forklift Systems, her boss, the company president, referred to Harris in derogatory terms, calling her "a dumb ass woman," and saying that the company "need[ed] a man as a rental manager" and "you're a woman, what do you know." Once he said to her, in front of others, "Let's go to the Holiday Inn to negotiate your raise." He also asked her and other women employees to retrieve coins from his front pants pocket. When she complained about his conduct, he apologized and said he was only joking and would stop. Based on his reassurances, she stayed on the job. His promise was soon forgotten, and he addressed more offensive remarks to her, saying to her, again in front of other employees, "What did you do, promise the guy some sex Saturday night?" She quit and filed a federal lawsuit.[68] At trial, he said he was only joking and everybody knew it. The lower courts found his comments vulgar and offensive, yet held they were not so serious as to interfere with her work performance or cause her psychological harm. The Supreme Court accepted the case for review to resolve a conflict among the circuits about whether plaintiffs must prove they suffered psychological damage in hostile environment cases.

Speaking for a unanimous Court, O'Connor stated that women were not required to demonstrate that the sexual harassment they complained of was so severe it led to psychological injury. The important issue, she explained, was whether the work environment was hostile or abusive and affected the employee's job performance, not whether the employee suffered psychological harm. "A discriminatorily abusive work environment," she stressed, "even one that does not seriously affect employees' psychological well-being, can and often will detract from employees' job performance, discourage employees from remaining on the job, or keep them from advancing in their careers. Moreover," she continued, "even without regard to these tangible effects, the very fact that the discriminatory conduct was so severe or pervasive that it created a work environment abusive to employees because of their race, gender, religion, or national origin offends Title VII's broad rule of workplace equality."[69]

O'Connor rejected the Sixth Circuit standard that Title VII plaintiffs must demonstrate psychological harm to prevail. Quoting *Vinson,* she reiterated that a Title VII violation occurs when the sexual harassment is severe or pervasive enough to "affect conditions of the victim's employment."[70]

The Court cited three factors to determine whether a workplace is hostile: "the frequency of the discriminatory conduct, its severity (whether physically threatening or humiliating), and whether it unreasonably interferes with an employee's work performance."[71] Psychological harm is relevant to the inquiry, O'Connor noted, but it is only one of several elements, with no single one necessary to prove the claim of harassment.

Harris was a victory for women's rights, yet the Court's use of a "reasonable person" test suggested that it was distancing itself from the Ninth Circuit "reasonable woman" standard.[72] However, because the high court had not explicitly rejected the "reasonable woman" standard, after *Harris* the lower courts were split about the correct standard to use. In 1995, the Ninth Circuit settled on a compromise, adopting a "reasonable person with the same fundamental characteristics" as the victim as the standard.[73]

The Clinton Lawsuit

The nation was again treated to a seminar on sexual harassment when Paula Jones, a twenty-four-year-old state employee, accused then-governor Clinton of Arkansas of lewd conduct in a Little Rock hotel room on May 8, 1991. In May 1994, after negotiations over a settlement broke down, she filed suit against him under federal and state law, alleging sexual harassment and emotional distress and defamation and seeking $700,000 in damages.[74]

Clinton claimed presidential immunity, arguing that a sitting president cannot be sued while in office. District Court judge Susan Webber Wright agreed and ordered the trial deferred until he left office. The Eighth Circuit reversed, explaining that the president is not entitled to special treatment and there was no precedent for delaying the trial. Most believed the Supreme Court would reverse the appeals court because of its position in *Nixon v. Fitzgerald,*[75] a 1982 decision in which it held that a "president is absolutely immune from civil damages liability for his official acts."[76]

However, in *Clinton v. Jones,*[77] decided on May 27, 1997, the high court unanimously held that there is no special immunity principle protecting a sitting president and rejected the president's argument to postpone the trial. The high court believed that the district court judge had not sufficiently considered the importance of bringing the plaintiff's suit to trial in a timely manner. The Court clearly miscalculated, however, when it denied that its ruling would result in undue interference with the duties and office of the presidency and "generate a large volume of politically motivated harassing and frivolous litigation."[78]

Her suit finally came to trial a year later, in May 1998. Ruling on Clinton's motion to dismiss, Wright held that even if he were guilty of the conduct she described, Jones had not stated a valid claim against him for either quid pro quo harassment or hostile environment harassment. In her view, "the conduct as alleged by the plaintiff describes a mere sexual proposition or encounter, albeit an odious one, that was relatively brief in duration, did not involve any coercion or threats of reprisals and was abandoned as soon as plaintiff made clear that the advance was unwelcome."[79]

In the end, Wright rejected Jones's evidence that she had suffered adverse job consequences after the incident because she did not receive flowers on Secretary's Day. The judge wrote that while "it is not clear why plaintiff failed to receive flowers on Secretary's Day in 1992, such an omission does not rise to a federal cause of action in the absence of evidence of some more tangible change in duties or working conditions."[80] Indeed, Wright noted, Jones had never complained to her supervisors and had even received merit raises after the incident. Her suit against Clinton was finally dismissed, but the victory was ephemeral for the president. The Jones lawsuit ultimately led to the revelations about Monica Lewinsky and to Clinton's impeachment. Although he was acquitted by the Senate, his presidency was permanently marred.

The Court handed down three significant sexual harassment rulings in 1998, clarifying a number of uncertainties in the law. In the first case, *Oncale v. Sundowner Offshore Services*,[81] the Court considered whether Title VII applies to harassment by persons of the same sex as the victim. The other two cases, *Burlington Industries v. Ellerth*[82] and *Faragher v. City of Boca Raton*,[83] attempted to resolve lingering questions of employer liability.

Same-Sex Harassment

Joseph Oncale, a twenty-one-year-old slightly built man, worked for a Louisiana offshore oil-drilling company. He claimed he had been abused by other male employees, including two who had supervisory authority over him; they insulted him and physically assaulted him, and one even threatened to rape him. The accused men were all heterosexual. Oncale quoted one of his tormentors as saying to him, "You know, you've got a cute little ass; I'm going to get you." The company defended its employees, saying they were simply hazing him, reflecting the male-only environment of the job.[84] Despite his complaints to the company, nothing was done, and he quit, later suing for sexual harassment. The lower federal courts ruled that Title VII does not apply to claims of same-sex harassment.

The Supreme Court accepted the case to decide whether Title VII's ban on discrimination "because of sex" should be interpreted to apply to situations in which the victim is harassed by members of the same sex. In a brief unanimous opinion by Scalia, the Court made it clear that Title VII does not automatically disqualify victims of same-sex harassment from the protection of the law. Scalia also noted that illegal conduct does not need to reflect sexual desire but can stem from hostility; what matters most, he stressed, is whether the conduct is sufficiently offensive that it affects the terms and conditions of employment. He noted that *Harris* had held that the conduct must be evaluated "from the perspective of a reasonable person in the plaintiff's position, 'considering all the circumstances.'"[85] Therefore, he concluded, it is important to apply common sense and social norms to determine whether the law is being violated. Because the courts below had not ruled on the merits of Oncale's claim, the Supreme Court remanded to allow the lower court to decide whether he had been sexually harassed.[86]

Employer Liability

Some months later, in June 1998 on the last day of the term, the Supreme Court handed down two 7 to 2 opinions, with Thomas and Scalia dissenting in both. The Court elaborated on *Vinson* and further defined the limits of the employers' liability for sexual harassment.[87] It was also forced to grapple with the intersection of the two kinds of sexual harassment: hostile environment and quid pro quo.[88]

Ellerth, brought as a quid pro quo case, revolved around a complaint by Kimberly Ellerth, a merchandising assistant in Burlington Industry's mattress fabric division in Chicago. She worked there for a little over a year, beginning in March 1993. She claimed that her supervisor, a company vice president operating out of New York, made sexual overtures to her, including offensive comments about parts of her body, and touched her inappropriately.[89] According to her, he said such things as, "You know, Kim, I could make your life very hard or very easy at Burlington," and "Are you wearing your shorter skirts yet, Kim, because it would make your job a whole heck of a lot easier?"[90] Unlike most other harassment scenarios, though, she never submitted to him, and his veiled threats were never carried out; indeed, she received a promotion. She eventually quit and sued the company for sexual harassment, despite the fact that there was no tangible effect on her job. She knew about Burlington's sexual harassment policy but never complained about his behavior to a company official.

The lower court dismissed her complaint, ruling that she needed to show she suffered adverse job consequences for a successful quid pro quo claim. The Seventh Circuit disagreed and, with eight separate opinions among the twelve judges, reinstated her suit.

Announcing the opinion for the high court, Kennedy explained that the Court must decide whether a company is liable when there is an unfulfilled threat by a supervisor. As in *Vinson,* the Court assessed the employer's liability for the acts of its supervisory employees, noting that the lower courts unanimously agree that under agency law, an employer is vicariously liable for a discriminatory act by a supervisor that leads to a tangible job consequence such as hiring, firing, or deprivation of a promotion or other benefit. Under this approach, the Court said, an employer is always liable when a supervisor is responsible for the harassment. However, when there are no tangible job consequences, the employer may escape a finding of vicarious liability by showing first "that [it] exercised reasonable care to prevent or correct promptly any sexually harassing behavior, and second, that the employee "unreasonably failed to take advantage" of any preventive or corrective opportunities provided by the employer or to avoid harm otherwise."[91] The Court sent the case back to the lower court to determine whether the employer satisfied the elements of the affirmative defense.

Beth Ann Faragher had worked as a lifeguard for the City of Boca Raton, Florida, for four years to help defray her college expenses. After she left, she sued the city and her two supervisors, both men, claiming they created a hostile work environment by repeatedly touching her and making lewd comments to her. She testified that one of them touched her shoulders and waist and patted her thigh and buttocks. The other one tackled her on the beach and talked about having sex with her. She never complained to city officials about their behavior during her employment, though she did tell another lifeguard supervisor, who advised her to ignore it since the city was unconcerned about such behavior. The city had adopted a sexual harassment policy, but it was not widely disseminated.

Souter's decision for the majority in *Faragher* further clarified the extent of the employer's liability when a supervisor creates a hostile work environment. Ruling that the notion of "scope of employment" is irrelevant in ascertaining the employer's liability, he said that under Title VII, the employer is strictly liable for the acts of supervisors who alter the terms and conditions of employees through sexual harassment. However, when there is no tangible job action, an employer may escape liability by showing it has a reasonable sexual harassment policy and that the employee unreasonably bypassed it.

In applying these principles, the Court believed that even though the city had a formal sexual harassment policy, it had not widely disseminated the policy to its employees, nor had officials attempted to make themselves aware of her supervisors' behavior. Moreover, as in *Vinson,* the city's sexual harassment policy specified that complaints must be reported to the employee's supervisor, and the city had neglected to inform their employees that they might bypass their supervisors when necessary. Thus, the Court concluded, the city had not exercised reasonable care in preventing the supervisors' harassing conduct.[92]

Faragher and *Ellerth* established a new standard of employer responsibility for harassment by supervisory personnel: the employer is strictly liable when a supervisor's harassment of a subordinate, regardless of the type of harassment involved, leads to a tangible job loss; when there is no tangible job action, the employer has an opportunity to escape liability if it can show it has an effective policy to deal with harassment complaints and the employee unreasonably failed to follow it. The burden is on the employer to show the employee acted unreasonably.

In deciding the extent to which employers would be held liable for the misconduct of supervisory personnel, the two rulings clarified that the type of harassment is no longer a determinative factor in assessing the employer's liability, thus focusing attention on the result of the supervisor's harassment of a subordinate more than on the behavior itself. In neither case did the Court specifically address employer liability for harassment by coworkers.

On June 21, 1999, the EEOC announced it would issue a new policy guidance entitled "Vicarious Employer Liability for Unlawful Harassment by Supervisors"; the document was intended to reflect the Court's new approach to the employer's vicarious liability announced in *Ellerth* and *Faragher.*[93] The revised guidance removed the provision applying strict liability to employers for supervisors' acts of sexual harassment.[94]

Employers' groups and women's rights advocates applauded the two decisions, saying that the Court had gone a long way toward clarifying a confusing area of law and underscoring the fact that employers would have to take responsibility when supervisory employees engage in sexual harassment. A women's rights attorney praised the decisions, calling them a "win-win for employers and for all the women of America." Her view was seconded by a lawyer for the U.S. Chamber of Commerce, who said "the court responded to our cries in the wilderness for clear, bright-line legal standards so employers will know what to do."[95]

In *Pennsylvania State Police v. Suders,*[96] a 2004 decision, the Court clarified the employer's liability in cases of constructive discharge, a situation in which an employee is not fired but resigns because of her supervisor's sexual harassment. Nancy Suders began working as a communications operator for the Pennsylvania State Police Department in

March 1998; from the start, her three supervisors continually harassed her with sexual remarks and óbscene physical gestures as well as derisive comments about her age. In June 1998, one of the supervisors charged her with removing a file from the office without authorization. She alerted the department's Equal Employment Opportunity (EEO) officer but did not follow up. Two months later (in August 1998), she told the EEO officer about the harassment and asked for assistance. The officer told her to file a complaint but provided no help in doing so.

A few days later, after Suders was arrested for theft, she resigned from the position. The arrest occurred after she accidentally discovered her computer-skills exams in a set of drawers located in the women's locker room and concluded that they had never been submitted for grading; her supervisors had repeatedly told her that she had failed these tests. She believed the tests were her property and removed them from the drawer. When she tried to return them, she found that they had dusted the drawer with a chemical that turned her hands blue. They arrested her, bringing her to an interrogation room in handcuffs. Although she offered to resign, they continued to question her; after some time, when she repeated the offer, they finally permitted her to leave.

She filed suit in federal court, claiming that she had been sexually harassed and constructively discharged. The trial court held that she had stated a valid claim for sexual harassment, but, citing *Faragher* and *Ellerth,* ruled against her because she had resigned only two days after she first complained of the harassment and therefore failed to avail herself of the department's grievance procedure. The court did not rule on her claim of constructive discharge.

The Third Circuit reversed, in part because the trial court erred in not addressing her constructive discharge claim. The appeals court ruled that the sexual harassment was the cause of the constructive discharge, which constituted a "tangible employment action" and, according to *Ellerth* and *Faragher,* barred the employer from offering an affirmative defense.[97]

The Supreme Court held that employers may be held responsible for an employee's constructive discharge under Title VII.[98] Announcing the 8 to 1 opinion for the Court, with Thomas dissenting, Ginsburg reviewed the constructive discharge doctrine and concluded that a claim for constructive discharge because of sexual harassment fell within Title VII.[99]

The Court held that a Title VII plaintiff must prove that "the conduct is sufficiently severe or pervasive" and the "working conditions [were] so intolerable that a reasonable person would have felt compelled to quit."[100] It explained that a constructive discharge may arise from a hostile environment caused by either coworkers or supervisors. When it involves supervisory personnel, the constructive discharge can be considered a tangible job action and preclude an affirmative defense. However, when "an official act does not underlie the constructive discharge," the employer may raise the affirmative defense described in *Ellerth* and *Faragher.*[101]

Two years after *Suders,* the Court addressed another contentious issue of employer liability in *Burlington Northern & Santa Fe Railway Co. v. White.*[102] Sheila White was hired to work as a track laborer, a job that included removing broken pieces of track and other debris from the tracks, in Burlington Northern's Tennessee Maintenance of Way Department in June 1997. Because of her previous experience as a forklift operator, she was quickly moved into that position, the only woman in her department.[103] A few months later, White complained to a company official that her supervisor made improper sexual comments to her in front of other workers and frequently stated that women should not work in this department. After an investigation, the company suspended the supervisor for ten days without pay and ordered him to attend a sexual harassment seminar.

At the end of the month, the supervisor who hired her informed her that he was transferring her back to the position of track laborer because her coworkers complained that the "less arduous and cleaner" forklift operator's job should be held by a "more senior man."[104] A few days later, she filed a complaint with the EEOC, charging the company with violating Title VII because the reassignment was based on discrimination and motivated by retaliation for her complaints about the supervisor.

She subsequently filed another retaliation charge with the EEOC.[105] Shortly thereafter, a disagreement between White and another supervisor led to a report of insubordination, and she was suspended indefinitely without pay. When she filed an internal grievance, after an investigation, Burlington Northern found she was not insubordinate and should not have been suspended; it reinstated her as a track laborer, giving her full backpay for the thirty-seven days of the suspension. Citing the suspension, she added a third EEOC charge and then filed suit in federal court, where a jury awarded her $43,500 in damages on the retaliation claims.[106] A three-judge panel of the Third Circuit reversed the trial court, but on rehearing the full circuit reinstated the jury award, agreeing that she had proved that the reassignment and suspension without pay constituted retaliatory action against her in violation of Title VII.[107]

The Supreme Court accepted the case to resolve a conflict among the circuits about the proper interpretation of Title VII's antiretaliation clause.[108]

Speaking for a unanimous Court, Breyer explained that the circuits varied widely in interpreting Title VII's antiretaliation protection, differing "about whether the challenged action has to be employment or workplace related and about how harmful that action must be to constitute retaliation."[109] Thus, he continued, at one extreme, some circuits required the plaintiff to show that the employer's retaliatory employment action negatively affected essential terms and conditions of her employment. At the other end, some circuits held employers liable for retaliation if the plaintiff showed that the retaliatory action was reasonably important to her employment status. The circuits in the middle found an employer guilty of retaliation if the action "materially" affected the terms and conditions of her employment.[110]

The railroad, supported by the Bush administration's solicitor general, advocated that the Court adopt the most restrictive approach, arguing that the antiretaliation provision of Title VII must be interpreted the same as its substantive provision, that is, it only banned retaliation that affects essential terms and conditions of employment.

Breyer disagreed, pointing to different language in the two sections of the law and maintaining that Congress intended them to be interpreted differently. The main section of Title VII, he said, is designed to prevent employment discrimination based on an employee's status; the antiretaliation provision is intended to "prevent harm to individuals based on what they do, *i.e.,* their conduct."[111]

In addition to the language, Breyer proclaimed that the purpose of the law would be hindered unless the antiretaliation section was interpreted more broadly because retaliation can hurt employees outside the workplace as well as inside. He cited an example of an employer filing trumped-up criminal charges against a worker who complained of employment discrimination. Breyer said there was no persuasive evidence (either in previous case law or in the EEOC guidelines) that a contrary view was preferable. Finally, he cited the broad interpretation of the antiretaliation provision of the National Labor Relations Act, an act often compared to Title VII.

In the end, the high court adopted a liberal interpretation of the antiretaliation clause, holding that "a plaintiff must show that a reasonable employee would have found the challenged action [the retaliatory act] materially adverse [to himself or herself]."[112] The purpose of the federal law, he reiterated, is to prevent companies from discouraging employees from complaining about discrimination in the workplace.[113]

The trial court judge had instructed the jury to find in White's favor if it believed that she "suffered a materially adverse change in the terms or conditions of her employment."[114] The Supreme Court upheld the award, ruling that it was reasonable for the jury to find that the reassignment and the suspension without pay were retaliatory actions within Title VII. Despite the backpay award, Breyer noted, a reasonable worker would be dissuaded from pursuing a complaint in the future after receiving such punishment, notwithstanding the eventual receipt of her salary. He added that the lower court judge's instructions had gone beyond the standard the high court had just announced, that is, that a jury need not even find that an employer's action affects the terms and conditions of employment. Alito, arguing for a narrower standard, said the Court went too far and that he would limit illegal retaliation to adverse employment actions.[115]

The Court revisited the issue of employer liability for retaliation in sexual harassment claims in *Crawford v. Metropolitan Government of Nashville and Davidson County, Tennessee*,[116] a 2009 ruling.

In 2002, the Nashville Metro government began investigating rumors that the school district's employee relations director was sexually harassing female employees. Crawford, a thirty-year veteran on the job, had not complained, but in the course of the inquiry, a Metro official asked her whether she had ever witnessed such behavior. She replied that he had made sexually inappropriate remarks and gestures to her; two other employees reported similar behavior.

Following the investigation, the employee relations supervisor received a verbal reprimand.[117] The three women who were interviewed were dismissed, with the government claiming Crawford was discharged for embezzlement. She charged that the dismissal was in retaliation for her report and filed a complaint with the EEOC, followed by lawsuit in federal court. The district court ruled for Metro, saying Crawford had not met her burden of proof in showing she was fired in retaliation for taking part in the investigation.

Speaking for a unanimous Court, Souter explained that Title VII prohibits employers from discriminating against employees because of their opposition to illegal employment practices or because they took part in an investigation. The first section is known as the "opposition clause," the other the "participation clause"; Crawford accused Metro of violating both. The district court ruled against her on both claims and the Sixth Circuit affirmed. Both courts held that the "opposition clause" requires that the employee take an active role in opposing an illegal employment practice and that simply answering questions during an investigation, as Crawford had, does not count. Moreover, they ruled, she failed to satisfy the "participation clause" because that only applies to employees who participate in an investigation resulting from a pending EEOC charge.[118]

The high court agreed to take the case to resolve another conflict among the circuits about the meaning of the retaliation clause in Title VII.[119] Noting that the law does not define these terms, the Court based its ruling on the dictionary definition and common understanding of the words. It said it found

> no reason to doubt that a person can "oppose" by responding to someone else's question just as surely as by provoking the discussion, and nothing in the statute requires a freakish rule protecting an employee who reports discrimination on her own initiative but not one who reports the same discrimination in the same words when her boss asks a question.[120]

To hold otherwise, it continued, would silence all employees who have knowledge of discriminatory practices in the workplace and discourage them from cooperating with an employer's attempt to rectify a harassing environment. Without addressing the meaning of the "participation clause," the Court reversed the courts below and remanded to allow the lower court to rule on Metro's defenses.[121]

Joined by Thomas, Alito concurred, but said he would impose a stricter view of the "opposition clause," requiring it to refer to conduct that is "active and purposive."[122]

Conclusion

Sexual harassment in the workplace typically arises from a power imbalance on the job, often in a male-dominated work environment. With a federal law against sex discrimination in place, women began filing suit in federal court in the early 1970s, arguing that sexual harassment on the job is sex discrimination prohibited by Title VII. The courts initially rejected their claims, refusing to hold employers accountable for the actions of their workers, even those in supervisory positions and even when the employee's refusal to accede to demands for sex resulted in negative job consequences. Similarly, the courts were reluctant to hold employers accountable when women complained of a hostile work environment.

In the late 1970s, the courts finally became more accepting of sexual harassment claims. In its first sexual harassment ruling in 1986, the Supreme Court sanctioned lawsuits against employers for harassment but was still hesitant to hold employers strictly liable for the acts of their employees. Over the next two decades, the high court clarified the employer's responsibility for sexual harassment in the workplace. And although it is still unwilling to hold employers liable in all instances of sexual harassment on the job, it imposed a strict standard of liability when the harassment led to a tangible job action.

Notes

1. The data are reported by fiscal year: FY 2009 began on October 1, 2008, and ended on September 30, 2009. The numbers include charges to the EEOC and state and local fair employment practices agencies that have shared working arrangements with the EEOC. U.S. Equal Employment Opportunity Commission, "Sexual Harassment Charges EEOC and FEPAs Combined: FY 1997–FY 2009," available at http://www.eeoc.gov//eeoc/statistics/enforcement/sexual_harassment.cfm?.

2. Catharine A. MacKinnon, *Sexual Harassment of Working Women* (New Haven: Yale University Press, 1979), chap. 3.

3. Cited in Barry S. Roberts and Richard A. Mann, "Sexual Harassment in the Workplace: A Primer," *Akron Law Review* 29 (1996): 269–289.

4. U.S. Merit Systems Protection Board, "Sexual Harassment in the Federal Workplace," available at http://www.mspb.gov/netsearch/viewdocs.aspx?docnumber =253661&version=253948&application=ACROBAT.

5. Joan Vermuelen, "Sexual Harassment," in Carol Lefcourt, ed., *Women and the Law* (New York: Clark Boardman, 1987), p. 7.

6. MacKinnon, *Sexual Harassment of Working Women,* chap. 3.

7. See Heather S. Murr's discussion of the relationship between quid pro quo harassment and "sexual extortion" by a supervisor. Murr, "The Continuing Expansive Pressure to Hold Employers Strictly Liable for Supervisory Sexual Extortion: An Alternative Approach Based on Reasonableness," *U.C. Davis Law Review* 39 (2006): 529–636.

8. See P. J. Murray, "Employer: Beware of 'Hostile Environment' Sexual Harassment," *Duquesne Law Review* 26 (1987): 461–484; Kerri Weisel, "Title VII: Legal Protection Against Sexual Harassment," *Washington Law Review* 53 (1977): 123–144; Vermuelen, "Sexual Harassment."

9. 13 Fair Employment Practice Cases, 123 (D.D.C. 1974).

10. 390 F. Supp. 161 (D. Ariz. 1975).

11. *Corne,* 390 F. Supp. at 163.

12. 422 F. Supp. 553 (D.N.J. 1976).

13. *Tomkins,* 422 F. Supp. at 556.

14. 418 F. Supp. 233 (N.D. Cal. 1976).

15. *Miller,* 418 F. Supp. at 234.

16. *Miller,* 418 F. Supp. at 236.

17. 413 F. Supp. 654 (D.D.C. 1976).

18. *Williams,* 413 F. Supp. at 657. This decision was reversed on other grounds in *Williams v. Bell,* 587 F.2d 1240 (D.C. Cir. 1978). The circuit court ruled that the district court judge erred in deciding the case on the basis of the administrative record and should have remanded to the district court for a new trial. On remand, the district court dismissed the supervisor's testimony as incredible and concluded that "submission to the sexual advances of the plaintiff's supervisor was a term and condition of employment in violation of Title VII." *Williams v. Civiletti,* 487 F. Supp. 1387, 1389 (D.D.C. 1980).

19. 561 F.2d 983 (D.C. Cir. 1977).

20. Shortly before *Barnes,* in *Garber v. Saxon Business Products,* 552 F.2d 1032 (4th Cir. 1977), the Fourth Circuit found a Title VII violation when women were required to submit to their superiors' sexual advances.

21. *Barnes,* 561 F.2d at 989–990.

22. 441 F. Supp. 459 (E.D. Mich. 1977).

23. 451 F. Supp. 1382 (D. Colo. 1978).

24. 568 F.2d 1044 (3d Cir. 1977).

25. *Tomkins,* 568 F.2d at 1048–1049.

26. Under the tort doctrine of respondeat superior, employers are held vicariously liable for torts committed by their servants who act within the scope of their employment.

27. *Miller v. Bank of America,* 600 F.2d 211, 213 (9th Cir. 1979).

28. *Miller,* 600 F.2d at 213.

29. EEOC interpretations are not binding on the courts.

30. On April 11, 1980, the EEOC published interim guidelines on sexual harassment as an amendment to the "Guidelines on Discrimination Because of Sex." After a sixty-day public comment period, the agency published the final guidelines as 29 C.F.R. Part 1604.11.

31. 29 C.F.R. § 1604.11(a).

32. 29 C.F.R. § 1604.11(c). This section was removed in 1999 to reflect the Supreme Court's revised approach to employer liability.

33. 29 C.F.R. § 1604.11(d).

34. *Bundy v. Jackson,* 19 Fair Employment Practice Cases, 828, 831 (D.D.C. 1979).

35. *Bundy,* 19 Fair Employment Practice Cases at 831.

36. *Bundy v. Jackson,* 641 F.2d 934, 946 (D.C. Cir. 1981). The Eleventh Circuit allowed a suit for workplace harassment a year later in *Henson v. City of Dundee,* 682 F.2d 897 (11th Cir. 1982), as did the Fourth Circuit the next year in *Katz v. Dole,* 709 F.2d 251 (4th Cir. 1983).

37. 477 U.S. 57 (1986).

38. *Vinson v. Taylor,* 23 Fair Employment Practice Cases, 37 (D.D.C. 1980).

39. *Vinson v. Taylor,* 753 F.2d 141 (D.C. Cir. 1985).

40. *Vinson,* 753 F.2d at 146.

41. Employer liability can be premised on several theories: agency law, tort law, or Title VII law. Title VII, as expressed in legislative intent, offers the broadest protection to workers. The doctrine of respondeat superior used by the *Miller* court arises from tort law. The problem with using tort law is that courts limit the reach of Title VII only to areas where employees can sue in tort. Traditionally, under tort and agency law, employers are exempt from liability when agents act outside the scope of their duty. By equating employers with their agents for purposes of Title VII, Congress indicated an intent to go beyond tort and agency law in assigning employer liability. In *Vinson,* the Supreme Court seemed to have adopted a position somewhere between agency law and Title VII law. Vermeulen, "Sexual Harassment," pp. 17–18.

42. The appellate court explained that the rules were derived from analysis of statutory language and interpretation rather than from common law tort principles of respondeat superior, which exempts employers from liability when the actions of their employers are outside the scope of their employment. *Vinson,* 753 F.2d at 149–152.

43. *Vinson,* 753 F.2d at 151.

44. *Vinson,* 477 U.S. at 64.

45. *Vinson,* 477 U.S. at 72.

46. *Vinson,* 477 U.S. at 77 (emphasis in the original).

47. 760 F. Supp. 1486 (M.D. Fla. 1991).

48. 924 F.2d 872 (9th Cir. 1991).

49. The original five-part formulation for judging sexual harassment complaints based on a hostile environment was articulated in *Henson,* 682 F.2d at 897. The *Henson* court cited the elements of racially based hostile environment cases and rejected the defendant's argument that the suit should be dismissed because the plaintiff had not alleged job-related consequences. The *Henson* test is the most commonly used one in all the circuits. Ann C. Juliano, "Did She Ask for It? The 'Unwelcome' Requirement in Sexual Harassment Cases," *Cornell Law Review* 77 (1992): 1558–1592.

50. Nell J. Medlin, "Expanding the Law of Sexual Harassment to Include Workplace Pornography: *Robinson v. Jacksonville Shipyards, Inc.,*" *Stetson Law Review* 21 (1992): 655–680.

51. Juliano, "Did She Ask for It?" See also Naomi R. Cahn, "The Looseness of Legal Language: The Reasonable Woman Standard in Theory and Practice," *Cornell Law Review* 77 (1992): 1398–1446. Saba Ashraf argues that this standard will hamper the effort to eradicate discrimination in the workplace. See Ashraf, "The Reasonableness of the 'Reasonable Woman' Standard: An Evaluation of Its Use in Hostile Environment Sexual Harassment Claims Under Title VII of the Civil Rights Act," *Hofstra Law Review* 21 (1992): 483–504.

52. Quoted in *Ellison,* 924 F.2d at 876; the lower court opinion is unpublished.

53. *Ellison,* 924 F.2d at 878.

54. *Ellison,* 924 F.2d at 879. In 1988, the EEOC had issued a notice stating that sexual harassment complaints should be judged from the perspective of a sex-neutral "reasonable person." Ashraf, "The Reasonableness of the 'Reasonable Woman' Standard," p. 490.

55. Juliano, "Did She Ask for It?" p. 1572.

56. Thomas became head of the EEOC during the Reagan administration in 1982; in 1990 he was appointed to the twelve-member District of Columbia Circuit Court, where he served until his appointment to the U.S. Supreme Court. Serving on the D.C. Circuit often leads to elevation to the high court.

57. *Congressional Quarterly Weekly,* July 6, 1991, p. 1851.

58. *Congressional Quarterly Weekly,* September 28, 1991, p. 2786.

59. Then-Senator Joseph Biden, Democrat from Delaware and chair of the Senate Judiciary Committee, claimed the committee had not simply ignored Hill's charges but had not revealed them because it promised her confidentiality.

60. See Jane Mayer and Jill Abramson, *Strange Justice: The Selling of Clarence Thomas* (Boston: Houghton Mifflin, 1994), for an account of the Thomas nomination.

61. *Congressional Quarterly Weekly,* October 12, 1991, p. 2948.

62. Forty-one of forty-three Republicans, including the lone woman Republican, Nancy Landon Kassebaum of Kansas, voted for Thomas; they were joined by eleven Democrats, seven from the South. The southern Democrats were concerned about losing support among the African Americans who favored Thomas's appointment.

63. *New York Times,* October 11, 1991.

64. In the *New York Times/CBS News* poll, almost two-thirds of those surveyed of both sexes indicated they believed Hill's charges would have been given more serious consideration had there been more women in the Senate. *New York Times,* October 11, 1991.

65. For a variety of reasons, women were considered attractive candidates and were more heavily recruited by the political parties; they were also more likely to win primary elections. See Clyde Wilcox, "Why Was 1992 the 'Year of the Woman'? Explaining Women's Gains in 1992," in C. Wilcox, S. Thomas, and E. Cook, eds., *The Year of the Woman: Myth or Reality* (Boulder, Colo.: Westview Press, 1994). Factors that may have contributed to women's increased support at the polls were the widely reported rape trials of boxer Mike Tyson and Kennedy nephew William Kennedy Smith, as well as the treatment of women at the naval aviators' Tailhook convention and allegations of sexual harassment of women Senate staffers. See *Congressional Quarterly Weekly,* November 7, 1992, p. 3559. Additionally, 1992 was a bad year for House incumbents, who were tainted by the check-writing and banking scandal; women challengers therefore had great advantages in that election.

66. There were twenty-eight women in the House of Representatives at the time of the Thomas hearings. Forty-eight women took seats in the House of Representatives as a result of the 1992 election. *Congressional Quarterly Almanac,* 1993, p. 4.

67. 510 U.S. 17 (1993).

68. *Harris,* 510 U.S. at 19.

69. *Harris,* 510 U.S. at 22. Without explicitly referring to *Ellison,* the Court adopted both an objective and subjective reasonable person test: "conduct that is not severe or pervasive enough to create an objectively hostile or abusive work environment— an environment that a reasonable person would find hostile or abusive—is beyond Title VII's purview. Likewise, if the victim does not subjectively perceive the environment to be abusive . . . there is no Title VII violation."

70. *Harris,* 510 U.S. at 22.

71. *Harris,* 510 U.S. at 23.

72. O'Connor specifically stated that the Court was not addressing the proposed EEOC regulation that had adopted the "reasonable woman" standard.

73. In "The Sweep of Sexual Harassment Cases," *Cornell Law Review* 86 (2001), pp. 582–584, Ann Juliano and Stewart J. Schwab report that most courts (well over three-quarters of their sample of cases) did not refer to a "reasonable standard" at all; when they did, the vast majority used the "reasonable person" standard. They found that plaintiffs succeeded slightly more often when the courts used the "reasonable woman" standard but concluded that there were too few cases in this category to predict the outcomes.

74. The charge against Clinton became public in February 1994, when Jones held a press conference sponsored by the Conservative Political Action Conference. *The Economist,* January 18, 1997.

75. 457 U.S. 731 (1982).

76. *Nixon,* 457 U.S. at 748.

77. 520 U.S. 681 (1997).

78. *Clinton v. Jones,* 520 U.S. at 708.

79. *Jones v. Clinton,* 990 F. Supp. 657 (E.D. Ark. 1998).

80. *Jones,* 990 F. Supp. at 674.

81. 523 U.S. 75 (1998).

82. 524 U.S. 742 (1998).

83. 524 U.S. 775 (1998).

84. *Washington Post,* December 4, 1997.

85. *Oncale,* 523 U.S. at 81.

86. Juliano and Schwab, in "The Sweep of Sexual Harassment Cases," p. 586, report that most complaints brought by men against heterosexual men lose, whereas

men complaining of harassment by women or homosexual men are as successful as women plaintiffs. Several years after *Oncale,* in *Rene v. MGM Grand Hotel,* 305 F.3d 1061 (9th Cir. 2002), the Ninth Circuit applied *Oncale* to a claim of same-sex harassment brought by a gay employee against a Las Vegas hotel. The plaintiff, Medina Rene, charged that he was sexually harassed by his coworkers and supervisor. The district court ruled against him, finding that he was harassed because of his sexual orientation and not because of his sex and that Title VII's prohibition against sex discrimination was not applicable to discrimination based on sexual orientation. The Ninth Circuit reversed, ruling that Rene had stated a valid claim for hostile environment harassment under Title VII, even though he also charged that the harassment was motivated by hostility toward him because of his sexual orientation. Gays have achieved moderate success when they claimed the harassment arises because they do not conform to gender norms; they have been less successful when they claim the harassment is based on their sexual orientation; see Tanya A. De Vos, "Sexuality and Transgender Issues in Employment Law," *Georgetown Journal of Gender and the Law* 10 (2009): 599–624.

87. Heather S. Murr argues that *Ellerth* and *Faragher* had negative consequences for victims of sexual extortion. Prior to these rulings, employers were held strictly liable for supervisors who engaged in "sexual extortion," a quid pro quo case of sexual harassment in which the employee submitted to the sexual acts to avoid the fulfillment of the supervisor's threats. After *Ellerth* and *Faragher,* the employer would be held vicariously liable for the behavior of the supervisor, but without a tangible job result, would be able to offer the two-part affirmative defense. Thus, after 1998, a company would escape strict liability for sexual extortion by a supervisor if the victim acquiesced and there was no tangible job result. See Murr, "The Continuing Expansive Pressure to Hold Employers Strictly Liable for Supervisory Sexual Extortion," pp. 529–636.

88. Christine Bradshaw notes that before *Ellerth* and *Faragher* were decided, the lower courts divided complaints of harassment into quid pro quo and hostile environment cases. Most found employers liable in cases of harassment by a supervisor, but some were reluctant to impose strict liability on employers even in cases of supervisory harassment, using a negligence standard instead and absolving employers from liability when they did not know (or could not have known) about the harassment. Others required the victim to show that the supervisor acted on authority granted by the employer. See Bradshaw, "A Revised Tangible Employment Action Analysis: Just What Is an Undesirable Reassignment?" *American University Journal of Gender, Social Policy, and the Law* 14 (2006): 385–411.

89. The Burlington vice president was a midlevel manager with authority over hiring and firing decisions.

90. *Ellerth,* 524 U.S. at 748.

91. *Ellerth,* 524 U.S. at 765.

92. Following the intent of Congress, the Court allowed the affirmative defense to encourage employers to protect their employees from sexual harassment. Alexis C. Knapp, "Driving Them Away—the Employee Who Quits in Response to Harassment: The Supreme Court *Suders* Decision—Constructive Discharge and the Affirmative Defense: Reviewing History to Find a Predictable Continuation of Sexual Harassment Jurisprudence and Employer Liability Under Title VII," *Houston Business and Tax Law Journal* 6 (2006): 280–328.

93. U.S. Equal Employment Opportunity Commission, "EEOC Issues Comprehensive Policy Guidance on Employer Liability for Harassment by Supervisors," available at http://www.eeoc.gov/eeoc/newsroom/release/archive/6-21-99.html.

94. In October 1999, another EEOC press release announced that the EEOC issued its "final rule rescinding subsection (c) of its guidelines on sex discrimination and national origin discrimination (29 C.F.R. Parts 1604.11 and 1606.8) to conform with recent Supreme Court rulings on employer liability for harassment by supervisors. The other sections of the guidelines remain in full effect. The deleted section had assigned responsibility to the employer for its acts and those of its agents and supervisory employees with respect to sexual harassment, regardless of whether the specific acts complained of were authorized or even forbidden by the employer and regardless of whether the employer knew or should have known of their occurrence." U.S. Equal Employment Opportunity Commission, "EEOC Updates Guidelines to Comply with Supreme Court Rulings on Employer Liability for Harassment by Supervisors," available at http://www.eeoc.gov/eeoc/newsroom/release/10-29-99.cfm.

95. *New York Times,* June 27, 1998.

96. 542 U.S. 129 (2004).

97. The Third and Eighth Circuits viewed a constructive discharge as a tangible job action; the Second and Sixth Circuits did not. See LeiLani J. Hart, *"Pennsylvania State Police v. Suders:* 124 S. Ct. 2342 (2004)," *American University Journal of Gender, Social Policy, and the Law* 13 (2005): 219–233.

98. Crystal L. Norrick, "Eliminating the Intent Requirement in Constructive Discharge Cases: *Pennsylvania State Police v. Suders,*" *William and Mary Law Review* 47 (2006): 1813–1839.

99. Some circuits required the employee to show that the events leading to the constructive discharge were deliberate; others permitted the employee to show only that it was foreseeable that the employee would resign as a result of the conduct; see Knapp, "Driving Them Away." Norrick, in "Eliminating the Intent Requirement," argues that the Court appeared to have removed the intent requirement.

100. *Suders,* 542 U.S. at 146–147.

101. *Suders,* 542 U.S. at 148. The employer must prove both elements of the *Ellerth* and *Faragher* affirmative defense.

102. 548 U.S. 53 (2006).

103. Lindsay Conway Thomas, *"Burlington Northern & Santa Fe Railroad Co. v. White:* Getting on the Right Track," *Mississippi College Law Review* 27 (2007–2008): 477–500.

104. *White,* 548 U.S. at 58.

105. The importance of Title VII's antiretaliation provision is demonstrated by the number of charges filed with the EEOC claiming retaliation: in FY 2009, the EEOC received 93,277 charges of employment discrimination. Of these, 28,948 (31 percent) were Title VII retaliation claims, and 33,613 (36 percent) were about retaliation more generally. U.S. Equal Employment Opportunity Commission, "Charge Statistics FY 1997 Through FY 2009," available at http://www.eeoc.gov/eeoc/statistics/enforcement/charges.cfm?.

106. The jury found, however, that she had not shown that the reassignment was based on sex discrimination. In defending itself against the retaliation claim, Burlington Northern unsuccessfully argued that the temporary suspension and job reassignment were not sufficiently adverse because her job description remained the same even though the track laborer job was more difficult and she had received all the pay owed her, including overtime pay and benefits, when the suspension was lifted; it also lost on the argument that she had not proven that the suspension and reassignment were related to her complaints to the EEOC. See Kaylin Redman Hart, "Employment Law—Title VII and the Anti-Retaliation Provision—Beyond Employment and the Workplace: The United States Supreme Court Resolves the

Split and Shifts the Balance. *Burlington Northern & Santa Fe Railroad Co. v. White,* 126 S. Ct. 2405 (2006)," *University of Arkansas at Little Rock Law Review* 29 (2007): 569–595.

107. Hart, in "Employment Law—Title VII and the Anti-Retaliation Provision," discusses the steps necessary to prove a Title VII claim of retaliation.

108. Section 704(a) of the 1964 Civil Rights Act, the antiretaliation section, provides: "It shall be an unlawful employment practice for an employer to discriminate against any of his employees or applicants for employment . . . because he has opposed any practice made an unlawful employment practice by this subchapter, or because he has made a charge, testified, assisted, or participated in any manner in an investigation, proceeding, or hearing under this subchapter." 42 U.S.C. § 2000e-3(a). In *Robinson v. Shell Oil Company,* 519 U.S. 337, 346 (1977), the Supreme Court declared that the "primary purpose" of the antiretaliation section was to permit "unfettered access to statutory remedial mechanisms."

109. *White,* 548 U.S. at 60–61.

110. The courts took three approaches to proving a retaliation claim: the Fifth and Eighth Circuits took the most restrictive, requiring the plaintiff to show that the employer's retaliatory action created an "adverse employment action" by affecting such essentials of the job as hiring, firing, and pay. The liberal views of the First, Seventh, Ninth, Eleventh, and D.C. Circuits and the EEOC varied somewhat, but in general, their approach required a plaintiff to point to an adverse action against her that would persuade a reasonable worker not to complain about future violations. The Second, Third, Fourth, and Sixth Circuits required the plaintiff to show an "adverse employment action" but did not define it as narrowly as the Fifth and Eighth Circuits. See Thomas, *"Burlington Northern & Santa Fe Railroad Co.";* Lauren LeGrand, "Proving Retaliation After *Burlington v. White," Saint Louis University Law Journal* 52 (2008): 1221–1247; Ernest F. Lidge, "What Types of Employer Actions Are Cognizable Under Title VII? The Ramifications of *Burlington Northern & Santa Fe Railroad Co. v. White," Rutgers Law Review* 59 (2007): 497–531.

111. *White,* 548 U.S. at 63.

112. *White,* 548 U.S. at 68.

113. Alex B. Long notes that almost all states also have laws against retaliation; he believes that despite the potential drawbacks to this duplication, workers benefit from the added protection. See Long, "Viva State Employment Law! State Law Retaliation Claims in a post–*Crawford/Burlington Northern* World," *Tennessee Law Review* 77 (2010): 253–298.

114. *White,* 548 U.S. at 70.

115. Lidge, in "What Types of Employer Actions Are Cognizable Under Title VII," argues that although the Court resolved some of the conflicts among the circuits, the ruling left open a number of questions, such as the precise relationship between the antiretaliation and substantive provisions of Title VII, the necessary level of severity of the employer's action, and the relationship between *White's* "materially adverse" standard and *Ellerth's* tangible job action standard. Bradshaw's analysis of lower court rulings indicated that the high court needed to clarify whether a transfer to an undesirable assignment constituted a tangible employment action. Bradshaw, "A Revised Tangible Employment Action Analysis."

116. 129 S.Ct. 846 (2009).

117. *New York Times,* January 27, 2009.

118. On June 29, 2010, the Supreme Court agreed to review a Sixth Circuit decision with a narrow interpretation of retaliation. Eric Thompson sued his former

employer for retaliation when it fired him three weeks after his fiancée, who worked for the same company, filed a complaint of sex discrimination against it with the EEOC. Thompson invoked the antiretaliation clause, claiming the company violated Title VII in retaliation for her complaint. The lower courts dismissed his complaint, ruling that he was not covered by the antiretaliation provision.

On January 24, 2011, in *Thompson v. North American Stainless,* 131 S.Ct. 863 (2011), Scalia announced the opinion for a unanimous Court. Conceding the uncertainty of determining which employees fall within the protection of the antiretaliation clause, the Court reiterated the broad interpretation of the clause it had recently announced in *White,* but refused to articulate a definitive standard. Scalia merely said that "a close family member will almost always" fall within the protection of the antiretaliation clause, but "inflicting a milder reprisal on a mere acquaintance will almost never do so" (*Thompson,* 131 S.Ct. at 868). The Court remanded the case to allow the trial court to determine whether his firing was in retaliation for her EEOC complaint and subsequent lawsuit against the company.

119. Three years earlier, the Court allowed a retaliation claim under Title IX in *Jackson,* 544 U.S. at 167. In 2008, the Court had expanded workers' protections under the retaliation clause of the ADEA in *Gomez-Perez v. Potter,* 553 U.S. 474 (2008), and in § 1981 of the 1866 Civil Rights Act in *CBOCS West, Inc. v. Humphries,* 553 U.S. 442 (2008); see Sue Ann Mota and Erin Elisabeth Waldman, "Employers Beware: Retaliation Prohibited by the Court in *Crawford v. Metropolitan Government of Nashville, CBOCS West, Inc. v. Humphries,* and *Gomez-Perez v. Potter,*" *Hamline Law Review* 33 (2010): 1–18. See also Megan E. Mowrey, "Discriminatory Retaliation: Title VII Protection for the Cooperating Employee," *Pace Law Review* 29 (2009): 689–737; John B. Lough, Jr., "Employers Still Cannot Retaliate: *Crawford v. Metropolitan Government of Nashville,*" *Hawaii Bar Journal* 13 (2009): 4–8.

120. *Crawford,* 129 S.Ct. at 852.

121. Mowrey, in "Discriminatory Retaliation: Title VII," argues that workers in Crawford's situation are protected under both clauses.

122. *Crawford,* 129 S.Ct. at 853.

5 Balancing Work and Family

On March 11, 2009, in one of his first actions after taking office, Obama signed an executive order creating a White House Council on Women and Girls. "The purpose of this Council," the president said, "is to ensure that American women and girls are treated fairly in all matters of public policy. . . . I want to be clear," he continued, "that issues like equal pay, family leave, child care, and others are not just women's issues, they are family issues and economic issues." Specifically, one of the aims of the council was "to ensure that the administration evaluates and develops policies that establish a balance between work and family."[1]

In the 1950s, most women entering the workforce were in their middle to late forties, without young children at home.[2] As the number of women in the nation's workforce has increased, so has the number of mothers with small children. In 2008, over three-quarters (77.5 percent) of mothers with children ages six to seventeen were in the labor force. Among mothers with children under six, almost two-thirds (63.6 percent) were in the workforce and 59.6 percent of mothers with children under three were in the labor force.[3] Thus, contrary to the belief that mothers have only tangential ties to the workforce, the "stay-at-home" Mom and working Dad applies to only a minority of two-parent families with children in the United States. In 2009, among families with children under eighteen, less than one-third (29.4 percent) conformed to the traditional image of the family; in contrast, almost two-thirds (58.9 percent) of families with children under eighteen had two wage earners.[4]

One of the Supreme Court's first opportunities to express an opinion about women's maternal roles was in *Muller,* the 1908 decision upholding a law that allowed the state to limit the hours of women laundry workers. The Court explained that the state's concern for women was justified because "healthy mothers are essential to vigorous offspring."[5]

159

The reasoning in *Muller* was eventually rejected, but a number of the Court's later opinions continued to reflect the view that women workers were primarily defined by their childbearing abilities and family roles.[6]

The Supreme Court and Pregnancy Policies

The Court became involved in pregnancy policies in the early 1970s, initially adjudicating challenges to laws restricting opportunities for pregnant women workers. By the early 1990s, its role in shaping pregnancy policies in the United States had greatly diminished. Table 5.1 presents the significant pregnancy policy cases decided by the Court from 1974 to 2009.

In *Cleveland Board of Education v. LaFleur*,[7] the Court considered the lawsuit brought by Jo Carol LaFleur and Ann Nelson. These two Cleveland junior high school teachers were forced out of the classroom because of a district policy requiring pregnant schoolteachers to take leave at least five months before their due date and not return until after their child was three months old; to return to work, women needed a doctor's certificate and, in some cases, a physical examination. Teachers with less than a year of seniority were simply dismissed at the beginning of their fifth month.

With Stewart delivering the majority opinion, the Court held that because the law was based on a presumption that all women were unfit to work after an arbitrarily selected date, it restricted their fundamental

Table 5.1 Supreme Court Rulings in Pregnancy Policy Cases, 1974–2009

Case	Date	Issue[a]	Ruling[b]
LaFleur	1974	Forced pregnancy leave	Expands employee rights
Geduldig	1974	Disability plan	Limits employee rights
Turner	1975	Unemployment compensation	Expands employee rights
Gilbert	1976	Disability plan	Limits employee rights
Satty	1977	Seniority system	Expands employee rights
Newport News	1983	Employees' wives	Expands employee rights
Guerra	1987	Pregnancy leave	Expands employee rights
Wimberly	1987	Unemployment compensation	Limits employee rights
Johnson Controls	1991	Fetal protection	Expands employee rights
Hulteen	2009	Retroactive benefits	Limits employee rights

Notes: a. Based on the major issue in the case.
b. Based on the overall outcome of the case.

freedom of choice in matters of marriage and family. Because the teachers were given no opportunity to present contrary medical evidence, the maternity leave policy "sweep[s] too broadly" and violates the Fourteenth Amendment's due process clause.[8] Stewart rejected the school district's argument that it was too burdensome to make "individualized" determinations of fitness for every teacher, saying administrative convenience cannot be used to justify a due process violation.

A year later, in *Turner v. Department of Employment Security*,[9] the Court considered whether the due process clause prevented Utah from denying pregnant women unemployment benefits from twelve weeks before the expected date of their delivery to six weeks after the birth of their child. Mary Ann Turner lost her job in November 1972 and collected unemployment benefits until March 1973, twelve weeks before her child was due. Like most states, Utah's unemployment compensation law required recipients to be capable of working. Also, as in most states, Utah law precluded pregnancy benefits for women workers for a period of time during and shortly after their pregnancy. Citing *LaFleur,* the Court held that the Utah statute also violated due process because it presumed that all women were unfit to work during the latter stages of pregnancy.

Despite the gains women made in *LaFleur* and *Turner,* the Court did not rule out the possibility that employers could impose special restrictions on pregnant women as long as the policies were not based on presumptions about women as a group and provided an opportunity for a woman to present evidence of her fitness for work.[10]

In the 1970s, women began to challenge pregnancy exclusions in disability insurance policies that compelled them and their families to bear all the economic and social costs of pregnancy. The Supreme Court rejected their claims of discrimination, subordinating gender equality in the workplace to the employer's cost considerations. *Geduldig v. Aiello,*[11] a 1974 ruling, represented the Court's initial reaction to pregnancy and disability benefits. The California disability insurance plan provided up to twenty-six weeks of payments to private sector employees. It was self-supporting and financed by contributions of 1 percent of workers' salaries (up to a maximum of $85 a year). Under the plan, employees were protected against loss of income arising from a wide variety of mental and physical disorders; virtually the only excluded condition was pregnancy.

Four women filed suit, charging the state with violating the Fourteenth Amendment's equal protection clause.[12] The state argued that providing disability benefits to pregnant women would jeopardize the fiscal integrity of the plan and that excluding pregnancy benefits allowed the plan to remain solvent and provide comprehensive coverage to employees at all levels of income. Including normal pregnancy within the plan, it insisted, would be "extraordinarily expensive" and force a drastic restructuring of the program—either by raising the contribution rate or reducing benefits.[13]

With Stewart announcing the opinion, the Court held that the exclusion was based on pregnancy, not sex; subjecting the law to the minimal scrutiny normally accorded economic and social welfare legislation, it found that the policy was rationally related to the state's interest in maintaining the plan under its current fiscal constraints.

The most memorable part of the decision was Stewart's discussion of pregnancy as a unique physical characteristic unrelated to sex. In the widely quoted Footnote 20, he declared that the California plan is not a sex-based classification because the state was merely selecting from among risks; it was justified in omitting the risk of pregnancy because of its unique features. To substantiate the fact that sex was not used as the basis for dividing potential beneficiaries, he explained that "there is no risk from which men are protected and women are not. Likewise, there is no risk from which women are protected and men are not."[14] Acknowledging that "only women can become pregnant," he denied the link between pregnancy and sex. Sex was not at issue, Stewart said, because the California scheme "divided potential recipients into two groups—pregnant women and nonpregnant persons. Although the first group is exclusively female, the second includes members of both sexes."[15] Because there were no differences in benefits available to nonpregnant persons, the plan does not discriminate on the basis of sex, even though all pregnant persons are women. Thus, Footnote 20 conveniently disposed of the confluence between pregnancy and sex.

Brennan's dissent criticized the majority for ignoring the obvious connection between pregnancy and sex. He found Stewart's logic unpersuasive because, in his view, pregnancy discrimination equated to sex discrimination. He argued the Court should have applied the strict scrutiny approach urged by the four-justice plurality in *Frontiero* a year earlier and that the state's desire to maintain the fiscal status quo did not justify excluding pregnancy benefits. Brennan reminded the Court that the disability program was intended to serve "broad humanitarian goals," providing a wide range of benefits for costly disabilities (like heart attacks), voluntary disabilities (like cosmetic surgery and sterilization), sex- and race-specific disabilities (like prostatitis and sickle-cell anemia), preexisting conditions (like arthritis or cataracts), and so-called normal disabilities (like impacted wisdom teeth). By singling out pregnancy disability, he said, the state limited benefits for disabilities pertinent to women but placed no restrictions on benefits for disabilities pertinent to men. "In effect," he charged, "one set of rules is applied to females and another to males."[16] Differentiating between men and women on the basis of a physical characteristic unique to one sex, Brennan insisted, is sex discrimination, a reality that is not altered by the fact that the characteristic is not found among all members of the affected sex. Brennan also pointed out that the Court's decision contradicted the EEOC's 1972 guidelines on pregnancy benefits.[17]

The most enduring effect of the *Geduldig* decision was the Court's surprising declaration of the distinction between pregnancy and sex. But in addition to the Court's verbal gymnastics, a more serious indictment is that the opinion indicated the Court's cavalier attitude toward women. By ignoring the effect of excluding pregnancy from employee disability plans, the Court failed to challenge the stereotypical view of women as marginal workers with loose ties to the workforce.[18]

Plaintiffs also challenged the pregnancy exclusion policies under Title VII, seemingly a wiser choice for a number of reasons. First, unlike the equal protection doctrine, in which a state may justify its policy on the basis of cost, Title VII does not allow employers to argue cost as a defense.[19] Second, an equal protection challenge requires evidence of intentional discrimination, in contrast to Title VII, where plaintiffs can succeed by showing that the pregnancy exclusion has an adverse impact upon women. Of course, if the Court continued to believe that singling out pregnancy does not implicate sex, Title VII challenges would also be unsuccessful.[20]

Ironically, despite *Geduldig,* women made progress in other states. Through statutes, state court rulings, and opinions of state attorneys general, several states included pregnancy benefits within disability insurance plans.[21] Based on its 1972 guidelines, the EEOC supported the principle that Title VII required pregnancy to be treated like other disabilities that keep workers off the job. Most lower federal courts agreed and refused to apply *Geduldig* to Title VII suits. By 1976, six circuits and eighteen district courts ruled that *Geduldig* only controlled in equal protection cases. In accordance with the EEOC guidelines, these courts held that a pregnancy exclusion violated Title VII's ban on sex discrimination.[22]

In *General Electric Company v. Gilbert,*[23] decided in 1976, the Supreme Court ruled on whether Title VII allowed employers to exclude pregnancy from company disability plans. General Electric's disability plan covered employees for a wide array of diseases, disabilities, and illnesses regardless of their effect, voluntariness, predictability, or cost. Moreover, as in the California plan upheld in *Geduldig,* the policy allowed benefits for conditions unique to men such as circumcisions, vasectomies, and prostatectomies. It excluded only disabilities arising from pregnancy, miscarriage, or childbirth, excluding as well any unrelated illnesses that appeared during pregnancy. Women sued General Electric, arguing that the pregnancy exclusion contravened the 1972 EEOC guidelines and violated Title VII.

General Electric presented a "cost differential defense," contending that it was spending at least as much on female employees as male employees and that adding pregnancy-related costs would significantly raise the cost of its disability insurance plan. The lower courts refused to accept this defense, ruling that it conflicted with Title VII's promise of equal opportunity in the workplace.[24]

Echoing *Geduldig*, Rehnquist announced the 6 to 3 majority opinion, once again drawing a distinction between pregnancy and sex. Quoting extensively from *Geduldig*, he said that General Electric's plan did not differentiate on the basis of sex because both men and women belonged to the class of nonpregnant persons. The case was about the classification of risks, and the plan covered both men and women for risks they shared in common. Removing pregnancy from the covered risks, he maintained, even though it only affected women, did not conflict with Title VII's prohibition of sex discrimination. Brushing aside evidence of the company's history of discriminating against women, the Court held that because pregnancy was sufficiently different from other disabilities, the company was entitled to treat it differently without violating Title VII. Rehnquist declared that

> discrimination does not result simply because an employer's disability-benefits plan is less than all-inclusive. For all that appears, pregnancy-related disabilities constitute an *additional* risk, unique to women, and the failure to compensate them for this risk does not destroy the presumed parity of the benefits accruing to men and women alike, which results from the facially evenhanded *inclusion* of risks.[25]

He also pointed out that the EEOC's 1972 guidelines were issued eight years after Title VII was enacted and they contradicted the agency's first guidelines on pregnancy disability benefits, which were promulgated only two years after the law was passed.

Stevens dissented, pointing out that pregnancy is not sex-neutral because "it is the capacity to become pregnant which primarily differentiates the female from the male." In a footnote, he rejected the Court's reliance on *Geduldig*'s classification of "pregnant women and nonpregnant persons." The proper distinction "is between persons who face a risk of pregnancy and those who do not."[26]

As in *Geduldig*, by refusing to equate pregnancy with other medical conditions necessitating brief interruptions from work and placing the burden of pregnancy solely on women and their families, the Court once again denigrated the importance of women's role in the workforce.

Nashville Gas Company v. Satty,[27] decided a year after *Gilbert*, involved a suit against a company policy that required women to take pregnancy leave but denied them disability benefits and their accumulated seniority when they returned to work. The plaintiff claimed the policy was discriminatory because she was being treated differently from employees who were absent from work for other reasons; they not only retained their seniority but continued to accrue it during the time away from the job.

With Rehnquist again delivering the majority opinion, the Court held that the seniority policy violated Title VII. This case was unlike *Gilbert*, he said, because there had been no evidence that General Electric's policy "favored men over women." In contrast, Nashville Gas "has not merely refused to extend to women a benefit that men cannot and do not receive, but has imposed on women a substantial burden that men need not suffer."[28] However, because the disability plan was virtually identical to the one upheld in *Gilbert*, the majority rejected the claim that it violated Title VII.[29]

Shortly after the Court approved General Electric's disability plan, a coalition of more than 300 groups, called the Campaign to End Discrimination Against Pregnant Workers, formed to lobby Congress to reverse the Court's decision. The campaign was dominated by union groups but also included members of NOW, the National Women's Political Caucus, and the Women's Equity Action League.[30]

The Pregnancy Discrimination Act

Both chambers of Congress reacted to *Gilbert* by introducing legislation to reverse it. On October 31, 1978, Carter signed the PDA into law; its passage had been held up because of differences between the House and Senate over anti-abortion language.[31]

As an amendment to Title VII, the law applied to employers with at least fifteen employees.[32] Reversing *Gilbert*, it equated discrimination on the basis of pregnancy with discrimination on the basis of sex and required employers to treat pregnancy-related disabilities the same as other temporary disabilities. The House committee report accompanying the bill emphasized that *Gilbert* was wrongly decided and "the dissenting Justices correctly interpreted the Act."[33]

At the time the PDA passed, less than half the states required disability coverage for pregnant women, primarily through state fair employment practices laws.[34] By providing a uniform interpretation of employment discrimination on the basis of pregnancy, the PDA's sponsors hoped it would end this piecemeal approach.

In enacting the PDA, Congress adopted an evenhanded approach to pregnancy, requiring employers to treat it as a condition that temporarily interrupted work and include it within their disability or sick leave policies. The PDA thus removed a significant impediment to women's full participation in the workforce but did not meet the needs of all women workers because it did not apply to women whose employers provided no disability insurance benefits to their employees.

The legislative history of the PDA suggests that Congress broadly envisioned it as an attempt to achieve greater parity between the sexes in the workforce. One of its Senate cosponsors, Democrat Alan Cranston of California, described the act as "fully compatible with the underlying objectives of Title VII to assure equality of employment opportunity and to eliminate those discriminatory practices which pose barriers to working women in their struggle to secure equality in the workplace."[35]

More than thirty years after the PDA's passage, some scholars wonder whether "modern workplace realities measure up to the lofty goals underlying the legislation," and although they acknowledge that the act made discrimination on the basis of pregnancy unlawful, they believe "we are still working through the ultimate contours and effect of that prohibition to this day."[36]

Despite the passage of the PDA and its ban on pregnancy discrimination, the EEOC received slightly more than 6,000 complaints of discrimination on the basis of pregnancy during FY 2009; the monetary benefits from those complaints, not counting litigation awards, totaled almost $17 million.[37] According to the National Partnership for Women and Families, discrimination on the basis of pregnancy is on the rise, especially among women of color. The organization reports that complaints about pregnancy discrimination increased by 65 percent in the fifteen years between 1992 and 2007. Most of the discrimination charges arise in predominantly female industries.[38]

Ironically, the Supreme Court's first PDA case, *Newport News Shipbuilding and Dry Dock Company v. EEOC*,[39] was brought by a man, John McNulty, who complained that the company provided more extensive pregnancy benefits for female employees than for the wives of male employees.

In September 1979, McNulty filed a discrimination charge with the EEOC; a month later, the United Steelworkers Union filed one on behalf of the other male employees in the shipbuilding company. The company responded with an action in federal court against McNulty, the EEOC, and the union, arguing that the less favorable pregnancy coverage for employees' wives did not violate the PDA because the law was intended to apply to women employees only.[40]

The Court disagreed, denying that the PDA was aimed at protecting women employees only. It stressed that the law's neutral approach barred employers from treating pregnancy differently from other medical conditions. Speaking for the Court, Stevens said, "For all Title VII purposes, discrimination based on a woman's pregnancy is, on its face, discrimination because of her sex."[41] The Court held that the disability plan was illegal because, by discriminating on the basis of pregnancy, it was inconsistent with congressional intent.

Preferential Treatment

A new debate over pregnancy policy emerged with the passage of the PDA. After their success in the struggle against pregnancy discrimination in disability, seniority, pensions, sick leave, and unemployment compensation, women's rights advocates soon found themselves divided over whether company policies must take pregnancy into account. The debate arose because of concerns that the PDA's nondiscrimination principle fails to acknowledge that pregnant working women have needs that differentiate them from other employees.

The controversy over the status of pregnancy in the workplace is fueled by ambiguities in the PDA. Intended to prohibit discrimination, the statute requires pregnancy to be treated like other disabilities. However, in reversing *Gilbert,* Congress stressed that it was also concerned about the financial burdens of pregnancy on women that impeded equality in the workplace. But the act did not spell out if it prohibited state laws mandating preferential treatment for pregnant women, tolerated them, or required them.

The Supreme Court again became involved in pregnancy policy in *California Federal Savings and Loan v. Guerra,*[42] a 1987 ruling that reflects society's ambivalence toward pregnancy and working women.

A number of states, such as Montana, Connecticut, and Massachusetts, enacted legislation requiring employers to allow pregnant women reasonable time off during pregnancy and to protect their jobs until they return.[43] California followed the lead of these states by enacting the Pregnancy Disability Leave Law (PDL) in September 1978. The California law compelled employers with five or more employees to provide women up to four months of unpaid pregnancy leave with a qualified guarantee of reinstatement. The sponsor of the legislation in the California State Assembly, Majority Leader Howard Berman, explained that denying pregnancy benefits "had potentially devastating economic consequences for millions of working women."[44]

Lillian Garland worked as a receptionist for the California Federal Savings and Loan Association for a number of years. The bank allowed employees to take unpaid leaves of absence for disabilities, including pregnancy, but it specified that it retained the right to discharge them if there were no similar positions available when they wanted to return to work.

When Garland became pregnant, she took leave, intending to return to work. When she tried to reclaim her job after eight weeks, she discovered that the bank had hired her replacement and there were no openings in similar positions. As a single mother, the loss of her job exemplified the devastating consequences that can arise when employees lack legal protection.[45]

Her complaint to the California Fair Housing and Employment Commission, the agency charged with enforcing civil rights, claimed that the bank violated California law by discharging her. But before the commission acted, the bank, joined by the Merchants and Manufacturers Association and the California Chamber of Commerce, filed suit in federal court, arguing that the California law (the PDL) favored women and was therefore inconsistent with the nondiscrimination principle of the federal law (the PDA). The district court sided with the bank, agreeing that by privileging women workers, the PDL conflicted with the PDA.[46]

Under the supremacy clause of the U.S. Constitution, a state law is preempted if it conflicts with a federal law, "either because 'compliance with both federal and state regulations is a physical impossibility' . . . or because the state law stands 'as an obstacle to the accomplishment and execution of the full purposes and objectives of Congress.'"[47]

The Ninth Circuit reversed the lower court, ruling that the PDA did not preempt the state law because the federal law set a minimum standard as "a floor beneath which pregnancy disability benefits may not drop—not a ceiling above which they may not rise."[48] The Supreme Court was asked to decide whether the California preferential treatment law conflicted with the PDA's nondiscrimination principle, in other words, whether the PDA preempted the California law.

The resolution of the preemption issue had far-reaching implications for pregnancy policy. If Title VII preempted the California law, all state preferential treatment laws would be considered illegal. But if the PDL could be reconciled with the nondiscrimination policy of the PDA, states would be free to follow California's lead and recognize the special needs of working pregnant women—at a minimum—through leaves of absence and assurances of job reinstatement.

The PDA specifies that it does not preempt a state law unless the state statute "purports to require or permit the doing of any act which would be an unlawful employment practice under this title," in other words, if it violates Title VII. With Marshall announcing the opinion, the Court rejected the bank's argument that by mandating pregnancy leaves, the law conflicts with the PDA's nondiscrimination policy. He articulated an expansive interpretation of the PDA, saying it does not "require" preferential treatment but neither does it "prohibit" it because Congress was aware of existing state preferential treatment statutes when deliberating passage of the PDA, and there was no indication that it intended to ban them.

Recalling the legislative history of Title VII, Marshall pointed out that it and, by extension, the PDA were aimed at allowing women to "'participate fully and equally in the workforce, without denying them the fundamental right to full participation in family life.'"[49] He endorsed the Ninth Circuit view that the PDA is "a floor beneath which pregnancy disability benefits may not drop—not a ceiling above which they may not rise."[50]

The California law has the same objective as the PDA, he said. "By 'taking pregnancy into account,' California's pregnancy disability-leave statute allows women, as well as men, to have families without losing their jobs."[51] Finally, he pointed out that because it was possible for an employer to comply with both laws at the same time by merely extending disability leaves and promises of reinstatement to all workers, there was no conflict between the two statutes and Title VII did not preempt the California law.

Concurring opinions by Stevens and Scalia expressed concern that the ruling would be interpreted as giving blanket approval to all state preferential treatment laws. Stevens cautioned that "the Court has not yet had occasion to explore the exact line of demarcation between permissible and impermissible preferential treatment under Title VII."[52]

Writing in dissent, White emphasized that the language of the PDA "leaves no room for preferential treatment of pregnant workers."[53] And, he added, the legislative history clearly supports his interpretation. He pointed out that Congress had been concerned with discrimination against pregnant women and had not considered the possibility of discrimination in their favor. Congressional silence on preferential treatment, he maintained, "cannot fairly be interpreted to abrogate the plain statements in the legislative history, not to mention the language of the statute, that equality of treatment was to be the guiding principle of the PDA."[54]

In *Wimberly v. Labor and Industrial Relations Commission,*[55] decided shortly after *Guerra,* the Court seemed to reverse course and shy away from a preferential treatment approach to pregnancy. Upon returning from her pregnancy leave, Linda Wimberly was told there were no positions available at J. C. Penney, her employer of three years; the store had granted her pregnancy leave but had made no commitment to reinstate her. When she applied for unemployment compensation, her claim was denied because she had left work voluntarily. Under Missouri law, unemployment compensation was only available to persons who quit their jobs for "good cause," that is, reasons related to the job or the employer. Leaving for any other reason, including childbirth, was not considered "good cause."

Wimberly argued that Missouri law contravened the 1935 Federal Unemployment Tax Act (FUTA), which prohibited states from denying unemployment compensation "solely on the basis of pregnancy or termination of pregnancy." She contended that FUTA required states to accommodate women who were unemployed because of pregnancy.[56]

Upholding the Missouri law in an 8 to 0 decision, the Court ruled that FUTA was intended "only to prohibit States from singling out pregnancy for unfavorable treatment."[57] With pregnancy only one of any number of reasons for denying a claim, the state could withhold her benefits without even knowing about her pregnancy.[58] Thus, because Missouri's statute is not aimed at workers who leave their jobs for pregnancy but encompasses all who leave for any reason other than "good cause," it does not conflict with FUTA.

Speaking for the Court, O'Connor pointed out that because FUTA allows states a great deal of discretion to determine eligibility for unemployment compensation benefits, state laws will vary. By banning pregnancy discrimination, FUTA was intended to forbid unemployment compensation schemes like the one in Utah, which the Court struck in *Turner.* It was not intended to obligate a state to accommodate a worker's pregnancy. The language in FUTA, she explained, should be construed "as prohibiting disadvantageous treatment, rather than as mandating preferential treatment."[59]

In her brief to the Supreme Court, Wimberly had argued that "the word 'solely' in the statute means that a state cannot 'deny compensation to an *otherwise eligible* woman' who 'left her job because of pregnancy.'"[60] But by construing FUTA narrowly, the Court held that states are permitted to deny unemployment benefits to women who leave work because of pregnancy.

The Supreme Court's ruling disagreed with a 1981 Fourth Circuit opinion, *Brown v. Porcher,*[61] in which the circuit court ruled that FUTA prohibits states from denying unemployment benefits to "otherwise eligible" pregnant women who leave their jobs and are able to return to work after childbirth. The appellate court held that it does not matter how the state deals with the claims of other disabled workers; it cannot deny benefits to women who are unable to work solely because of pregnancy.[62] However, in *Wimberly,* the high court chose to disregard the fact that the state unemployment compensation scheme has a disproportionate effect on women "who leave work to have children or who are forced to become unemployed due to pregnancy."[63] As in *Geduldig,* the Court refused to recognize society's responsibility to working women, subordinating equality in the workplace to the state's overriding interest in its fiscal policy.

Passage of the PDA touched off a new round of controversy about whether the law requires pregnancy to be accorded preferential treatment and mandates benefits for pregnant women that are unavailable to other employees. The high court left this question open by ruling that the PDA permits preferential treatment but does not require it.

The question was also addressed by the Montana Supreme Court in ruling on the validity of the 1975 Montana Maternity Leave Act (MMLA), a law that prohibited employers from firing women because of pregnancy and required them to allow women "a reasonable leave of absence." Tamara Buley was hired as a sales clerk in the Three Sisters store owned by Miller-Wohl in 1979. During her first month, she started missing work because of pregnancy-related morning sickness. Company policy entitled all full-time employees with one year of seniority to five paid days of sick leave per year and unpaid leaves of absence for longer periods. Because she was not eligible for any leave, she was fired for her absences. There was no evidence that the company treated her differently from the way it treated men who failed to appear for work. Buley filed a complaint with the Montana Labor and Industry Commission, claiming her employer violated the MMLA. After a hearing, the commission agreed.

The company reacted to her suit by filing an action in federal court, arguing that the MMLA violated the equal protection clause of the Fourteenth Amendment because it granted benefits to pregnant women that are not accorded to disabled men. The district court disagreed, saying that, on the contrary, by removing "pregnancy-related disabilities as a legal grounds for discharge from employment, the MMLA places men and women on more equal terms."[64]

Ironically, the court cited *Geduldig*'s reasoning that a pregnancy classification differs from a sex-based classification. Although it appears aimed at women only, the court stated, the intent of the law was neutral as to sex because the legislature recognized that in many families both parents are employed. The statute therefore "protect[s] the right of husband and wife, man and woman alike, to procreate and raise a family without sacrificing the right of the wife to work and help support the family after her pregnancy."[65]

The court held that the PDA did not preempt the Montana law because the latter did not require employers to violate the federal law. Rather, they could easily comply with both statutes by allowing reasonable leave time to first-year employees of both sexes who miss work for disability-related reasons. Miller-Wohl appealed, and the Ninth Circuit Court of Appeals dismissed the case.[66]

When Miller-Wohl challenged the commissioner's decision in the Montana state court, the court ruled that the MMLA was discriminatory because it favored nondisabled pregnant employees over disabled nonpregnant women and disabled men and was preempted by the PDA. On appeal to the state supreme court, the state, supported by briefs from California and California women's rights organizations, urged the court to uphold the MMLA, arguing that preferential treatment is consistent with Title VII. In a joint brief, the ACLU, NOW, and the League of Women Voters argued that the MMLA was inconsistent with the PDA and asked the court to order it extended to all workers. Miller-Wohl simply argued that the MMLA was invalid because it was preempted by the PDA.[67]

Announcing its decision in December 1984, the Montana high court upheld the state commission, finding Miller-Wohl's no-leave rule "facially neutral" yet "subject[ing] pregnant women to job termination on a basis not faced by men."[68] Therefore, notwithstanding the MMLA, Miller-Wohl's policy violated the PDA because it had a disparate impact on women. Additionally, the court ruled, the purpose of the PDA and the MMLA was to promote equality between the sexes, and employers could effectuate both laws by simply extending leaves to first-year employees of both sexes. Because they could be reconciled, the PDA did not preempt the MMLA.

The Montana court also delivered a message to the Montana legislature, which was scheduled to meet shortly. It suggested that further debate over preferential treatment of pregnancy could be halted if the legislature followed its suggestion and expanded the provisions of the MMLA to temporarily disabled employees of either sex.

On appeal to the U.S. Supreme Court, the high court vacated the state supreme court decision without explanation and remanded the case to the state court for reconsideration in light of its decision in *Guerra*.[69] Confessing uncertainty about why the case was remanded, the state court noted that *Guerra* reinforced its view that the MMLA was not preempted by the PDA. The court reinstated its earlier judgment in Buley's favor.[70]

These cases suggest that the Court is hesitant about articulating a consistent approach to pregnancy in the workplace. Its rulings range from minimally endorsing the preferential treatment law in *Guerra* to refusing to express an opinion on the more far-reaching maternity leave policy in *Miller-Wohl* to narrowly construing the federal statute banning discrimination on the basis of pregnancy in *Wimberly*. Perhaps the Court's interpretation of the PDA reflects society's ambivalence toward working women and their families.

Feminists are divided about the wisdom of preferential treatment for pregnancy.[71] Concerned about its implications, some argue that legislation such as the MMLA renews visions of protectionist laws finally laid to rest in the early days of Title VII litigation. Others argue that ignoring pregnancy denigrates women's roles as workers and that society must intervene to help women overcome inequities in the workforce caused by pregnancy.[72]

Joan Williams and Nancy Segal sum up the controversy by asking "whether workplaces will continue to be designed around the bodies and life patterns of men, with 'accommodations' offered to women, or whether workplace norms will be redesigned to take into account the reproductive biology and social roles of women and family caregivers, as well." In their view, "equality is not achieved when women are offered equal opportunity to live up to ideals framed around men. True equality requires new norms that take into account the characteristics— both social and biological—of women."[73]

Fetal Protection Policies

During the 1970s, women began to enter into the higher-paying industrial jobs that had traditionally been closed to them.[74] Some of this work necessitated possible risks to their unborn children from "hazardous" or "toxic" chemicals. In response, employers adopted so-called fetal protection policies that barred women from exposure to such materials unless they provided evidence of their infertility. Defending themselves in the Title VII suits brought against them, the employers argued that they were justified in banning women of childbearing age.

The rhetoric used to justify the policies proclaimed employers as champions of worker and fetal safety, with women portrayed as selfishly pursuing their narrow economic interests. "By couching the debate in terms of the protection of the health and safety of pregnant women and their children, major corporations . . . won the support of a wide range of people in state government, the business and medical communities and some labor unions."[75]

Many believe that these policies resemble outdated protectionist laws because they "reinforce the perception of women as marginal workers and stereotype women as nurturers first and workers second."[76] Critics claim they harm women in a number of ways: (1) they are more likely to be aimed at women working in higher-paying industrial jobs, where they can easily be replaced by men, than at women in lower-paying jobs where women predominate, even when the risks of the job are comparable; (2) they are more likely to be aimed at women rather than men, even if the risks of harm to the adults and their offspring are alike; and (3) they reduce the employer's incentive to decrease workplace hazards.[77]

Others acknowledge the undisputed risks to pregnant women from toxic chemicals in the workplace and argue that such policies justifiably seek to avoid harm to the next generation. They urge, for example, that women be allowed to move out of high-risk jobs during their pregnancies or in contemplation of pregnancy.[78]

Workers challenged the sex-specific fetal protection policies, claiming they violated Title VII and the PDA. More narrowly, they asked the courts to decide whether, as the employers argued, the exclusion was justified on the basis of business necessity (it "bears a demonstrable relationship to successful performance of the jobs for which it is used") or a BFOQ (it is "reasonably necessary to the normal operation of that particular business"). Under traditional Title VII analysis, the less stringent business necessity defense is used in disparate impact cases; the more difficult (for the employer) BFOQ defense is used in disparate treatment cases in which the policy is discriminatory on its face, that is, there is an explicit sex-based classification.

Several circuits ruled on the Title VII challenges to fetal protection policies.[79] However, despite the explicit references to sex in the policies, the courts assessed them under a disparate impact analysis. This approach allowed the employers to argue—in some cases, successfully—that fear for the health of the employee's fetus constituted a business necessity.

Johnson Controls, based in Milwaukee, Wisconsin, manufactured car batteries, a job that involved exposure to lead, causing potential harm to the fetus. Prior to Title VII's ban on sex discrimination, the company simply excluded women from such jobs. For a period of time after Title VII became law, it merely warned women of the possible danger of lead exposure. In 1982, it reinstated its policy of exclusion, restricting all women of childbearing age from working in areas where they would be exposed to high levels of lead, excepting only those who could provide medical evidence that they were unable to bear children. The union sued, arguing that because lead can be transmitted through both parents, it was wrong to bar only women from the lead-exposed areas. It also claimed that most women did not get pregnant, and the company had an obligation to eliminate or decrease the risk of fetal harm in the workplace.[80]

In *International Union, United Auto Workers v. Johnson Controls,*[81] decided in 1989, the Seventh Circuit followed the lead of the other circuits and established a modified business necessity defense as the appropriate measure with which to balance the interests of the employer, the employee, and the fetus. The three-part test for the business necessity defense inquired whether there is a substantial health risk to the fetus, whether it is only transmittable through the woman, and whether there is an equally effective nondiscriminatory policy that serves the employer's business interests, in this case, avoiding harm to the fetus.

Applying the three-part test, the circuit court ruled in favor of Johnson Controls for several reasons: (1) both sides agreed on the risk of harm to the fetus through lead exposure, (2) the plaintiffs had not presented sufficient evidence to show that the father's exposure to lead harmed the fetus, (3) the plaintiffs had not offered an equally effective alternative policy.[82] The court held that Johnson Controls thereby satisfied the business necessity defense.

Turning to the BFOQ defense, the court also ruled for the company. It broadly held that industrial safety was part of the "essence" of the business and that the fetal protection plan was "reasonably necessary" to promote it. The court believed that the company's interest in avoiding the risk of birth defects outweighed the woman's right to self-determination in the workplace. Indeed, it seemed to disapprove of the plaintiffs for their willingness to risk their "unborn child's life" to further their own economic interests.[83]

Judge Richard Easterbrook argued in dissent that because the policy was sex-specific, it must be analyzed under the disparate treatment approach, restricting the employer to the BFOQ defense only. And in his view, the defense failed because the employer's concern for fetal health was unrelated to the job of making batteries. Posner, another dissenter, agreed that it was a disparate treatment case, requiring the employer to offer a BFOQ defense. But he believed that a serious concern with tort liability might constitute a BFOQ that would allow a company to exclude women from certain positions or require sterility as a condition of employment. Charging that women were being "protected" out of jobs for their own good, women's rights advocates warned that unless the decision were reversed by the high court, "it will institutionalize the second-class employment status of all fertile women."[84]

In 1990, the Sixth Circuit contradicted the prevailing view of the circuits by holding, in *Grant v. General Motors Corporation,*[85] that the company's fetal protection policy discriminated against women of childbearing age. It criticized the other circuits for ignoring the language and intent of Title VII and the PDA. However, although it agreed with the dissent in *Johnson Controls,* the court refused to categorically rule out all fetal protection policies.

The Supreme Court's ruling in *International Union, United Auto Workers v. Johnson Controls,*[86] in 1991, resolved the conflict among the circuits about the proper framework for the Title VII analysis. Writing for a unanimous Court, Blackmun declared that "the bias in Johnson Control's policy is obvious. Fertile men, but not fertile women, are given a choice as to whether they wish to risk their reproductive health for a particular job."[87] Because it was facially discriminatory, the Court ruled the company was required to satisfy the more stringent BFOQ defense. Consistent with Title VII case law, the Court interpreted the BFOQ narrowly, requiring the company to show that ensuring fetal safety "went to the core of the employee's job performance" or "involved the central purpose of the enterprise."[88]

Acknowledging that Johnson Controls exhibited "deep social concern" for fetal safety, the Court did not accept it as "an essential element of batterymaking."[89] Blackmun declared that

> Johnson's Controls professed moral and ethical concerns about the welfare of the next generation do not suffice to establish a BFOQ of female sterility. Decisions about the welfare of future children must be left to the parents who conceive, bear, support, and raise them rather than to the employers who hire those parents.[90]

He concluded that that was Congress's intention in enacting Title VII and the PDA. Ultimately, the company could not satisfy the BFOQ test because there was no evidence that fertile women were less capable than men of working safely and effectively in producing batteries. The Court did not rule out the possibility that tort liability could be a BFOQ, but believed it unlikely that the employer would be liable if it conformed to federal work safety guidelines and warned workers of the risk involved.[91]

Four of the justices agreed that the company had not met the requirements of the BFOQ defense but were unwilling to go as far as Blackmun and the others in defining its scope. They believed that the manufacturer could argue that it had a valid BFOQ if it could show there was a high risk that it might be liable to the fetus.[92] Under this analysis, an employer's concern for incurring a substantial cost in a lawsuit could justify infertility as a BFOQ.

In ruling against the company's fetal protection policy and telling women they were free to decide to further their economic interests, the Court reflected the nondiscrimination principle of Title VII and the PDA. However, the decision leaves unanswered questions about the employer's (and the government's) responsibility to ensure a safer workplace for this generation of workers as well as the next. Moreover, it also raises concerns about whether the equal treatment approach that simply allows women to coexist in the workplace with men is adequate for the special needs of pregnancy. It removes the company's obligation to accommodate pregnant women who choose not to risk harming their fetus by working in potentially hazardous areas.[93]

The PDA and Retroactivity

Almost two decades later, with the urging of the Bush administration, the Court agreed to review another PDA case with roots going back to the decade before the PDA was enacted.

Noreen Hulteen and three other women working at AT&T had taken maternity leave between 1968 and 1976, before the PDA protected them from job discrimination. At the time, the company considered pregnancy leave as "personal" time away from the job. Employees on disability leave accrued full service credit for the entire time of their absence; however, employees on leave for "personal reasons," which included pregnancy, were limited to a maximum of thirty days of credit, even if they became disabled while on pregnancy leave for non-pregnancy-related reasons.

Additionally, pregnant women were often required to take pregnancy leave at the company's option, rather than their own choice.[94]

In 1977, AT&T adopted a Maternity Payment Plan policy that granted pregnant employees maximum credit benefits of thirty days before delivery and six weeks after delivery. Following the passage of the PDA, the company instituted a new plan that treated pregnancy and other temporary disabilities alike, but it made no provisions for women, like Noreen Hulteen, who had been on pregnancy leave before April 29, 1979, the day the law went into effect.

When Hulteen retired against her will, a victim of AT&T's involuntary layoff policy, she discovered that she had not received credit for seven months toward her retirement benefits. She had required surgery while out on maternity leave and missed a total of 240 days of work, losing 210 days of service credit. The other plaintiffs in the suit against AT&T had similar experiences of losing service credit for time spent on pregnancy leave. They filed suit in federal court, arguing that the PDA required the company to adjust the service credit calculations related to their pregnancy leaves. Echoing the plaintiff's argument in *Ledbetter*, they maintained that the company engaged in a new act of discrimination each time they received their retirement checks. AT&T contended that Congress had not specified that the PDA was retroactive and because its disability plan was legal when the women took leave, it should not be required to raise their retirement benefits.

The district court ruled in Hulteen's favor, a panel of the Ninth Circuit reversed, and the Ninth Circuit, sitting en banc, reversed the panel.[95] Hulteen's attorney described the case as "the second generation of pregnancy discrimination," saying, "women who were discriminated against back in the '70s are being discriminated against again."[96] Bush justice department attorneys, arguing on the company's behalf, urged the Court to reverse the appellate court, claiming that because of limited resources, other employees might lose benefits if the company increased the plaintiffs' retirement benefits.

Souter delivered the opinion for the 7 to 2 Court in *AT&T Corporation v. Hulteen*.[97] Citing the now-discredited *Gilbert*, he reiterated that AT&T's limitations on service credits for pregnancy leaves were lawful under Title VII. He characterized the pension plan as a "function of a seniority system," explaining that differential treatment of a pregnancy leave would violate Title VII at the present time, but that "a seniority system does not necessarily violate the statute when it gives current effect to such rules that operated before the PDA."[98]

Under Title VII, he said, an employer may compensate employees differently on the basis of a bona fide seniority system as long as there is no intent to discriminate on the basis of race, sex, or other protected classifications. Hulteen argued that the PDA's command of equal treatment of pregnancy in "fringe benefit programs" supercedes the employer's right to set different levels of pay on the basis of seniority systems. Souter disagreed, saying Congress could not have intended to permit pregnancy discrimination alone (as opposed to discrimination based on race or color, for example) to vitiate the employer's rights under the seniority provision. Rather, he declared that the section of the PDA quoted by the plaintiff meant that Congress wanted to ward off the possibility that a court might interpret the ambiguously worded Bennett Amendment to allow discrimination in pay based on pregnancy in the future.

Hulteen claimed that AT&T's seniority system violated Title VII because it was facially discriminatory, even if not intentionally so. She cited the Court's statement in *Johnson Controls* that a finding of facial discrimination in a policy does not depend on whether the employer intends to discriminate, but on the terms of the policy. *Johnson Controls* does not apply, said Souter. That company's policy was established after the PDA was enacted and was facially discriminatory by singling out pregnant women for exclusion from specified work areas. In contrast, AT&T's seniority system was not discriminatory because there was no barrier to singling out pregnancy at the time it was in place. Finally, the Court refused to apply the PDA retroactively, finding no indication of congressional intent to do so.

Stevens concurred. He declared that although he largely agreed with Ginsburg's dissent, he was forced to concur with the majority because AT&T's policy was not discriminatory until Congress enacted the PDA.

Ginsburg's dissent (for herself and Breyer) began by noting that before *Gilbert,* the lower courts as well as the EEOC had agreed that pregnancy discrimination violated Title VII. She acknowledged that the PDA did not compel companies to provide relief for their former discriminatory leave policies, but, she insisted, the law "does protect women . . . against repetition or continuation of pregnancy-based disadvantageous treatment."[99] But the Court is doing precisely that, she charged; by sanctioning AT&T's pension plan, it allows *Gilbert's* discriminatory spirit to survive. In her view, AT&T "committed a current violation of Title VII, when post-PDA, it did not totally discontinue reliance upon a pension calculation premised on the notion that pregnancy-based classifications display no gender bias."[100]

The discrimination will only cease, she declared, when the company stops relying on a system that reflects a time when it was acceptable to discriminate against pregnant women. She ended by saying that in her view, the Court should finally overrule *Gilbert.*

The Family and Medical Leave Act

Most feminists believe that the workplace must be restructured to accommodate the needs of women with children, including pregnant women.[101] The Supreme Court's interpretation of the PDA as a floor, not a ceiling, in *Guerra* permits the government to enact laws that require employers to acknowledge the needs of pregnant workers, as California did by passing the PDL. In 1993, the federal government took an important step in recognizing women's needs by passing family leave legislation. But despite its efforts to secure greater equality in the workplace, the policy falls short of a true commitment to equal opportunity for women workers for a number of reasons.

During the 1980s, about half the states required certain employers to provide some type of parental or sick leave for their workers. The state policies were generally divided into three categories: laws treating pregnancy like other disabilities, laws distinguishing pregnancy by mandating affirmative rights for pregnant women, and laws allowing either or both parents to take unpaid leave.[102] A national parental leave policy, modeled after the third approach to pregnancy, emerged in 1993 after being stalled in Congress for almost a decade and vetoed twice by the president.

Congress's first attempt to enact family leave legislation began in 1986. This early version, H.R. 4300, would have required public and private employers with fifteen or more workers to grant up to eighteen weeks of unpaid "family" leave to women and men for a variety of circumstances, including birth, adoption, or the serious illness of a child or parent. Employees would be permitted to take up to twenty-six weeks of unpaid disability leave for medical reasons for themselves, with their employers continuing their health insurance benefits during the leave time and ensuring they would be able to return to their jobs with seniority and other benefits intact. The bill also proposed establishing a commission to study the issue of income replacement during leaves.

When the bill was introduced in Congress, maternity or parental leave policies were common in most industrialized nations, with varying lengths of time from the job and some form of income replacement during the time off. By 2008, with the exception of the United States and

Australia, most countries in western Europe, as well as Japan, New Zealand, and Canada, offered a combination of paid and unpaid leave to mothers, fathers, or both. Compared to those policies, the U.S. policies were far less generous in providing replacement salaries and length of time allowed on leave.[103]

Representative Patricia Schroeder, Democrat from Colorado, spoke of the need for parental leave legislation in the United States, commenting that "it is time that we drag ourselves into the 1980s and update our personnel policies to make work and family more compatible."[104] Supported by labor, women's rights, and health groups, the bill faced strong opposition from the business community, which called it anticompetitive and expensive; it warned the law would harm women by making them more expensive to employ and cause employers to refuse to hire them.[105] A letter to members of Congress from the U.S. Chamber of Commerce and other business groups argued that the proposed legislation "is contrary to the voluntary, flexible and comprehensive benefit system that the private sector has developed."[106] Despite the strong opposition from business groups, H.R. 4300 was approved in a voice vote by the House Education and Labor Committee but was never considered by the full House.

A year later, in the 100th Congress, Schroeder and her fellow Democrat, William Clay of Missouri, again proposed family leave legislation, introducing H.R. 925, an updated version of the 1986 bill. A Senate version, S. 249, was introduced by Christopher Dodd, Democrat from Connecticut. The bills were accompanied by intense lobbying on both sides: NOW organized its supporters to send more than 25,000 Mother's Day cards to congressional leaders. Testifying against the bill at a Senate subcommittee hearing, a member of the Chamber of Commerce gloomily predicted that the legislation would cost more than $20 billion a year. The General Accounting Office (GAO) rejected this figure, saying that the estimate was based on "a variety of unrealistic assumptions."[107]

The final House version of H.R. 925 set the threshold size of a covered business at fifty employees, with the number dropping to thirty-five after three years unless Congress disapproved.[108] Employees could take leaves of absence to care for others, including children and ill parents, for ten weeks over a two-year period; they could take up to fifteen weeks a year for their own disabilities. The employee had to work for a minimum of twenty hours a week for at least a year, and employers could refuse to reinstate the highest-paid 10 percent of their workforce.[109]

The bill was approved by a House committee in November 1987 but failed to pass out of Congress that year. The next year, a Senate version stalled in a filibuster, and despite the fact that parental leave formed part of a pro-family package, along with child care and protection against child pornography, it failed to clear Congress in 1988 as well.

In what was becoming a customary congressional exercise, a slightly different version of parental leave legislation was again introduced in both the House and Senate in February 1989, also requiring companies to provide up to ten weeks every two years to new parents and workers with ill parents or children. The bills differed slightly in that the House version, H.R. 770, was more generous, allowing fifteen weeks of medical leave; the Senate measure, S. 345, permitted workers to take up to thirteen weeks of individual medical leave in a year for a serious illness. The GAO estimated that each bill would cost approximately $200 million a year.[110] Critical of the House bill, Representative Dick Armey, Republican from Texas, argued that only well-to-do couples who could afford the loss of income would be able to take advantage of the bill. "This is yuppie welfare—a perverse redistribution of income from the poor to the rich," he said.[111] He did not, however, offer a substitute measure to provide paid parental leave, a move that would have met his ostensible goal of allowing lower-income workers to benefit from the law.

Both House and Senate bills were approved by four congressional committees over the next two months.[112] But in a letter to Utah senator Orrin Hatch, ranking Republican on the Labor and Human Resources Committee, Labor Secretary Elizabeth Dole indicated that she would advise the president to veto the bill if it landed on his desk. She stated, "We strongly believe this [benefit program] can be best achieved voluntarily; therefore, the administration strongly opposes the mandated approach to employee benefits."[113] The Bush White House reiterated its opposition to the bill, saying it supported parental and medical leave but felt that decisions about employee fringe benefits should be left to the private sector.[114]

H.R. 770 passed the House in a 237 to 187 vote on May 10, 1990. Just before the vote, White House chief of staff John Sununu told business leaders at a White House meeting that "if Congress passed a measure requiring parental leave, Mr. [George H.W.] Bush would veto it because he opposed Government's dictating fringe benefits."[115] The bill was later approved in a voice vote by the Senate on June 14, 1990.

Over time, the bill had been steadily weakened in an effort to appease the business community. In the final version of H.R. 770, employers with fifty or more employees would have to offer twelve weeks of unpaid medical or parental leave. The medical leave could be used to provide care for an ill child, a parent, or a spouse. Workers would be eligible for the released time if they were employed for at least 1,000 hours over the course of a year. Employers would continue to provide health coverage for employees on leave and place returning employees in their previous jobs or equivalent positions.[116]

On June 29, 1990, as promised, Bush vetoed the legislation. In his veto message, he said,

> I want to emphasize my belief that time off for a child's birth or adoption or for family illness is an important benefit for employers to offer employees. I strongly object, however, to the Federal Government mandating leave policies for America's employers and work force. HR 770 would do just that.[117]

Almost one month later, on July 25, 1990, the House failed to override the president's veto. Members of Congress vowed to keep sending family leave legislation to the president until they succeeded. Paraphrasing from a civil rights movement song, Schroeder vowed, "We will override someday."[118] Dodd, the bill's chief sponsor in the Senate, promised that "George Bush is going to have a family leave bill on his desk every year he's in office." A member of Bush's own party, Marge Roukema, House member from New Jersey, expressed amazement at the presidential veto. "It's beyond my understanding why the President vetoed this," she said, adding, "What compelling national interest prompted this veto?" Celebrating its victory in defeating the legislation, an official of the National Federation of Independent Businesses said, "From our standpoint, it's a great day."[119]

A year later, H.R. 2 and S. 5, introduced in their respective chambers, were met with renewed veto threats. But despite approval by voice vote in the Senate and a vote of 253 to 177 in the House, the bills lacked sufficient support to defeat the promised presidential veto and were shelved. In 1992, the scenario was repeated. The Senate succeeded in overriding the veto, but the House was unable to produce the requisite votes.[120] In his veto message of the family leave bill, Bush reiterated that he would support a family policy that imposed no requirements on employers to grant leaves, claiming that he wished "those members of Congress who have joined me in the past in opposing government mandates to work with me again."[121]

The likelihood that the bill would pass increased after the November 1992 election, with Democratic control of Congress and the White House, especially as it was one of Clinton's chief campaign issues. On February 5, 1993, a few weeks after Clinton was sworn into office, H.R. 1, the Family and Medical Leave Act (FMLA), was signed into law as the first piece of legislation enacted in the new Clinton administration.[122] In signing the FMLA in a Rose Garden ceremony, Clinton declared, "Now millions of our people will no longer have to choose between their jobs and their families."[123]

Representing an amalgam of the earlier versions, the FMLA provides that workers in companies with fifty or more employees within a 75-mile radius are entitled to twelve weeks of unpaid leave during any twelve-month period for the birth or adoption of a child; the illness of a child, spouse, or parent; or a worker's own serious health condition that requires absence from the job. To be eligible, an employee must have worked for the same employer for one year for at least 1,250 hours (an average of twenty-five hours a week) during the year. The employer must maintain health care benefits for employees during the leave time, and workers are guaranteed a return to their former jobs or their equivalents. If both parents work for the same employer, they may only take a total of twelve weeks of leave between them. Employers can deny leave to the highest-paid 10 percent of the workforce if their absence would cause "serious and grievous injury." The act allows intermittent or periodic leave and encourages employers to offer their employees more generous leave programs. Enforced by DOL, the law went into effect on August 5, 1993; it allows workers to sue noncompliant employers for damages and injunctive relief.

Its legislative history indicates that Congress was concerned that women's familial responsibilities for children or parents affected their employment status. This concern is reflected in the act's stated goal of "promot[ing] . . . equal employment opportunity for women and men [by] balanc[ing] the demands of the workplace with the needs of families . . . in a manner that . . . minimizes the potential for employment discrimination on the basis of sex." The purpose of the FMLA, to allow men and women to balance the needs of work and family, furthers the principle of equal opportunity in the workplace. However, in guaranteeing only unpaid leave, the FMLA falls short of its goal of helping women accommodate work and family.[124]

One explanation for the shortfall is that almost half of the workers in the United States do not meet the eligibility requirements. According to a study conducted by DOL in 2000, almost 40 percent of the workforce is outside the protection of the FMLA, either because they work in smaller than fifty-employee establishments or do not meet the hours and time in service requirements. When examining eligibility rates of workers according to their annual incomes, the study shows that workers with incomes of less than $20,000 have the lowest eligibility rate (only 39 percent eligible).

In contrast, 74 percent of workers with annual incomes of $100,000 and higher were found eligible for leave under the FMLA.[125]

Aside from the problem of eligibility, an important concern about the law is that even when eligible, most women cannot avail themselves of the leave because it is unpaid. Surveys found that at least 60 percent of the respondents indicated that they could not afford to take leave or were forced to take only partial leave because they were unable to get by without their earnings. Ironically, one study suggests that the law is especially aimed at women who have the means to do without their salaries for the period of the leave, primarily middle-class and married workers.[126]

Finally, studies also show that, despite its neutral language, women chiefly avail themselves of the option of taking time off from work, indicating that they still assume primary responsibility for family care. In part because the leave is unpaid, fathers, who are more likely to earn higher salaries than mothers, are less likely to absent themselves from their jobs, especially when money is scarce following the birth of a child or the onset of a family member's serious illness.[127]

Additionally, it is reported that men who attempt to absent themselves from the workplace under their employer's family leave policy are subjected to derision, if not outright hostility.[128] Thus, although it was a positive step toward equal opportunity, the FMLA represents only the initial stages in creating a more egalitarian workplace.[129]

The Supreme Court and the Family and Medical Leave Act

Since its passage, the Court has only issued two rulings interpreting the FMLA, each requiring it to consider Congress's intent and purpose in enacting the law. Table 5.2 presents these cases. As the lead FMLA enforcement agency, DOL issues necessary regulations to enforce the act. The courts will customarily defer to the agency if they believe the regulation is consistent with congressional intent.[130]

Ragsdale v. Wolverine[131] proved to be an exception to this principle. *Ragsdale* revolved around DOL regulations requiring the employer to inform its employees of the relationship between the employer's leave policy and the FMLA as well as to post information about the employee's rights and obligations under the act. In addition to posting the information, the regulations stated that employers with more generous leave policies than the FMLA must notify the employee what portion of the absence is covered by the FMLA and what portion is attributable to the

Table 5.2 Supreme Court Rulings on the FMLA, 2002–2003

Case	Date	Issue[a]	Ruling[b]
Ragsdale	2002	DOL regulation	Limits act
Hibbs	2003	State immunity	Expands act

Notes: a. Based on the major issue in the case.
b. Based on the overall outcome of the case.

employer's policy.[132] The penalty for failing to apprise the employee of this information was that the leave did not count against the employee's twelve-week FMLA entitlement, in effect, granting the employee an additional twelve weeks of leave.[133]

Tracy Ragsdale began working at Wolverine World Wide, Inc., a footwear manufacturing company, in March 1995; she was diagnosed with Hodgkin's disease in February 1996 and required time away from work for surgery and radiation treatment. Entitled to seven months of unpaid sick leave, her requests for leave in thirty-day increments were granted until the seven months had elapsed. Her employer never told her that she could take twelve weeks of her leave as FMLA leave. Because she could not return to work after the thirty weeks of leave, she asked for additional time off or permission to work part-time; Wolverine denied both requests and discharged her when she did not return to work.

Ragsdale filed suit in federal court, seeking backpay and reinstatement. Additionally, she claimed that because the company had not informed her that she could count twelve of the thirty weeks as FMLA leave, as required by the DOL regulation, she was entitled to another twelve weeks of leave. Wolverine acknowledged that it had not conveyed the requisite information to her but argued that by giving her thirty weeks of leave, it had complied with the federal law; indeed, it emphasized, it had even exceeded it.

The district court ruled in the company's favor, holding that the regulation's penalty provision conflicted with the FMLA because it would allow the employee to have more than twelve weeks of leave during a single year. The Eighth Circuit affirmed the lower court.

Kennedy announced the majority opinion for himself and Stevens, Scalia, Thomas, and Rehnquist. He began by praising Wolverine for complying with the spirit of the FMLA by allowing Ragsdale thirty weeks of leave as well as maintaining her health benefits and paying six months of her premiums. He seemed to chide Ragsdale for suing the company in the face of its generosity, charging her with seeking more leave simply "because Wolverine was in technical violation" of DOL regulations.[134]

The Court's major concern with the penalty provision was that it conclusively presumed that employees' rights are abridged by the employer's failure to provide the requisite information, allowing employees to avoid the act's requirement that they prove prejudice (that is, injury) resulting from their employer's failure to comply with the regulation. Additionally, the Court held, by granting employees an extra twelve weeks, the penalty provision is at variance with Congress's determination that twelve weeks of leave represents the best compromise between employees and employers. The majority believed that the penalty provision subverted Congress's intent of limiting leave time to twelve weeks and found it invalid because it was contrary to the act and exceeded the secretary of labor's authority. The Court also expressed concern that enforcing the penalty provision would discourage employers from providing more generous leave policies than the FMLA to avoid the stringent consequences of the designation requirement. Parenthetically, the Court expressed no opinion on whether the notice provisions are within the secretary's regulatory authority, merely holding that the penalty provision is not.[135]

Speaking for herself, Souter, Ginsburg, and Breyer, O'Connor dissented. In her view, the secretary could reasonably believe that the act requires employers to notify employees about the intersection of their FMLA leave with company leave and that the specified penalty is an effective means of enforcing the requirement. She denied that the regulation conflicted with the law by requiring employers to provide more than twelve weeks leave if they fail to tell employees which portion of their leave is FMLA-qualified. A simple way to avoid the problem, she said, is to comply with the designation requirement.

A year later, the Court decided a case questioning whether Congress had the authority to hold states accountable under the FMLA. A manifestation of its "new federalism" jurisprudence of the 1990s, the issue revolved around the high court's interpretation of the Eleventh Amendment and its relationship to the Fourteenth Amendment.[136]

In 1997, William Hibbs, a state worker, requested intermittent leave under the FMLA to care for his injured wife. Later, he requested paid "catastrophic leave," which he was told would run concurrently, not consecutively, with his FMLA leave. When the twelve-week leave expired and he did not return to work, his employer, the Nevada Department of Human Resources, eventually dismissed him. Hibbs argued that the state violated the FMLA by dismissing him from his job while he was on leave. The state maintained that the Eleventh Amendment barred him from collecting damages. It contended that because the act was not intended to enforce the equal protection guarantees of the Fourteenth Amendment, it exceeded Congress's authority under section 5 of the Fourteenth Amendment.[137] Most courts agreed with this position, ruling that because the law was sex-neutral, Congress had not intended it to redress discrimination based on sex.[138] The district court determined that the state had provided Hibbs with adequate notice that his leave had ended and it could fire him for staying away from the job.

On appeal, in the Ninth Circuit, the state claimed immunity under the Eleventh Amendment, arguing that the "family care" provision of the FMLA was unrelated to Congress's intent in eradicating sex discrimination and therefore beyond its authority to enforce the Fourteenth Amendment's equal protection clause under section 5. A unanimous three-judge panel reversed the lower court, ruling that Congress intended the FMLA to alleviate women's disproportionate burden of caring for sick family members.[139] In part, the court pointed to the language of the act that explicitly allows employees to file suit "against any employer (including a public agency) in any Federal or state court."[140]

The principal questions before the Supreme Court on appeal were whether the FMLA was within Congress's authority to enact legislation under the Fourteenth Amendment or if the Eleventh Amendment insulated states from suits for money damages. In *Nevada Department of Human Resources v. Hibbs,*[141] the Court voted 6 to 3 that the FMLA validly abrogated the state's Eleventh Amendment immunity and that state workers may sue their employers for violating the law. In a strongly worded ruling that surprised most observers because it departed from its recent pattern of support for states' rights, the Court cited the history of discrimination against women workers by states. The opinion announced by Rehnquist stated that "according to evidence that was before Congress when it enacted the FMLA, States continue to rely on invalid gender stereotypes in the employment context, specifically in the administration of leave benefits."[142]

The Court distinguished the FMLA from other laws in which Congress was viewed as exceeding its authority to enact remedial legislation because Congress had "significant evidence of a long and extensive history of sex discrimination with respect to the administration of leave benefits." Moreover, Rehnquist continued, "the impact of the discrimination targeted by the FMLA, which is based on mutually reinforcing stereotypes that only women are responsible for family caregiving and that men lack domestic responsibilities, is significant."[143]

Hibbs's attorney, pleased with the opinion, was quoted as saying that it "reflects and elaborates on the court's strong commitment to sex equality. The court identifies discrimination at the fault line between work and family as a key area of continuing and intractable sex discrimination."[144]

Family Leave Policies

The FMLA seemed to end the debate over preferential treatment for pregnant women by transforming pregnancy leave into parental leave. However, the difficulties of balancing work with family persist, especially for women in lower-income jobs for whom paid leave is a necessity. Recognizing that neither the federal government nor the courts would remedy the inequities resulting from the limited protection of the FMLA, women's rights leaders focused their attention on the states again, which, as in the past, demonstrated their capacity for creating innovative family policies.

By 2008, twelve states (California, Connecticut, Hawaii, Maine, Minnesota, New Jersey, New York, Oregon, Rhode Island, Vermont, Washington, and Wisconsin) and the District of Columbia exceeded the provisions of the FMLA by providing residents either partial paid leave or more generous FMLA benefits such as reducing the number of workers to below fifty for eligibility or extending the allowable time away on leave. A few rely on temporary disability insurance plans to provide benefits for mothers who give birth.[145] However, by 2011, only California and New Jersey had paid parental leave programs in which workers received varying dollar amounts to miss work while caring for newborn or newly adopted children or sick relatives. Some of the other states include limited wage replacement for some workers for pregnancy-related illnesses as part of their disability insurance programs. Paid leave policies have been proposed in other states but have not achieved legislative approval yet. Much of the success in highlighting the need for state parental leave policies is attributable to the efforts of the National Partnership for Women and Families, an organization devoted to expanding parental leave programs for workers throughout the nation.[146]

California offers the most comprehensive leave coverage in the nation, with four laws, including the federal FMLA, as well as the state disability insurance program, providing overlapping benefits. The PDL, at issue in *Guerra,* requires employers with at least five employees to allow pregnant workers to take up to four months of unpaid leave for pregnancy, childbirth, or a related medical condition, both before and after the birth of the child. Like the FMLA, the PDL provides job guarantees, but unlike the FMLA, it does not protect the employee's health benefits. If eligible, the employee can take simultaneous leave under the FMLA, and the employer will be required to continue health coverage under the federal law. Moreover, if the woman pays into the state disability insurance plan, she is entitled to receive disability payments for the entire leave under the PDL.[147]

The California Family Rights Act (CFRA), passed two years before the FMLA, is the state variant of the federal law, allowing eligible employees to take twelve weeks of unpaid job-protected leave to care for a sick family member (or oneself) or bond with a newborn or adopted or foster child.[148]

In 2002, California's Democratic governor Gray Davis made the state the first in the nation to enact paid leave legislation by signing the Family Temporary Disability Insurance Law, also called the Paid Family Leave Act (PFLA). Taking effect in 2004, the PFLA allows workers six weeks' leave to care for a newborn or newly adopted child or an ailing relative. While on leave, they receive 55 percent of their weekly wages up to a maximum benefit, which changes each year, depending on inflation; in 2009, the maximum benefit was $959 a week. It was estimated that the law would cover the majority of California workers (about 13 million of a total of 16 million), and be financed entirely by employee payroll deductions. Employees pay a maximum of $64 a year; employers pay nothing.

As Davis said during the signing ceremony, "This bill will help millions of California workers meet their responsibilities to both their families and their employers." Labor unions and women's groups greeted the law with enthusiasm, but employers were less sanguine about it, predicting that it would eventually require contributions from businesses to meet the costs of the program and warning of hidden costs such as overtime pay and training expenses for temporary workers. Reflecting the pressure from the business community, the duration of the leave was reduced in the final days of passage from the originally proposed twelve weeks to six weeks, and employer contributions were eliminated.[149]

The PFLA does not guarantee the worker's position or require the employer to provide health benefits during the paid family leave, but workers who qualify for leave under the FMLA or the CFRA have job protection and remain under their employer's health insurance policy. Unlike the federal law, workers are eligible for benefits under the PFLA if they pay into the state disability insurance program; benefits are determined by the amount paid into the state plan.

The Family Leave Insurance provision of the New Jersey Temporary Disability Benefits Law also allows cash benefits for up to six weeks to bond with a newborn or newly adopted child or to provide care for a seriously ill family member. Created in 2008, it is financed by payroll deductions of approximately $33 a year. Workers began drawing benefits on July 1, 2009, receiving two-thirds of their salaries up to a maximum $524 a week in 2009.[150]

The state of Washington's Paid Family Leave Program, slated to go into effect on October 1, 2009, was delayed for three years for budgetary reasons. It is now scheduled to go into effect on October 1, 2012. Unlike the California and New Jersey plans, Washington's is a parental leave program limited to birth and adoptive parents. It allows those who regularly work thirty-five hours or more a week in the year before the leave to take five weeks of leave and receive up to $250 a week in benefits. The state has still not determined how it will pay for the program if, indeed, it does become a reality.

A number of changes were made to the FMLA during 2008 and 2009. On January 28, 2008, Bush signed the National Defense Authorization Act, amending the FMLA to create a new category of leave for members of the armed forces and their families.[151] It entitles servicemembers to take either "Qualifying Exigency Leave" for twelve weeks or "Service-member Family Leave" for twenty-six weeks. The twelve-week leave is available to an employee if a specified exigency occurs because a family member is on active duty or has been called to active duty. Eligible employees are permitted to take up to twenty-six weeks of leave to care for a servicemember with a "serious injury or illness."[152] On October 28, 2009, Obama signed the National Defense Authorization Act for FY 2010 to expand the provisions of the 2008 act for members of the military and their families.[153]

In November 2008, as the Bush administration was preparing to leave the White House following the 2008 election, DOL announced that new regulations, first proposed in April 2008, were forthcoming.[154] The primary effect of these rules was to tighten the standard for defining "serious health condition," restricting employees' access to leave. The rules also required employees to provide more extensive documentation of their medical conditions, mandating that they be recertified by physicians more frequently at their own expense, and authorizing employers to discuss their medical conditions without the employees' knowledge or permission. The president of the American Postal Workers Union sharply criticized the regulations: "These onerous regulations are yet another burden the Bush administration is imposing on America's working families. . . . We will not sit idly by while a lame-duck president issues rules that favor the Chamber of Commerce at the expense of America's workers."[155]

The final regulations became effective on January 16, 2009, and on April 29, 2009, Representative Carol Shea-Porter, Democrat from New Hampshire, introduced the FMLA Restoration Act. The purpose of the bill, H.R. 2161, was "to nullify certain regulations promulgated under the Family and Medical Leave Act of 1993 and restore prior regulations." Specifically, it would have repealed a segment of the new regulations and, among other things, modified the new certification and recertification requirements. The bill was referred to committee, and no action was taken on it by the end of the 111th Congress, leaving the Bush-era restrictive regulations in place.[156]

In another attempt to expand family leave benefits, on June 4, 2009, the House approved a bill entitled the Federal Employees Paid Parental Leave Act of 2009, amending the FMLA to provide federal and congressional employees the benefit of paid leave. The law, H.R. 626, would have granted federal workers four weeks of leave with pay when they were absent from the job for reasons of birth or adoption or to care for a seriously ill relative or for their own serious medical condition. The leave would be available for FMLA-eligible employees and would have to be taken as part of the twelve-week FMLA leave. The Congressional Budget Office estimated that the law would cost $67 million in 2010 and a total of $938 million from 2010 to 2014.[157] After passing the House, H.R. 626 was sent to the Senate on October 19, 2009, but after being referred to committee there, no further action was taken on it.

In the most recent change to the FMLA, on December 21, 2009, Obama signed the Airline Flight Crew Technical Corrections Act.[158] The purpose of the law was to clarify eligibility requirements for airline flight crews, that is, to calculate the hours of service these individuals must complete to be eligible for leave under the act.[159] It specified that flight attendants or flight crew members were eligible for leave if they worked or had been paid for 60 percent of the monthly requirement and at least 504 hours over the year.

Conclusion

Working women struggled to eliminate discriminatory policies based on pregnancy, and the Supreme Court initially supported their efforts to remove restrictions on their work, ruling it was unfair to make assumptions about their inability to work while pregnant. But the Court allowed pregnancy to be excluded from disability insurance plans, making the startling observation that pregnancy is unrelated to sex.

Congress reversed the high court by enacting the PDA, intending it to create a more evenhanded approach to pregnancy in the workplace. Ironically, the neutrality principle of the PDA soon led to controversy among feminists and public policymakers about preferential treatment for pregnant women. And when asked, the Supreme Court ruled that such treatment was permissible but not required.

Passage of the FMLA seemed to end the debate over preferential treatment by transforming pregnancy leave into family leave. The sex-neutral policy allows eligible workers to take twelve weeks of unpaid leave and, for the most part, guarantees their jobs upon their return. Although a positive step, it provides little benefit for workers in low-wage jobs whose salaries are essential to their family's survival. Some states established family leave policies, two providing paid leave, but this piecemeal approach is far short of the family leave policy workers require.

Notes

1. The White House, Office of the Press Secretary, "President Obama Announces White House Council on Women and Girls," March 11, 2009, available at http://www.whitehouse.gov/the-press-office/president-obama-announces-white-house -council-women-and-girls.

2. Joanna L. Grossman, "Pregnancy, Work, and the Promise of Equal Citizenship," *Georgetown Law Journal* 98 (2010): 573.

3. U.S. Department of Labor, Bureau of Labor Statistics, "Labor Force Participation of Women by Presence and Age of Youngest Child, March 1975–2008," available at http://www.bls.gov/opub/ted/2009/ted_20091009 _data.htmb; U.S. Department of Labor, Bureau of Labor Statistics, "Labor Force Participation Rates Among Mothers by Age of Youngest Child, March 1975–March 2008," available at http://www.bls.gov/opub/ted/2010/ted_20100507.htm.

4. Employment figures were apt to be skewed in 2009 because of the high rate of unemployment, especially among African American and Hispanic families. U.S. Department of Labor, Bureau of Labor Statistics, "Table 4: Families with Own Children: Employment Status of Parents by Age of Youngest Child and Family Type, 2008–09 Annual Averages," available at http://www.bls.gov/news.release/ pdf/famee.pdf.

5. *Muller,* 208 U.S. at 421.

6. Congress also singled women out for special attention by passing the Sheppard-Towner Act in 1921. The law provided funds to states to improve health care for women and their children; the program survived for less than a decade.

7. 414 U.S. 632 (1974).

8. *LaFleur,* 414 U.S. at 644.

9. 423 U.S. 44 (1975).

10. See Katharine T. Bartlett, "Pregnancy and the Constitution: The Uniqueness Trap," *California Law Review* 62 (1974): 1532–1566.

11. 417 U.S. 484 (1974).

12. *Geduldig,* 417 U.S. at 494. Shortly before the lower court's ruling, in another case brought by a woman disabled by an abnormal pregnancy, the California Court of Appeal held that the state plan must provide disability payments to women missing work because of complications from abnormal pregnancies. As a result of the California court decision, the disability program was revised so that the three women with the abnormal pregnancies were given benefits for time lost from work; the fourth woman, disabled by normal pregnancy, was not. The only issue before the Supreme Court was the exclusion of benefits for normal pregnancy.

13. Under a stricter standard of review, the Court would have demanded more evidence from the state that the cost of adding pregnancy disability benefits insurance would have severely disrupted the disability insurance program. Even if such evidence were available, under a stricter form of scrutiny, the Court would have been less willing to accept financial exigency as a basis for discrimination. See Ann Scales, "Towards a Feminist Jurisprudence," *Indiana Law Journal* 56 (1980–1981): 375–444; Harriet Hubacker Coleman, "Barefoot and Pregnant—Still: Equal Protection for Men and Women in Light of *Geduldig v. Aiello*," *South Texas Law Journal* 16 (1975): 211–240.

14. *Geduldig,* 417 U.S. at 496–497.

15. *Geduldig,* 417 U.S. at 496–497 n. 20.

16. *Geduldig,* 417 U.S. at 501.

17. According to the 1966 EEOC guidelines, it was not discriminatory to exclude pregnancy from disability plans. In March 1971, the agency abruptly reversed itself and, a year later, issued guidelines reflecting this change. The 1972 guidelines, classifying pregnancy with other temporary disabilities, prohibited employers from refusing to hire qualified women because they were pregnant or *might become* pregnant, required employers to treat pregnancy like other temporarily disabling conditions, and barred employers from disproportionately firing women for absences from the job caused by pregnancy unless doing so was justified by business needs. Mark A. Lies II, "Current Trends in Pregnancy Benefits—1972 EEOC Guidelines Interpreted," *DePaul Law Review* 24 (1974): 127–142; Barnard and Rapp, "Pregnant Employees."

18. Diane L. Zimmerman, "*Geduldig v. Aiello:* Pregnancy Classifications and the Definition of Sex Discrimination," *Columbia Law Review* 75 (1975): 441–482.

19. Phillip Nollin Cockrell, "Pregnancy Disability Benefits and Title VII: Pregnancy Does Not Involve Sex," *Baylor Law Review* 29 (1977): 266.

20. Scales, "Towards a Feminist Jurisprudence," pp. 380–381.

21. See Zimmerman, "*Geduldig v. Aiello.*"

22. Patricia Huckle, "The Womb Factor: Policy on Pregnancy and the Employment of Women," in Ellen Boneparth and Emily Stoper, eds., *Women, Power, and Policy,* 2d ed. (New York: Pergamon Press, 1988), p. 135.

23. 429 U.S. 125 (1976).

24. Barnard and Rapp, "Pregnant Employees," p. 208.

25. *Gilbert,* 429 U.S. at 138–139 (emphasis in the original).

26. *Gilbert,* 429 U.S. at 162 n. 5.

27. 434 U.S. 136 (1977).

28. *Satty,* 434 U.S. at 142.

29. Shortly after *Satty,* in *Los Angeles Department of Water and Power v. Manhart,* 435 U.S. 702 (1978), the Court found the city violated Title VII by requir-

ing women to make higher contributions than men to the pension fund; unlike in *Gilbert,* the Court explained, the pension plan discriminated on the basis of sex.

30. Joyce Gelb and Marian Lief Palley, *Women and Public Policies,* 2d ed. (Princeton: Princeton University Press, 1987).

31. The final bill specified that employers are not required to pay for abortions, unless the life of the woman is endangered.

32. 42 U.S.C. § 2000e(k). The PDA specifies that "women affected by pregnancy, childbirth, or related medical conditions shall be treated the same for all employment-related purposes . . . as other persons not so affected but similar in their ability or inability to work." The law does not require employers to accommodate a pregnant woman when she is unable to perform the duties of the job. It is up to the woman to prove that other disabled individuals are given more favorable treatment; see Barnard and Rapp, "Pregnant Employees," for cases illustrating the limits of the PDA.

33. H. Rep. No. 948, 95th Cong., 2d sess. (1978), p. 2.

34. H. Rep. No. 948, 95th Cong., 2d sess. (1978), pp. 10–11.

35. *Congressional Record,* 95th Cong., 1st sess., Vol. 123 (1977): S29663.

36. Barnard and Rapp, "Pregnant Employees," pp. 200–201; Grossman, "Pregnancy, Work, and the Promise of Equal Citizenship."

37. U.S. Equal Employment Opportunity Commission, "Pregnancy Discrimination Charges EEOC and FEPAs Combined: FY 1997–FY 2009," available at http://www.eeoc.gov/eeoc/statistics/enforcement/pregnancy.cfm.

38. National Partnership for Women and Families, "The Pregnancy Discrimination Act: Where We Stand 30 Years Later," October 2008, available at http://www.nationalpartnership.org/site/DocServer/Pregnancy_Discrimination_Act_-_Where_We_Stand_30_Years_L.pdf?docID=4281.

39. 462 U.S. 669 (1983).

40. See discussion of the case in Sherri Thornton, "Title VII: The Equalization of Spousal Benefits in View of the Pregnancy Discrimination Act of 1978 *Newport News Shipbuilding and Dry Dock Co. v. Equal Employment Opportunity Commission,*" *Howard Law Journal* 27 (1984): 653–680.

41. *Newport News,* 462 U.S. at 684.

42. 479 U.S. 272 (1987).

43. See Mary DeLano, "The Conflict Between State Guaranteed Pregnancy Benefits and the Pregnancy Discrimination Act: A Statutory Analysis," *Georgetown Law Journal* 74 (1986): 1743–1768.

44. Quoted in Patricia A. Shiu and Stephanie M. Wildman, "Pregnancy Discrimination and Social Change: Evolving Consciousness About a Worker's Right to Job-Protected, Paid Leave," *Yale Journal of Law and Feminism* 21 (2009), p. 128.

45. See Shiu and Wildman, "Pregnancy Discrimination and Social Change," for details of Garland's personal life, including the loss of her child, whom she was unable to support without a job.

46. *California Federal Savings and Loan v. Guerra,* 1984 U.S. Dist. LEXIS 18387 (C.D. Cal.)

47. *Guerra,* 479 U.S. at 281.

48. *Guerra,* 758 F.2d 390, 396 (9th Cir. 1985).

49. *Guerra,* 479 U.S. at 289, quoting *Congressional Record,* 95th Cong., 1st sess., Vol. 123 (1977): S29658.

50. *Guerra,* 479 U.S. at 285.

51. *Guerra,* 479 U.S. at 289.

52. *Guerra,* 479 U.S. at 294 n. 4.

53. *Guerra,* 479 U.S. at 297.

54. *Guerra,* 479 U.S. at 300.

55. 479 U.S. 511 (1987).

56. FUTA was amended in 1976 in part to prevent federal funds under the act from going to states that denied assistance to individuals solely on the basis of pregnancy. See H. Irene Higginbotham, "Pregnancy Discrimination in Unemployment Benefits: Section 3304(a)(12) Merely an Antidiscrimination Provision," *Stetson Law Review* 17 (1987): 219–247.

57. *Wimberly,* 479 U.S. at 516.

58. Logically, in order to determine whether an individual is eligible for unemployment compensation benefits, the state has to know why an employee left his or her job; thus, it knew that pregnancy was the reason in Wimberly's case. Higginbotham, "Pregnancy Discrimination in Unemployment Benefits," p. 234, citing Brief for Petitioner in *Wimberly.*

59. *Wimberly,* 479 U.S. at 517.

60. Brief for Petitioner at 7, *Wimberly,* cited in Higginbotham, "Pregnancy Discrimination in Unemployment Benefits," p. 234 (emphasis in the original).

61. 660 F.2d 1001 (4th Cir. 1981).

62. *Brown,* 660 F.2d at 1004.

63. Higginbotham, "Pregnancy Discrimination in Unemployment Benefits," p. 233, citing Brief for Petitioner in *Wimberly.*

64. *Miller-Wohl Company v. Commissioner of Labor and Industry,* 515 F. Supp. 1264, 1266 (D. Mont. 1981).

65. *Miller-Wohl,* 515 F. Supp. at 1266–1267.

66. *Miller-Wohl Company v. Commissioner of Labor and Industry,* 685 F.2d 1088 (9th Cir. 1982).

67. See Wendy Williams, "Equality's Riddle: Pregnancy and the Equal Treatment/Special Treatment Debate," *New York University Review of Law and Social Change* 13 (1984–1985): 325–380.

68. *Miller-Wohl Company v. Commissioner of Labor and Industry,* 692 P.2d 1243, 1252 (Mont. 1984).

69. *Miller-Wohl Company v. Commissioner of Labor and Industry,* 479 U.S. 1050 (1987). On remand, the company argued that the issue was moot because it had already paid damages to Buley by giving her back pay plus penalties and interest. The court, however, agreed with her that she was entitled to attorney's fees and sent the case to the lower court for a determination of the fees. *Miller-Wohl Company v. Commissioner of Labor and Industry,* 744 P.2d 871 (Mont. 1987).

70. *Miller-Wohl,* 744 P.2d at 872 n. 2.

71. See discussion in Shiu and Wildman, "Pregnancy Discrimination and Social Change," for groups on both sides of the debate in *Guerra,* some of which filed briefs for the state and some against the state. NOW, for example, supported the bank's position, whereas Planned Parenthood opposed it.

72. During the 1980s, many feminists joined in the debate about the wisdom and legality of preferential treatment for pregnancy in the workplace. See, for example, Williams, "Equality's Riddle"; Elizabeth Duncan Koontz, "Childbirth and Childrearing Leave: Job-Related Benefits," *New York University Law Forum* 17 (1971): 480–502; Linda J. Krieger and Patricia N. Cooney, "The Miller-Wohl Controversy: Equal Treatment, Positive Action, and the Meaning of Women's Equality," *Golden Gate University Law Review* 13 (1983): 513–572; Lucinda M. Finley, "Transcending Equality Theory: A Way Out of the Maternity and the Workplace Debate," *Columbia Law Review* 86 (1986): 1118–1182; Herma Hill Kay,

"Equality and Difference: The Case of Pregnancy," *Berkeley Women's Law Journal* 1 (1985): 1–38; Scales, "Towards a Feminist Jurisprudence."

73. Joan C. Williams and Nancy Segal, "Beyond the Maternal Wall: Relief for Family Caregivers Who Are Discriminated Against on the Job," *Harvard Women's Law Journal* 26 (2003): 84–85; see Shiu and Wildman, "Pregnancy Discrimination and Social Change"; Barnard and Rapp, "Pregnant Employees"; Grossman, "Pregnancy, Work, and the Promise of Equal Citizenship."

74. Suzanne Uttaro Samuels, *Fetal Rights, Women's Rights: Gender Equality in the Workplace* (Madison: University of Wisconsin Press, 1995), chap. 1 discusses the effect of fetal protection policies on women's employment opportunities, especially their access to higher-paying jobs.

75. Cynthia Daniels, "Competing Gender Paradigms: Gender Difference, Fetal Rights, and the Case of *Johnson Controls*," *Policy Studies Review* 10 (1991–1992): 58.

76. Pendelton Elizabeth Hamlet, "Fetal Protection Policies: A Statutory Proposal in the Wake of *International Union, UAW v. Johnson Controls, Inc.*," *Cornell Law Review* 75 (1990): 1110.

77. Hamlet, "Fetal Protection Policies," p. 1125; see Mary Becker, "From *Muller v. Oregon* to Fetal Vulnerability Policies," *University of Chicago Law Review* 53 (1986): 1219–1268, who discusses similarities between the old and new forms of protectionist policies and Daniels, "Competing Gender Paradigms," who discusses the types of jobs from which women are most likely to be excluded.

78. See Daniels, "Competing Gender Paradigms," for a discussion of types of fetal protection policies.

79. *Zuniga v. Kleberg County Hospital,* 692 F.2d 986 (5th Cir. 1982); *Wright v. Olin Corporation,* 697 F.2d 1172 (4th Cir. 1982); *Hayes v. Shelby Memorial Hospital,* 796 F.2d 1543 (11th Cir. 1984).

80. There are numerous arguments against directing exclusionary policies only at women. It has been known for several decades that exposing men to lead can directly harm them and indirectly harm their future children. Joan I. Samuelson, "Employment Rights of Women in the Toxic Workplace," *California Law Review* 65 (1977): 1113–1142; Daniels, "Competing Gender Paradigms."

81. 886 F.2d 871 (7th Cir. 1989).

82. Specifically, the court granted summary judgment to the defendant, a ruling issued before a trial on the merits when the court finds there are "no genuine issues of material fact."

83. Samuels, *Fetal Rights, Women's Rights,* chap. 7.

84. *New York Times,* October 3, 1989.

85. 908 F.2d 1303 (6th Cir. 1990).

86. 499 U.S. 187 (1991).

87. *Johnson Controls,* 499 U.S. at 197.

88. *Johnson Controls,* 499 U.S. at 203.

89. *Johnson Controls,* 499 U.S. at 204.

90. *Johnson Controls,* 499 U.S. at 206.

91. At that time, forty states allowed recovery for a prenatal injury, but only in cases of negligence or wrongful death, neither of which was likely to apply to an employer who complied with federal law and warned employees of the possible dangers involved in the job. *Congressional Quarterly Weekly,* March 23, 1991, p. 749.

92. Most employers are not liable in tort to employees because of worker's compensation laws in which employees waive the right to sue their employers; they may be liable to a third party such as a fetus.

93. See Daniels, "Competing Gender Paradigms," for a discussion about the problems of designing a workplace that reflects egalitarian principles yet does not ignore the realities of reproductive safety. Grossman, "Pregnancy, Work, and the Promise of Equal Citizenship," notes that the decision disproportionately affects lower-income women who cannot afford to quit their jobs despite the possible hazards to their children.

94. AT&T's Net Credit Service system, used to compute retirement and pension benefits, was based on the initial date of employment and adjusted for the employee's absence, when no service credit accrued. See Maria Greco Danaher, "Pension Service Credit That Excludes Pregnancy Leave Violates Title VII," *Lawyers Journal* (September 28, 2007).

95. In *Pallas v. Pacific Bell*, 940 F.2d 1324 (9th Cir. 1991), the Ninth Circuit ruled that Pacific Bell violated Title VII by calculating retirement benefits of women who had taken pregnancy-related leave before the passage of the PDA differently from employees on other disability leaves. However, in *Hulteen v. AT&T Corporation*, 441 F.3d 653 (9th Cir. 2006), the three-judge panel decided that AT&T, the successor to Pacific Bell, did not violate Title VII even though the service credit policies were identical. The Ninth Circuit panel believed that *Pallas* did not govern because it conflicted with the Supreme Court's approach against giving retroactive effect to statutes. In *Hulteen v. AT&T Corporation*, 498 F.3d 1001 (9th Cir. 2007), the en banc Ninth Circuit rejected the panel's conclusion about the effect of the Supreme Court's retroactivity principles, holding that, as in *Pallas,* the discriminatory act of calculating Hulteen's benefits was made subsequent to the PDA's passage and that each time it applied the discriminatory policy in calculating an employee's benefits, it engaged in intentional discrimination. In *Ameritech Benefit Plan Committee v. Communication Workers of America*, 220 F.3d 814 (7th Cir. 2000), the Seventh Circuit had made a contrary decision, ruling that workers did not have the right to retroactive credit toward seniority for the time spent on pregnancy leave. The Ninth Circuit criticized the Seventh Circuit decision. The Sixth Circuit agreed with the Seventh in *Leffman v. Sprint Corporation*, 481 F.3d 428 (6th Cir. 2007).

96. *Washington Post*, June 24, 2008.

97. 129 S.Ct. 1962 (2009).

98. *AT&T Corporation v. Hulteen*, 129 S.Ct. at 1968.

99. *AT&T Corporation v. Hulteen*, 129 S.Ct. at 1975.

100. *AT&T Corporation v. Hulteen*, 129 S.Ct. at 1975.

101. See Barnard and Rapp, "Pregnant Employees," for a discussion of bias against working mothers.

102. *New York Times*, May 8, 1990; see Eva A. Cicoria, "Pregnancy and Equality: A Precarious Alliance," *Southern California Law Review* 60 (1987): 1345–1374; and Christine Neylon O'Brien and Gerald A. Madek, "Pregnancy Discrimination and Maternity Leave Laws," *Dickinson Law Review* 93 (1989): 311–337, for a discussion of state maternity policies.

103. For current policies, see Rebecca Ray, *A Detailed Look at Parental Leave Policies in 21 OECD Countries* (Washington, D.C.: Center for Economic and Policy Research, September 2008), available at http://www.cepr.net/documents/publications /parental-app_2008_09.pdf; Rebecca Ray, Janet C. Gornick, and John Schmitt, *Parental Leave Policies in 21 Countries: Assessing Generosity and Gender Equality* (Washington, D.C.: Center for Economic and Policy Research, September 2008, revised June 2009), available at http://www.cepr.net/documents/publications/ parental_2008_09.pdf. For earlier policies, see Eschel M. Rhoodie, *Discrimination Against Women: A Global Survey* (Jefferson, N.C.: McFarland, 1989).

104. *Congressional Quarterly Weekly,* June 14, 1986, p. 1361.

105. The dire warnings about the cost of the bill and its negative effect on women employees have failed to materialize; see Lisa Bornstein, "Inclusions and Exclusions in Work-Family Policy: The Public Values and Moral Code Embedded in the Family and Medical Leave Act," *Columbia Journal of Gender and Law* 10 (2000): 77–124, who notes that despite employers' initial opposition, they report many positive effects that have resulted from the law.

106. *Congressional Quarterly Weekly,* June 28, 1986, p. 1485. As originally proposed and approved by the House Education and Labor Subcommittee in a 9 to 6 vote, the bill would have reached employers with as few as five workers; *Congressional Quarterly Weekly,* June 14, 1986, p. 1361.

107. *Congressional Quarterly Weekly,* May 16, 1987, p. 999; *Congressional Quarterly Weekly,* November 21, 1987, p. 2884.

108. Marjorie Jacobson, "Pregnancy and Employment: Three Approaches to Equal Opportunity," *Boston University Law Review* 68 (1988): 1019–1045.

109. *Congressional Quarterly Weekly,* November 21, 1987, p. 2884. According to a GAO study, the fifty-employee cutoff would exempt 95 percent of the nation's employers from the bill. The remaining 5 percent of employers covered by the bill employ 39 percent of the workforce, about 42 million people.

110. *Congressional Quarterly Weekly,* March 4, 1989, p. 439.

111. *Congressional Quarterly Weekly,* March 11, 1989, p. 519.

112. *Congressional Quarterly Weekly,* April 22, 1989, p. 892.

113. *Congressional Quarterly Weekly,* April 22, 1989, p. 892.

114. *New York Times,* May 8, 1990.

115. *New York Times,* May 8, 1990.

116. *Congressional Quarterly Weekly,* June 16, 1990, p. 1873; *Congressional Quarterly Weekly,* June 30, 1990, p. 2055. The bill would have given federal workers eighteen weeks of parental leave and twenty-six weeks of medical leave. House workers would have gotten the same benefits as private employees; Senate workers were not included in this version of the bill.

117. *Congressional Quarterly Weekly,* July 7, 1990, p. 2178.

118. *Congressional Quarterly Weekly,* July 28, 1990, p. 2405.

119. *New York Times,* July 26, 1990.

120. *Congressional Quarterly Weekly,* November 16, 1991, p. 3385; *Congressional Quarterly Weekly,* December 7, 1991, p. 3593; *New York Times,* August 11, 1992; *New York Times,* September 10, 1992; *New York Times,* September 24, 1992.

121. *Congressional Quarterly Weekly,* September 26, 1992.

122. 29 U.S.C. § 2601.

123. Bureau of National Affairs, *Daily Labor Report,* February 8, 1993.

124. See Ray, *A Detailed Look at Parental Leave Policies in 21 OECD Countries;* Ray, Gornick, and Schmitt, *Parental Leave Policies in 21 Countries,* p. 103; Bornstein, "Inclusions and Exclusions in Work-Family Policy," pp. 79–80.

125. Ray, Gornick, and Schmitt, *Parental Leave Policies in 21 Countries,* p. 8.

126. Deborah J. Anthony, "The Hidden Harms of the Family and Medical Leave Act: Gender-Neutral Versus Gender-Equal," *American University Journal of Gender, Social Policy, and the Law* 16 (2008): 459–501.

127. Heather A. Peterson, "The Daddy Track: Locating the Male Employee Within the Family and Medical Leave Act," *Washington University Journal of Law and Policy* 15 (2004): 253–284; Anthony, "The Hidden Harms of the Family and Medical Leave Act."

128. Rosemarie Feuerbach Twomey and Gwen E. Jones, "The Family and Medical Leave Act of 1993: A Longitudinal Study of Male and Female Perceptions," *Employee Rights and Employment Policy Journal* 3 (1999): 232–236; see Jeremy I. Bohrer, "You, Me, and the Consequences of Family: How Federal Employment Law Prevents the Shattering of the 'Glass Ceiling,'" *Washington University Journal of Urban and Contemporary Law* 50 (1996): 401–421, for a discussion of the reasons why the FMLA is incapable of breaking the glass ceiling.

129. In May 2007, the EEOC indicated its concern with discrimination against family caregivers by releasing an enforcement guidance on workers with caregiving responsibilities. Although the guidance made it clear that discrimination against caregivers is not prohibited by federal law, it cited numerous examples of how discrimination against women caregivers could violate Title VII. These examples included comments about the deficiencies of working mothers, changes in the status of a pregnant worker, or questions about a woman's child care arrangements. U.S. Equal Employment Opportunity Commission, "Enforcement Guidance: Unlawful Disparate Treatment of Workers with Caregiving Responsibilities," 2007, available at http://www.eeoc.gov//policy/docs/caregiving.html. In 2009, the agency issued a document on best practices for treating workers with caregiving responsibilities. U.S. Equal Employment Opportunity Commission, "Employer Best Practices for Workers with Caregiving Responsibilities," 2009, available at http://www.eeoc.gov/policy/docs/caregiver-best-practices.html.

130. See John E. Matejkovic and Margaret E. Matejkovic, "If It Ain't Broke . . . Changes to FMLA Regulations Are Not Needed; Employee Compliance and Employer Enforcement of Current Regulations Are," *Willamette Law Review* 42 (2006): 413–438; Caitlyn M. Campbell, "Overstepping One's Bounds: The Department of Labor and the Family and Medical Leave Act," *Boston University Law Review* 84 (2004): 1077–1102.

131. 535 U.S. 81 (2002).

132. 29 C.F.R. § 825.208.

133. 29 C.F.R. § 825.700(a).

134. *Ragsdale,* 535 U.S. at 84.

135. The penalty provision was removed after *Ragsdale* was decided.

136. See Gabriel R. MacConaill, *"Nevada Department of Human Resources v. Hibbs:* Does Application of Section 5 Represent a Fundamental Change in the Immunity Abrogation Rules of 'New Federalism,' or Have the Burdens Simply Shifted?" *Penn State Law Review* 109 (2005): 831–855; Allison K. Slagle, *"Nevada Department of Human Resources v. Hibbs:* Regulation or Simply Encouragement?" *Capital University Law Review* 33 (2005): 869–895; Stephanie C. Bovee, "The Family Medical Leave Act: State Sovereignty and the Narrowing of Fourteenth Amendment Protection," *William and Mary Journal of Women and Law* 7 (2001): 1011–1037.

137. With some exceptions, the Eleventh Amendment bars a private individual from suing a state for monetary damages, that is, grants states immunity from damage awards. The Supreme Court has held that § 5 of the Fourteenth Amendment, authorizing Congress to enact appropriate legislation to enforce it, abrogates (nullifies) the state's immunity under the Eleventh Amendment. In *City of Boerne v. Flores,* 521 U.S. 507 (1997), the Court specified that Congress may pass laws under the authority of § 5 if it has evidence that the state violated the Fourteenth Amendment and that the law intends to remedy the violations. In the absence of such evidence, the Court held that the Eleventh Amendment shields states from

damage suits even if they violate the law. In *Kimel v. Florida Board of Regents,* 528 U.S. 62 (2000), and *Board of Trustees of the University of Alabama v. Garrett,* 531 U.S. 356 (2001), the Court ruled that Congress lacked the authority under the Fourteenth Amendment to abrogate state immunity in the ADEA and Section 1 of the ADA, thus shielding states from damage awards in suits brought to enforce these laws. See Susan Gluck Mezey, "The U.S. Supreme Court's Federalism Jurisprudence: *Alden v. Maine* and the Enhancement of State Sovereignty," *Publius: The Journal of Federalism* 30 (2000): 21–38.

138. See, for example, *Chittister v. Department of Community and Economic Development,* 226 F.3d 223 (3d Cir. 2000); *Hale v. Mann,* 219 F.3d 61 (2d Cir. 2000); *Sims v. University of Cincinnati,* 219 F.3d 559 (6th Cir. 2000); *Kazmier v. Widmann,* 225 F.3d 519 (5th Cir. 2000). In contrast, the courts rejected the state's claim of immunity from suit in actions brought to enforce the Equal Pay Act. See, for example, *Varner v. Illinois State University,* 150 F.3d 706 (7th Cir. 1998); *Hundertmark v. Florida Department of Transportation,* 205 F.3d 1272 (11th Cir. 2000); *Kovacevich v. Kent State University,* 224 F.3d 806 (6th Cir. 2000).

139. *Hibbs v. Department of Human Resources,* 273 F.3d 844 (9th Cir. 2001).

140. 29 U.S.C. § 2617(a)(2).

141. 538 U.S. 721 (2003).

142. *Nevada Department of Human Resources v. Hibbs,* 538 U.S. at 730.

143. *Nevada Department of Human Resources v. Hibbs,* 538 U.S. at 722.

144. David L. Hudson, Jr., "Court Surprises with Family Leave Act Ruling," *American Bar Association Journal eReport* 2 (May 30, 2003): 21–22.

145. See Ray, *A Detailed Look at Parental Leave Policies in 21 OECD Countries;* Julie Weber, "Policy Briefing Series, Work-Family Information for State Legislators," Sloan Work and Family Research Network, 2009, available at http://wfnetwork.bc.edu/pdfs/policy_makers17.pdf.

146. See National Partnership for Women and Families, "The Pregnancy Discrimination Act."

147. See Labor Project for Working Families, *Know Your Rights: Family Leave Laws in California,* 2009, available at http://www.working-families.org/learnmore/ca_family_leave_guide.pdf, for a discussion of the interaction of these family policies; Ray, *A Detailed Look at Parental Leave Policies in 21 OECD Countries;* see also Shiu and Wildman, "Pregnancy Discrimination and Social Change."

148. See Shiu and Wildman, "Pregnancy Discrimination and Social Change."

149. *San Diego Union Tribune,* September 24, 2002; *New York Times,* September 24, 2002.

150. *New York Times,* April 8, 2008.

151. Pub. Law No. 110-181.

152. See Marcy Karin, "Time Off for Military Families: An Emerging Case Study in a Time of War . . . and the Tipping Point for Future Laws Supporting Work-Life Balance?" *Rutgers Law Record* 33 (2009): 46–64.

153. Pub. Law No. 111-84.

154. 29 C.F.R. Part 825.

155. American Postal Workers Union, "Bush's Lame-Duck Labor Department to Implement Onerous FMLA Rule Changes," November 17, 2008, available at http://www.Apwu.org/news/webart/2008/08108-fmla-081110.htm.

156. Ashley Hawley, "Taking a Step Forward or Backward? The 2009 Revisions to the FMLA Regulations," *Wisconsin Journal of Law, Gender, and Society* 25 (2010): 137–159.

157. See U.S. House of Representatives, "Federal Employees Parental Leave Act of 2009," report accompanying H.R. 626, H. Rep. No. 111–116, Part I, 111th Cong., 1st sess., May 18, 2009.

158. Pub. Law No. 111-119.

159. In July 2009, H.R. 912 and S. 1422 were introduced in Congress as proposed amendments to the FMLA. The House approved H.R. 912 in a voice vote on February 9, 2009; the Senate passed S. 1422, also in a voice vote, on December 2, 2009.

6 Attaining Abortion Rights

The struggle over abortion rights has occupied the nation's attention for much of the twentieth century, with neither side able to declare final victory.[1] As this clash over cultural values persists, the courts continue to play a major role in determining the contours of abortion policy.

In 1973, abortion rights proponents were elated when the Supreme Court announced that the constitutional right to privacy includes a woman's right to choose to terminate her pregnancy. For the most part, over the next decade, the majority on the high court rejected legislative attempts to restrict access to abortion for adult women.[2] However, when the composition of the Court became more conservative, advocates of abortion rights began to realize that they could no longer take the right to choose for granted. Table 6.1 presents the Supreme Court's abortion rights rulings from 1973 to 1989.

The Right to Abortion Develops

Abortion may be one of the most controversial legal, political, and social issues of our time. It was not always so. Prior to the 1800s, abortion was widely practiced; it was even considered a relatively safe medical procedure, especially before quickening, the time at which fetal movement is detectable (generally around the fourth or fifth month of pregnancy). Prescriptions for home abortion remedies were widely used and freely advertised. Criminal charges, rare in any event, were never brought against the woman. By 1880, however, the law had changed, and legal abortions were no longer attainable in the United States.

Increasing pressure for abortion reform developed in the 1950s and 1960s. In 1962, the nation watched as Phoenix celebrity Sherri Finkbine, star of a children's television show, was unable to obtain a legal abortion after she had taken thalidomide, a tranquilizer drug found to cause

Table 6.1 Supreme Court Abortion Rights Rulings, 1973–1989

Case	Date	Issue[a]	Ruling[b]
Roe	1973	Abortion ban	Expands access to abortion
Doe	1973	Abortion restrictions	Expands access to abortion
Danforth	1976	Minors' rights	Expands access to abortion
Beal	1977	Public funding	Limits access to abortion
Maher	1977	Public funding	Limits access to abortion
Poelker	1977	Public funding	Limits access to abortion
Bellotti	1979	Minors' rights	Expands access to abortion
Harris	1980	Public funding	Limits access to abortion
H.L.	1981	Minors' rights	Limits access to abortion
City of Akron	1983	Informed consent	Expands access to abortion
Thornburgh	1986	Informed consent	Limits access to abortion
Webster	1989	Viability testing	Limits access to abortion

Notes: a. Based on the major issue in the case.
b. Based on the overall outcome of the case.

severe birth defects. Under Arizona law, the only reason for a legal abortion was to save the life of the woman. Ultimately, Finkbine was forced to travel to Sweden for her abortion.

Also during this time, an outbreak of German measles—a disease often leading to blindness, deafness, or mental retardation in infants—further focused the public's attention on the restrictiveness of abortion laws when women with the disease were denied legal abortions. The German measles epidemic led to the birth of thousands of severely disabled children.[3]

Women's rights activists began to lobby for abortion reform as a necessary condition for sexual equality. As a California activist explained,

> when we talk about women's rights, we can get all the rights in the world . . . and none of them means a doggone thing if we don't own the flesh we stand in, if we can't control what happens to us, if the whole course of our lives can be changed by somebody else that can get us pregnant by accident, or by deceit, or by force. So I consider the right to elective abortion, whether you dream of doing it or not, is the cornerstone of the woman's movement. . . . if you can't control your own body you can't control your future, to the degree that any of us can control futures.[4]

Pressure for reform of restrictive abortion laws increased as abortions were a reality for millions of American women. The number of illegal abortions performed can only be estimated, but studies have concluded that in the years before legalization in 1973, there were approximately 1 million illegal abortions performed each year in the United

States.[5] Many members of the medical profession also favored legalizing abortion because they believed medical judgments should control the decision.

Between 1967 and 1970, abortion reform legislation was enacted in twelve states, including Colorado (the first), New York, California, Hawaii, North Carolina, Alaska, and Georgia. The laws differed, but most comported with the Model State Abortion Law drafted by the American Law Institute (ALI) in 1959, permitting abortions for victims of rape or incest, in cases of severe fetal deformity, or when the woman's life or health was threatened. Going beyond the ALI model, the New York law allowed abortion for any reason during the first twenty-four weeks of pregnancy.[6]

By 1973, although a number of states were allowing women easier access to abortion, some, such as Texas, still banned all abortions except to save the woman's life. In Georgia, abortions were permitted when the pregnancy endangered the life of the woman or would lead to serious and permanent health problems. When the Texas and Georgia laws were challenged in the Supreme Court in *Roe v. Wade*[7] and *Doe v. Bolton*,[8] the Court was forced to determine whether they violated the right to privacy guaranteed by the U.S. Constitution.

The foundation for *Roe* and *Doe* was laid in two earlier decisions: *Griswold v. Connecticut*,[9] decided in 1965, and *Eisenstadt v. Baird*,[10] decided in 1972. In *Griswold,* in a 7 to 2 vote, the Court invalidated a Connecticut law prohibiting the use of contraceptives by married couples on the grounds that various amendments to the Constitution created a "zone of privacy" that is protected from intrusion by the government. Because the marital relationship lies within that zone, a law forbidding the use of contraceptive devices constitutes an unconstitutional invasion of that privacy.

A few years later, in *Eisenstadt,* the Court struck a Massachusetts law prohibiting the distribution of contraceptive devices or materials to single persons. Speaking for the majority, Brennan stated that a married couple's privacy, established in *Griswold,* belongs to single persons as well. Perhaps laying the foundation for *Roe* less than a year later, he explained that "if the right of privacy means anything, it is the right of the *individual,* married or single, to be free from unwarranted governmental intrusion into matters so fundamentally affecting a person as the decision whether to bear or beget a child."[11]

In *Roe,* the Court was asked to decide whether the privacy right articulated in *Griswold* extends to the right to decide whether to terminate a pregnancy. Norma McCorvy, an unmarried, pregnant carnival worker, sought an abortion in her home state of Texas in 1969. McCorvy consulted a doctor, who informed her that abortion was illegal in Texas and suggested she might try going to another state. With no money to travel, she sought an attorney to arrange a private adoption and was referred to two Dallas–Fort Worth attorneys, Linda Coffee and Sarah Weddington. It was a fortuitous meeting because Coffee and Weddington had been looking for a plaintiff to challenge the Texas abortion law in federal court. They accepted her case, arguing that restricting the right to abortion unconstitutionally infringes on a woman's fundamental right to privacy.[12]

Speaking for the 7 to 2 majority, Blackmun agreed that the right to privacy "is broad enough to encompass a woman's decision whether or not to terminate her pregnancy."[13] This right, he emphasized, is fundamental, but not absolute, and a woman may not "terminate her pregnancy at whatever time, in whatever way, and for whatever reason she alone chooses."[14] He proclaimed that the woman's right must be balanced against the state's interest in regulating abortions.

Texas argued that the abortion law was intended to protect women from the medical risks of abortion and protect prenatal life.[15] Agreeing that these interests were important, the Court pointed to the established principle that limits on fundamental rights "may be justified only by a 'compelling state interest.'"[16]

McCorvey's attorneys argued that the state did not have a compelling interest in banning abortion, and the government countered that protecting prenatal life is always a compelling reason to prohibit abortion in the absence of a threat to a woman's life. The Supreme Court rejected both views.

Texas contended that the fetus is a person, protected by the Fourteenth Amendment. The Court said there was no evidence that the framers of the Constitution had ever contemplated protecting the unborn. Texas also maintained that life began at conception and its compelling interest in prenatal life arose at that point and continued throughout the pregnancy. Citing the dispute among religious, medical, and philosophical perspectives about when life begins, the Court declared itself unable to define the onset of life and refused to accept the state's unproven theory of life as a justification for its abortion regulation.

Rejecting the state's claim that its interests in maternal health and fetal life are compelling throughout the pregnancy, the Court granted that each becomes compelling at a specific stage. To accommodate these interests, the Court adopted a trimester approach based on the principle that abortion regulations should vary with the trimester, or stage, of pregnancy.

Because abortion carries almost no medical risk when performed in the first three months of pregnancy, the state has no compelling reason to regulate the procedure; it may only require the physician to be licensed. Thus, during the first trimester, Blackmun said,

> the attending physician, in consultation with his patient, is free to determine, without regulation by the State, that, in his medical judgment, the patient's pregnancy should be terminated. If that decision is reached, the judgment may be effectuated by an abortion free of interference by the State.[17]

Although the Court would later retreat from this sweeping statement, with about 90 percent of abortions performed during the first trimester, Blackmun's avowal had enormous consequences for a woman's abortion decision.[18]

The state's "important and legitimate interest" in maternal health becomes compelling at "approximately the end of the first trimester." During the second trimester, the state "may regulate the abortion procedure to the extent that the regulation reasonably relates to the preservation and protection of maternal health."[19] A regulation specifying the place where the abortion may be performed (that is, in a hospital or clinic) would be permissible according to this standard.

Last, the "State's important and legitimate interest in potential life" becomes compelling at viability, when "the fetus . . . presumably has the capability of meaningful life outside the mother's womb."[20] The Court located viability at about seven months (twenty-eight weeks) but noted that it may occur even earlier, possibly at twenty-four weeks. In protecting the fetus during the last trimester, the state "may go so far as to proscribe abortion . . . except when it is necessary to preserve the life or health of the mother."[21]

After applying this standard to the Texas abortion law, the Court declared it unconstitutional. A law that permits abortion only to save a woman's life, makes no distinctions among the stages of pregnancy, and acknowledges no competing interests with the state's interest in fetal life violates the Fourteenth Amendment's due process clause by interfering with the woman's right to privacy.

In *Doe,* the Court determined the constitutionality of Georgia's abortion statute.[22] The Georgia law exempted certain "necessary" abortions from criminal penalties: if the pregnancy endangered the woman's life or would cause serious and permanent injury; if the fetus would be born with a "grave, permanent, and irremediable mental or physical defect"; or if the pregnancy resulted from rape. In addition to the woman's physician, two other doctors were required to examine her and certify in writing that the abortion was "necessary." All abortions had to be performed in licensed and accredited hospitals and required advance approval from at least three members of the hospital's abortion committee. The law authorized hospitals to deny admittance to abortion patients and allowed physicians or staff members to refuse to participate in abortions. It also specified that the woman seeking the abortion must be a Georgia resident.[23]

Applying the standard developed in *Roe,* with the same 7 to 2 majority, the Court held that the state could not require all abortions to be performed in hospitals because it had no compelling interest in first trimester abortions; it also ruled that the hospital-committee approval and two-physician requirement served no legitimate state interest and "unduly" restricted a woman's right to privacy, and that the residency requirement abridged her constitutional right to travel and was irrational as well.[24]

Rehnquist dissented, disputing the majority's conclusion that abortion is a fundamental right, entitled to strict scrutiny and meriting the compelling state interest test. Conceding that the right to privacy is a liberty protected by the Fourteenth Amendment, he emphasized that the "liberty is not guaranteed absolutely against deprivation, only against deprivation without due process of law." The traditional test to assess the constitutionality of economic or social legislation, such as an abortion law, is whether the law is rationally related to a "valid state objective," that is, to apply minimal scrutiny.[25] By using minimal scrutiny, he said, the Court would appropriately entrust abortion policy to the judgments of state legislators.

Also dissenting, White accused the majority of allowing a woman to terminate her pregnancy for almost any reason "or for no reason at all" and without having to demonstrate any risk to her health. Before viability, he said, the Court shows more concern for "the convenience, whim, or caprice of the putative mother . . . than [for] the life or potential life of the fetus."[26] Like Rehnquist, he charged the Court with creating a new constitutional right for pregnant women and said he found no constitutional justification for usurping the power of elected state representatives to decide how to protect human life.

Following *Roe* and *Doe,* almost 200 bills were introduced in state legislatures across the nation, and within two years after the Court's ruling, thirty-two states enacted a total of sixty-two abortion-related laws. The laws revolved around seven categories: regulations specifying where abortions could be performed and by whom, informed consent requirements, record-keeping and reporting requirements, advertising prohibitions, funding restrictions, conscience laws (allowing hospitals or physicians to refuse to perform abortions), and fetal protection policies.[27] Largely aimed at second trimester abortions, most of these laws were quickly challenged in federal court.

In June 1974, the Missouri General Assembly approved a law directed at second trimester abortions.[28] Its most significant features were the requirement that second trimester abortions be performed in hospitals and the ban on the saline amniocentesis method of abortion, the most popular second trimester abortion procedure at the time.[29]

Three days after the act went into effect, Planned Parenthood and two Missouri physicians challenged it in federal court on behalf of themselves and their female patients.[30] When the case reached the Supreme Court, it became clear that the Court had become more divided on the issue of abortion rights than it had been in *Roe*. In a 5 to 4 opinion, in *Planned Parenthood of Central Missouri v. Danforth*,[31] the Court rejected the state's claim that its regulation furthered maternal health. Other second trimester abortion procedures were not readily available, and the Court found it illogical to ban a safe abortion procedure and force women to undergo a more dangerous method under the guise of protecting their health.

Minors' Rights

Shortly after *Roe*, states began to impose restrictions on a minor woman's access to abortion, usually by requiring one or both parents to consent to the procedure.[32] Beginning in 1976, the Court handed down rulings determining the limits of the minor's right to privacy, weighing it against the parents' interest in the welfare of their child and the state's interest in the health of the minor and the integrity of the family.[33]

The Missouri law challenged by Planned Parenthood required an unmarried woman under eighteen to obtain her parent or guardian's written consent, unless a licensed physician certified that the abortion was needed to save her life. A married woman needed her husband's consent. Known as a "blanket veto," this law took the decision away from the woman and gave it to her parents or husband.

The Court struck both provisions. Recalling that the abortion decision is between the physician and the woman, the Court held that "the State does not have the constitutional authority to give a third party an absolute, and possibly arbitrary, veto over the decision of the physician and his patient to terminate the patient's pregnancy, regardless of the reason for withholding the consent."[34] Conceding that parents have an "independent interest" in their minor daughter's pregnancy, the Court believed her right to privacy should prevail. Missouri argued that the statute "safeguard[ed] the family unit" and promoted "parental authority," but Blackmun said he doubted that it accomplished either goal.

Stewart and Powell indicated their concerns about how much autonomy a minor should be allowed to have in deciding whether to have an abortion. They stressed that their objection to the parental consent provision stemmed from its "absoluteness" and that a law that included a procedure for allowing a child to seek a judge's consent instead of the parent's (a "judicial bypass" procedure) would be acceptable to them.

As in *Roe,* White dissented, stressing that the law was aimed at furthering the parents' interest in their child. There is nothing novel, or unconstitutional, he insisted, when a state seeks "to protect children from their own immature and improvident decisions."[35] Stevens also dissented from the majority's stand on parental consent because, in his view, the state's interest in the welfare of minors entitles it to compel them to obtain the "advice and moral support of a parent." Unlike the other dissenters, however, he did not believe the law was intended to be an anti-abortion measure. He assumed that some parents will "advise" abortions that should not be performed and others will "prevent" those that should be performed. He felt that "the overriding consideration is that the right to make the choice be exercised as wisely as possible."[36]

With the "blanket" veto imposed by the Missouri law forbidden, states began to incorporate judicial bypass procedures into their consent laws. Under such a provision, a minor who was unable to secure her parent's consent (or was unwilling to ask) could seek consent from a judge. Under most bypass procedures, the teenager had to prove that she was sufficiently mature to make her own decision or that the abortion was in her "best interests."

Bellotti v. Baird,[37] decided in 1979, clarified the Court's view on the judicial bypass process. It revolved around a 1974 Massachusetts law requiring parental consent for unmarried minors under eighteen; if one or both parents refused to consent, a judge could, after a hearing, supply the necessary permission. If a parent had died or deserted the family, the other's consent was sufficient. The law specified criminal penalties for physicians who performed abortions without the requisite consent.

The Supreme Court was sharply divided.[38] Although there was only one dissent, the others were unable to agree on the reasoning. Powell, writing for a plurality of four, recognized the state's important interest in furthering the "guiding role of parents in the upbringing of their children."[39] But he believed that the state must accommodate a minor's right to privacy by creating an alternate route for obtaining consent; it must also allow a young woman to demonstrate that she is mature enough to make an abortion decision on her own or that the abortion is in her best interests. Powell articulated three criteria that became the standard for determining a proper judicial bypass procedure: it must allow a minor to show either that she is mature enough to decide to have an abortion or, if she is not, that an abortion would be in her best interests; it must ensure her anonymity; and it must allow an expedited appeal.[40]

Stevens's concurring opinion simply found the law unconstitutional because, like the Missouri law in *Danforth,* it subjected a minor's abortion decision to an "absolute veto" by a third party. In all situations, he said, regardless of how mature she is, either her parents or a judge controlled her decision.

In many states, the battle over abortions for minors shifted from consent requirements to notification provisions. Under such laws, physicians and hospitals are required to notify the parents of pregnant teenagers that their daughters are seeking abortions. The Court ruled on the constitutionality of a Utah notice law in *H. L. v. Matheson,*[41] decided in 1981. The statute required a physician to "notify, if possible, the parents or guardian of the woman upon whom the abortion is to be performed, if she is a minor, or the husband of the woman, if she is married."[42] There was no judicial bypass procedure.

The law was initially challenged in state court by a fifteen-year-old, pregnant, unmarried teenager living at home with her parents, who wanted to obtain an abortion without notifying them. The Court limited its ruling to the facts of the case, holding that a state may require a physician to notify the parents of an immature and dependent minor seeking an abortion and is not obligated to provide a bypass procedure for such teenagers.[43] With a 6 to 3 majority, with Burger announcing the decision, the Court held that the law did not establish veto power in the parents, nor did it deter a minor from seeking an abortion. Instead, it furthered the state's interest in promoting the family unit and protected the teenager by allowing her parents to supply her physician with her medical records, as well as her emotional and psychological history. The Court concluded that "the Utah statute is reasonably calculated to protect minors in appellant's class by enhancing the potential for parental consultation concerning a decision that has potentially traumatic and permanent consequences."[44]

Marshall dissented, arguing that the notice requirement unduly burdened the girl's right to abortion. He denied that the statute served

Utah's asserted purpose of providing relevant medical information to physicians because the law did not require the parents to communicate medical history or other information to the physician. A physician placing a telephone call to the parents a few minutes before the abortion was scheduled to be performed would satisfy the statute. He also contended that the statute was "plainly overbroad." Parental consultation, he said, is inappropriate when incest or other physical abuse is involved or when a teenager is afraid that the notice will prevent her from obtaining the abortion she seeks. He doubted that a parental notification requirement would strengthen the family, and in any event, he argued, a state's desire to establish parental authority should not be permitted to override the young woman's fundamental right to privacy as guaranteed by the Fourteenth Amendment.

Public Funding

Another area in which the Court was asked to approve governmental restrictions on the right to abortion was in the area of public funding. Here, the issue was not whether a woman could secure an abortion but whether the government had to pay for it if she could not afford it. This issue had arisen because *Roe* established a "negative [right]—limiting state power to forbid abortions—rather than creating a positive state obligation to implement abortion."[45]

Many states had reacted to *Roe* by limiting payment for abortion expenses in their state medical assistance programs for indigent women. Medicaid is a joint federal-state program administered by the states and subject to the rules of Title XIX of the Social Security Act.[46] It was estimated that in 1977, almost 3 million women who were eligible for Medicaid assistance were at risk of having an unwanted pregnancy.[47] According to Bayh, restrictions on abortion funding under Medicaid meant that society was "saying that those who have the resources to enjoy their constitutional right to decide to have an abortion may do so. Those who do not have the financial resources have the constitutional right, but," he added, "a right without the ability to use it is absolutely worthless."[48] On the contrary, said Senator John Stennis, Democrat from Mississippi, the restrictions meant that government would not be "spending millions of tax dollars for the unnecessary slaughter of innocent unborn children."[49]

Most lower federal courts found the funding regulations illegal.[50] On June 20, 1977, the Supreme Court handed down a trio of rulings, *Beal v. Doe*,[51] *Maher v. Roe*,[52] and *Poelker v. Doe*,[53] revealing its approach to public funding of abortions. The question was whether the state's interest in childbirth justified its refusal to fund medically unnecessary (nontherapeutic) abortions. Abortion rights advocates charged that states were misusing their authority over medical assistance programs to assert their opposition to abortion, forcing poor women to have unwanted children by denying them access to legal and safe abortions. They argued that the funding regulations were aimed at discouraging abortions and that withholding funds for poor women's abortions restricted access to abortion as effectively as the Texas law struck down in *Roe*.[54]

In *Beal*, the Court held that Title XIX allowed the state of Pennsylvania to fund only "medically necessary" abortions. Speaking for the Court, Powell noted that it was "hardly inconsistent with the objectives of the Act [Title XIX] for a State to refuse to fund *unnecessary*— though perhaps desirable—medical services."[55] Acknowledging that abortions were cheaper and safer than childbirth, Powell held that a state's "strong and legitimate interest" in childbirth justified its refusal to fund abortions.

In his dissent, Brennan predicted that the majority opinion "can only result as a practical matter in forcing penniless pregnant women to have children they would not have borne if the State had not weighted the scales to make their choice to have abortions substantially more onerous."[56] Marshall also dissented, accusing the state of abusing its power. "It is all too obvious," he charged, "that the governmental actions in these cases, ostensibly taken to 'encourage' women to carry pregnancies to term, are in reality intended to impose a moral viewpoint that no State may constitutionally enforce." He contended that anti-abortionists were using "every imaginable means to . . . impose their moral choices upon the rest of society"; the result, he predicted, will be that nearly all poor women will be denied access to "safe and legal abortions."[57]

Maher, the most important and comprehensive of the three rulings, was the only one decided on constitutional grounds. The plaintiffs claimed that the Connecticut regulation restricting Medicaid funds to "medically necessary" abortions violated the equal protection clause by differentiating among women on the basis of wealth.[58]

Powell rejected this argument, explaining that "the regulation places no obstacles—absolute or otherwise—in the pregnant woman's path to an abortion. . . . The indigency that may make it more difficult—and in some cases, perhaps, impossible—for some women to have abortions is neither created nor in any way affected by the Connecticut regulation." Admitting that a woman living in poverty may be less likely to be able to afford an abortion, Powell insisted that the decision "signals no retreat from Roe."[59]

The last of the trio, *Poelker,* arose from a St. Louis, Missouri, policy banning elective abortions in public hospitals. In a brief unsigned opinion, echoing *Maher,* the majority held that public hospitals are not required to provide or even permit elective abortions. The Court stressed that the policy reflected the views of the people's representatives on the city council and could be reversed if a majority of people were opposed to it. Again, the Court ruled that the government may adopt a funding policy that expresses its preference for childbirth over abortion.

In a press conference following these rulings, Carter defended the Court, saying, "There are many things in life that are not fair, that wealthy people can afford and poor people can't. But I don't believe that the federal government should take action to try to make those opportunities exactly equal, particularly when there is a moral factor involved."[60] By the end of 1978, only ten states and the District of Columbia were paying for abortions for poor women.[61]

Congress entered the policymaking arena on Medicaid funding for abortions by enacting the Hyde Amendment, named after the abortion opponent in the House who made no secret of the fact that the law was aimed at restricting access to abortions.[62] In 1977, Hyde proclaimed, "I certainly would like to prevent, if I could legally, anybody having an abortion, a rich woman, a middle-class woman, or a poor woman. Unfortunately, the only vehicle available is the . . . Medicaid bill."[63] A year later, his cosponsor, Representative Robert Bauman, Republican from Maryland, said, "I think without the availability of Federal funds there would definitely be a decrease in abortions. That is what we seek."[64]

The first assault on the Hyde Amendment came when Planned Parenthood of New York City filed suit in federal court. The lower court judge, asserting that his decree affected the Hyde Amendment nationwide, ordered all states to pay for "medically necessary" abortions.[65] On appeal to the Supreme Court, his order was vacated, and the case sent back for rehearing in light of the June 1977 decisions.[66] On January 15, 1980, the lower court held that the Hyde Amendment violated women's First and Fifth Amendment rights.

On appeal, Stewart announced the opinion for the 5 to 4 Court in *Harris v. McRae.*[67] He compared the Hyde Amendment to the law upheld in *Maher,* stressing that neither interfered with a woman's constitutionally protected right to an abortion. Echoing *Maher,* he explained that

> although government may not place obstacles in the path of a woman's exercise of her freedom of choice, it need not remove those not of its own creation. . . . The financial constraints that restrict an indigent woman's

ability to enjoy the full range of constitutionally protected freedom of
choice are the product not of governmental restrictions on access to abortions, but rather of her indigency.[68]

As in *Maher,* the Court rejected the equal protection challenge,
holding that Congress did not discriminate against poor women by
refusing to pay their abortion expenses. The dissent argued that the
Hyde Amendment imposed a moral code on poor women only and
denied their ability to exercise their right to privacy just as effectively as
the laws had done in the days before *Roe.* Marshall predicted that
women seeking abortions would be forced to resort to dangerous methods to secure them; he contended that the majority opinion was a
"retreat" from *Roe* and a "cruel blow to the most powerless members of
our society."[69] With some variations, the Hyde Amendment has
remained in place for over three decades.[70]

Restrictive Abortion Regulations

In February 1978, the city council of Akron, Ohio, enacted the most
restrictive set of abortion regulations yet devised.[71] The ordinance,
authored by the counsel for the Ohio Right to Life Society, who later
argued the case in front of the Supreme Court, contained seventeen provisions regulating the performance of abortions, including a variety of
consent and notice requirements affecting first trimester abortions.
Perhaps the most important section required all abortions after the first
trimester to be performed in hospitals rather than clinics or doctors'
offices. Because of the inaccessibility of hospital abortions and the cost
involved, this provision significantly reduced access to abortions for
Ohio women.

The sections on informed consent and waiting periods required a
physician to obtain a woman's written consent and wait twenty-four hours
after obtaining the consent before performing the abortion; the doctor
must also notify the child's father (or parents if she was underage). To
ensure that her consent is "informed," the doctor must describe to her "in
detail the anatomical and physiological characteristics of the particular
unborn child at the gestational point of development at which time the
abortion is to be performed," explaining that "the unborn child is a human
life from the moment of conception" and can feel pain. The doctor's lecture must state that an "abortion is a major surgical procedure, which can
result in serious complications" and inform her that it "may worsen any

existing psychological problems she may have, and can result in severe emotional disturbances."[72]

The ordinance was immediately challenged by the ACLU on behalf of an Akron physician and several abortion clinics. Powell announced the 6 to 3 opinion for the Court in *City of Akron v. Akron Center for Reproductive Health*[73] in 1983. Abortion rights advocates were especially pleased that Powell rejected the solicitor general's efforts to persuade the Court to adopt a lower form of scrutiny in reviewing abortion regulations.[74] He reiterated the Court's commitment to strict scrutiny, insisting that states must demonstrate a compelling reason to restrict abortion. Despite the outcome, the ruling revealed that cracks were developing in the edifice constructed by *Roe* ten years earlier.

The Court found that the hospital requirement created a "significant obstacle" to a woman seeking an abortion because it more than doubled the cost; moreover, Akron hospitals rarely performed second trimester abortions. The city conceded that its regulation erected a barrier for a pregnant woman, yet defended the ordinance as a reasonable health measure. But Powell explained that the hospital requirement, like any second trimester regulation, is constitutional "only if it is reasonably designed" to advance the state's compelling interest in maternal health, and a regulation that "depart[s] from accepted medical practice" cannot reasonably advance the state's interest.[75]

At the time *Roe* was decided, health considerations had prompted the American Public Health Association (APHA) and the American College of Obstetricians and Gynecologists (ACOG) to recommend that all abortions performed during or after the second trimester be performed in hospitals. Based on these views, *Roe* had cited a hospitalization requirement as a possible example of a permissible second trimester abortion regulation. In the intervening decade since *Roe,* however, second trimester abortions (at least up to sixteen weeks) were being safely performed in abortion clinics, making it unnecessary to go to a full-service hospital. By 1983, the two medical organizations had abandoned their recommendation for hospital abortions during the first sixteen weeks of pregnancy.[76] And because the Akron regulation now "departed from accepted medical practice," the Court found it unconstitutional, declaring that the city could not reasonably require all second trimester abortions to be performed in hospitals.[77]

The twenty-four-hour waiting period and informed consent requirements of the Akron ordinance regulated first trimester abortions, as well as those occurring later in the pregnancy. Despite the Court's statement in *Roe* that first trimester abortions were largely beyond state regulation,

Powell explained in *City of Akron* that first trimester abortion regulations may be valid as long as they "have no significant impact on the woman's exercise of her right . . . [and are] justified by important state health objectives."[78] But the Court found that the waiting period in the Akron ordinance led to scheduling delays that increased a woman's risk and did not further a legitimate state interest. With appropriate counseling and informed written consent, the Court held, no purpose is served by an arbitrary twenty-four-hour delay.

Attorneys for the city characterized the mandatory lecture to the pregnant woman as an attempt to ensure that her consent is informed. The Court found instead that the information it characterized as "a parade of horribles" was intended to influence her choice against an abortion.[79] And by specifying the content of the warning, the Court believed that the city was also intruding on the physician's ability to practice medicine.

Many eyes were on O'Connor. This was her first abortion case, and prior to her confirmation hearings, she had been attacked by anti-abortion groups who feared that her views on reproductive rights diverged from theirs. Members of Congress questioned her very closely about her views on *Roe*.

Her opinion in *City of Akron* suggested that the fears of abortion opponents were largely unfounded. Her dissent characterized *Roe*'s trimester approach as technologically outmoded. She called it "unworkable" because medical knowledge was simultaneously advancing the state's interest in potential life by moving the point of viability to an earlier stage in the pregnancy and delaying the state's interest in maternal health by making abortions safer at a later stage in the pregnancy. She even suggested that viability might move up to the first trimester.[80] These technological changes, she contended, meant the *Roe* framework was "on a collision course with itself."[81]

O'Connor argued it was inappropriate to divide the state's interests into trimesters because the state has a compelling interest in maternal health and fetal life throughout the pregnancy. "Potential life," she said, "is no less potential in the first weeks of pregnancy than it is at viability or afterwards. At any stage in pregnancy," she continued, "there is the *potential* for human life."[82]

She urged the Court to limit itself to one question only: is the regulation "unduly burdensome" on a pregnant woman's right to abortion? If it does not "unduly" burden her abortion decision, O'Connor said she would apply minimal scrutiny and merely require the state to show that the law is rationally related to a legitimate purpose, reserving strict scrutiny for regulations that impose an undue burden on a woman's right to abortion. Seeking to restrain the Court's interference with state law-making, she urged it to pay "careful attention" to a state legislature's judgments about an abortion regulation and ask whether the law imposed an undue burden or merely "inhibit[ed]" access to abortion.[83] She judged none of the provisions of the Akron ordinance as unduly burdensome and, applying minimal scrutiny, found each rationally related to a legitimate state interest and constitutionally valid.

A new drama began to unfold in 1985 when the Supreme Court agreed to review Pennsylvania and Illinois abortion laws. The Illinois case was dismissed on procedural grounds, but despite procedural irregularities in the Pennsylvania case, the Court chose to rule on it.[84]

After the Court struck its earlier abortion law, Pennsylvania enacted another, the 1982 Pennsylvania Abortion Control Act. Similar to the Akron ordinance, this law was also the product of an anti-abortion group. It contained provisions on second trimester abortions, informed consent, the physician's responsibilities, record-keeping and reporting, a twenty-four-hour waiting period, public funding, and parental consent for minors.[85] On June 11, 1986, in *Thornburgh v. American College of Obstetricians and Gynecologists*,[86] the last major abortion case decided by the Burger Court, the Court announced its decision on informed consent, the physician's duty, and reporting requirements. Blackmun delivered the 5 to 4 majority opinion, frequently referring to the statute's aim to limit abortions.[87]

The law required seven kinds of information to be given to the woman, five by the physician personally. Along with the usual medical information about risks associated with the procedure, a doctor had to tell a woman "that there may be detrimental physical and psychological effects which are not accurately foreseeable." The law also required the physician to inform her that she might be entitled to financial support from the state and the father of her child.

The woman also had to read (or be read) a card informing her that adoption agencies were available to help her and that she was "strongly urged" to contact them. The material had to describe the "probable anatomical and physiological characteristics of the unborn child at two-week gestational increments from fertilization to full term, including any relevant information on the possibility of the unborn child's survival."[88] After receiving the information, she was required to wait twenty-four hours before she could legally give consent. The Court found that, like the "parade of horribles" in *City of Akron*, the informed consent provision of the Pennsylvania law was intended to deter abortions. It seemed "to be nothing less than an outright attempt to wedge the Commonwealth's message discouraging abortion into the privacy of the informed-consent dialogue between the woman and her physician."[89]

Rather than ensuring informed consent, the information would likely increase a woman's anxiety and tension about the upcoming procedure and harm the doctor-patient relationship. Furthermore, because much of the information was not relevant to informed consent, it served "no legitimate state interest." The Court concluded that these provisions were designed to prevent a woman from exercising her choice freely instead of assisting her in making her decision. And "states are not free under the guise of protecting maternal health or potential life, to intimidate women into continuing pregnancies."[90]

The law required physicians, under the threat of losing their licenses, to file detailed reports of the abortion, including the basis for their determination that the fetus was not viable. Although the reports were not supposed to become public records, they were to be made available for public inspection and copying. The woman's name would not be part of the record, but because of the breadth of information called for, it would be possible to identify her. Blackmun concluded that the information required in the Pennsylvania law exceeded health-related concerns and served no legitimate interest. This reporting regulation was different from the one in *Danforth*, he said, because the Missouri law kept the records confidential except for public health officers and was designed for statistical purposes only.

The Pennsylvania law also instructed physicians performing an abortion on a viable fetus to exercise the same degree of care they would with a child intended to be born alive. The physician was ordered to use a technique that "would provide the best opportunity for the unborn child . . . unless . . . [it] would present a significantly greater medical risk to the life or health of the pregnant woman."[91] The penalty for violating the law was a possible seven-year prison sentence and a $15,000 fine. The Court found this provision unconstitutional because it promoted an impermissible tradeoff between the woman's health and fetal life.

Another section required the presence of a second physician at an abortion after viability to preserve the child's life. The Court had upheld a similar provision in a previous case because that statute contained an "implicit" exception to prevent an increased risk to a woman's health if an abortion were delayed to await a second physician. But because the Pennsylvania law provided no exception for life-threatening situations, the Court found the provision unconstitutional for its effect on "chilling the performance of a late abortion, which, more than one performed at an earlier date, perhaps tend to be under emergency conditions."[92]

Blackmun ended with an impassioned plea to preserve the right to abortion. He acknowledged that abortion "raises moral and spiritual questions over which honorable persons can disagree sincerely and profoundly." Yet, he insisted that

> few decisions are more personal and intimate, more properly private, or more basic to individual dignity and autonomy, than a woman's decision— with the guidance of her physician and within the limits specified in *Roe*— whether to end her pregnancy. A woman's right to make that choice freely is fundamental. Any other result, in our view, would protect inadequately a central part of the sphere of liberty that our law guarantees equally to all.[93]

In dissent, Burger accused the majority of exceeding the bounds of *Roe*. It is not possible, he said, that the Court would forbid a state from giving a woman "accurate medical information" about the procedure she is about to undertake. How can the Court refuse to allow the state to impose conditions for obtaining consent for a medical procedure, he asked rhetorically? Moreover, he stressed, the second physician requirement was merely a means of realizing the state's compelling interest in fetal life after viability. Pennsylvania was entitled to assume, he said, that the Court meant what it said in *Roe* that the state had a legitimate interest in a viable fetus.

O'Connor devoted the bulk of her dissent to attacking the procedural irregularities of the decision. But more important, she continued to advocate the undue burden standard, which, she stressed, the Court had relied on in past cases. She accused the Court of going "well beyond distortion" of that standard. "It [now] seems," she said, "that the mere possibility that some women will be less likely to choose to have an abortion by virtue of the presence of a particular state regulation suffices to invalidate it."[94]

O'Connor had indicated in *City of Akron* that she would apply a stricter scrutiny to legislation that unduly burdened a woman's decision to abort but did not suggest what type of regulation she would regard as unduly burdensome. With her acceptance of the Pennsylvania restrictions on a woman's access to abortion, she indicated that her threshold was a high one.

White's was the major dissent in *Thornburgh*. He urged the majority to acknowledge that *Roe* was wrongly decided and to overrule it. He insisted that abortion is not a fundamental right. But, he added, even if it were, the Pennsylvania law is within constitutional bounds because it furthers the state's compelling interest in the fetus before and after viability. The right to personal autonomy recognized in *Griswold* and *Eisenstadt* does not extend to abortion, he contended. The decision to abort a fetus is distinct, he said, from the decision not to conceive it in the first place. Because a life is involved, a woman's decision to abort is "different in kind from other decisions the Court has protected under the rubric of personal or family privacy and autonomy."[95] He charged that by identifying abortion as a fundamental right, the majority was infusing the Constitution with its own values. Reiterating that the primary responsibility for abortion policy should be left to the states, he urged the Court to defer to the views of state legislators when reviewing abortion regulations.

White argued that Pennsylvania's informed consent regulation, unlike Akron's, merely represents the state's attempt to present truthful information to a woman considering an abortion. He defended the reporting requirements because they furthered the state's medical knowledge of fetal and maternal health and believed the state to be within its authority to require a physician to preserve the life of a viable fetus. If a state can prohibit an abortion entirely during the last trimester except to save a woman's life, surely, he said, it can compel a procedure that gives the fetus the greatest chance of survival.

Abortion opponents believed that the Reagan-Bush justices appointed throughout the 1980s and early 1990s would undermine the Court's commitment to *Roe* and allow states greater latitude to restrict a woman's access to abortion. They anxiously awaited the Court's decision in another Missouri case, *Webster v. Reproductive Health Services,*[96] hoping that the *Thornburgh* dissenters would attract more votes to allow an anti-abortion majority to uphold the law.

On July 4, 1989, a *New York Times* banner headline read, "Supreme Court, 5–4, Narrowing *Roe v. Wade,* Upholds Sharp State Limits on Abortions."[97] In a sharply divided—and often bitterly worded—opinion, the Supreme Court sparked renewed interest in the abortion debate by raising serious doubts about *Roe*'s future.

The 1986 Missouri abortion law was challenged by doctors, nurses, abortion clinics, and Planned Parenthood. Following a three-day trial, the district court declared seven provisions of the act unconstitutional; the circuit court affirmed the lower court on all but one of these.

The Supreme Court heard oral arguments in *Webster* on April 26, 1989. Public demonstrations to attempt to influence the courts are uncommon, but two weeks earlier, at least 300,000 abortion rights advocates marched in Washington. They carried signs proclaiming, "My body, my baby, my business" and "Keep your laws off my body." The rally drew counter-demonstrators to the scene, shouting, "What about the babies?" and "Life, life, life." The Court received 200,000 pieces of mail before the argument day.[98] And on the day of the argument, demonstrators from both sides gathered outside the Supreme Court building with signs and loud voices.

The Court listened to arguments by Attorney General William L. Webster; Frank Susman of the ACLU, representing Missouri abortion clinics; and former U.S. solicitor general Charles Fried, representing the Bush administration. Fried urged the Court to "reconsider and overrule its decision in *Roe v. Wade.*" He stressed that he was "not asking the Court to unravel the fabric of unenumerated and privacy rights." Rather, he said, he was merely "asking the Court to pull this one thread." Susman argued that the right to abortion was an integral part of the right to privacy and procreation. He accused Fried of being "disingenuous" by insisting that he was "not seek[ing] to unravel the whole cloth of procreational rights, but merely to pull a thread. It has always been my personal experience," Susman said, "that when I pull a thread, my sleeve falls off. There is no stopping."[99]

The Court considered the constitutionality of four sections of the Missouri law: a preamble declaring life begins at conception, a required test to determine fetal viability, a ban on the use of public funds to encourage or counsel women to have abortions not necessary to save their lives, and a prohibition on the use of public facilities and public employees to perform abortions that are unnecessary to save women's lives.[100]

The preamble to the law stated that human life "begins at conception" and that "unborn children have protectable interests in life, health, and well-being." The state characterized the preamble as abortion-neutral, saying it merely extended the protections of tort, property, and criminal law to the unborn. Moreover, it argued, the law had no effect on abortion policy because it explicitly stated that it must be interpreted in a manner consistent with Supreme Court decisions.

Rehnquist's plurality opinion for himself, White, and Kennedy declined to resolve the issue, holding that the Court need not decide on this provision because it did not purport to regulate abortion but was merely expressing the state's preference for childbirth over abortion. Because it did not impinge on abortion in "some concrete way," the preamble was too abstract to require the Supreme Court to rule on its constitutionality.[101]

In 1985, Truman Medical Center in Kansas City, Missouri, performed 97 percent of all Missouri hospital abortions at sixteen weeks or later. Although it was a private hospital primarily staffed by private physicians, with no public funds expended on abortions performed there, it was considered a "public facility" because it was on land leased from the state.[102]

Rehnquist found no constitutional problem in the ban on abortions at Truman. If a state may prefer childbirth to abortion by withholding funds, he said, "surely it may do so through the allocation of other public resources, such as hospitals and medical staff."[103] He explained that the state had not created a barrier to abortion by withholding its facilities and personnel. It merely left women in the same position as if it had chosen not to operate a public hospital in the first place, and any restriction caused by a woman's physician being affiliated with Truman or another public hospital was "easily remedied."

As with the preamble, the Supreme Court found it unnecessary to rule on the provision of the law forbidding the use of public funds, employees, and facilities to encourage or counsel abortions. The appellate court found the entire provision unconstitutional, but the state appealed only a portion of the lower court ruling to the Supreme Court. The issue before the high court was whether the state could constitutionally ban the use of public funds to encourage women to seek abortions.

Missouri argued that the provision was not aimed at persons engaged in abortion counseling (a possible First Amendment violation); rather, it was intended to prevent hospital administrators from allocating funds for abortion counseling. Given the state's narrow interpretation of the law, the plaintiffs withdrew their challenge, and the Court never decided whether the law restricted freedom of speech by preventing physicians from discussing abortion with their patients.[104]

The most significant part of the law, the viability testing section, provided that

> before a physician performs an abortion on a woman he has reason to believe is carrying an unborn child of twenty or more weeks gestational age, the physician shall first determine if the unborn child is viable by using and exercising that degree of care, skill, and proficiency commonly exercised by the ordinarily skillful, careful, and prudent physician. . . . In making this determination of viability, the physician shall perform . . . such medical examinations and tests as are necessary to make a finding of the gestational age, weight, and lung maturity of the unborn child.[105]

The appellate court had held that because these tests were costly and potentially dangerous to the woman and the fetus, the provision was unconstitutional. Speaking for the same plurality of himself, White, and Kennedy, Rehnquist reversed the circuit court. He construed the law as requiring doctors to test for lung maturity, age, and weight only when, in their professional judgment, they believed such tests were useful to determine viability. He rejected the view that the law required the tests in all situations when a physician believed a woman was at least twenty weeks pregnant. Rehnquist acknowledged that the Missouri law clashed with *Roe* by prescribing viability tests during the second trimester. But instead of forthrightly overruling *Roe,* the Rehnquist plurality utilized a "backdoor approach [that] allowed it to eviscerate *Roe* without explicitly overruling" it.[106] Rather than attacking *Roe* head-on, Rehnquist proposed to resolve the conflict between *Roe* and the Missouri law by abandoning "the rigid trimester" approach that he said had made "constitutional law in this area a virtual Procrustean bed."[107]

The plurality approved the fetal test provision because it furthered the state's interest in fetal life. Conceding that the ruling would allow government regulations that would have been forbidden under *Roe,* Rehnquist invited legislatures to challenge the continuing vitality of *Roe.* He repeated his oft-stated assertion that abortion is not a fundamental right but only a narrowly defined "liberty interest," implying that the Court will not require the state to show a compelling interest in the future. In denying that the Court was overruling *Roe,* Rehnquist insisted that the facts in the two cases were distinct and *Webster* offered the Court "no occasion to revisit the holding of *Roe.*" But, he added, "to the extent indicated in our opinion, we would modify and narrow *Roe* and succeeding cases."[108]

O'Connor found the plurality's interpretation of the fetal viability section persuasive and agreed that the viability tests did not impose an undue burden on a woman's abortion right. But she disputed Rehnquist's contention that the viability testing section was inconsistent with *Roe* because, in her view, *Roe* was not implicated and the plurality did not have to address it. "When the constitutional invalidity of a State's abortion statute actually turns on the constitutional validity of *Roe v. Wade,* there will be time enough to reexamine *Roe.* And to do so carefully."[109]

Scalia also concurred, attacking the plurality for failing to explicitly overrule *Roe* and criticizing O'Connor, saying her refusal to reconsider *Roe* "cannot be taken seriously."[110] He charged that the plurality had vitiated *Roe* but was afraid to admit it. Characterizing the Court's decision as "stingy" because it did not forthrightly address the constitutionality of abortion, Scalia argued that by refusing to dismantle *Roe,* the Court had chosen the "least responsible" path. "It thus appears," he complained, "that the mansion of constitutionalized abortion-law, constructed overnight in *Roe v. Wade,* must be disassembled door-jamb by door-jamb, and never entirely brought down, no matter how wrong it may be."[111]

In a passionate dissent, Blackmun charged that the plurality and Scalia "would return to the States virtually unfettered authority to control the quintessentially intimate, personal, and life-directing decision whether to carry a fetus to term." He accused the plurality of "implicitly invit[ing] every state legislature to enact more and more restrictive abortion regulations . . . in the hope that sometime down the line the Court will return the law of procreative freedom to the severe limitations that generally prevailed in this country before January 22, 1973."[112]

In language rarely heard in judicial opinions, Blackmun accused the plurality of breeding "disregard for the law." He focused his attack on the fetal testing provision, which he insisted, contrary to the plurality's assertion, directed the doctor to determine the age, weight, and lung maturity of every twenty-week fetus. By requiring doctors to impose risks on the woman and the fetus by performing the tests, he continued, the law was not rationally related to the state's interest in protecting fetal life or maternal health.

Blackmun defended the trimester approach he articulated almost twenty years ago, describing it as a tool for evaluating and balancing a woman's constitutional right to procreational privacy against the state's competing interests. *Roe*'s trimester approach and the dividing line of viability, he claimed, still represented the most effective and sensible way to balance a state's interest in regulation and a woman's interest in privacy.

Given the result in *Webster*, Blackmun predicted dire consequences for the future, warning that

> hundreds of thousands of women, in desperation, would defy the law, and place their health and safety in the unclean and unsympathetic hands of back-alley abortionists, or they would attempt to perform abortions on themselves, with disastrous results. Every year, many women, especially poor and minority women, would die or suffer debilitating physical trauma, all in the name of enforced morality or religious dictates or lack of compassion, as it may be.[113]

He concluded somberly, "For today, at least, the law of abortion remains undisturbed. For today, the women of this Nation still retain the liberty to control their destinies. But the signs are evident and very ominous, and a chill wind blows."[114]

The Court's opinion galvanized abortion rights proponents into action. Their efforts were matched by invigorated activity from abortion opponents.[115] The battles following *Webster* reflected the importance of the state as an arena for the abortion debate. Abortion played a key role in the 1990 New Jersey and Virginia governors' races as well as the congressional elections.[116] Shortly after *Webster* was decided, a number of states, including Florida, Idaho, Louisiana, and Pennsylvania, as well as the territory of Guam, considered restrictive abortion laws, hoping to provoke a challenge that would lead to the Supreme Court overturning *Roe*.[117]

In November 1989, Democratic Pennsylvania governor Robert P. Casey signed the first post-*Webster* state abortion law. The Pennsylvania Abortion Control Act of 1989—an amendment to the 1982 law—banned most abortions in public hospitals, required that the woman notify her husband of a planned abortion, required a minor to get her parent's consent, imposed a twenty-four-hour waiting period, and ordered the doctor to inform the woman about fetal development. In 1992, the Supreme Court would hear arguments about this law in a case that again had the nation wondering about the future of *Roe*. Before then, however, the Court turned its attention to a pair of stringent parental involvement laws in Minnesota and Ohio.

Conclusion

Women's rights groups achieved a major victory when the Supreme Court declared in *Roe* that the constitutional right to privacy guaranteed a woman's choice to terminate her pregnancy. But the Court struck a balance between the woman's control over her body and the state's interest in regulating the abortion procedure. It crafted a compromise by creating a trimester framework in which the state's interest was weighed against the woman's during each stage of the pregnancy.

Unwilling to accept a woman's right to choose, anti-abortion activists lobbied the state legislatures and Congress, seeking to have their elected officials undo the Court's ruling by imposing restrictions on abortion rights. They were most successful in restricting state funding for abortion and limiting the rights of minors.

For over a decade, the Court supported abortion rights, at least for adult women who could afford to pay for their abortions. However, when the Reagan-Bush appointees (Scalia, O'Connor, Kennedy, and Thomas) took their seats on the Court, *Roe*'s future looked very uncertain. And when the Court announced its decision in *Webster,* although it had not formally overruled *Roe,* it was clear that it had become more sympathetic to states' efforts to limit women's access to abortion.

Notes

1. For accounts of the past political struggles over abortion policy, see James R. Bowers, *Pro-Choice and Anti-Abortion* (Westport, Conn.: Praeger Publishers, 1994);

Mark A. Graber, *Rethinking Abortion: Equal Choice, the Constitution, and Reproductive Politics* (Princeton: Princeton University Press, 1996).

2. During this time, however, the Court refused to order the government to pay for abortions, essentially reserving the right to terminate a pregnancy to women who could afford it.

3. It was common for women to be denied therapeutic abortions by physicians and hospital review committees, despite the known effects of the disease on the fetus. A number of women who contracted German measles and were refused abortions brought "wrongful life" lawsuits when their children were born with multiple birth defects. Most did not succeed. See Leslie J. Reagan, "Rashes, Rights, and Wrongs in the Hospital and in the Courtroom: German Measles, Abortion, and Malpractice Before *Roe* and *Doe*," *University of Illinois Law and History Review* 27 (2009): 241–284. A 2010 Oklahoma law provides that a woman cannot recover damages from a doctor whose failure to inform her of her child's defects played a role in her decision to carry the fetus to term. See also Hyman Rodman, Betty Sarvis, and Joy Walker Bonar, *The Abortion Question* (New York: Columbia University Press, 1987), p. 5.

4. Kristen Luker, *Abortion and the Politics of Motherhood* (Berkeley: University of California Press, 1984), p. 97.

5. Rodman, Sarvis, and Bonar, *The Abortion Question,* p. 23.

6. One of the most important sources of information on early abortion policy in the United States is James C. Mohr, *Abortion in America* (Oxford: Oxford University Press, 1978). See also Luker, *Abortion and the Politics of Motherhood;* Marian Faux, *Roe v. Wade* (New York: Mentor Books, 1988); Eva Rubin, *Abortion, Politics, and the Courts* (Westport, Conn.: Greenwood Press, 1987), for an overview of U.S. policy before 1973.

7. 410 U.S. 113 (1973).

8. 410 U.S. 179 (1973).

9. 381 U.S. 479 (1965). *Griswold* was the first case to formally declare a constitutional right to privacy.

10. 405 U.S. 438 (1972).

11. *Eisenstadt,* 405 U.S. at 453 (emphasis in the original).

12. The lower court ruled in her favor, finding that a woman's right to terminate a pregnancy was constitutionally protected. But while declaring the law unconstitutional, it refused to order the state to cease enforcement. Coffee and Weddington were forced to go to the U.S. Supreme Court to attain their final victory.

13. *Roe,* 410 U.S. at 153. The district court grounded its belief in the woman's right to privacy in the Ninth Amendment; the Supreme Court found it "in the Fourteenth Amendment's concept of personal liberty and restrictions upon state action."

14. *Roe,* 410 U.S. at 153.

15. The Court first resolved the procedural issues in the case, primarily whether the mootness doctrine compelled dismissal. The federal mootness doctrine requires a live controversy when the case is reviewed by a court. But because the litigation process will almost always outlast a pregnancy and because pregnancy will "always be with us," the Court concluded that it "provides a classic justification for a conclusion of nonmootness." *Roe,* 410 U.S. at 125.

16. *Roe,* 410 U.S. at 155. As with a suspect category in equal protection analysis, when a fundamental right is involved, the state must offer a compelling reason to restrict it. Fundamental rights arise out of the guarantee of liberty protected by the due process clause of the Fourteenth Amendment.

17. *Roe*, 410 U.S. at 163. In *Connecticut v. Menillo*, 423 U.S. 9 (1975), the Supreme Court upheld a Connecticut statute requiring abortions to be performed by licensed physicians. In *Sendak v. Arnold*, 429 U.S. 968 (1976), the Supreme Court affirmed an Indiana three-judge district court ruling that struck a statute requiring first trimester abortions to be performed by physicians in hospitals or other licensed facilities.

18. Paul Reidinger, "Will *Roe v. Wade* Be Overruled?" *American Bar Association Journal* (July 1988): 68.

19. *Roe*, 410 U.S. at 163.

20. *Roe*, 410 U.S. at 163.

21. *Roe*, 410 U.S. at 163–164.

22. The abortion committee at Atlanta's Grady Memorial Hospital had denied Mary Doe's application for an abortion because she failed to meet the criteria for a medically necessary abortion. Doe was twenty-two years old, had three children—two in foster care and one given up for adoption; she also had a history of mental illness. The Georgia law was challenged by Doe, as well as social workers, nurses, and clergy, in federal district court.

23. *Doe*, 410 U.S. at 183–184.

24. *Doe*, 410 U.S. at 194–200.

25. *Roe*, 410 U.S. at 173.

26. *Doe*, 410 U.S. at 221.

27. Rubin, *Abortion, Politics, and the Courts*. For discussions of efforts to minimize the effect of *Roe*, see Ann E. Fulks, "*Thornburgh:* The Last American Right-to-Abortion Case?" *Journal of Family Law* 26 (1987–1988): 775–776; Rodman, Sarvis, and Bonar, *The Abortion Question*, chap. 7; and Frederick S. Jaffe, Barbara L. Lindheim, and Philip R. Lee, *Abortion Politics: Private Morality and Public Policy* (New York: McGraw-Hill, 1981), chap. 9.

28. There were also parental and spousal consent requirements, as well as record-keeping and reporting rules that were not specific to any trimester. Physicians were also charged with a duty to preserve a viable fetus or face manslaughter charges and civil suits for damages.

29. The process involved a saline solution being introduced into the amniotic sac, causing premature labor. This procedure could not be performed earlier than sixteen weeks. Nancy K. Rhoden, "Trimesters and Technology: Revamping *Roe v. Wade*," *Yale Law Journal* 95 (1986): 644.

30. Plaintiffs are generally not permitted to sue on behalf of others. In abortion cases, however, the Court allows physicians to assert the rights of their patients because the relationships are sufficiently intertwined. See *Singleton v. Wulff*, 428 U.S. 106 (1976).

31. 428 U.S. 52, 63 (1976).

32. A survey conducted by the Alan Guttmacher Institute in 2008 reported that 58 percent of women obtaining abortions were in their twenties; the next largest group (22 percent) comprised women in their thirties. Most (85 percent) of the abortions were performed on never-married women; most women in the survey (61 percent) had at least one child, about half of them had two or more children. Rachel K. Jones, Lawrence B. Finer, and Susheela Singh, "Characteristics of U.S. Abortion Patients, 2008" (New York: Alan Guttmacher Institute, May 2010), available at http://www.guttmacher.org/pubs/US-Abortion-Patients.pdf.

33. The Court had generally been moving toward a convergence of rights enjoyed by adults and children, yet some differences remained. In 1969, in *Tinker v. Des Moines*, 393 U.S. 503 (1969), the Court proclaimed that students do not shed their constitutional rights at the schoolhouse door and overturned the suspension of

three Des Moines students who wore black armbands to school to protest the Vietnam War. But in *Bethel School District No. 403 v. Fraser,* 478 U.S. 675 (1986), the Court upheld a restriction on a student's nonobscene speech that it would not have allowed for an adult. Then in *Hazelwood School District v. Kuhlmeier,* 484 U.S. 260 (1988), the Court curtailed freedom of the press in public schools by upholding a principal's regulation of the student newspaper. And in *New Jersey v. TLO,* 469 U.S. 325 (1985) the Court allowed a school search on grounds that would not have satisfied Fourth Amendment standards for a search of adults. In each case, the Court balanced the minor's constitutional right against the state's authority over education and discipline in schools.

34. *Danforth,* 428 U.S. at 74.

35. *Danforth,* 428 U.S. at 94–95.

36. *Danforth,* 428 U.S. at 104.

37. 443 U.S. 622 (1979).

38. The same case had been in the Supreme Court three years earlier, and in *Bellotti v. Baird,* 428 U.S. 132 (1976), the Court unanimously vacated the district court ruling, holding that the court should have allowed the state court to construe the law. It reappeared in the Massachusetts Supreme Court and was appealed to the U.S. Supreme Court again.

39. *Bellotti,* 443 U.S. at 637.

40. *Bellotti,* 443 U.S. at 644–645.

41. 450 U.S. 398 (1981).

42. *H. L.,* 450 U.S. at 400.

43. The Court addressed the constitutionality of the Utah statute only as it applied to teenagers in the plaintiff's class.

44. *H. L.,* 450 U.S. at 412.

45. Thomas Dickinson, "Limiting Public Funds for Abortions: State Response to Congressional Action," *Suffolk University Law Review* 13 (1979): 926.

46. Title XIX requires states to provide medical assistance to persons with inadequate "income and resources" to pay for their "necessary" medical care, allowing states to establish "reasonable standards" for the amount of the aid. Distinguishing between medically necessary (therapeutic) and elective (nontherapeutic) abortions, states generally denied funding for the latter.

47. Alan Guttmacher Institute, *Abortions and the Poor: Private Morality, Public Responsibility* (New York: Alan Guttmacher Institute, 1979), p. 8.

48. Alan Guttmacher Institute, *Abortions and the Poor,* p. 9.

49. Alan Guttmacher Institute, *Abortions and the Poor,* p. 34.

50. Note, "Abortion, Medicaid, and the Constitution," *New York University Law Review* 54 (1979): 124; see Angela Benzo Norman, *"Beal v. Doe, Maher v. Roe,* and Non-Therapeutic Abortions: The State Does Not Have to Pay the Bill," *Loyola University Law Journal* 9 (1977): 288–311.

51. 432 U.S. 438 (1977).

52. 432 U.S. 464 (1977).

53. 432 U.S. 519 (1977).

54. Michael Perry, "The Abortion Funding Cases: A Comment on the Supreme Court's Role in American Government," *Georgetown Law Journal* 66 (1978): 1201.

55. *Beal,* 432 U.S. at 444–445 (emphasis in the original).

56. *Beal,* 432 U.S. at 454.

57. *Beal,* 432 U.S. at 454–455.

58. The Court cited *Dandridge v. Williams,* 397 U.S. 471 (1970) and *San Antonio School District v. Rodriguez,* 411 U.S. 1 (1973), in which it held that wealth

is not a suspect category for equal protection analysis. The Court refused to apply strict scrutiny to wealth classifications, using a rationality test to scrutinize a state welfare policy and a school financing plan.

59. *Maher*, 432 U.S. at 474–475.

60. Jaffe, Lindheim, and Lee, *Abortion Politics*, p. 132.

61. Some of the states were New York, Colorado, Idaho, Michigan, and Maryland. Of the thirty-nine other states participating in the Medicaid program, eighteen adopted the precise language of the Hyde Amendment, sixteen limited Medicaid funding to women in life-endangering situations, and five paid for abortions in life-threatening situations or cases of reported rape or incest. Seven of the thirty-nine states, including California and Massachusetts, were prevented from enforcing their funding restrictions by court order. See Alan Guttmacher Institute, *Abortions and the Poor*, pp. 22–23.

62. See Roger Davidson, "Procedures and Politics in Congress," in Gilbert Y. Steiner, ed., *The Abortion Dispute and the American System* (Washington, D.C.: Brookings Institution, 1983); Susan Tolchin, "The Impact of the Hyde Amendment on Congress: Effects of Single Issue Politics on Legislative Dysfunction, June 1977–June 1978," *Women and Politics* 5 (1985): 91–106.

63. *Congressional Record*, 95th Cong., 1st sess., Vol. 123 (1977): H19700.

64. *Congressional Record*, 95th Cong., 2d sess., Vol. 124 (1978): H17260.

65. *McRae v. Califano*, 491 F. Supp. 630 (E.D.N.Y. 1980). "Medically necessary" abortions referred to abortions based on physical, psychological, emotional, and familial considerations.

66. In November 1976, the Supreme Court had refused to block enforcement of the court's order. *New York Times*, November 9, 1976. See Albie Sachs and Joan Hoff Wilson, *Sexism and the Law* (New York: Free Press, 1978), chap. 4.

67. 448 U.S. 297 (1980). The Court based its ruling on the current version of the Hyde Amendment, applicable for fiscal year 1980, which banned funding for abortions unless a woman's life was in danger or in cases of rape or incest. The Court noted that this version was more inclusive than the fiscal year 1977 approach, which did not include the rape or incest exception. It was narrower than the one used in most of fiscal year 1978 and all of fiscal year 1979, which allowed federal funding for abortions in which physical and long-lasting damage to health would result if the pregnancy were continued. In sum, the operative version of the Hyde Amendment prohibited funding unless a woman's life was threatened by the pregnancy. Medically necessary abortions were not funded by Medicaid because they did not rise to the requisite degree of danger.

68. *Harris*, 448 U.S. at 316.

69. *Harris*, 448 U.S. at 338.

70. Abortion opponents scored a major victory at the end of 2009 when they succeeded in maintaining the restrictions on federal funding for abortion in the House and Senate health care reform measures. Anti-abortion Democrats threatened to withhold their votes, charging that the new law could allow federal subsidies for insurance policies that provide abortion services as well as for federally subsidized community health centers. Obama was able to win their support for the final bill by promising to sign an executive order to specify that the new law banned the use of federal money for abortion. In the end, they voted for the bill. Abortion rights Democrats were forced to decide whether to vote for an anti-abortion measure or vote against the entire health care bill. In the end, they also voted for the bill, which, despite its limits on abortion, provided more accessible health care for the entire nation. After passing the Senate, the bill was passed in the House in a close vote of

219 to 212, with no Republican support. On March 23, 2010, Obama signed the Patient Protection and Affordable Care Act; see Jon O. Shimabukuro, "Abortion and the House- and Senate-Passed Health Reform Measures," *Congressional Research Service,* January 15, 2010; *New York Times,* April 10, 2010; March 23, 2010; March 21, 2010; *Washington Post,* March 25, 2010; March 22, 2010; *Congressional Quarterly Weekly,* March 29, 2010, p. 748. After the passage of the law, anti-abortion activists quickly turned their attention to preventing certain private health insurance plans sold though state insurance exchanges from covering abortions. Their efforts have succeeded in a number of states. *New York Times,* March 11, 2011.

71. In 1981, with a population of 237,000 people, Akron had five abortion clinics, which performed a total of 7,685 abortions. *New York Times,* December 1, 1982.

72. *City of Akron v. Akron Center for Reproductive Health,* 462 U.S. 416, 423 n. 5 (1983).

73. *City of Akron,* 462 U.S. at 416.

74. *New York Times,* December 1, 1982.

75. *City of Akron,* 462 U.S. at 434.

76. By the time this case was decided, advances in medical knowledge meant that abortions performed up to sixteen weeks were now safer than carrying a child to term. Rhoden, "Trimesters and Technology," p. 649.

77. The vast majority of abortions take place before the end of the second trimester, and most are performed during the first trimester. Reidinger, "Will *Roe v. Wade* Be Overruled?" p. 68.

78. *City of Akron,* 462 U.S. at 430.

79. *City of Akron,* 462 U.S. at 445.

80. O'Connor's belief about viability was not based on the current medical evidence. The medical community believed that fetal viability was unlikely to ever move back earlier than twenty-three or twenty-four weeks because fetal lung development required at least that length of time. According to a study published two years after *City of Akron* was decided, more than one-quarter of infants born between twenty-four and twenty-six weeks were born with a severe handicap. Only about 40 percent of infants born between the twenty-sixth and twenty-eighth weeks of pregnancy survived, and many of them suffered numerous handicaps; at twenty-eight weeks, an infant's chances improved remarkably. Another study showed that 83 percent of infants born at twenty-eight weeks survived. Reidinger, "Will *Roe v. Wade* Be Overruled?" p. 69. See studies reported in Rhoden, "Trimesters and Technology," pp. 660–662.

81. *City of Akron,* 462 U.S. at 458.

82. *City of Akron,* 462 U.S. at 461 (emphasis in the original).

83. *City of Akron,* 462 U.S. at 464.

84. In *Diamond v. Charles,* 476 U.S. 54 (1986), the Court unanimously held that the petitioner, an anti-abortion pediatrician, did not have standing to bring an appeal to the Supreme Court. Among other provisions, the law had an informed consent provision requiring physicians to inform their patients that certain drugs and intrauterine devices are "abortifacient[s]" that cause fetal death by preventing the fertilized egg from attaching to the uterine wall.

85. Fulks, "*Thornburgh:* The Last American Right-to-Abortion Case?" p. 780.

86. 476 U.S. 747 (1986).

87. David Fernandez, "*Thornburgh v. American College of Obstetricians:* Return to *Roe?*" *Harvard Journal of Law and Public Policy* 10 (1987): 714.

88. *Thornburgh,* 476 U.S. at 761.

89. *Thornburgh,* 476 U.S. at 762.

90. *Thornburgh,* 476 U.S. at 759.

91. *Thornburgh,* 476 U.S. at 768.

92. *Thornburgh,* 476 U.S. at 771.

93. *Thornburgh,* 476 U.S. at 772.

94. *Thornburgh,* 476 U.S. at 829.

95. *Thornburgh,* 476 U.S. at 792.

96. 492 U.S. 490 (1989).

97. *New York Times,* July 4, 1989.

98. *New York Times,* April 10, 1989; *Congressional Quarterly Weekly,* April 29, 1989, pp. 973–975.

99. *New York Times,* April 27, 1989.

100. *Webster,* 492 U.S. at 490. The lower court struck the provision of the state law requiring all abortions at sixteen weeks' gestational age to be performed in hospitals. The appellate court affirmed, and the state did not appeal the lower court's ruling on this issue to the Supreme Court.

101. In her concurring opinion, O'Connor rejected the argument that the preamble made postfertilization contraceptive choices and in-vitro fertilization (during which fertilized ova may be destroyed) illegal. Recognizing that earlier rulings protected such choices, she said there was nothing in the record to indicate that the preamble would have such an effect.

102. *Webster,* 492 U.S. at 539 n. 1.

103. *Webster,* 492 U.S. at 510.

104. For a discussion of the First Amendment implications of the Missouri law challenged in *Webster,* see Rachel Pine, "Abortion Counseling and the First Amendment: Open Questions After *Webster,*" *American Journal of Law and Medicine* 15 (1989): 189–197.

105. *Webster,* 492 U.S. at 513.

106. Walter Dellinger and Gene B. Sperling, "Abortion and the Supreme Court: The Retreat from *Roe v. Wade,*" *University of Pennsylvania Law Review* 138 (1989): 83.

107. *Webster,* 492 U.S. at 517.

108. *Webster,* 492 U.S. at 521.

109. *Webster,* 492 U.S. at 526.

110. *Webster,* 492 U.S. at 532.

111. *Webster,* 492 U.S. at 537.

112. *Webster,* 492 U.S. at 538.

113. *Webster,* 492 U.S. at 557–558.

114. *Webster,* 492 U.S. at 560.

115. See Malcolm L. Goggin, "Understanding the New Politics of Abortion," *American Politics Quarterly* 21 (1993): 4–30.

116. *Congressional Quarterly Weekly,* March 10, 1990, pp. 765–775.

117. *New York Times,* October 12, 1989.

7

Preserving Abortion Rights

Webster signaled abortion rights advocates that they could no longer regard the Supreme Court as their ally in their efforts to defeat restrictive abortion regulations. After 1990, the Court was chiefly occupied with cases concerning parental involvement laws and limits on abortion procedures. Table 7.1 presents the high court's rulings on women's access to abortion from 1990 to 2007.

Parental Involvement Laws

During the 1980s, an increasing number of state legislatures enacted parental involvement laws, and by 1988, twenty-five states had notice or consent laws involving at least one parent; most included a judicial bypass procedure. Proponents of notice laws said that parents had a right to know about their daughter's decision to have an abortion and that parental involvement reduced teen pregnancy. Opponents said that most pregnant teens informed their parents anyway and that it is unrealistic and harmful to assume that every teen benefits from a parent's involvement.[1] In her critique of such laws, Janet Benshoof, former director of the Reproductive Freedom Project of the ACLU, argues that they are counterproductive and result in a "survival of the fittest" effect because mature, well-connected, and more affluent minors will be able to secure abortions. "The minors who do not get the abortions are the younger, more immature teenagers, those least prepared for the emotional and physical rigors of pregnancy and childbirth."[2]

On June 26, 1990, the Supreme Court considered the constitutionality of parental involvement laws in Minnesota and Ohio. The Minnesota law amended the Minors' Consent to Health Services Act, a law authorizing minors to give valid consent to health care services for pregnancy, venereal disease, and alcohol or drug abuse.

233

Table 7.1 Supreme Court Abortion Rights Rulings, 1990–2007

Case	Date	Issue[a]	Ruling[b]
Hodgson	1990	Minors' rights	Limits access to abortion
Akron Center	1990	Minors' rights	Limits access to abortion
Casey	1992	Informed consent	Limits access to abortion
Lambert	1997	Minors' rights	Limits access to abortion
Carhart I	2000	Abortion procedures	Expands access to abortion
Ayotte	2006	Minors' rights	Limits access to abortion
Carhart II	2007	Abortion procedures	Limits access to abortion

Notes: a. Based on the major issue in the case.
b. Based on the overall outcome of the case.

Subdivision Two of the amendment required a physician to notify both parents of an unemancipated minor before performing an abortion. There was no exemption for teens whose parents were divorced or separated or for those whose parent deserted the family. There were a few exceptions: if the parent were deceased or could not be found after "reasonably diligent effort," if there was an emergency, if both parents consented in writing to the abortion, or if there was a record of sexual or physical abuse. The physician was required to wait for forty-eight hours after providing notice.

Subdivision Six of the law specified that a judicial bypass procedure took effect if a court declared Subdivision Two unconstitutional. The bypass procedure allowed the pregnant minor to attempt to convince a judge that she was sufficiently mature to make the abortion decision herself or that an abortion without notice was in her best interest.

In 1986, after a five-week trial, the district court upheld the challenge brought by Dr. Jane Hodgson and the other plaintiffs. A year later, a three-judge panel of the Eighth Circuit affirmed, but the en banc court later reversed in a 7 to 3 vote. The majority held that "considering the statute as a whole and as applied to all pregnant minors, the two-parent notice requirement does not unconstitutionally burden the minor's abortion right."[3] It also upheld the forty-eight-hour waiting period. The court's ruling indicates the importance of presidential appointments to the federal bench. Six of the seven judges in the majority were appointed by Reagan; the three dissenting judges were Johnson appointees.[4]

On appeal, in *Hodgson v. Minnesota*,[5] five members of the Supreme Court found Subdivision Two unconstitutional because it was not reasonably related to a legitimate state interest. A different five-justice majority sustained Subdivision Six, thereby allowing the state to impose the two-parent notice provision as long as it included a judicial bypass. Four justices said they would have found the entire law constitutional—even without a bypass procedure. The Court also upheld the forty-eight-hour waiting period.

Speaking for the Court on Subdivision Two, Stevens distinguished this case from earlier cases addressing the constitutionality of a notice or consent requirement. "None of the opinions in any of those cases," he explained, "focused on the possible significance of making the consent or the notice requirement applicable to both parents instead of just one."[6] He highlighted the district court's findings that only about half the minors in Minnesota lived with both biological parents and that notifying the absent parent may be harmful to the teenager. Even when both parents are present, Stevens said, criminal reports show there is a realistic danger of violence against the teen. Additionally, he cited the lower court's finding that even though most petitions were granted, the bypass procedure was often traumatic for the teenager.

Stevens denied that the two-parent notice furthered the state's interests in the teen, the parent, or the family. The state could fulfill its obligation to the minor by notifying a parent and permitting that parent to decide whether to notify the other. He was not persuaded by the state's contention that the family functions best if both parents are involved in a teenager's abortion decision, saying that the state cannot legitimately seek to mold the family into its idealized image.

Dissenting from the majority's ruling on Subdivision Six, Stevens explained that the judicial bypass procedure in the Minnesota law differed from those upheld in previous cases.

> A judicial bypass that is designed to handle exceptions from a reasonable general rule, and thereby preserve the constitutionality of that rule, is quite different from a requirement that a minor—or a minor and one of her parents—must apply to a court for permission to avoid the application of a rule that is not reasonably related to legitimate state goals.[7]

O'Connor agreed that Subdivision Two was unconstitutional yet maintained that Subdivision Six saved the two-parent notice requirement "because the interference with the internal operation of the family required by Subdivision 2 simply does not exist where the minor can avoid notifying one or both parents by use of the bypass procedure."[8] However, although she "broke rank" with the other Reagan appointees, she "demonstrated once again that she is not prepared to climb off the fence she has long straddled on abortion issues."[9]

In *Ohio v. Akron Center for Reproductive Health,*[10] decided the same day as *Hodgson,* the Court upheld an Ohio law with a one-parent notice requirement and a bypass procedure. The law specified that before performing an abortion, the physician was required to give twenty-four hours' notice to a parent. Another relative could be notified if the teenager and the relative filed an affidavit in juvenile court that the minor feared physical or emotional abuse if the parent were told. The law also provided a bypass procedure that allowed the teenager to attempt to prove to a juvenile court judge that she was mature enough to make the decision without notifying her parent or that notification was not in her best interest.

Both district and appellate courts declared the Ohio law unconstitutional. On appeal, the high court left open the question of whether all parental notification laws must be accompanied by judicial bypass procedures. Speaking for the Court, Kennedy merely held that because the Ohio statute satisfied the criteria listed in *Bellotti* for consent statutes, it must logically be sufficient for a notice statute as well. He concluded that because the Ohio law placed a lesser burden on young women seeking abortions, it was not an undue burden on their right to abortion.

Shortly after *Hodgson* and *Akron Center* were decided, in an effort to reinforce abortion rights through legislation, congressional abortion rights supporters introduced a one-page bill entitled the Freedom of Choice Act. Essentially codifying *Roe,* the bill prohibited states from "restrict[ing] the right of a woman to choose to terminate a pregnancy before fetal viability, or at any time, if such termination is necessary to protect the life or health of the woman." Subsequent versions of the bill were introduced in following years, but it was never approved and eventually died in the chamber. Its opponents charged that the law would have gone beyond *Roe* by curtailing the state's ability to impose a parental consent or notice requirement.[11]

A few years later, in *Lambert v. Wicklund,*[12] a 1997 decision, the high court ruled on another challenge to a judicial bypass procedure in a parental notification law, this time in Montana.[13] The law allowed the young woman to seek a court's approval to bypass notice to her parents by showing either that she was sufficiently mature to decide whether to have an abortion, she had been subjected to abuse, or that notifying her parent or guardian was not in her best interest. The issue was whether the third condition was too narrow to satisfy her constitutional right to obtain an abortion. The plaintiffs challenging the law argued that past rulings required the notice requirement to be waived whenever an abortion was in the woman's best interest, not just when notification was not in her best interests. In a brief unsigned opinion, the Court found the Montana law constitutional, comparing it to laws it upheld in *Bellotti* and *Akron Center.*

Parental involvement laws appear to be popular with the American people. A survey conducted by CNN/*USA Today*/Gallup in 2005 found that 69 percent of those surveyed approved of laws requiring teens to obtain parental consent before undergoing an abortion, with only 28 percent opposed.[14] Not surprisingly, a majority of state legislatures enacted laws involving at least one parent in a minor's abortion decision, and by 2010, the number had climbed to thirty-four. Of these, twenty required consent (two from both parents), ten required notification only (one to both parents), and four required both consent and notice.[15] A number of other states had enacted parental involvement laws, but legal challenges had prevented them from being enforced. Only six states and the District of Columbia had no such laws.[16]

A recent analysis of parental involvement found that the majority of teenagers (60 percent) talk to their parents when considering an abortion— whether they live in a state requiring it or not. Of the other 40 percent, many indicated that they feared physical harm if they informed their parents of their pregnancy or proposed getting an abortion. The studies also found that state involvement laws did not affect the teen pregnancy rate.[17]

In the late 1990s, Congress sought to enact a federal law to reinforce state parental involvement laws. In 1998, the Republican-controlled House approved a bill that made it a federal crime for an adult to transport a pregnant minor across state lines to evade the home state's parental involvement law to obtain an abortion—except to save her life. The bill never became law despite Republican efforts to win support in the Senate. In July 2006, the measure passed the Senate when its sponsor, John Ensign, Republican of Nevada, was able to secure sixty-five votes for his bill, the Child Interstate Abortion Notification Act (S. 3). The House version (H.R. 748), which contained criminal and civil penalties for doctors who performed abortions in violation of the law, had passed a year earlier. The measure ultimately died when Senate Republicans failed to muster the necessary votes to invoke cloture on a vote to concur with the stricter regulations in the House bill.[18] The bill was subsequently reintroduced in the House, but the Senate did not vote on it again.

With polls showing that most people agreed with parental involvement laws, it is not surprising that state legislatures have continued to enact laws restricting minors' rights to abortion. And because the courts believe that minors are not entitled to the same degree of privacy as adults, for the most part, these laws are upheld.

Informed Consent

In October 1990, Souter became the newest associate justice, replacing Brennan, the staunch abortion rights supporter. In his confirmation hearings, Souter expressed support for the right to privacy, yet refused to answer questions about his views on abortion or *Roe*. In the meantime, states continued to enact restrictive abortion measures, and both sides of the abortion debate anxiously awaited the next case to see if the Court, especially the newest justice, would allow states to impose further limits on access to abortion. Shortly thereafter, Thomas was appointed to the bench to replace Marshall, who, like Brennan, was resolutely in favor of abortion rights for women. Thomas's confirmation hearings were the subject of a great deal of controversy, not the least of which revolved around his denial of having any views on *Roe* or admitting that he had ever discussed the case. For a number of reasons, it seemed clear to many that Thomas would be a staunch foe of abortion rights.

The suspense ended in 1992 when the Court announced its decision in *Planned Parenthood of Southeastern Pennsylvania v. Casey.*[19] The case revolved around the 1982 Pennsylvania Abortion Control Act, amended in 1988 and again in 1989, the latter partially in response to the *Webster* plurality's invitation to limit abortion rights, making the law one of the most restrictive in the nation. Because it included provisions that had been declared unconstitutional by the Court in *City of Akron* and *Thornburgh,* it clearly was an attempt to provoke the Court into overruling or, at least, constraining *Roe.*[20]

The law primarily regulated the conduct of physicians.[21] Under the general heading of informed consent, it required doctors to inform women about the risks of abortion and childbirth at least twenty-four hours before performing the abortion.[22] It obligated a married woman to present a signed statement that she had notified her husband of the planned abortion, unless he was not the father of the baby, or if the pregnancy resulted from a reported case of sexual assault, or if she believed that she would be subjected to "bodily injury." Women who lied about the notification could be imprisoned for up to a year, and doctors who failed to obtain these statements could have their licenses suspended or revoked and be liable for civil damages. Additionally, the law required minors to obtain their parents' consent and ordered the physician to present the same information to the parent that had to be presented to the adult woman. Notification was not required only in medical emergencies necessary "to avert her death or for which a delay will create serious risk of substantial and irreversible impairment of major bodily function."[23]

A number of abortion providers challenged the constitutionality of five provisions of the law, arguing that they infringed on a woman's fundamental right to privacy. After a three-day trial, the district court agreed and struck the law. Applying the "compelling state interest" test, the court ruled that the informed consent, parental consent, spousal notice, and reporting and record-keeping requirements violated the due process clause of the Fourteenth Amendment.[24]

On appeal, a three-judge panel of the circuit court found that rulings subsequent to *Roe,* especially *Webster* and *Hodgson,* indicated that the Supreme Court no longer considered abortion a fundamental right. Because of this, the appeals court continued, it would not apply the "compelling state interest" test to the abortion regulations. Instead, the court held that the appropriate test was O'Connor's "undue burden" standard, defined as a regulation that "imposed an absolute obstacle or severe limitation on the abortion decision." The court characterized this standard as the "common denominator" among the high court justices and held that, unlike *Roe*'s "compelling state interest" test, it represented the approach that "a majority of the justices . . . would agree" should be used to determine the constitutionality of abortion regulations.[25] Applying the new standard, the circuit court reversed the lower court on all but the spousal notification requirement, finding that it alone imposed an undue burden on women seeking to exercise their right to abortion.

Both sides appealed to the Supreme Court, with the Bush administration entering on the side of the state and asking the Court to overturn *Roe.* On January 22, 1992, *Roe*'s nineteenth anniversary, the Court agreed to hear the case. Once again, abortion rights proponents feared, and anti-abortion advocates hoped, that the ruling would signify a return to the pre-*Roe* era, in which each state was free to restrict access to abortion. With four justices—Rehnquist, White, Scalia, and Kennedy—on record as wanting to limit, if not overturn, *Roe*—and O'Connor at best lukewarm—the odds were not in favor of the abortion rights advocates. At a minimum, they believed that the Court would grant states a great deal more latitude to regulate.[26]

In the oral arguments, Planned Parenthood attorney Kathryn Kolbert reminded the Court that since *Roe,* abortion had been considered a fundamental right, relied on by millions of women. Moreover, she indicated, the Court had already determined in *City of Akron* and *Thornburgh* that the twenty-four-hour waiting period and the physician's lecture infringed on this constitutional right.

Attorney General Ernest Preate exhorted the Court to uphold the entire statute, arguing that all provisions were consistent with *Webster.*[27]

He urged the Court to adopt the "undue burden" standard, but if the statute could not be upheld under this standard, the Court should overrule *Roe*. Kenneth Starr, solicitor general in the Bush administration, sought to convince the Court to judge the statute within the framework of the *Webster* plurality opinion, identifying it as a "rational basis standard." In his view, the state had a compelling interest in the fetus throughout the pregnancy, not, as *Roe* stipulated, only in the third trimester.[28] Kolbert's and Starr's positions were diametrically opposed. In an all-or-nothing strategy, she was asking the Court to keep *Roe* intact; he asked that it be overruled. The state was primarily interested in having the Court uphold its regulations, arguing that the law did not unduly interfere with a woman's right to abortion.

The Court addressed these key questions: Should a woman's fundamental right to abortion be retained? What standard should be used to judge abortion regulations? Should the state's interest in fetal life extend throughout the entire pregnancy? Can the Pennsylvania law be saved without abandoning *Roe*? Can *Roe* be partially dismantled without going back to the pre-*Roe* status of virtually unlimited state regulation of abortion?

The Court issued a lengthy and complex ruling in *Casey* on June 29, 1992, revealing that a new (and somewhat surprising) consensus had been forged among O'Connor, Kennedy, and Souter, who jointly authored the opinion; Scalia and Rehnquist, joined by White and Thomas, partially concurred and partially dissented, as did Stevens and Blackmun, although on different grounds.

The joint opinion began with support for *Roe*, saying, "After considering the fundamental constitutional questions resolved by *Roe*, principles of institutional integrity, and the rule of stare decisis, we are led to conclude this: the essential holding of *Roe* should be retained and once again reaffirmed."[29] The opinion identified three essential elements of *Roe*. First, the state may not unduly interfere with an abortion of a previable fetus. Second, a state can prohibit an abortion of a viable fetus if it allows exceptions to protect the woman's life or health. Third, the state's interest in maternal and fetal life commences at the start of the pregnancy. The authors stressed that the Court's commitment to individual liberty as well as the need to preserve its legitimacy in the eyes of the nation led them to conclude that *Roe* must be reaffirmed.

Attempting to strike a balance between the woman's constitutional right to abortion and the state's interest in the fetus throughout the pregnancy, the Court drew a line at viability. In doing so, it abandoned *Roe*'s trimester framework, saying it was not "essential" to *Roe*, and replaced it with two stages of pregnancy: pre- and post-viability.[30] Before viability, a state can ensure that the abortion decision is "thoughtful and informed," but it "may not strike at the right itself." The Court stressed that the trimester framework had prevented the state from enacting any regulation to further its interest in fetal and maternal health before viability. Under the new standard, the state's "substantial interest in potential life leads to the conclusion that not all regulations must be deemed unwarranted [and] not all burdens on the right to decide whether to terminate a pregnancy will be undue."[31] The Court acknowledged that in ensuring a "thoughtful and informed" decision, the law may have an "incidental effect of increasing the cost or decreasing the availability" of abortion.[32]

The Court stressed that the state's legitimate interest in protecting "potential human life" throughout the pregnancy entitled it to regulate abortion at all times, but it may not impose an "undue burden" on the woman before viability. "A finding of an undue burden," it clarified,

> is a shorthand for the conclusion that a state regulation has the purpose or effect of placing a substantial obstacle in the path of a woman seeking an abortion of a nonviable fetus. A statute with this purpose is invalid because the means chosen by the State to further the interest in potential life must be calculated to inform the woman's free choice, not hinder it.

"And," it continued, "a statute which, while furthering the interest in potential life or some other valid state interest, has the effect of placing a substantial obstacle in the path of a woman's choice cannot be considered a permissible means of serving its legitimate ends."[33]

The Court further explained that the "undue burden" standard, replacing the "compelling state interest" test, was a means of balancing *Roe* with the state's interest in "potential life." In promoting this interest, the state can ensure that a woman's choice is informed and may attempt to persuade her to choose childbirth over abortion. But even though states may protect the woman's health and safety, "unnecessary health regulations that have the purpose or effect of presenting a substantial obstacle to a woman seeking an abortion impose an undue burden on the right."[34] Thus, the Court reaffirmed *Roe,* holding that states may impose reasonable health measures, but they "may not prohibit any woman from making the ultimate decision to terminate her pregnancy before viability."[35]

Echoing *Roe,* the Court held that when the fetus is viable, "the State . . . may, if it chooses, regulate, and even proscribe, abortion except where it is necessary, in appropriate medical judgment, for the preservation of the life or health of the mother."[36]

Based on these principles, the Court found most parts of the statute constitutional and overruled *City of Akron* and *Thornburgh* on the twenty-four-hour delay and informed consent provisions. The plurality expressed concern that the twenty-four-hour waiting period may impose burdens on some women, particularly those who must travel long distances to medical facilities. In the end, however, the justices believed the regulation was not unduly burdensome, explaining that "the fact that a law which serves a valid purpose, one not designed to strike at the right itself, has the incidental effect of making it more difficult or more expensive to procure an abortion cannot be enough to invalidate it."[37]

The high court concurred with the circuit court that a state may not require a woman to notify her husband of her intention to have an abortion. Citing the detailed findings of fact made by the district court on domestic violence, the opinion concluded that women who do not want to inform their husbands are likely to have a legitimate reason. Thus, the Court concluded, "in a large fraction of the cases in which § 3209 [the spousal notification provision] is relevant, it will operate as a substantial obstacle to a woman's choice to undergo an abortion."[38] Applying the new undue burden test, the Court held that the spousal notification provision was unconstitutional.

The Court's interpretation of the "large fraction" analysis favored the plaintiffs. The state claimed that the notification provision would only burden a minuscule number of women who seek to obtain abortions, and, among them, some might not be subject to domestic violence or would be able to avoid notification on other grounds. Therefore, it contended, the statute did not erect a substantial obstacle to women's right to abortion because it would affect only a small number of women who did not wish to notify their husbands, in other words, a small fraction of women in the state.

The Court disagreed, explaining that the law "must be judged by reference to those for whom it is an actual rather than an irrelevant restriction." Thus, it believed that the undue burden test must be applied to the small number of women who could be harmed by the spousal notice provision, not to all women, or even all married women, seeking abortions. In this case, the relevant group was "married women seeking abortions who do not wish to notify their husbands of their intentions and who do not qualify for one of the statutory exceptions to the notice requirement."[39]

Each of the other justices concurred and dissented in part. Calling the joint opinion "an act of personal courage and constitutional principle," Blackmun exulted that "just when so many expected the darkness to fall, the flame has grown bright." He gloomily continued, however, "I fear for the darkness as four Justices anxiously await the single vote necessary to extinguish the light."[40]

Four justices believed the entire law constitutional, including the notice provision. Speaking for them, Rehnquist criticized the opinion for "retain[ing] the outer shell of *Roe* . . . but beat[ing] a wholesale retreat from the substance of that case." He continued, "We believe that *Roe* was wrongly decided and should be overruled . . . [and] we would adopt the approach of the plurality in *Webster* and uphold the challenged provisions of the Pennsylvania statute in their entirety."[41]

In the end, *Casey* retained the woman's right to choose yet allowed states greater latitude in regulating abortions, gratifying neither side of the abortion debate. On the day the decision was announced, the president of the National Right to Life Committee said, "We are disappointed by today's Supreme Court decision to affirm *Roe v. Wade,* the 1973 decision which legalized abortion on demand."[42] The president of the Women's Legal Defense Fund called the ruling "a dark omen," declaring that American women were being deprived of the fundamental right to make decisions about their own lives.[43] Each side vowed to continue the fight.

Although the nation's battle over reproductive rights was far from over, *Casey* effectively ended the debate over the future of *Roe*—at least for the near future. And, as it turned out, the Court's compromise in *Casey* moved the battle over abortion rights center stage in the 1992 presidential election.

Abortion Protestors

While *Casey* was on its way to the Supreme Court, anti-abortion activists were staging increasingly violent demonstrations in front of abortion clinics in an effort to disrupt their activity.[44] In the summer of 1991, anti-abortion protests lasting over a month took place at clinics in Wichita, Kansas. Federal court judge Patrick Kelly ordered the protestors to cease blocking clinic entrances and called out federal marshals to enforce the order.[45] As it turned out, Kelly himself required marshals when he received death threats following his ruling.[46] The protests continued, accompanied by a mounting number of arrests. At the direction of Bush attorney general Richard Thornburgh, the local U.S. attorney filed a brief arguing that the federal court did not have the authority to enforce abortion rights.

In other parts of the nation, protests, also often leading to violence and numerous arrests, disrupted clinic activities. As a result, abortion rights advocates became more and more concerned that women's access to abortion was threatened by their opponents' determination to engage in physical and verbal harassment. The clinics sought help from the federal courts when local law enforcement officials were unwilling or unable to curb the violence at the clinics.[47] They claimed that the Ku Klux Klan Act, a 1871 Reconstruction-era federal civil rights law, required the courts to prevent protestors from trespassing or obstructing access to clinics. This law barred conspiracies by persons seeking to deprive "any persons or class of persons" of equal rights. The protestors, led by Operation Rescue, an anti-abortion group formed in 1987, argued that the 1871 statute was enacted to guarantee the rights of newly freed slaves and did not apply to a woman's right to obtain an abortion.[48] The Bush administration sided with the protestors.

The Supreme Court settled the matter in *Bray v. Alexandria Women's Health Clinic,*[49] a 6 to 3 decision announced by Scalia. In this 1993 opinion, the Court held that women seeking abortions were not within the class of people intended to be protected by the federal law and barred federal court judges from invoking the 1871 act to stop the protests aimed at clinics and reproductive health care centers.

From 1977 to 1994, abortion clinics reported more than 1,000 violent incidents, including 36 bombings, 81 fires, 131 death threats, 84 assaults, 2 cases of kidnapping, and 2 physician shootings.[50] Concerned about the implications of *Bray* as well as the growing violence of anti-abortion protestors, Charles Schumer, a New York Democrat, and Constance Morella, a Republican from Maryland, introduced a bill in the House to protect women seeking abortions as well as abortion providers. At a news conference, Schumer announced that "the bill gives the federal government the power to act when abortion protestors move from the legitimate expression of their views to acts of violence against those who have made other choices."[51]

Congress enacted the Freedom of Access to Clinic Entrances Act (FACE) in response to the problems presented by blockades of abortion clinics and the inability of local law enforcement agencies to keep clinic doors open. The law was passed in early May and signed into law by Clinton on May 26, 1994. At the signing ceremony, the president said, "We simply cannot—we must not—continue to allow the attacks, the incidents of arson, the campaigns of intimidation upon law-abiding citizens that has given rise to this law."[52]

FACE makes it a federal crime to use force, the threat of force, or physical obstruction, such as sit-ins, to interfere with, injure, or intimidate clinic workers or women seeking abortions or other reproductive health services. Violent offenders are subject to fines of up to $100,000 and a year in prison for a first conviction; a subsequent conviction is punishable by a fine of $250,000 and three years of imprisonment. Nonviolent offenders can be sentenced to six months in prison and a $10,000 fine for a first offense and eighteen months and a $25,000 fine for a second offense; the law also authorizes civil suits by private citizens. The drama was heightened when during debate over the bill, two physicians who performed abortions were shot, one fatally, by anti-abortion activists near the entrances to their clinics.[53] Shortly after the law was enacted, the Clinton administration announced that six demonstrators were arrested for violating FACE at a Milwaukee abortion clinic. The protestors used chains and containers filled with concrete to attach themselves to two cars to block the entrance to the clinic.[54] Media reports indicate that as a result of FACE, "obstructive" abortion protests appreciably diminished, allowing women to exercise their constitutional right to reproductive freedom in greater safety.[55]

Other efforts were made in the courts to restrain illegal protest activity. *National Organization for Women v. Scheidler,*[56] a case that endured in the federal courts for over two decades, revolved around NOW's suit against abortion protestors accused of disrupting women's access to abortions. NOW claimed that the anti-abortion activists could be held accountable under the 1970 Racketeer Influenced and Corrupt Organizations Act (RICO). RICO, enacted as part of the Organized Crime Control Act of 1970, was originally intended as a weapon against organized crime. In 1984, it was amended to apply it more broadly—to conduct unrelated to organized criminal activity.

RICO is a powerful weapon that enables the government to file criminal charges as well as allowing private individuals to sue for damages. It prohibits persons engaged in interstate commerce "from conducting the affairs of the enterprise through a pattern of racketeering activity" or engaging in a conspiracy to do so. The law defines an "enterprise" as a group of associated individuals, and a "pattern of racketeering activity" requires proof of at least two actions (known as predicate offenses) that violate specified state or federal laws such as murder, extortion, or fraud. It is unnecessary to show that the acts resulted in a conviction. In addition to allowing the government to file criminal charges, RICO permits suits by private individuals who, if successful, are entitled to collect triple damages and costs, including attorneys' fees.[57]

In 1986, NOW filed a civil RICO action against Operation Rescue and its founder; the Pro-Life Action Network (PLAN) and its director, Joseph Scheidler; as well as a number of other anti-abortion groups and activists. NOW, which filed the lawsuit on behalf of the Delaware Women's Health Organization in Wilmington and the Summit Women's Health Organization in Milwaukee, charged that anti-abortion protestors were involved in a nationwide conspiracy to close abortion clinics by engaging in racketeering activities that included blocking clinic entrances, arson, harassment of clinic personnel and clients, destruction of property, physical injuries, bombings, extortion, threats, and intimidation. They alleged that in doing so, the defendants violated the 1948 Hobbs Act, a federal law prohibiting "actual or attempted robbery or extortion affecting interstate or foreign commerce."

The district court held that RICO could not be used against defendants seeking to further ideological or political motives rather than economic gain. In *National Organization for Women v. Scheidler*,[58] the Seventh Circuit agreed, ruling that NOW must show that the defendants were economically motivated.

The Supreme Court unanimously reversed the appeals court. Speaking for the Court, Rehnquist stressed that RICO "contains no economic motive requirement."[59] Although he also noted that such suits against anti-abortion protestors might interfere with their First Amendment rights to express their beliefs, he held that this issue was not before the Court at the time. Souter, joined by Kennedy, however, explicitly pointed out that "nothing in the Court's opinion precludes a RICO defendant from raising the First Amendment in its defense in a particular case." He continued, "I think it prudent to notice that RICO actions could deter protected advocacy and to caution courts applying RICO to bear in mind the First Amendment interests that could be at stake."[60]

Four years later, on April 20, 1998, a federal court jury in Chicago found the defendants guilty of violating numerous counts of the Hobbs Act. After a seven-week trial and three days of deliberation, the jury awarded the plaintiffs $85,926. Under the terms of RICO, this amount was tripled, resulting in a judgment of slightly over $250,000 to compensate the clinics for their expenses in enhancing security. The district court judge also issued a nationwide order barring PLAN from blocking access to clinics, trespassing, damaging clinic property, and threatening or using violence against clinic personnel or patients.[61]

PLAN appealed to the Seventh Circuit, arguing that it had not violated the Hobbs Act because it had not "obtained" clinic property and therefore was not guilty of extortion. In *National Organization for Women, Inc. v. Scheidler*,[62] the Seventh Circuit rejected PLAN's argument, ruling that individuals may be found guilty of violating the Hobbs

Act for disrupting or interfering with the victim's business; it is unnecessary that the defendants physically "obtain" the victim's property. The appellate court affirmed the jury award.

The Supreme Court agreed to hear the case, leaving aside the issue of whether the law infringed on the protestors' First Amendment freedoms. In *Scheidler v. National Organization for Women, Inc.,*[63] the high court reversed the appellate court.

Speaking for the Court in an 8 to 1 decision, Rehnquist held that PLAN did not commit extortion because it did not "obtain" the abortion providers' property as required under the Hobbs Act; interference with, or disruption of, such property does not constitute extortion, even if it closes down a clinic, said the Court. Rehnquist concluded that because PLAN had not committed any acts of extortion, it had not violated the Hobbs Act, and therefore the judgment against it must be reversed. The Court overturned the jury verdict in NOW's favor and vacated the district court's order restricting PLAN from blockading abortion clinics and harassing abortion providers and their patients.

After the Supreme Court absolved the defendants of the extortion charge, NOW argued that their violent acts against people and property associated with abortion clinics violated the Hobbs Act and satisfied the requirements of RICO. Therefore, NOW claimed, the district court order was still valid. Because NOW had not raised this issue before the Supreme Court, the appellate court remanded the case to allow the district court to determine whether the threats or acts of violence constituted crimes under the Hobbs Act. The anti-abortion groups sought Supreme Court review of this decision, and the Court agreed to hear the case.

In 2006, the Supreme Court ruled again on the limits on protests at abortion clinics in *Scheidler v. National Organization for Women, Inc.*[64] Once again, the high court ruled against NOW. Speaking for a unanimous Court, Breyer stated that threatening or committing acts of physical violence that were unrelated to extortion or robbery did not violate the Hobbs Act. According to the Court, the "plan or purpose" specified in the statute must be interpreted as a "plan or purpose" that affects interstate commerce through robbery or extortion, not simply a "plan or purpose" related to commerce. Thus ended NOW's attempt to use civil RICO to halt the actions of the protestors whose aim was to stop women from obtaining abortions.

Anti-abortion protestors claimed that the First Amendment guaranteed their right to protest at clinic sites. *Madsen v. Women's Health Center*[65] squarely addressed the conflict between the First Amendment rights of demonstrators and women's constitutional right to obtain abortions. It arose out of a legal confrontation between the Aware Woman Center for Choice in Melbourne, Florida, and Operation Rescue and other anti-abortion groups.[66]

The center was singled out by anti-abortion protestors (as many as 400 at a time) in 1991. They blocked clinic doors, marched on the street with bullhorns, approached patients, and demonstrated at the home of clinic staff members. Responding to the center's suit, in September 1992, a state court judge ordered the protestors to refrain from trespassing on center property, blocking entrances, and physically abusing persons entering or leaving the building; the court specified that its order was not aimed at limiting the protestors' First Amendment rights.

After six months, as the demonstrations continued and protestors violated the court order, the court modified the order to establish a 36-foot buffer zone around the clinic entrances and driveways (including the public sidewalk), within which all anti-abortion speech was banned, and to prohibit excessive noise ("singing, chanting, whistling, shouting, yelling, and the use of bullhorns, auto horns, sound amplification equipment or other sounds or images observable to or within earshot of the patients inside") during the hours of morning surgery and recovery.[67] Additionally, the court created a 300-foot zone to prevent protestors from approaching patients without their consent and a 300-foot demonstration-free zone at the homes of clinic staff members.

The Florida Supreme Court unanimously upheld the lower court, declaring that the protestors' activity conflicted with the state's concern for public safety as well as women's right to abortion.[68] The anti-abortion groups had also gone to federal court, and shortly before the Florida Supreme Court issued its opinion, the federal court ruled that the state court injunction was unconstitutional.[69]

The key issue before the Supreme Court was the 36-foot buffer zone, with the protestors claiming the state court order was content-based and viewpoint-based and therefore impermissible under the First Amendment; they did not challenge the 300-foot zone in which only invited speech was allowed.[70]

The protestors argued that anti-abortion beliefs were targeted by the court order, since only they were arrested for being in the buffer zone. The center contended that the injunction was a proper "time, place, and manner" restriction that indicated no views on abortion and served to protect a variety of government interests, including public safety. Each side asked the Court to apply the level of scrutiny that would lead to the desired outcome: the protestors advocated the use of strict scrutiny, whereas the center requested the lower level of intermediate scrutiny customarily applied to "time, place, and manner" restrictions.[71]

The Court's 6 to 3 ruling, announced by Rehnquist, first addressed the proper form of scrutiny to apply to the restrictions imposed by the state court order. The Court rejected the protestors' claims that the injunction was aimed only at anti-abortion speech. Every injunction, explained the Court, is aimed at a party involved in a particular dispute. Because abortion rights supporters were not demonstrating, it was pointless to curb their activities in the buffer zone. Moreover, he said, the restrictions were not aimed at the content of the speech but at the demonstrators who had repeatedly violated the earlier injunction; the order, he stressed, applied to all persons engaged in such activities, regardless of their message. Agreeing that the injunction was content-neutral and did not merit the strict scrutiny the demonstrators sought, the Court still imposed a higher standard of review than it normally applied to "time, place, and manner" laws.

Applying the heightened standard, the majority upheld the 36-foot buffer zone around the clinic entrances and driveway to preserve access to and from the clinic and to allow the flow of traffic on the street; it also allowed the noise abatement restrictions. It found, however, that the restrictions imposed on access to private property at the back and side of the clinic, as well as the one forbidding the protestors from flashing signs and pictures to patients, imposed greater burdens on speech than necessary. Similarly, the 300-foot no-approach buffer zone around the clinic and outside staff homes was too broad to allow the peaceful expression of protestors' views and burdened their speech beyond the permissible limits of the government's interests in ensuring access to the clinic and preventing intimidation of the patients and staff.

In *Schenck v. Pro-Choice Network of Western New York,*[72] the Court again addressed permissible limitations on the so-called sidewalk counseling engaged in by anti-abortion protestors. In response to a suit by abortion providers in upstate New York, including doctors, hospitals, and clinics, a federal court judge issued an order that established a 15-foot buffer zone outside the clinic entrances and driveways and prohibited "counselors" from being within 15 feet of persons or vehicles entering or leaving the clinic.[73] The order permitted two "counselors" to come closer to have a nonthreatening conversation but required that they end the discussion at the patient's request. The demonstrators characterized their activities as peaceful persuasion, but as the Supreme Court opinion indicated, the injunction had been granted after seventeen months of protests and numerous contempt hearings to keep access to the clinics open by preventing protestors from demonstrating within 15 feet of clinic entrances. The protestors lost their appeal in the circuit court in a 13 to 2 vote and took their case to the Supreme Court.[74]

The high court examined the factual circumstances of the dispute and, in a 6 to 3 vote, held that the demonstrators' behavior justified establishing the 15-foot buffer at the clinic entrances and parking lots to maintain public safety, allow traffic to flow freely, and ensure women's access to medical care. In an 8 to 1 vote, however, the Court rejected the "floating buffer zone" that the lower court allowed around individuals and cars.[75] Applying the *Madsen* standard, the high court held that this part of the injunction infringed on the First Amendment rights of the protestors because it placed an unnecessary burden on speech.

Despite the characterization of such encounters as turning "into 'in your face' yelling, and sometimes into pushing, shoving, and grabbing"[76] when women objected, the Court found this "floating buffer" zone unconstitutional because it prevented activists from expressing their views peacefully by handing out leaflets and communicating their message in normal conversational tones. In the end, the Court did not decide whether requiring the "counselors" to cease their attempts at persuasion when asked unconstitutionally restricted their speech.

The Court again was asked to resolve a conflict over "sidewalk counseling" in *Hill v. Colorado* in 2000.[77] Here, the issue was the validity of a 1993 Colorado statute, enacted before FACE, that established a 100-foot zone around health care facilities and barred persons inside this zone from moving closer than 8 feet to pass out literature, display signs, or engage in "sidewalk counseling" without the listener's consent. Violating the law could result in a fine of up to $750 or six months in jail. In a challenge brought by three anti-abortion activists, the Colorado Supreme Court ruled in February 1999 that the law did not violate their First Amendment rights.[78]

On appeal before the U.S. Supreme Court, the Clinton administration supported the state court decision. Lawyers for the state and the administration argued that the 8-foot barrier did not impede speech or debate because it allowed the protestors to have a conversation with clinic patients. In another vote reflecting the 6 to 3 division, the Supreme Court upheld the statute against the First Amendment challenge. The Court first noted that each side had undisputed interests in this conflict: the protestors in the First Amendment and the state in protecting the health and safety of its citizens, especially at medical care facilities. Signaling the direction of the Court, Stevens, who delivered the opinion, indicated that the statute was not aimed at restricting speakers or at the dissemination of any particular views. He stressed the importance of "recogniz[ing] the significant difference between state restrictions on a speaker's right to address a willing audience and those that protect listeners from unwanted communication. This statute," he added, "deals only with the latter."[79]

After a lengthy analysis, Stevens agreed with the Colorado court that the statute was a content-neutral "time, place, and manner" restriction because (1) it did not regulate speech, just the place where the speech occurred; (2) it was not passed to restrict a particular message; and (3) the state's interests were not related to the content of the speech. The Court also found the restriction narrowly tailored, allowing communication of the protestors' message to listeners—either verbally or with signs and pictures. The distance did not preclude the "counselors" from offering leaflets or other written material to individuals walking by them. Last, he noted, as with schools and courthouses, the state had a special interest in regulating the area surrounding a health care facility.

Limits on Abortion Procedures

Perhaps the most contentious issues in the political and legal struggle over abortion rights revolve around the methods generally known as "dilation and evacuation" (D&E) or "intact dilation and extraction" (D&X). The D&X procedure, a variant of the commonly used D&E procedure for second trimester abortions, is rarely performed, occurring when physicians believe that it is the safest method for a woman with severe health conditions of her own or with a fetus that has developed severe abnormalities.[80] Beginning in the 1990s, the battle over the method—called "partial-birth" abortion by abortion opponents—raged for many years, encompassing the federal courts and Congress as well as the executive branch.[81]

In 1995, Congress debated a bill (H.R. 1833) that would have criminalized an abortion in which the doctor "partially vaginally delivers a living fetus before killing the fetus and completing the delivery."[82] Lynn Woolsey, Democrat from California, warned her colleagues that the bill "with all of the emotional rhetoric, with all of the graphic pictures, with all of the exaggerated testimony—is the first frontal attack on *Roe versus Wade* by the new majority. Plain and simple. The new majority wants to do away with *Roe;* the radical right wants to do away with *Roe*."[83]

When the bill was approved by both houses and sent to Clinton in March 1996, the final version subjected doctors to federal charges, with up to two years' imprisonment or $250,000 in fines, unless they could prove the procedure was necessary to save the woman's life and no other procedure would be effective; it also allowed the father, if married to the woman at the time she received the abortion, and her parents, if she were a minor, to sue the doctor.

In vetoing the legislation, Clinton said that he disapproved of such abortions but could not sign the bill because it allowed an exception only to save the woman's life and provided no exemption for situations in which a woman's health was at risk. His veto message charged that Congress "fashioned a bill that is consistent neither with the Constitution nor with sound public policy."[84] Although the House narrowly succeeded in overriding the president's veto, the override vote failed in the Senate.

Despite their failure to pass the law, abortion opponents succeeded in turning public attention away from the issue of a woman's constitutional right established in *Roe* and focusing it on a particular procedure that much of the public found disagreeable. They also succeeded in ensuring that the president's support for abortion rights would be an issue in the 1996 presidential election.

In March 1997, another battle to limit abortion was underway, involving a new House bill (H.R. 1122) identical to the one passed the year before. Charges and countercharges flew back and forth, with abortion rights advocates claiming the bill's supporters ultimately wanted to outlaw all abortions and were merely beginning with this procedure first. They feared that banning this method would eventually lead to restrictions on other second trimester abortions. The bill easily passed, with a vote large enough to override the anticipated veto from the president.

With new support from the American Medical Association (AMA) in exchange for expanded protection for doctors, the Senate approved the measure as well; the sixty-four votes in favor were three votes shy of the two-thirds necessary to override.[85] Again, after the House voted to accept the Senate version, the bill was sent to the president. In October 1997, Clinton vetoed it again, reiterating that he was opposed to the procedure but would not deny it to women who needed it. He refused to sign HR 1122, he said, because it "does not contain an exception . . . that would adequately protect the lives and health of a small group of women in tragic circumstances who need an abortion performed at a late stage of pregnancy to avert death or serious injury." He had "asked Congress repeatedly," he added, to enact a law "that includes a limited exception for the small number of compelling cases where use of this procedure is necessary to avoid serious health consequences."[86]

Once again, the House voted to override; the Senate did not, and the measure died. In 1999, both houses of Congress again cleared legislation to prohibit this abortion method but took no further action because the Supreme Court agreed to review a lower court ruling on a Nebraska law.

While the battle had been raging between Congress and the White House, more than half the states enacted bans on this type of abortion procedure; most did not survive constitutional challenges because they were unconstitutionally vague or imposed an undue burden on women. The courts ruled that because the D&X procedure is safer for a woman than any other method in some circumstances, the ban would place some women's health at risk.

Dr. Leroy Carhart, a Nebraska physician, challenged the state law that automatically revoked the medical license of a doctor who "partially delivers vaginally a living unborn child before killing the unborn child and completing the delivery." The law was aimed at pre-viability abortions; another statute prohibited post-viability procedures. It also subjected doctors to felony charges, including up to twenty years in prison, a $25,000 fine, or both. Carhart argued that because the D&X procedure is the safest method of abortion for women under certain circumstances, the law imposed an undue burden on women. Additionally, he claimed that it was unconstitutionally vague because it did not precisely define the prohibited conduct.[87]

In September 1999, the Eighth Circuit ruled in *Carhart v. Stenberg*[88] that the Nebraska law was so broadly written that in addition to prohibiting the D&X method of abortion, it also barred doctors from performing abortions by the most common and safest method of second trimester abortion, the D&E.[89] Thus, it imposed an undue burden on women and was unconstitutional.

Shortly after the Eighth Circuit ruled, the Seventh Circuit decided the opposite in *Hope Clinic v. Ryan*,[90] holding that the Illinois and Wisconsin laws prohibiting D&X procedures were not unconstitutionally vague. The appeals court stressed, however, that the state courts must construe the statutes in a way that did not impinge on procedures other than the D&X method and that clearly marked the bounds of the physician's liability. The court believed that the statutes would be interpreted this way because the state attorneys general declared that the laws were limited to the D&X procedure and were not aimed at outlawing the D&E method.[91]

This conflict among circuits made it more likely that the Supreme Court would accept a case in which a state's ban on a D&X procedure was challenged. In accepting the Nebraska case for review, the Court effectively placed the national debate over such abortions on hold.

In determining whether the Nebraska statute violated the Constitution, the high court focused on whether the statute required an exception for women's health and whether it was vague. The ruling in *Stenberg v. Carhart (Carhart I)*[92] in June 2000 was the Rehnquist Court's first major abortion opinion in eight years.

In announcing the opinion for the 5 to 4 majority, Breyer clearly indicated that he believed the ruling was within the parameters determined by *Casey.* He identified three principles that had been established in *Casey* and *Roe* and upon which the Court now based its decision: (1) a woman has a right to terminate her pregnancy before viability; (2) a state cannot place an undue burden on a woman's right to terminate her pregnancy before viability; and (3) after viability, the state may regulate and even prohibit abortion, unless the procedure is necessary to preserve the life or health of the woman.

After apologizing for the clinical nature of the discussion, Breyer described several abortion methods, focusing on those performed during the second trimester, in which approximately 10 percent of abortions are performed.[93] Echoing the courts below, he cited two factors that convinced the majority that the Nebraska law was unconstitutional. First, quoting *Casey,* he noted that the law did not contain an exception for the health of the mother. Second, he held that because it also limited a woman's ability to obtain a D&E abortion, it imposed an undue burden on her right to abortion.

Emphasizing that all abortion regulations must contain a health exception, Breyer noted that the Court has repeatedly held that the state must not risk the woman's health by regulating the method of abortion. He rejected the state's contention that outlawing this procedure would not create any risks for the woman because other methods were available, stressing that the medical testimony in the record indicated that there were situations in which the D&X method was the safest for the woman. He found the state's arguments to the contrary "insufficient to demonstrate that Nebraska's law needs no health exception."[94]

The second consideration revolved around the relationship between the two abortion procedures. The state conceded that the statute would place an undue burden on a woman's right to abortion if it applied to the D&E as well as the D&X procedure. Reiterating the findings of the circuit court, Breyer held that the plain language of the statute did not distinguish between the two procedures and was so broadly written that it encompassed both. Whether the state intended to ban only the D&X was not the issue, he maintained; the issue was whether the law reached other types of procedures, including the commonly used D&E. The answer, he said, was that it could be applied to both.

The Nebraska attorney general argued that he interpreted the statute to ban only the D&X procedure, but Breyer was not persuaded. In part, he pointed out that the attorney general's opinion did not bind the state courts, which might not accept his view, nor did it bind the county prosecutors, who would be responsible for enforcing the law. Moreover, the attorney general's interpretation of the law was flatly contradicted by its text. The state urged the Supreme Court to accept the view that "partial-birth" abortion as used in the statute was limited to the D&X procedure. But because the law did not single out the D&X procedure, the Court believed that it would allow state law enforcement officials to "pursue physicians who use 'D&E' procedures."[95]

Stevens's concurring opinion was brief, questioning "how a state has any legitimate interest in requiring a doctor to follow any procedure other than the one that he or she reasonably believes will best protect the woman" who chooses to exercise her right to abortion. He added that for the state to distinguish between abortion procedures and claim that one was closer to "infanticide" than the other was "simply irrational."[96] Similarly, Ginsburg wrote to question the motives of the legislators who, she believed, were using the law to "chip away at the private choice shielded by *Roe v. Wade,* even as modified by *Casey.*"[97]

O'Connor concurred as well, agreeing that a health exception was required. But she also suggested that the outcome might well have been different had it been clear that the law only applied to D&X abortions and included a health exception.

Rehnquist, Scalia, Kennedy, and Thomas dissented, arguing that the majority had wrongly applied *Casey* and was expanding the right to abortion beyond the principles articulated there. They expressed their shock and horror about the procedure, describing it in great detail; they also voiced concern that the ruling would foreclose all abortion regulations. Kennedy's dissent suggested that although he was probably still committed to preserving *Roe,* he was willing to allow states greater latitude to regulate abortion.

Proponents of the ban vowed to fight on, but they appeared unwilling to add a health exception to such laws because they believed it would give women virtually unfettered access to D&X abortions. Women's rights advocates countered that women should not have to be near death before doctors could perform this procedure. The struggle continued, with *Carhart I* providing a temporary lull in the conflict as both sides geared up for more legal and political battles ahead.

Minors' Rights

After a five-year hiatus in abortion rulings, the high court agreed to hear a challenge to New Hampshire's Parental Notification Prior to Abortion Act. Passed in 2003, the law required a physician to notify a parent in writing forty-eight hours before performing an abortion on a minor unless the procedure was necessary to "prevent the minor's death." Unlike most parental consent and notice laws, New Hampshire's lacked an explicit health exception. The teen could avoid notification by requesting a hearing from a state court judge who must determine whether she is sufficiently mature to give informed consent or that performing an abortion without notice to her parent was in her best interest. The judge had seven calendar days in which to issue a ruling. A physician who failed to comply with the law faced civil and criminal penalties.

Before the bill was signed, Planned Parenthood challenged the law on its face, arguing that because it lacked an exception for medical emergencies to preserve the health of the teen, the law contravened *Casey* by placing an undue burden on a minor's right to abortion. Two days before the law was to take effect, the district court found it unconstitutional.[98]

On appeal before the First Circuit in *Planned Parenthood of Northern New England v. Heed,*[99] the state argued that the appellate court should apply the "no set of circumstances" test from *United States v. Salerno,*[100] a 1987 Supreme Court decision in which the high court ruled that a plaintiff who challenges a law on its face "must establish that no set of circumstances exists under which the Act would be valid."

The First Circuit disagreed, emphasizing that in *Casey,* the Court had applied the "large fraction" test to determine whether the Pennsylvania law was unconstitutional. The appellate court explained that five justices (consisting of the plurality of O'Connor, Souter, and Kennedy, plus Stevens and Blackmun) had held that "an abortion regulation is facially invalid if 'in a large fraction of cases in which [the regulation] is relevant, it will operate as a substantial obstacle to a woman's choice to undergo an abortion,' thus imposing an undue burden."[101] Noting that the Supreme Court had never resolved the inconsistency between *Salerno* and *Casey,* the First Circuit held that most circuits now agreed that *Casey* had replaced *Salerno* as the standard for deciding facial challenges in abortion rights cases and that the Court's decisions in *Casey* and *Carhart I* had reflected this.

The state also contended that its interest in ensuring parental involvement in their daughters' abortion decisions excused it from including an explicit health exception. Moreover, it declared, the Court had upheld parental involvement laws without them. Not persuaded, the appeals court responded that each time the high court had explicitly considered laws lacking a health exception, it had ruled in the plaintiffs' favor. Moreover, it cited two circuit court decisions that had recently struck laws in Colorado and Idaho because they lacked health exceptions.

The appeals court also ruled that in allowing abortions to be performed only to prevent the minor's death, the law placed physicians in the unenviable position of having to wait until their patients were near death to perform the abortion or risk exposing themselves to civil and criminal penalties by performing the procedure without the requisite notification to the parents. Finally, the First Circuit rejected the state's argument that the law did not require an explicit health exception because there were other state laws that would be interpreted to allow the abortion to be performed if the minor's health were endangered.

Citing *Roe, Casey,* and *Carhart I,* the appeals court noted that the high court had held in those cases that state abortion regulations must include exceptions to preserve women's health—at all stages of pregnancy. In the end, the circuit court concluded that the statute imposed an undue burden on a "large fraction" of minors seeking abortions and struck the law as an unconstitutional restriction on the rights of teenagers facing medical emergencies that required immediate abortions.

Attorney General Kelly Ayotte (who replaced Peter Heed as attorney general and was subsequently elected as the Republican senator from New Hampshire in the 2010 election) appealed to the Supreme Court, and the Court handed down its ruling in January 2006, after hearing oral arguments in November 2005. The Bush administration urged the high court to reverse the circuit court and uphold the law. With Roberts in place as the new chief justice (following Rehnquist's death) and O'Connor's upcoming retirement from the Court, the case received a great deal of attention from the media as well as from both sides of the abortion debate.[102]

The Court devoted its ruling entirely to the appropriateness of the lower court's remedy of striking the entire statute; it avoided resolving the inconsistency between *Salerno* and *Casey* in the proper interpretation of facial challenges.

In a narrow opinion—O'Connor's last one—she began by establishing the parameters of the decision, saying

> we do not revisit our abortion precedents today, but rather address a question of remedy: If enforcing a statute that regulates access to abortion would be unconstitutional in medical emergencies, what is the appropriate judicial response? We hold that invalidating the statute entirely is not always necessary or justified, for lower courts may be able to render narrower declaratory and injunctive relief.[103]

The Court agreed with the lower courts that the law was unconstitutional because it lacked an explicit health exception. O'Connor presented the three governing principles ("two legal and one factual") guiding the decision: (1) states may enact parental notification laws; (2) states may not restrict access to abortions that are "necessary, in appropriate medical judgment, for the preservation of the life or health of the mother";[104] and (3) a small number of pregnant teens require immediate abortions to prevent serious health injuries.

The state acknowledged that it cannot "subject minors to significant health risks" but argued that teenagers were protected by the judicial bypass procedure and physicians were shielded from legal liability in emergencies by the state "competing harms statute" that would allow them to justify their actions.[105] Because the lower courts found these alternatives insufficient, they struck the law.[106] But, O'Connor stressed, courts should refrain from invalidating statutes wholesale, adding "the courts below chose the most blunt remedy—permanently enjoining the enforcement of New Hampshire's parental notification law and thereby invalidating it entirely."[107] And in doing so, they nullified its effect on all teenagers, including the majority whose health would not be affected by the notice provision.

O'Connor agreed with the state that the courts should not have applied the blunt remedy because there would be only a few instances in which the absence of a health exception would risk harm to the teenager. Instead, she said, the lower court should have considered a limited remedy that would invalidate the law only for those few minors whose health would be adversely affected by it.

In devising an appropriate remedy, she continued, the court must also abstain from interfering with the legislature's authority and avoid rewriting a law to make it constitutional. Thus, to determine the proper remedy when a portion of a statute is unconstitutional, a court must ascertain the legislature's intent: "Would the legislature have preferred what is left of its statute to no statute at all?"[108] Noting that the parties differed with each other over the legislature's intent, the Court remanded the case to allow the appeals court to decide whether the state would have preferred to enact a law with a proper health exception or not enact the law at all if a health exception were required.[109] The state soon indicated its preference by repealing the parental notification law.[110]

More Limits on Abortion Procedures

Despite *Carhart I,* by 2003, more than half the states had enacted statutes prohibiting the D&X abortion method.[111] Most such laws lacked a health exception for the mother and were struck at the district court level. With Bush's election in 2000, congressional Republicans received assurances that the bill they had attempted to pass twice since 1995 would be signed.[112] On July 24, 2002, the House passed the Partial-Birth Abortion Ban Act of 2002 (H.R. 4965) in a 274 to 151 vote. In a statement released before the vote, on July 8, 2002, ACOG had criticized the bill for interfering with the doctor-patient relationship and for failing to allow a physician to use his or her best judgment about the most appropriate procedure for the patient.[113] The bill was never brought to the Senate floor for a vote in the Democratic-controlled chamber.

The next year, when the Republicans controlled the Senate, it approved S. 3, a bill sponsored by Pennsylvania Republican Rick Santorum. The Senate vote, taking place on March 13, 2003, was 64 to 33; sixteen Democrats voted in favor, with three Republicans and an Independent voting against it. On June 4, 2003, the House passed its version of the bill (H.R. 760) in a vote of 282 to 139.[114]

In the midst of congressional deliberations, groups from all perspectives joined in the fray, urging passage or defeat of the bill. Groups such as ACOG, already on record against it, the AMA, and the National Abortion Rights Action League (NARAL) Pro-Choice America warned that Congress was making inroads into *Roe* and that a legislature should not determine proper medical procedures. They pointed out that the D&X procedure is used sparingly, only when the woman's health or future fertility is at risk and the doctor determines it is the safest method of abortion. Doctors expressed concern that the bill did not distinguish between the types of abortion procedures and that they may begin an abortion intending to perform a D&E, but that conditions may arise that would indicate the D&X was more appropriate to safeguard the woman's health.

Planned Parenthood, the National Abortion Federation (NAF), an association of abortion providers, and the ACLU Reproductive Freedom Project all promised to file suit to block enforcement of the law as soon as the president signed it. On the other side, the U.S. Conference of Catholic Bishops, the National Right to Life Committee, the Family Research Council, and Concerned Women for America viewed the legislation as an opportunity to limit women's access to abortion and take a stand against abortion rights. They characterized the ban as a step forward in protecting women's health and called the procedure "barbaric," saying it was dangerous for women.[115]

The bill went to conference, with both chambers approving the conference report at the end of October. The Partial-Birth Abortion Ban Act of 2003 was signed into law by Bush on November 5, 2003, and was scheduled to take effect the next day. During the signing ceremony, the president said the country "owes its children a different and better welcome." He continued, "for years, a terrible form of violence has been directed against children who are inches from birth, while the law looked the other way. Today, at last, the American people and our government have confronted the violence and come to the defense of the innocent child." He also promised that the executive branch would vigorously defend the law in the courts.[116]

Like the Nebraska law struck in *Carhart I,* the federal ban applied to second trimester abortions of pre-viable fetuses. However, Congress attempted to differentiate it from the state statute struck in *Carhart I* with extensive findings of fact. In the lengthy "Findings" section, the law defined a "partial-birth" abortion as one in which the person performing the abortion "deliberately and intentionally vaginally delivers a living fetus until, in the case of a head-first presentation, the entire fetal head is outside the mother's body or in the case of a breech presentation, any part of the fetal trunk past the navel is outside the mother's body." Congress hoped that specifying these "anatomical landmarks" would ensure that the statute would not suffer the fate of the ill-defined Nebraska law.

Congress explicitly rejected the Nebraska district court's findings that the procedure is safest for women in certain circumstances, which the high court had relied on in *Carhart I.* Instead it declared there was "substantial" evidence to conclude "that a ban on partial-birth abortion is not required to contain a 'health' exception, because the facts indicate that a partial-birth abortion is never necessary to preserve the health of a woman, poses serious risks to a woman's health, and lies outside the standard of medical care."[117] The law provided for a fine and imprisonment of a doctor who "knowingly" performs such a procedure unless it is necessary "to save the life of a mother"; additionally, it allowed the father of the child (if married to the mother) or the parents of a minor under eighteen to file a civil suit and collect monetary damages from the physician.

Most opponents (and many neutral observers) of the ban considered the law unconstitutional because it failed to conform to the requirements of *Carhart I* by omitting a health exception. Moreover, they argued that like the Nebraska law, it was unconstitutionally vague because it could also apply to the D&E procedure. Proponents contended that the specificity of the language in the federal law sufficiently distinguished it from the vague law struck in *Carhart I* and that Congress had adequately shown that there is no need for a health exception because the procedure is never medically necessary to protect a woman's health.

Before the bill was signed, Planned Parenthood and NAF, represented by the ACLU, sued the federal government (with Attorney General John Ashcroft named as the defendant) in San Francisco and New York federal district courts; in Nebraska, Carhart and three other doctors, represented by the Center for Reproductive Rights, filed suit in a Nebraska federal district court. All three courts issued temporary injunctions to halt enforcement of the law.

The question of the constitutionality of the law primarily revolved around the absence of a health exception. The government argued that Congress had legitimately concluded that a health exception was unnecessary because prohibiting the D&X method posed only insignificant health risks to women and therefore did not impose an undue burden on them. The challengers insisted that since *Roe* was decided, the Court had made it clear that all abortion regulations must include an exception for a woman's life and health.

As the trials were about to begin, the parties engaged in a skirmish with the Justice Department, which demanded hundreds of hospital medical records of women who had obtained abortions in New York, Philadelphia, Chicago, and Ann Arbor, Michigan. Ashcroft claimed the records were a necessary part of the government's case in defending the law.[118] Many hospitals resisted, refusing to release the records to the government, and the courts eventually agreed that releasing them would infringe on the women's privacy, even if their names were redacted.

The three trials began at the end of March, and in each case, citing *Carhart I,* the district court judges ruled in the plaintiffs' favor, all declaring the law unconstitutional because it lacked a health exception. The first to decide, California federal district court judge Phyllis Hamilton, handed down her decision in *Planned Parenthood Federation of America v. Ashcroft*[119] on June 1, 2004. A few months later, on August

26, 2004, Judge Richard Conway Casey issued his opinion in *National Abortion Federation v. Ashcroft*.[120] Last, on September 12, 2004, Nebraska federal court judge Richard Kopf also ruled against the federal government in *Carhart v. Ashcroft*,[121] declaring that the congressional finding that the procedure was never necessary was "unreasonable."

The government was no more successful in the appeals courts: all the circuits affirmed the trial courts and continued the injunctions on the law, preventing it from going into effect. The Ninth Circuit ruled in *Planned Parenthood Federation of America, Inc. v. Gonzales;*[122] the Second Circuit in *National Abortion Federation v. Gonzales;*[123] and the Eighth Circuit in *Carhart v. Gonzales*.[124]

The Nebraska trial court judge had struck the law because it lacked a health exception and placed an undue burden on women. The Eighth Circuit ruling was narrower, focusing only on the absent health exception. The Ninth Circuit found the law unconstitutional on several grounds: it lacked a health exception, placed an undue burden on a woman's ability to obtain a second trimester abortion because it did not sufficiently distinguish the D&X from the more commonly used D&E, and was vague in defining the banned method. Despite the unanimity among six lower courts and its own 2000 ruling in *Carhart I,* the high court accepted the federal statute for review in the same week it announced its ruling in *Ayotte*. It heard oral arguments on November 8, 2006.[125]

The four justices in the *Carhart I* majority (Ginsburg, Souter, Stevens, and Breyer) were almost certain to vote against the federal law, but the composition of the Court had changed in the seven years since that case was decided. Four votes in favor of the law (Scalia, Thomas, Roberts, and Alito) seemed just as certain; of course, Scalia and Thomas had long expressed their desire to see *Roe* overturned. Roberts's replacement of Rehnquist was unlikely to affect the outcome of the case, but Alito's replacement of O'Connor would almost certainly have a significant impact. Kennedy's was the unknown vote. He had jointly authored *Casey,* reaffirming *Roe,* and had insisted that state regulations must contain exceptions to protect the woman's health. However, more recently, his heated dissent in *Carhart I,* calling the D&X method one that "many decent people find so abhorrent as to be among the most serious of crimes against human life," signaled a likely vote to uphold the federal ban.[126] The high court issued its ruling in *Gonzales v. Carhart (Carhart II)*[127] on April 18, 2007, with Kennedy announcing the opinion for the five-justice majority consisting of himself, Scalia, Thomas, Roberts, and Alito.

After discussing first and second trimester abortion procedures (noting that 90 percent of abortions are performed during the first trimester),

Kennedy focused at length on the D&X method, describing it in great detail. He pointed out that Congress had reacted to *Carhart I* in at least two ways: (1) making its own factual findings and concluding that a "consensus" exists that "partial-birth" abortion "is a gruesome and inhumane procedure that is never medically necessary" and (2) explicitly defining the banned procedure in a way that the Nebraska law had not.[128] Signaling the outcome of the case, Kennedy declared that according to *Casey,* "the government has a legitimate and substantial interest in preserving and promoting fetal life," which, he said, "would be repudiated were the Court now to affirm the judgments of the Courts of Appeals."[129]

The plaintiffs argued that the law was vague because it did not sufficiently describe the proscribed behavior and would lead to arbitrary enforcement. Not so, said Kennedy; the law defines the illegal act precisely by establishing anatomical landmarks. In contrast, the Nebraska statute had defined the banned procedure as any delivery of a "substantial portion" of the fetus. Additionally, he explained, the federal law clearly excludes other abortion procedures and imposes criminal liability only if the physician uses the D&X method "deliberately and intentionally" and follows it with an overt act that destroys the fetus. The same standards, he pointed out, govern the behavior of the authorities, thus eliminating the possibility of arbitrary enforcement.

Kennedy next addressed the challengers' claim that, like the Nebraska law in *Carhart I,* the federal law is invalid on its face because it imposes an undue burden on women by extending the ban to other methods of second trimester abortions. He also rejected this argument, insisting that the law as written applies only to the D&X method and does not encompass other second trimester abortions.[130] And, he added, even if a physician performing a D&E method abortion accidentally produces a partially delivered fetus, there is no criminal liability if the physician does not intend that result. In any event, he noted, according to their own testimony, most doctors who perform the D&X method do so purposefully, not accidentally.

Acknowledging that the Court was bound by *Casey,* Kennedy nevertheless dismissed the plaintiffs' other argument that the law creates "a substantial obstacle" for a woman seeking an abortion of a pre-viable fetus. They maintained that Congress had no legitimate purpose in enacting the law, that its aim was to hinder women from obtaining abortions. Kennedy, however, found that Congress had several legitimate reasons. First, he said, by prohibiting an inhumane practice, "the Act expresses respect for the dignity of human life."[131] Second, Congress wanted to preserve the integrity of the medical profession by preventing members of the medical community from performing acts that society considered repugnant. To this end, Kennedy stressed that "the state may use its regulatory power to bar certain procedures, all in furtherance of its legitimate interests in regulating the medical profession in order to promote respect for life, including life of the unborn."[132]

Congress, he continued, was within its authority to single out a method that many consider tantamount to infanticide. He conceded that other methods of abortion, such as the D&E, may also appear to devalue human life, but citing the congressional findings, he held that the legislature might legitimately conclude that the banned procedure is distinctly different from all others and warrants special regulation.

In language that angered many abortion rights supporters, Kennedy also proclaimed that the law furthered Congress's legitimate interest in women's well-being by preventing them from being traumatized by their decisions.[133] He explained that almost certainly "severe depression and loss of esteem can follow" from some abortions. Knowing this, he said, many doctors are reluctant to fully inform women about the intended method. "It is self-evident," he continued,

> that a mother who comes to regret her choice to abort must struggle with grief more anguished and sorrow more profound when she learns, only after the event, what she once did not know: that she allowed a doctor to pierce the skull and vacuum the fast-developing brain of her unborn child, a child assuming the human form.[134]

Additionally, he noted, the law serves the state's purpose of deterring women from having an abortion, thereby leading to fewer of them. Moreover, he said, the ban may encourage the medical community to look for a less shocking method of performing a second trimester abortion.

Satisfied that the law furthered Congress's legitimate interests, Kennedy admitted that he had not resolved the question of whether it imposed an undue burden on women by not permitting the procedure when needed to protect women's health as required by *Casey* and *Ayotte*.

Unlike *Ayotte*, in which both parties agreed that New Hampshire's parental notice statute required a health exception to prevent the possibility of grave injury to the young woman, Kennedy pointed out that there was a dispute among medical experts about whether the D&X was the safest abortion method for some women. Noting that the lower courts were split on this issue as well, he explained that the California and Nebraska district courts had both concluded that the D&X was the safest method for some women in some circumstances, but that the New York trial court judge differed, saying that he did not believe that the testimony presented at trial showed the D&X was medically necessary. Nevertheless, the trial judge struck the law, Kennedy pointed out, because he found that the D&X may be safer than the D&E for some women.

The crucial question, however, is whether the variance among medical opinions about the risks to women arising from the ban on the D&X procedure doomed the act. No, Kennedy said, it is well established that legislatures may act in the face of conflicting medical opinion. This "medical uncertainty over whether the Act's prohibition creates significant health risks provides a sufficient basis to conclude in this facial attack that the Act does not impose an undue burden."[135]

Furthermore, he added, other factors also support the conclusion that the act does not create significant health risks to women and thus a facial challenge is inappropriate.[136] First, other procedures remain available, including the most commonly used method, the D&E; second, in a situation in which the D&X is "truly necessary," the doctor may inject the fetus and cause its death while still in the womb and then perform the procedure.[137] He concluded that the act is not facially invalid merely because there is disagreement over whether the banned procedure is ever needed to safeguard a woman's health, as long as other abortion methods exist.

Kennedy faulted the plaintiffs for challenging the law on its face, charging that they should have brought an "as-applied" challenge instead. He acknowledged that the Court had not settled the matter of whether to apply the *Salerno* "no set of circumstances" test in facial challenges, but, he added, the Court need not resolve that dispute here because the plaintiffs had not even satisfied the more lenient standard used in *Casey*.[138]

He ended by noting that the plaintiffs could bring a pre-enforcement "as-applied" challenge to the law with evidence that the prohibition on the D&X method imposes an undue burden on a specific woman suffering from a specified health condition.[139] In the event there is such evidence, he emphasized, the proper approach is an "as-applied" challenge rather than a facial challenge.[140] Thus, the high court repudiated the circuit courts' rulings in all respects, finding that the government has a legitimate interest in passing the law, that the law is not vague, and that its lack of a health exception does not render it invalid on its face.

In her dissent for herself, Breyer, Stevens, and Souter, Ginsburg expressed dismay at the decision, characterizing it as "alarming" for "refus[ing] to take *Casey* and *Stenberg* [*Carhart I*] seriously. It tolerates, indeed applauds, federal intervention to ban nationwide a procedure found necessary and proper in certain cases" according to many medical professionals. Moreover, she continued, "it blurs the line, firmly drawn in *Casey,* between previability and postviability abortions. And, for the first time since *Roe,* the Court blesses a prohibition with no exception safeguarding a woman's health."[141]

Ginsburg passionately reminded the majority that its ruling was allowing moral and ethical objections to abortion to take precedence over women's long-established fundamental rights. She quoted Kennedy's own words in *Casey* and *Lawrence v. Texas,* in which the Court declared the Texas same-sex sodomy law unconstitutional: "Our obligation is to define the liberty of all, not to mandate our own moral code."[142]

Citing the Court's solicitude for preserving women's health manifested in its rulings in *Thornburgh, Casey,* and *Ayotte* (among others), she took great exception to the majority's cavalier dismissal of women's health concerns. She charged the majority with wrongly applying the *Casey* "large fraction" test. According to *Casey,* she said, plaintiffs must show that an abortion regulation imposes an undue burden on "a large fraction" of relevant women. The relevant group in this case, she insisted, is women requiring a D&X procedure because their doctors judge it to be the safest method for them and whose health would be at risk otherwise; it is not all women seeking abortions who comprise the relevant group.

> It makes no sense to conclude that this facial challenge fails because respondents [plaintiffs] have not shown that a health exception is necessary for a large fraction of second-trimester abortions, including those for which a health exception is unnecessary: The very purpose of a health exception is to protect women in exceptional cases.[143]

Moreover, she stressed, *Carhart I* had clearly indicated "that as long as 'substantial medical authority supports the proposition that banning a particular abortion procedure could endanger women's health,' a health exception is required."[144] Ginsburg criticized the Court for disregarding its commitment to the rule of law and stare decisis and allowing Congress to simply override its constitutional jurisprudence by passing a law patently designed to erode abortion rights.

Abortion Regulations After *Carhart II*

Carhart II also set the stage for state and local governments as well as the federal government to devise new abortion regulations, secure in the knowledge that the courts will likely sanction their efforts.[145] Anti-abortion activists, encouraged by the federal Partial-Birth Abortion Ban Act, increased their efforts to limit women's access to abortion, in part by imposing new requirements on abortion providers. The Center for Reproductive Rights concluded that in 2010, state legislatures "considered and enacted some of the most extreme restrictions on abortion in recent memory, as well as passing laws creating dozens of other significant new hurdles."[146] Such laws had a twofold purpose. The immediate goal was to reduce the number of abortions through restrictive regulations. As one abortion opponent stated, "Those opposed to abortion are finding new and different ways to increase the roadblocks and the hoops [that] providers and patients have to jump through." The other tactic was to continue the long-term goal of passing laws directly contradictory to *Roe,* hoping that a challenge would eventually reach the Supreme Court.[147] Known as trigger laws, myriad abortion regulations arose in over twenty states.[148]

The Democratic governor of Louisiana, Kathleen Blanco, signed a law that would ban all abortions except when the woman's life was in danger or when childbirth would permanently harm her. Doctors who violated the Louisiana law could receive fines of up to $100,000 and face ten years in jail. Such laws are largely symbolic because they directly contradict *Roe* and could only go into effect if *Roe* were overturned.[149]

One of the most extreme measures was South Dakota's Women's Health and Human Life Protection Act (HB 1215), a law that would have banned almost all abortions in the state. South Dakota governor Mike Rounds, calling it a "full frontal attack on *Roe,*" signed it into law on March 6, 2006.[150] As written, the law would have banned abortion in all circumstances, including a pregnancy that resulted from rape or incest or one that threatened the woman's health; the only exception was "to prevent the death of a pregnant mother," and, in such cases, doctors were required to attempt to save the life of the fetus as well. Physicians who violated the law would be guilty of a felony and could be imprisoned for up to five years and have to pay a $5,000 fine.[151]

Ironically, even before Rounds signed the bill, it was extremely difficult to obtain an abortion in South Dakota; only about 800 were performed each year. There was only one clinic in the state, staffed by a rotating group of four Minnesota doctors who each flew in once a week.[152]

Instead of filing a lawsuit to challenge the law, opponents of the measure collected the requisite number of signatures to submit it to the voters on the ballot in the 2006 election; it was rejected by a 56 to 44 percent vote. Two years later, in a 55 to 45 percent vote, the citizens of South Dakota again rejected an abortion regulation, this one containing exceptions for rape and incest or when the mother's life or health was at risk. Abortion restrictions on the ballot in 2008 in Colorado and

California also failed. One of the most extreme, the Colorado proposal, would have included fertilized eggs (prior to implantation in the womb, which the AMA regards as the starting point of pregnancy) within the meaning of the word "person" in the state constitution. It lost in a vote of 73 to 27 percent.[153]

Although the anti-abortion activists had failed to persuade the Supreme Court to overturn *Roe,* the steady stream of anti-abortion regulations demonstrated their success at the state level. In 2008 alone, state legislatures deliberated on 400 abortion regulations.[154] The pace quickly accelerated: from January to March 2010, 825 measures were introduced in state legislatures that had convened at the start of the year.[155]

Increasingly, abortion opponents focused on the "informed consent" doctrine. Patients must always be given sufficient information to allow them to give valid consent before undergoing a medical procedure, but these laws seemed designed to make a woman waver in her decision to proceed with the abortion.[156] South Dakota's version of an informed consent law requires the doctor to tell the woman, among other things, that the abortion will "terminate the life of a whole, separate, unique, living human being."[157] In 2006, Indiana legislators proposed a law that would have required women to be told that "life begins at conception."[158]

A number of states adopted laws requiring physicians to perform ultrasounds (sonograms) on women, ostensibly to ensure that their consent was truly informed; the laws varied on whether the physician had to describe the fetus and whether women were required to look at the images.[159] As of July 2010, twenty-three states had laws pertaining to ultrasound procedures on the books.[160]

The strictest in the nation, a proposed 2008 Oklahoma law, not only required the ultrasound monitor to be placed so that the woman could view it but also required the doctor to give the woman a detailed description of the fetus, regardless of her objections. Passed by the Republican-controlled state legislature over Democratic governor Brad Henry's veto, the ultrasound bill was put on hold by a county court judge in August 2009, and the Oklahoma Supreme Court eventually ruled against it, holding that it violated the state constitution's single subject rule, limiting laws to addressing one subject only.[161] In vetoing the law, Henry, who was not known for supporting abortion rights, called it "an unconstitutional attempt by the Oklahoma legislature to insert government into the private lives and decisions of its citizens." The government "should never mandate," he added, "that a citizen be forced to undergo any medical procedure against his or her will, especially when such a procedure could cause physical or mental trauma."[162] In April 2010, the Oklahoma legislature, again overriding Henry's veto, cured the violation by enacting the ultrasound bill as a separate law.

The federal government also sought to test the limits of judicial support for the principles of *Roe* and *Casey*. At the end of 2006, the Republican-controlled House of Representatives almost succeeded in passing the Unborn Child Pain Awareness Act, a national fetal pain law, and by 2008, five states (Arkansas, Georgia, Oklahoma, Louisiana, and Minnesota) had laws requiring physicians to inform women seeking abortions that the fetus may feel pain; at least five other states have variations of such laws. Nebraska went a step further by citing fetal pain as a reason for enacting a law that bans abortions after twenty weeks. Departing from the touchstone measure of viability, the legislature justified the law by claiming there was "substantial evidence that abortion methods used at or after twenty weeks would cause substantial pain to an unborn child."[163] The Nebraska Women's Health Protection Act (LB 1103) went into effect on October 15, 2010.

Taking his example from the law passed in his home state, Republican senator Mike Johanns of Nebraska revived an attempt to enact a national fetal pain law by introducing the Unborn Child Pain Awareness Act of 2010 (S. 14) into the 111th Congress. It would require physicians to tell women seeking abortions after twenty weeks that the fetus could feel pain, a highly contested proposition, and that the woman may ask the doctor to administer anesthesia directly to the fetus.[164]

On August 5, 2010, the U.S. Senate confirmed Obama's nomination of Elena Kagan to the Supreme Court to replace Stevens. Most presume Kagan supports abortion rights, yet like other nominees to the high court, she refrained from indicating her position on *Roe* except to acknowledge, as most others have done, that she recognizes it as settled law. In August 2009, Obama's first nominee, Sonia Sotomayor, had taken her seat on the bench. Her views on abortion are also largely unknown and little attention was paid to the issue during her confirmation hearings. Most assume that both justices are likely to be sympathetic to the goal of preserving women's access to abortion.

With the Supreme Court's support for abortion rights uncertain, and Republicans controlling numerous state legislatures and governors' mansions around the nation following their sizable victory in the mid-term 2010 election, anti-abortion groups eagerly looked forward to a new wave of state abortion regulations such as those enacted in Oklahoma and Nebraska. Likely expressing the views of many anti-abortion activists, the head of the anti-abortion group Operation Rescue was quoted as saying, "I feel like a little boy on Christmas morning—which package do you open up first?"[165]

Supporters of abortion rights feared that states' efforts to restrict access to abortion would intensify once these public officials, some of whom campaigned on the issue, assumed office. Their fears were realized when, buoyed by their victories in the November election, legislative majorities in numerous states approved measures intended to limit access to abortion by erecting barriers for women and their physicians to surmount. Most appear to be of questionable constitutionality, intended to force a confrontation in the U.S. Supreme Court about *Roe*'s continuing validity. Thus, at this time, the only certainty is that the Court will revisit the issue of women's abortion rights when it is asked to rule on one or more of these state laws.

Conclusion

Following *Webster,* state legislatures adopted new abortion regulations, and soon after, the Supreme Court agreed to decide the constitutionality of a Pennsylvania law. To the surprise of many, the Court's ruling was a compromise, upholding the bulk of the law while reaffirming the continuing validity of *Roe.*

The strategy that ultimately netted anti-abortion activists one of their most important victories was the focus on a specific abortion procedure, the D&X method. Each side geared up for battle when a Nebraska law reached the courts. A majority of the high court voted to strike it, in part, because it did not contain an exception to protect the woman's health. Six years later, the Court ruled on a challenge to a New Hampshire parental notification law that lacked a health exception, unanimously holding that the law was deficient in not including an explicit health exception but that the lower court went too far in striking the entire statute.

In 2007, a 5 to 4 majority of the high court upheld a federal ban on "partial-birth" abortions and also seemed to move closer to restricting the availability of facial challenges to anti-abortion laws. As a result of the victories of anti-abortion activists in the November 2010 election, state legislatures took center stage again by enacting new regulations that threatened women's continued access to safe and legal abortions. Many of these laws were designed to deliberately challenge the principles established in *Roe* and *Casey.*

Notes

1. *Congressional Quarterly Weekly,* May 19, 1990, p. 1575.

2. Janet Benshoof, "The Legacy of *Roe v. Wade,*" in Jay L. Garfield and Patricia Hennessey, eds., *Abortion* (Amherst: University of Massachusetts Press, 1984), p. 42.

3. *Hodgson v. Minnesota,* 853 F.2d 1452, 1465 (8th Cir. 1988).

4. *New York Times,* August 9, 1988.

5. 497 U.S. 417 (1990).

6. *Hodgson,* 497 U.S. at 437.

7. *Hodgson,* 497 U.S. at 457.

8. *Hodgson,* 497 U.S. at 461.

9. *Washington Post,* June 26, 1990.

10. 497 U.S. 502 (1990).

11. *Congressional Quarterly Weekly,* August 25, 1990, pp. 2713–2719.

12. 520 U.S. 292 (1997).

13. In 1999, the Court let stand a federal appeals court ruling that upheld a Virginia parental notice requirement. Although the lower courts have imposed some conditions on judicial bypass procedures (such as requiring expedited review by the court), laws mandating parental involvement in a minor woman's abortion decision are almost always upheld.

14. *CNN.com,* November 29, 2005.

15. Alan Guttmacher Institute, "State Policies in Brief: Parental Involvement in Minors' Abortions," New York: Alan Guttmacher Institute, July 2010, available at http://www.guttmacher.org/statecenter/spibs/spib_PIMA.pdf.

16. *Washington Post,* May 24, 2005.

17. Alan Guttmacher Institute, "Parental Involvement Laws Have Little, If Any, Impact on Abortion Rates," New York: Alan Guttmacher Institute, March 11, 2009, available at http://www.guttmacher.org/media/nr/2009/03/11/index.html.

18. *Congressional Quarterly Weekly,* January 1, 2007, p. 66; December 18, 2006, p. 3336.

19. 505 U.S. 833 (1992).

20. *New York Times,* October 25, 1989.

21. In 1979, in *Colautti v. Franklin,* 439 U.S. 379 (1979), the Supreme Court ruled on an earlier version of the law that had imposed criminal penalties on physicians who failed to preserve the life of a viable fetus or one they had "sufficient reason to believe" was viable by requiring them to use the abortion technique most likely to save the fetus unless another technique was necessary to preserve the woman's life or health. In a 6 to 3 decision, the Court had found the duty imposed on the physician unconstitutionally vague because it did not indicate when the doctor's duty to the fetus came into play and how the risks of the survival of the fetus and the survival of the woman should be balanced. Such a law, Blackmun said, intimidates physicians from performing abortions.

22. This information had to be presented by the doctor performing the abortion or the referring doctor. Other information, such as the availability of printed material on fetal development, the legal obligation of the father to support the child, and the opportunity for medical assistance from the state for childbirth, could be presented by a "qualified nonphysician."

23. The law also imposed new record-keeping and reporting requirements on physicians. See L. Anita Richardson, "Parsing *Roe v. Wade*: Will the Court Reaffirm the Right to Choose but Make It Easier for States to Regulate?" *American Bar*

Association Preview of United States Supreme Court Cases (May 15, 1992), for an analysis of the legal issues in *Casey.*

24. *Planned Parenthood of Southeastern Pennsylvania v. Casey,* 744 F. Supp. 1323 (E.D. Pa. 1990).

25. *Planned Parenthood of Southeastern Pennsylvania v. Casey,* 947 F.2d 682, 694 (3d Cir. 1991).

26. *Congressional Quarterly Weekly,* January 25, 1992, pp. 167–171.

27. Rehnquist, Scalia, White, and Kennedy had applied a less stringent test for abortion regulations in *Webster* but did not give it a formal name; O'Connor has used the "undue burden" standard since she formulated it in *City of Akron* in 1983.

28. *New York Times,* April 23, 1992.

29. *Casey,* 505 U.S. at 845–846.

30. The Court essentially collapsed *Roe*'s first two trimesters into the pre-viability stage.

31. *Casey,* 505 U.S. at 876.

32. *Casey,* 505 U.S. at 874.

33. *Casey,* 505 U.S. at 877.

34. *Casey,* 505 U.S. at 878.

35. *Casey,* 505 U.S. at 879.

36. *Casey,* 505 U.S. at 879, quoting *Roe,* 410 U.S. at 164–165.

37. *Casey,* 505 U.S. at 874.

38. *Casey,* 505 U.S. at 895.

39. *Casey,* 505 U.S. at 894. See Jill Hamers, "Reeling in the Outlier: *Gonzales v. Carhart* and the End of Facial Challenges to Abortion Statutes," *Boston University Law Review* 89 (2009): 1069–1101; Joshua C. Howard, "'No Set of Circumstances' v. 'Large Fraction of Cases': Debate Resolved—*Gonzales v. Carhart,* 127 S. Ct. 1610 (2007)," *Nebraska Law Review* 87 (2009): 759–792.

40. *Casey,* 505 U.S. at 922–923.

41. *Casey,* 505 U.S. at 944.

42. *New York Times,* June 30, 1992.

43. *New York Times,* June 30, 1992.

44. See John Henn and Maria Del Monaco, "Civil Rights and RICO: Stopping Operation Rescue," *Harvard Women's Law Journal* 13 (1990): 251–277, for a description of the tactics of those abortion protestors; see also Laurence Tribe, *Clash of Absolutes* (New York: Norton, 1992).

45. See Georgia M. Sullivan, "Protection of Constitutional Guarantees Under 42 U.S.C. Section 1985(3): Operation Rescue's 'Summer of Mercy,'" *Washington and Lee Law Review* 49 (1992): 237–262.

46. *New York Times,* August 8, 1991.

47. Clinics play an important role in the delivery of abortion services: they are cheaper, more easily accessible, and generally have more supportive staff than hospitals.

48. Operation Rescue emerged during the late 1980s as the predominant anti-abortion protest group; see *National Organization for Women v. Operation Rescue,* 726 F. Supp. 1483 (E.D. Va. 1989), for a discussion of the organization and its goals. The group is perhaps best known for its demonstrations in Atlanta during the 1988 Democratic National Convention. See Henn and Monaco, "Civil Rights and RICO."

49. 506 U.S. 263 (1993).

50. *New York Times,* June 7, 1994.

51. *Congressional Quarterly Weekly,* February 6, 1993, p. 271.

52. *New York Times,* May 27, 1994.

53. See *New York Times,* May 27, 1994; *Congressional Quarterly Weekly,* April 30, 1994, p. 1070; September 10, 1994, p. 56.

54. *New York Times,* June 7, 1994.

55. *New York Times,* January 18, 1998.

56. 510 U.S. 249 (1994).

57. A civil RICO suit requires a plaintiff to prove that "(1) the defendant (2) through the commission of two or more acts (3) constituting a pattern (4) of racketeering activity (5) directly or indirectly invest[ed] in, or maintain[ed] an interest in (6) an enterprise (7) the activities of which affect[ed] interstate or foreign commerce." Geri Yonover, "Fighting Fire with Fire: Civil RICO and Anti-Abortion Activists," *Women's Rights Law Reporter* 12 (1990): 156–157.

58. 968 F.2d 612 (7th Cir. 1992).

59. *National Organization for Women,* 510 U.S. at 262.

60. *National Organization for Women,* 510 U.S. at 263–264.

61. The prospect of collecting any damages from these largely judgment-proof defendants was very slim. *Chicago Tribune,* April 21, 1998. Abortion providers had won millions of dollars in judgments since the mid-1990s but were unable to collect their awards; similarly, the government was owed millions of dollars in contempt fines from individuals in anti-abortion groups who were skilled at ridding themselves of assets. *New York Times,* June 11, 1994.

62. 267 F.3d 687 (7th Cir. 2001).

63. 537 U.S. 393 (2003).

64. 547 U.S. 9 (2006).

65. 512 U.S. 753 (1994).

66. Judy Madsen and the other named parties in the cases claimed not to be members of Operation Rescue.

67. *Madsen,* 512 U.S. at 760.

68. *Operation Rescue v. Women's Health Center, Inc.,* 626 So.2d 664 (Fla. 1993).

69. *Cheffer v. McGregor,* 6 F.3d 705 (11th Cir. 1993).

70. The Florida Supreme Court opinion was the case on appeal before the Supreme Court.

71. See *Ward v. Rock Against Racism,* 491 U.S. 781 (1989); *Frisby v. Schultz,* 487 U.S. 474 (1988); *Perry Education Association v. Perry Local Educators' Association,* 460 U.S. 37 (1983), for discussions of the standards applied to content-neutral and content-based restrictions on speech.

72. 519 U.S. 357 (1997).

73. By 1997, such buffer zones applied to about one-third of the nation's 900 abortion clinics. *New York Times,* February 20, 1997.

74. *Pro-Choice Network of Western New York v. Schenck,* 67 F.3d 377 (2d Cir. 1995); the appellate court upheld the injunction in its entirety.

75. As in *Madsen,* the dissent consisted of Scalia, Thomas, and Kennedy; the eight-justice majority on the "floating buffer" issue included all but Breyer.

76. *Schenck,* 519 U.S. at 363.

77. 530 U.S. 703 (2000).

78. *Hill v. City of Lakewood,* 973 P.2d 1246 (Colo. 1999).

79. *Hill,* 530 U.S. at 715–716.

80. See *Carhart v. Stenberg,* 192 F.3d 1142 (8th Cir. 1999), for a discussion of the two procedures. Dilation and evacuation is the most common method used during the second trimester. The difference between the two is chiefly in the technique; in both types of procedures, the intent is to terminate the pregnancy, and both are performed in the second trimester. In the D&E, fetal demise takes place entirely

within the woman's body as a result of dismemberment of the fetus with sharp instruments; in the D&X, the fetus is partially delivered into the vagina, usually in a breech position, and the doctor collapses the skull so that it fits through the opening of the cervix. Doctors say the D&X is preferable in some cases because it does not involve invasion of the uterus with sharp implements, thus lessening the possibility of infection, excessive blood loss, and damage to the uterus, which could compromise the woman's health or fertility. Other abortion techniques, considered riskier to women by most medical personnel, involve causing fetal demise by injecting a substance into the womb before starting the abortion or inducing labor. *New York Times,* April 25, 2003. According to the Alan Guttmacher Institute, an estimated thirty-one providers performed 2,200 dilation and extraction abortions in 2000, and 0.17 percent of the 1.3 million abortions performed that year used this method. See Lawrence B. Finer and Stanley K. Henshaw, "Abortion Incidence and Services in the United States in 2000," *Perspectives on Sexual and Reproductive Health* 35 (2003): 6–16, available at http://www.guttmacher.org/pubs/psrh/full/3500603.pdf.

81. The term "partial-birth" has no medical meaning; it is largely a rhetorical device created by abortion rights opponents to conjure up images of infanticide.

82. The law uses terms that are not medically recognized. *New York Times,* March 28, 1996.

83. *Congressional Record,* 104th Cong., 1st sess., Vol. 141 (1995): H11461.

84. *Congressional Quarterly Weekly,* April 13, 1996, p. 1009.

85. *New York Times,* May 21, 1997.

86. *Congressional Quarterly Weekly,* October 18, 1997, p. 2563.

87. The Nebraska law ostensibly only applied to the D&X procedure.

88. *Carhart,* 192 F.3d at 1142.

89. The appellate court declined to rule on the vagueness argument because the law failed on undue burden grounds.

90. 195 F.3d 857 (7th Cir. 1999).

91. The Seventh Circuit conceded that if the law reached the D&E method of abortion, it would be an undue burden on the woman and therefore unconstitutional.

92. 530 U.S. 914 (2000).

93. *Carhart I,* 530 U.S. at 924–929. The Supreme Court largely relied on the findings of the lower court, also citing Carhart's testimony as well as medical textbooks.

94. *Carhart I,* 530 U.S. at 934.

95. *Carhart I,* 530 U.S. at 945–946.

96. *Carhart I,* 530 U.S. at 946–947.

97. *Carhart I,* 530 U.S. at 952. This view was first expressed by Posner in his dissent in *Hope Clinic* in 1999.

98. *Planned Parenthood of Northern New England v. Heed,* 296 F. Supp. 2d 59 (D.N.H. 2003).

99. 390 F.3d 53 (1st Cir. 2004).

100. 481 U.S. 739, 745 (1987).

101. *Heed,* 390 F.3d at 57, quoting *Casey,* 505 U.S. at 895. The operation of the *Salerno* test differs from the application of the overbreadth doctrine, which states that if a law could be applied unconstitutionally in any possible case, it is unconstitutional. The overbreadth doctrine is primarily used in First Amendment cases, but the Court has also used it in facial challenges to abortion laws, most notably, in *Casey.* C. Casey and Vered Jona, "Cleaning Up for Congress: Why Courts Should Reject the Presumption of Severability in the Face of Intentionally Unconstitutional Legislation," *George Washington Law Review* 76 (2008): 698–724.

The undue burden doctrine is consistent with the overbreadth doctrine; see Natasha Plumly, "The United States Supreme Court Could Have Been Stuck Between a Rock and a Hard Place: *Ayotte v. Planned Parenthood of Northern New England*," *Florida Coastal Law Review Special Supplement* 7 (2006): 72–80.

102. As the Court announced its decision on January 18, 2006, the Senate was preparing to hold hearings to consider O'Connor's replacement.

103. *Ayotte v. Planned Parenthood of Northern New England*, 546 U.S. 320, 323 (2006).

104. *Ayotte*, 546 U.S. at 327–328, quoting *Casey*, 505 U.S. at 879, and *Roe*, 410 U.S. at 164–165.

105. *Ayotte*, 546 U.S. at 328.

106. Caitlin E. Borgmann, in "Holding Legislatures Constitutionally Accountable Through Facial Challenges," *Hastings Constitutional Law Quarterly* 36 (2009): 563–610, argues that legislatures sometimes intentionally enact laws they know to be unconstitutional and, in such circumstances, the courts should invalidate the entire law to protect individual rights from legislative overreaching.

107. *Ayotte*, 546 U.S. at 330. O'Connor admitted that the Court had previously invalidated entire statutes in the same circumstances, as recently as *Carhart I*.

108. *Ayotte*, 546 U.S. at 330.

109. The bill was narrowly approved by the New Hampshire House in a 187 to 181 vote; the Senate vote was 12 to 11. During debate, the opposition argued that the Supreme Court's decision in *Carhart I* indicated the law must contain a health exception. Its supporters objected, contending that doctors would easily be able to claim medical emergencies to escape the penalties of the notification law in appropriate cases; *New York Times*, November 29, 2005.

The state argued that the statute's severability clause indicated that the legislature preferred a statute with a health exception to no statute at all. The other side disagreed. Some commentators view *Ayotte* as a complete rejection of *Casey* and a direction to lower courts to abandon the overbreadth doctrine in abortion cases and apply severance instead. See Sarah Danielle Kohrs, "What's *Ayotte* Left for *Casey*? The Newest Supreme Court Precedent in the Area of Abortion," *Georgetown Journal of Law and Public Policy* 5 (2007): 725–766.

110. The repeal of the statute (RSA 132:24–RSA 132:28) took effect in June 2007. In a later action, Planned Parenthood claimed it was entitled to attorneys' fees and court costs. In *Planned Parenthood of Northern New England v. Ayotte*, 571 F. Supp. 2d 265 (D.N.H. 2008), the district court agreed.

111. For the list of states, see Alan Guttmacher Institute, "State Policies in Brief: Bans on 'Partial-Birth' Abortions," New York: Alan Guttmacher Institute, October 2010, available at http://www.guttmacher.org/statecenter/spibs/spib_BPBA.pdf. The success rate in challenging these laws is mixed, with victories for abortion rights proponents in the lower courts frequently reversed on appeal. An Ohio district court ruling in *Planned Parenthood Cincinnati Region v. Taft*, 2004 U.S. Dist. LEXIS 19933 (D. Ohio), in favor of the plaintiffs was later reversed by the Sixth Circuit in *Planned Parenthood Cincinnati Region v. Taft*, 444 F.3d 502 (6th Cir. 2006). A Virginia federal district court judge found a similar Virginia law unconstitutional in *Richmond Medical Center for Women v. Hicks*, 301 F. Supp. 2d 499 (E.D. Va. 2004). The Virginia ruling was affirmed by a three-judge panel of the Fourth Circuit but later reversed by the circuit sitting en banc in *Richmond Medical Center for Women v. Herring*, 570 F.3d 165 (4th Cir. 2009). The Bush administration filed a brief in the Ohio case to urge the appeals court to uphold the law.

112. In another effort to appeal to anti-abortion groups, Congress enacted the Born-Alive Infants Protection Act (Public Law No. 107-207). The law, signed by Bush in August 2002, was only tangentially related to abortion, declaring that infants born alive should be treated as persons under federal law.

113. The American College of Obstetricians and Gynecologists, "The American College of Obstetricians and Gynecologists on the Subject of Partial-Birth Abortion Bans," July 8, 2002, available at http://www.acog.org.

114. *Congressional Quarterly Weekly,* March 15, 2003, p. 616; June 7, 2003, p. 1385.

115. *New York Times,* March 11, 2003; March 14, 2003; April 25, 2003; June 5, 2003.

116. *New York Times,* November 6, 2003.

117. The statute noted that Congress has the authority to rely on its own findings of fact and is not bound by the findings of the district court as the Supreme Court was in *Carhart I.*

118. *New York Times,* February 13, 2004.

119. 320 F. Supp. 2d 957 (N.D. Cal. 2004).

120. 330 F. Supp. 2d 436 (S.D.N.Y. 2004).

121. 331 F. Supp. 2d 805 (D. Neb. 2004).

122. 435 F.3d 1163 (9th Cir. 2006). Alberto Gonzales's name was substituted for John Ashcroft's as the defendant in the case when Gonzales replaced Ashcroft as the U.S. attorney general.

123. 437 F.3d 278 (2d Cir. 2006).

124. 413 F.3d 791 (8th Cir. 2005).

125. The Court first granted certiorari in *Gonzales v. Carhart,* the Eighth Circuit case, and four months later in *Gonzales v. Planned Parenthood,* the Ninth Circuit decision. Although Planned Parenthood sought to have the two cases consolidated, the Court refused and heard arguments in the two cases separately; see *Washington Post,* June 20, 2006.

126. *Carhart I,* 530 U.S. at 979.

127. 550 U.S. 124 (2007).

128. *Carhart II,* 550 U.S. at 141.

129. *Carhart II,* 550 U.S. at 146.

130. Ironically, Kennedy did not accept this interpretation of the Nebraska law when he voted to uphold it when it was before the Court in 2000.

131. *Carhart II,* 550 U.S. at 158.

132. *Carhart II,* 550 U.S. at 158.

133. Abortion rights supporters were angered at what they considered Kennedy's paternalistic and condescending tone. They also charged that his use of the phrase, "abortion doctors," was demeaning and indicated his attitude toward abortion in general, which, they say, had apparently undergone some alteration since *Casey;* see the *Nation,* May 14, 2007; *Washington Post,* May 13, 2007.

134. *Carhart II,* 550 U.S. at 159–160.

135. *Carhart II,* 550 U.S. at 164.

136. Since 1987, the Court has required that a successful facial challenge must show that "no set of circumstances exists under which the Act would be valid" (*Carhart II,* 550 U.S. at 167, quoting *Salerno,* 481 U.S. at 745). In *Casey,* the Court instead applied the "large fraction" test: a statute is unconstitutional if "it would impose an undue burden [that is, place a substantial obstacle in the path of women seeking abortion] in a large fraction of the cases in which [it] is relevant" (*Carhart II,* 550 U.S. at 167, quoting *Casey,* 505 U.S. at 895). In *Carhart II,* the Court chose

not to decide which standard was the appropriate one, finding that the challengers had met neither one. See Howard, "No Set of Circumstances"; Hamers, "Reeling in the Outlier."

137. Acknowledging that the Court ordinarily defers to the legislature, Kennedy noted that it need not "place dispositive weight on Congress' findings," adding that Congress erred in declaring that there is a consensus that the D&X procedure is "never medically necessary." *Carhart II,* 550 U.S. at 165.

138. The Court assessed the relevant group differently in determining the constitutionality of the spousal notice provision in *Casey.*

139. The Roberts Court has made clear its opposition to facial challenges and its preference for "as-applied" challenges but has not decided on the proper standard to use in either case. Gillian E. Metzger, "Facial and As-applied Challenges Under the Roberts Court," *Fordham Urban Law Journal* 36 (2009): 773–801; see Borgmann, "Holding Legislatures Constitutionally Accountable."

140. An "as-applied" challenge pertains to the effect of the law in a particular situation. Kennedy seems to minimize the difficulty that a doctor would have in raising an "as-applied" challenge when a D&X abortion would be safest for a patient with a grave medical condition. During oral arguments, he asked Solicitor General Paul Clement, who argued the case for the government, how a pregnant woman whose physician informed her that the best procedure for her would be a D&X procedure, could bring an "as-applied" challenge if the abortion needed to be done quickly. Clement replied that doctors could file a pre-enforcement as-applied challenge and try to prove that the procedure is safest for pregnant women with a specified medical condition. If the court agreed, it could enjoin the ban for women with those conditions and have it apply to all others—all before the law takes effect. Apparently Kennedy was satisfied with this response; see Hamers, "Reeling in the Outlier."

141. *Carhart II,* 550 U.S. at 164.

142. *Carhart II,* 550 U.S. at 182, quoting *Casey,* 505 U.S. at 850, and *Lawrence v. Texas,* 539 U.S. 558, at 571 (2003). Kennedy composed this line in *Casey,* according to Linda Greenhouse, *New York Times,* April 20, 2007.

143. *Carhart II,* 550 U.S. at 188–189.

144. *Carhart II,* 550 U.S. at 174, quoting *Carhart I,* 530 U.S. at 938.

145. See Christopher Mirakian, "*Gonzales v. Carhart:* A New Paradigm for Abortion Legislation," *University of Missouri Kansas City Law Review* 77 (2008): 197–225.

146. *Washington Post,* December 28, 2010.

147. *Washington Post,* August 29, 2005.

148. Most of these states simply retained their pre-*Roe* abortion regulations, relying on them to restrict abortions as they had before *Roe* went into effect. Alan Guttmacher Institute, "State Policies in Brief: Abortion Policy in the Absence of *Roe,*" New York: Alan Guttmacher Institute, July 2010, available at http://www .guttmacher.org/statecenter/spibs/spib_APAR.pdf.

149. *New York Times,* June 7, 2006.

150. Rounds said he doubted the wisdom of an all-out attack on *Roe.* He believed it might be more prudent to regulate abortion through restrictive laws instead. See *New York Times,* February 22, 2006; November 1, 2006.

151. South Dakota was not alone; more than a dozen other states enacted similar legislation. See Janessa L. Bernstein, "The Underground Railroad to Reproductive Freedom: Restrictive Abortion Laws and the Resulting Backlash," *Brooklyn Law Review* 73 (2008): 1463–1508.

152. *Washington Post,* February 23, 2006.

153. *CNN.com,* November 7, 2008.

154. *Washington Post,* June 8, 2009.

155. Alan Guttmacher Institute, "News in Context," New York: Alan Guttmacher Institute, April 13, 2010, available at http://www.guttmacher.org/media/inthenews /2010/04/13/index.html.

156. See Robert M. Godzeno, "The Role of Ultrasound Imaging in Informed Consent Legislation Post–*Gonzales v. Carhart,*" *Quinnipiac Law Review* 27 (2009): 285–325, for an analysis of informed consent laws and the likely impact of *Carhart II* on the constitutionality of such laws.

157. After several rounds in the courts, the injunction was lifted by a South Dakota federal court in *Planned Parenthood Minnesota, North Dakota, South Dakota v. Rounds,* 650 F. Supp. 2d 972 (D.S.D. 2009).

158. *CNN.com,* February 11, 2006.

159. Carol Sanger, "Seeing and Believing: Mandatory Ultrasound and the Path to a Protected Choice," *UCLA Law Review* 56 (2008): 351–408. Although states began passing such laws in the 1980s, the pace picked up in the 1990s and continued into the new century. *Washington Post,* August 19, 2009. In 2007, Congress considered passage of the Ultrasound Informed Consent Act.

160. Alan Guttmacher Institute, "State Policies in Brief: Requirements for Ultrasound," New York: Alan Guttmacher Institute, July 2010, available at http://www.guttmacher.org/statecenter/spibs/spib_RFU.pdf.

161. The law contained no exceptions for women who became pregnant as a result of rape or incest. Absent a medical emergency, it required the ultrasound to be performed at least one hour before the abortion, with a "simultaneous explanation" of the image displayed on the screen, including "the dimensions of the embryo or fetus, the presence of cardiac activity if present and viewable, and the presence of external members and internal organs, if present and viewable." Additionally, the screen had to be positioned so that the woman could view it, but she was permitted to avert her eyes if she chose. The woman had to certify in writing that these requirements were met, and the doctor had to retain the record for seven years. A physician who failed to comply with the law was subject to civil suit and criminal penalties and liable to have his or her license suspended or revoked. When it was too early in the pregnancy to obtain the ultrasound in the traditional way by passing a transducer (a wand) over the woman's abdomen, the law ordered the doctor to obtain the ultrasound image vaginally, a painful and invasive process; see Sanger, "Seeing and Believing."

162. *CNN.com,* April 27, 2010.

163. See Harper Jean Tobin, "Confronting Misinformation on Abortion: Informed Consent, Deference, and Fetal Pain Laws," *Columbia Journal of Gender and Law* 17 (2008): 111–152, who reviews the medical literature and questions the accuracy of such assertions. See also S. J. Lee, H. J. Ralston, E. A. Drey, J. C. Partridge, and M. A. Rosen, "Fetal Pain: A Systematic Multidisciplinary Review of the Evidence," *Journal of the American Medical Association* 294 (2005): 947–954; *Washington Post,* October 15, 2010.

164. Johanns introduced the bill on September 29, 2010. *Congressional Record,* 111th Cong., 2d sess., Vol. 156 (2010): S7791. Representative Christopher Smith, Republican from New Jersey, introduced H.R. 5276, a bill with the same title, on May 11, 2010; *Congressional Record,* 111th Cong., 2d sess., Vol. 156 (2010): H3309. See *Washington Post,* October 15, 2010.

165. *New York Times,* November 8, 2010.

8 Is Equality Still Elusive?

The primary purpose of this book has been to explore the role of law in expanding gender equality in the United States. Considering the results from the vantage point of early 2011, there is cause for optimism in the signs that U.S. society is moving toward a higher level of gender equality. At the same time, a number of alarming trends suggest reasons for pessimism. To briefly summarize the findings, as expected, there were encouraging indicators that women are becoming better educated, earning higher wages, and making progress in taking their rightful places alongside men in fields such as medicine, law, higher education, and the military and corporate worlds. However, a great deal more needs to be done. First, despite the fact that the number of working women with children has grown steadily since the 1960s, policies to alleviate the burden of combining pregnancy with work are rather ineffectual and, at best, reach only a minority of the families needing them. Equally troubling is the fact that the wage gap between men and women persists after more than fifty years of legislation and litigation to combat it. And, in the area of reproductive rights, there are disturbing indications of concerted efforts to enact policies designed to restrict women's opportunities to control their reproductive autonomy.

The Courts and Social Change

In the latter part of the twentieth century, in part reacting to pressure from the women's movement, Congress enacted several key pieces of legislation: the Equal Pay Act of 1963, the 1964 Civil Rights Act, Title IX of the 1972 Education Amendments, the Pregnancy Discrimination Act, the 1991 Civil Rights Act, and the Family and Medical Leave Act. Although each of these laws made important contributions to eradicating discrimination on the basis of sex, they also demonstrated that legis-

279

lation often only marks the first step in progress toward equal rights because in many cases, legislative victories require judicial implementation for effective enforcement.

The feminist movement, following in the path of earlier social movement activists, turned to the courts, predominantly the federal courts, to secure their rights, relying on litigation in their fight to expand sexual equality. Consequently, women's rights litigation served as a focal point in the debate over the status of women in society, and the victories were barometers of feminists' success in furthering social reform.

It is not surprising that women turned to the courts. Because most reform movements in the United States are infused with concepts of legal equality, the courts frequently serve as the arena for the debate over social change. Women's rights litigants mounted legal challenges against state and federal laws based on traditional and stereotypical notions of men and women's roles. They used litigation for two ends: to cement legislative or administrative gains in antidiscrimination policy and to challenge restrictive laws and policies at the state and federal levels, primarily grounding their claims in equal protection and the right to privacy. Women's demands for equal treatment under the law were frequently met, as the courts struck laws based on stereotypical generalizations about women and men's roles. In ruling such laws unconstitutional, the courts recognized that society had become more complex and that women were assuming new roles as citizens and wage earners.

Despite the gains in constitutional equality doctrines and case law, as this study demonstrates, the courts remain unwilling to strike laws related to biological sex differences, allowing societal norms governing such laws to survive. Thus, when their review should be most rigorous, the courts relax their inquiry, refusing to probe the cultural biases behind such laws and merely requiring that there be a reasonable basis for the legislation, not an important or compelling one. In doing so, the courts help ensure that physical sex differences will continue to play a role in structuring the nation's laws and further enshrine stereotypical beliefs about men's and women's roles.

The attempt to secure equal rights, once again appearing in the guise of the renewed efforts to ratify the federal Equal Rights Amendment, might alleviate this concern, but it has been unable to gain the momentum needed to ensure its passage. The attempt failed in part because many believe the ERA is unneeded—except perhaps for symbolic reasons—and in part because it is mirrored in a good number of state constitutional provisions or judicial interpretations. Ironically, its opponents have resurfaced, exchanging their old arguments that an ERA would eliminate

women's favorable treatment under the law—for such claims do not res-
onate anymore (not the least because the so-called favorable treatment no
longer exists, if it ever did)—for new warnings that the ERA would prevent states from denying the right to same-sex marriage.

Women's demands for educational equity have led to more egalitarianism in the nation's schools, yet in a number of ways, girls are still treated
differently—and usually less favorably—than boys. Despite Title IX and
judicial rulings against sex-based educational policies, school customs and
policies are often still structured by sex. Single-sex schools, once argued
by some as a panacea to fight inequality, are no longer considered desirable
by most—for reasons both legal and financial.

An ongoing controversy in high school districts and colleges around
the country revolves around claims of inequitable athletic opportunity.
Title IX has greatly enhanced women's opportunities on the athletic field,
but, more than thirty years later, it has not achieved its stated goal of banning discrimination in schools. Although the number of women in sports
activities has seen tremendous growth since Title IX was enacted, many
problems remain. Indeed, there are alarming indications that the developing trend toward equity has been halted, and just as disheartening, most
victories for women's sports activities are seen as defeats for men's
activities and are portrayed as coming at the expense of men's teams.

Title IX has also played an important role in combating a growing
problem for schoolchildren that often has deleterious effects on their
ability to learn. In a number of key decisions, the courts allowed victims
of sexual harassment to hold schools accountable for instances of sexual
harassment, whether committed by school officials or children sitting in
the next seat in class or on the bus. Yet in setting a high standard of
"deliberate indifference" for determining the school's liability, the
courts made it more difficult for plaintiffs to prevail.

The number of women in the labor force has grown exponentially
over the past decades, and the courts became an integral part of the
movement toward equality at work. Women's rights litigants were largely
successful in removing so-called protective legislation barring women
from employment without regard to their talents and skills, minimizing
the use of the BFOQ defense, eliminating sex-segregated advertising,
ruling out sex-plus hiring policies, and precluding employers from relying on irrelevant height and weight requirements.

However, as the high court became increasingly conservative over
time, the justices were less willing to restrict employers' use of "mixed-
motive" employment decisions and interpreted Title VII to hinder most
litigants in disparate impact suits. Women's rights advocates suffered

another major defeat when the Court interpreted Title VII to bar most employees from filing suit for wage discrimination. Reaching the limits of litigation, feminists turned to the legislative branch and succeeded in persuading Congress to reverse these decisions.

While the earnings gap between men and women has narrowed over time, the pace has been very slow, with full-time women workers earning only about 80 cents for every dollar men earn. Even more disturbing is that the gap between men and women's pay is wider among the more educated, higher-earning wage groups. Thus, despite its usefulness in curtailing employment discrimination on the basis of sex, the limits of litigation are made clear when the courts refuse to interpret employment discrimination laws to remedy the underlying problem of a sex-segregated workforce and resulting wage differences. In these cases, the courts uniformly indicated their unwillingness to interfere with so-called neutral market forces, accepting employers' arguments that they are not required to redress pay inequity they did not cause.

Women have made most progress through litigation in their efforts to hold employers accountable for sexual harassment in the workplace, once the courts finally acknowledged that it was a form of sex discrimination. Since the early 1990s, the courts have expanded the protection offered to victims of sexual harassment in several ways, primarily by clarifying and expanding employer liability when employees are harassed, including limiting affirmative defenses in situations when supervisors' actions result in tangible job consequences or, more recently, when employers are responsible for constructive discharge. Notwithstanding these impressive litigation successes, the EEOC receives thousands of sexual harassment complaints a year, and most agree that there are many more unreported instances of sexual harassment in the workplace.

Another issue that feminists confront is the increasing number of employed women with children and the conflicting demands of family and work. In the beginning, women's rights advocates challenged laws that treated pregnant women less favorably than other workers, laws that denied them benefits solely on the basis of their pregnancy. After Congress stepped in to reaffirm that discrimination on the basis of pregnancy constituted discrimination on the basis of sex, pregnant woman could no longer be treated as an anomaly of the workplace, banished for the duration of their pregnancy and denied benefits granted to other workers.

The passage of the Pregnancy Discrimination Act, at first considered a victory for women's rights advocates, led to controversy over whether its nondiscrimination principle precluded policies that enhanced women's opportunities to combine pregnancy and work. Feminists recognized that the workplace must be restructured to allow men and women to share responsibilities for work and family but disagreed among themselves about the extent to which employers should make special provisions for pregnant women. The courts were largely neutral on the subject, interpreting the act to allow states that wished to establish policies, such as job protection and time off to accommodate the needs of pregnancy in the workplace, to do so.

Passage of the gender-neutral Family and Medical Leave Act in 1993 appeared to put an end to the controversy over preferential treatment of pregnant women, but a closer look at the law and its implementation, especially with restrictive regulations put in place at the end of the second Bush administration, indicate that it does not serve the women who need it most. Moreover, the law itself reflects a class bias in that only women who can afford to take time off from work without pay are able to take advantage of it.

Women with children are firmly attached to the labor force. But while those with greater resources have an easier time juggling the often conflicting demands placed on them, the vast majority of women—no matter what their income bracket—must struggle to balance work with family, especially during their pregnancy. It is true that an increasing number of men now confront many of the same issues as women, but society still expects women to be the "first responders" in the home, to shoulder most of the responsibility there. Until it learns to accommodate the needs of working women, the promise of equal opportunity in the workplace will be a hollow one.

Finally, although a number of states relaxed their restrictions on women's access to abortion during the late 1960s, progress was slow and uneven. In the early 1970s, women's rights advocates adopted a litigation strategy in the federal courts, arguing that women's right to choose to terminate their pregnancy falls within the parameters of their constitutional right to privacy, forcing states to articulate a compelling reason to impose restrictions. Amid rumblings that abortion reform should have been left to the states—despite evidence that many had no interest in increasing access to abortion—the litigation strategy proved highly successful. Beginning in 1973, the courts took a leading role in advancing abortion rights. Not all benefited from the rulings because states were permitted to maintain restrictions on teens and low-income women, but most women achieved the ability to exercise control over their reproductive decisions, at least largely free from the state's control.

With the increasingly conservative viewpoints of Supreme Court appointees during the 1980s and early 1990s, the high court began to accept more regulations on women's access to abortion, including restrictive parental notification and consent statutes. Moreover, the rulings against abortion rights prompted states, as well as the federal government, to continue to impose more limitations, hoping to eventually entice the high court to reverse *Roe v. Wade*.

By the early 1990s, it appeared that the Court had put an end to the continual legal skirmishes over abortion rights, but the battle merely took a new form. Opponents successfully exploited anti-abortion rhetoric and succeeded in passing laws aimed at outlawing certain abortion procedures. Failing to convince the courts at first, they took advantage of an anti-abortion president and majority in Congress to enact federal legislation intended to achieve the same result. The high court proved it could no longer be considered an ally of abortion rights advocates when it upheld the federal partial-birth abortion ban and, of even greater concern, seemed to impose restrictions on raising challenges to abortion regulations. Heartened by their victory in the high court and in the state and federal legislative races in the 2010 election, abortion opponents broadly proclaimed their intentions to regulate abortion out of existence to the extent they can. Far from resolved, the battle over abortion rights continues, with supporters seeking new allies in the fight to preserve women's reproductive freedom. And even though, for the most part, women still retain the right to choose, the signs are not favorable and, to quote Justice Blackmun, "a chill wind blows."

Elusive Equality

The women's movement has played a critical role in propelling U.S. society toward greater gender equality, and litigation has been crucial in achieving that end. However, as this study has demonstrated, significant work needs to be done to further advance the movement's goals, and feminists cannot be complacent about their successes. Although society has become more egalitarian, gender still plays an important role in structuring our public and private lives, and it is clear that despite the progress that has been made, gender equality remains elusive.

Bibliography

Aaron, Henry, and Cameran M. Lougy. *The Comparable Worth Controversy.* Washington, D.C.: Brookings Institution, 1986.

Alan Guttmacher Institute. *Abortions and the Poor: Private Morality, Public Responsibility.* New York: Alan Guttmacher Institute, 1979.

———. "News in Context." New York: Alan Guttmacher Institute, April 13, 2010, available at http://www.guttmacher.org/media/inthenews/2010/04/13/index.html.

———. "Parental Involvement Laws Have Little, If Any, Impact on Abortion Rates." New York: Alan Guttmacher Institute, March 11, 2009, available at http://www.guttmacher.org/media/nr/2009/03/11/index.html.

———. "State Policies in Brief: Abortion Policy in the Absence of *Roe.*" New York: Alan Guttmacher Institute, July 2010, available at http://www.guttmacher.org/statecenter/spibs/spib_APAR.pdf.

———. "State Policies in Brief: Bans on 'Partial-Birth' Abortions." New York: Alan Guttmacher Institute, October 2010, available at http://www.guttmacher.org/statecenter/spibs/spib_BPBA.pdf.

———. "State Policies in Brief: Parental Involvement in Minors' Abortions." New York: Alan Guttmacher Institute, July 2010, available at http://www.guttmacher.org/statecenter/spibs/spib_PIMA.pdf.

———. "State Policies in Brief: Requirements for Ultrasound." New York: Alan Guttmacher Institute, July 2010, available at http://www.guttmacher.org/statecenter/spibs/spib_RFU.pdf.

Aldridge, Joseph M. "Pay-Setting Decisions as Discrete Acts: The Court Sharpens Its Focus on Intent in Title VII Actions in *Ledbetter v. Goodyear Tire and Rubber Co.,* 127 S. Ct. 2162 (2007)." *Nebraska Law Review* 86 (2008): 955–986.

Allessandra, Anita. "When Doctrines Collide: Disparate Treatment, Disparate Impact, and *Watson v. Fort Worth Bank and Trust.*" *University of Pennsylvania Law Review* 137 (1989): 1755–1790.

American Association of University Women (AAUW). *Beyond the "Gender Wars": A Conversation About Girls, Boys, and Education.* Washington, D.C.: American Association of University Women Educational Foundation, 2001, available at http://www.aauw.org/research/upload/BeyondGenderWar.pdf.

———. *Gender Gaps: Where Schools Still Fail Our Children.* Executive Summary. Washington, D.C.: American Association of University Women Educational Foundation, 1998, available at http://www.aauw.org/research/upload/GGES.pdf.

————. *Hostile Hallways: The AAUW Survey on Sexual Harassment in America's Schools.* Washington, D.C.: AAUW Educational Foundation, 1993.

————. *Hostile Hallways: Bullying, Teasing, and Sexual Harassment in School.* Washington, D.C.: AAUW Educational Foundation, 2001.

————. *How Schools Shortchange Girls: A Study of Findings on Girls and Education.* Executive Summary. Washington, D.C.: American Association of University Women Educational, 1992, available at http://www.aauw.org/research/upload/hssg.pdf.

————. *Separated by Sex: A Critical Look at Single-Sex Education for Girls.* Washington, D.C.: American Association of University Women Educational Foundation, 1998, available at http://www.aauw.org/research/upload/SeparatedBySex.pdf.

————. *Where The Girls Are: The Facts about Gender Equity in Education.* Washington, D.C.: American Association of University Women Educational Foundation, 2008, available at http://www.aauw.org/research/upload/whereGirlsAre.pdf.

American College of Obstetricians and Gynecologists. "The American College of Obstetricians and Gynecologists on the Subject of Partial-Birth Abortion Bans." July 8, 2002, available at http:/www.acog.org.

American Federation of Labor–Congress of Industrial Organizations. "Working Women: Equal Pay—Facts About Working Women." 1998, available at http://www.afl-cio.org/women/wwfacts.htm.

American Postal Workers Union. "Bush's Lame-Duck Labor Department to Implement Onerous FMLA Rule Changes." November 17, 2008, available at http://www.Apwu.org/news/webart/2008/08108-fmla-081110.htm.

Anderson, Ann M. "Whose Malice Counts? *Kolstad* and the Limits of Vicarious Liability for Title VII Punitive Damages." *North Carolina Law Review* 78 (2000): 799–830.

Anderson, Paul, and Barbara Osborne. "A Historical Review of Title IX Litigation." *Journal of Legal Aspects of Sport* (2008): 127–164.

Anthony, Deborah J. "The Hidden Harms of the Family and Medical Leave Act: Gender-Neutral Versus Gender-Equal." *American University Journal of Gender, Social Policy, and the Law* 16 (2008): 459–501.

Arthurs, Rich. "State Legislatures See Flood of Comparable Worth Proposals." *Legal Times,* October 15, 1984.

Ashraf, Saba. "The Reasonableness of the 'Reasonable Woman' Standard: An Evaluation of Its Use in Hostile Environment Sexual Harassment Claims Under Title VII of the Civil Rights Act." *Hofstra Law Review* 21 (1992): 483–504.

Baldez, Lisa, Lee Epstein, and Andrew D. Martin. "Does the U.S. Constitution Need an Equal Rights Amendment?" *Journal of Legal Studies* 35 (2006): 243–281.

Baram-Blackwell, Inessa. "Separating Dick and Jane: Single-Sex Public Education Under the Washington State Equal Rights Amendment." *Washington Law Review* 81 (2006): 337–362.

Barnard, Thomas H., and Adrienne L. Rapp. "Pregnant Employees, Working Mothers, and the Workplace: Legislation, Social Change, and Where We Are Today." *Cleveland State Journal of Law and Health* 32 (2009): 197–239.

Barnes, Jeffrey A. "The Supreme Court's 'Exceedingly [Un]persuasive' Application of Intermediate Scrutiny in *United States v. Virginia.*" *University of Richmond Law Review* 31 (1997): 523–548.

Baron, Ava. "Feminist Legal Strategies: The Powers of Difference." In Beth B. Hess and Myra Marx Ferree, eds., *Analyzing Gender.* Beverly Hills: Sage Publications, 1987.

Bartlett, Katharine T. "Pregnancy and the Constitution: The Uniqueness Trap." *California Law Review* 62 (1974): 1532–1566.

Bayes, Jane. "Women, Labor Markets, and Comparable Worth." *Policy Studies Review* 5 (1986): 776–799.

Bayh, Birch. "Personal Insights and Experiences Regarding the Passage of Title IX." *Cleveland State Law Review* 55 (2007): 463–471.

Becker, Mary. "From *Muller v. Oregon* to Fetal Vulnerability Policies." *University of Chicago Law Review* 53 (1986): 1219–1268.

Bednarek, Lucy. "The Gender Wage Gap: Searching for Equality in a Global Economy." *Indiana Journal of Global Legal Studies* 6 (1998): 213–236.

Benshoof, Janet. "The Legacy of *Roe v. Wade.*" In Jay L. Garfield and Patricia Hennessey, eds., *Abortion.* Amherst: University of Massachusetts Press, 1984.

Bergmann, Barbara. *The Economic Emergence of Women.* New York: Basic Books, 1986.

Bernstein, Janessa L. "The Underground Railroad to Reproductive Freedom: Restrictive Abortion Laws and the Resulting Backlash." *Brooklyn Law Review* 73 (2008): 1463–1508.

Berry, Mary Frances. *Why ERA Failed: Politics, Women's Rights, and the Amending Process of the Constitution.* Bloomington: Indiana University Press, 1986.

Bird, Carolyn. *Born Female.* New York: Pocket Books, 1970.

Blau, Francine D., and Marianne A. Ferber. "Occupations and Earnings of Women Workers." In Karen Shallcross Koziara, Michael H. Moskow, and Lucretia Dewey Tanner, eds., *Working Women: Past, Present, Future.* Washington, D.C.: Bureau of National Affairs, 1987.

Blumrosen, Alfred. "The Legacy of *Griggs:* Social Progress and Subjective Judgments." *Chicago-Kent Law Review* 63 (1987): 1–41.

———. "Single-Sex Public Schools: The Last Bastion of 'Separate but Equal'?" *Duke Law Journal* (1977): 259–276.

———. "Strangers in Paradise: *Griggs v. Duke Power Co.* and the Concept of Employment Discrimination." *Michigan Law Review* 71 (1972): 59–110.

Blumrosen, Ruth. "Wage Discrimination, Job Segregation, and Title VII of the Civil Rights Act of 1964." *University of Michigan Journal of Law Reform* 12 (1979): 399–502.

Bohrer, Jeremy I. "You, Me, and the Consequences of Family: How Federal Employment Law Prevents the Shattering of the 'Glass Ceiling.'" *Washington University Journal of Urban and Contemporary Law* 50 (1996): 401–421.

Boles, Janet K. *The Politics of the Equal Rights Amendment: Conflict and the Decision Process.* New York: Longman, 1979.

Borgmann, Caitlin E. "Holding Legislatures Constitutionally Accountable Through Facial Challenges." *Hastings Constitutional Law Quarterly* 36 (2009): 563–610.

Bornstein, Lisa. "Inclusions and Exclusions in Work-Family Policy: The Public Values and Moral Code Embedded in the Family and Medical Leave Act." *Columbia Journal of Gender and Law* 10 (2000): 77–124.

Boushey, Heather. *The New Breadwinners.* Center for American Progress, October 16, 2009, available at http://www.americanprogress.org/issues/2009/10/pdf/awn/chapters/economy.pdf.

Bovee, Stephanie C. "The Family Medical Leave Act: State Sovereignty and the Narrowing of Fourteenth Amendment Protection." *William and Mary Journal of Women and Law* 7 (2001): 1011–1037.

Bowers, James R. *Pro-Choice and Anti-Abortion.* Westport, Conn.: Praeger Publishers, 1994.

Bowsher, David K. "Cracking the Code of *United States v. Virginia.*" *Duke Law Journal* 48 (1998): 305–339.

Bradshaw, Christine. "A Revised Tangible Employment Action Analysis: Just What Is an Undesirable Reassignment?" *American University Journal of Gender, Social Policy, and the Law* 14 (2006): 385–411.

Brauer, Carl M. "Women Activists, Southern Conservatives, and the Prohibition of Sex Discrimination in Title VII of the 1964 Civil Rights Act." *Journal of Southern History* 49 (1983): 37–56.

Brejcha, Barrie L. "*Grove City College v. Bell:* Restricting the Remedial Reach of Title IX." *Loyola University Law Journal* 16 (1985): 319–358.

Bridge, Diane L. "The Glass Ceiling and Sexual Stereotyping: Historical and Legal Perspectives of Women in the Workplace." *Virginia Journal of Social Policy and the Law* 4 (1997): 581–643.

Brown, Barbara, Thomas Emerson, Gail Falk, and Ann E. Freedman. "The Equal Rights Amendment: A Constitutional Basis for Equal Rights for Women." *Yale Law Journal* 80 (1971): 871–985.

Brown, Barbara, Ann Freedman, Harriet Katz, and Alice Price. *Women's Rights and the Law.* New York: Praeger Publishers, 1977.

Brown, Judith, Phyllis Tropper Baumann, and Elaine Millar Melnick. "Equal Pay for Jobs of Comparable Worth: An Analysis of the Rhetoric." *Harvard Civil Rights–Civil Liberties Law Review* 21 (1986): 127–170.

Butler, Elisa M. "Civil Rights—No Hitting Back: Schools Have to Play by the Title IX Rules: *Jackson v. Birmingham Board of Education,* 544 U.S. 167 (2005)." *Wyoming Law Review* 7 (2007): 577–603.

Cahn, Naomi R. "The Looseness of Legal Language: The Reasonable Woman Standard in Theory and Practice." *Cornell Law Review* 77 (1992): 1398–1446.

Campbell, Caitlyn M. "Overstepping One's Bounds: The Department of Labor and the Family and Medical Leave Act." *Boston University Law Review* 84 (2004): 1077–1102.

Cary, Eve, and Kathleen Willert Peratis, eds. *Woman and the Law.* Skokie: National Textbook Company, 1977.

Case, Mary Anne. "Discrimination and Inequality Emerging Issues 'The Very Stereotype the Law Condemns': Constitutional Sex Discrimination Law as a Quest for Perfect Proxies." *Cornell Law Review* 85 (2000): 1447–1491.

Casey, C., and Vered Jona. "Cleaning Up for Congress: Why Courts Should Reject the Presumption of Severability in the Face of Intentionally Unconstitutional Legislation." *George Washington Law Review* 76 (2008): 698–724.

Chamallas, Martha. "Mothers and Disparate Treatment: The Ghost of *Martin Marietta.*" *Villanova Law Review* 44 (1999): 337–354.

Chi, Keon. "Comparable Worth in State Government: Trends and Issues." *Policy Studies Review* 5 (1986): 800–814.

Cicoria, Eva A. "Pregnancy and Equality: A Precarious Alliance." *Southern California Law Review* 60 (1987): 1345–1374.

Clinton, Bill. "Executive Order 13160—Nondiscrimination on the Basis of Race, Sex, Color, National Origin, Disability, Religion, Age, Sexual Orientation, and

Status as a Parent in Federally Conducted Education and Training Programs." *Weekly Compilation of Presidential Documents,* June 27, 2000, available at http://frwebgate3.access.gpo.gov/cgi-bin/TEXTgate.cgi?WAISdocID= 17713014877+0+1+0&WAISaction=retrieve.

————. "Remarks on Signing a Memorandum Strengthening Enforcement of Title IX." *Weekly Compilation of Presidential Documents,* June 17, 1997, available at http://frwebgate1.access.gpo.gov/cgi-bin/TEXTgate.cgi?WAISdocID= 175497237357+0+1+0&WAISaction=retrieve.

Cockrell, Phillip Nollin. "Pregnancy Disability Benefits and Title VII: Pregnancy Does Not Involve Sex." *Baylor Law Review* 29 (1977): 257–281.

Cohen, Robert H. "Pay Equity: A Child of the 80s Grows Up." *Fordham Law Review* 63 (1995): 1461–1493.

Coleman, Harriet Hubacker. "Barefoot and Pregnant—Still: Equal Protection for Men and Women in Light of *Geduldig v. Aiello.*" *South Texas Law Journal* 16 (1975): 211–240.

Collins, Gail. *When Everything Changed: The Amazing Journey of American Women from 1960 to the Present.* New York: Little, Brown, 2009.

Collins, Kathy Lee. "Student-to-Student Sexual Harassment Under Title IX: The Legal and Practical Issues." *Drake Law Review* 46 (1998): 789–834.

Colopy, Katie J., Sandra K. Dielman, and Michelle A. Morgan. "Women and the Law: Gender Discrimination in the Workplace: 'We've Come a Long Way, Baby.'" *The Advocate* 49 (2009): 11–17.

Corbett, Christianne, Catherine Hill, and Andresse St. Rose. *Where the Girls Are: The Facts About Gender Equity in Education.* Executive Summary. Washington, D.C.: American Association of University Women Educational Foundation, 2008, available at http://www.aauw.org/research/upload/whereGirlsAre_exec Summary.pdf.

Corcoran, Mary, and Greg Duncan. "Work History, Labor Force Attachment, and Earnings Differences Between the Races and Sexes." *Journal of Human Resources* 14 (1979): 3–20.

Costain, Anne. "Eliminating Sex Discrimination in Education: Lobbying for Implementation of Title IX." In Marian Lief Palley and Michael Preston, eds., *Race, Sex, and Policy Problems.* Lexington: Lexington Books, 1979.

Danaher, Maria Greco. "Pension Service Credit That Excludes Pregnancy Leave Violates Title VII." *Lawyers Journal,* September 28, 2007.

Daniels, Cynthia. "Competing Gender Paradigms: Gender Difference, Fetal Rights, and the Case of *Johnson Controls.*" *Policy Studies Review* 10 (1991–1992): 51–68.

Daughtrey, Martha Craig. "Women and the Constitution: Where We Are at the End of the Century." *New York University Law Review* 75 (2000): 1–25.

Davidson, Roger. "Procedures and Politics in Congress." In Gilbert Y. Steiner, ed., *The Abortion Dispute and the American System.* Washington, D.C.: Brookings Institution, 1983.

Davis, Martha F. "The Equal Rights Amendment: Then and Now." *Columbia Journal of Gender and Law* 17 (2008): 419–459.

Dean, Virginia. "Pay Equity/Comparable Worth." In Carol Lefcourt, ed., *Women and the Law.* New York: Clark Boardman, 1987.

DeLano, Mary. "The Conflict Between State Guaranteed Pregnancy Benefits and the Pregnancy Discrimination Act: A Statutory Analysis." *Georgetown Law Journal* 74 (1986): 1743–1768.

Delchin, Steven A. "*United States v. Virginia* and Our Evolving 'Constitution': Playing Peek-a-boo with the Standard of Scrutiny for Sex-Based Classifications." *Case Western Reserve Law Review* 47 (1997): 1121–1155.

Dellinger, Walter, and Gene B. Sperling. "Abortion and the Supreme Court: The Retreat from *Roe v. Wade*." *University of Pennsylvania Law Review* 138 (1989): 83–118.

Denning, Brannon P., and John R. Vile. "Necromancing the Equal Rights Amendment." *Constitutional Commentary* 17 (2000): 593–602.

Denvir, John. *Democracy's Constitution: Claiming the Privileges of American Citizenship*. Urbana: University of Illinois Press, 2001.

De Pauw, Linda Grant. *Battle Cries and Lullabies: Women in War from Prehistory to the Present*. Norman: University of Oklahoma Press, 1998.

De Vos, Tanya A. "Sexuality and Transgender Issues in Employment Law." *Georgetown Journal of Gender and the Law* 10 (2009): 599–624.

Dickinson, Thomas. "Limiting Public Funds for Abortions: State Response to Congressional Action." *Suffolk University Law Review* 13 (1979): 923–959.

Dill, Terri L. "*St. Mary's Honors Center v. Hicks:* Refining the Burden of Proof in Employment Discrimination Litigation." *Arkansas Law Review* 48 (1995): 617–637.

Douglas, Elizabeth A. "*United States v. Virginia:* Gender Scrutiny Under an 'Exceedingly Persuasive Justification Standard.'" *Capital University Law Review* 26 (1997): 173–199.

Eason, Heather Larkin. "Gender Equality and Single-Sex Education: *United States v. Virginia,* 116 S.Ct. 2264 (1996)." *University of Arkansas at Little Rock Law Journal* 20 (1997): 191–211.

Eidman, Kathryn A. "*Ledbetter* in Congress: The Limits of a Narrow Legislative Override." *Yale Law Journal* 117 (2008): 971–979.

Eisenberg, Deborah Thompson. "Shattering the Equal Pay Act's Glass Ceiling." *Southern Methodist University Law Review* 63 (2010): 17–69.

Enloe, Cynthia. *Does Khaki Become You?* Boston: South End Press, 1983.

Epstein, Lee, Andrew D. Martin, Lisa Baldez, and Tasina Nitzschke Nihiser. "Constitutional Sex Discrimination." *Tennessee Journal of Law and Policy* 1 (2004): 11–68.

Evans, Sara, and Barbara Nelson. "Comparable Worth: The Paradox of Technocratic Reform." *Feminist Studies* 15 (1989): 171–190.

Evanson, Kymberly K. "Employment Law Chapter: Title VII of the Civil Rights Act of 1964." *Georgetown Journal of Gender and the Law* 7 (2006): 981–998.

Faux, Marian. *Roe v. Wade*. New York: Mentor Books, 1988.

Feldberg, Roslyn. "Comparable Worth: Toward Theory and Practice in the United States." *Signs* 10 (1984): 311–328.

Feldstein, Merrill D. "*Watson v. Fort Worth Bank and Trust:* Reallocating the Burdens of Proof in Employment Discrimination Litigation." *American University Law Review* 38 (1989): 919–951.

Fenner, Lorry M., and Marie E. DeYoung. *Women in Combat: Civic Duty or Military Liability?* Washington, D.C.: Georgetown University Press, 2001.

Fernandez, David. "*Thornburgh v. American College of Obstetricians:* Return to *Roe?*" *Harvard Journal of Law and Public Policy* 10 (1987): 711–727.

Ferrin, Leigh E. "Pencil Me In: The Use of Title IX and §1983 to Obtain Equal Treatment in High School Athletics Scheduling." *American University Modern American* 3 (2007): 15–22.

Finer, Lawrence B., and Stanley K. Henshaw. "Abortion Incidence and Services in the United States in 2000." *Perspectives on Sexual and Reproductive Health* 35 (2003): 6–16, available at http://www.guttmacher.org/pubs/psrh/full/3500603.pdf.

Finley, Lucinda M. "Transcending Equality Theory: A Way Out of the Maternity and the Workplace Debate." *Columbia Law Review* 86 (1986): 1118–1182.

Fishel, Andrew, and Janice Pottker. *National Politics and Sex Discrimination in Education.* Lexington: Lexington Books, 1977.

Fiss, Owen. "Groups and the Equal Protection Clause." *Philosophy and Public Affairs* 5 (1976): 107–177.

Frank, Abigail. "Education Law Chapter: Athletics and Title IX of the 1972 Education Amendments." *Georgetown Journal of Gender and the Law* 9 (2008): 769–794.

Freedman, Ann E. "Sex Equality, Sex Differences, and the Supreme Court." *Yale Law Journal* 92 (1983): 913–968.

Freeman, Jo. *A Room at a Time: How Women Entered Party Politics.* Lanham, Md.: Rowman and Littlefield, 2002.

———. "How 'Sex' Got into Title VII: Persistent Opportunism as a Maker of Public Policy." *Law and Inequality: A Journal of Theory and Practice* 9 (1991): 163–184.

Fulks, Ann E. "*Thornburgh:* The Last American Right-to-Abortion Case?" *Journal of Family Law* 26 (1987–1988): 771–792.

Gelb, Joyce, and Marian Lief Palley. *Women and Public Policies.* 2d ed. Princeton: Princeton University Press, 1987.

Ginsburg, Ruth Bader. "The Burger Court's Grapplings with Sex Discrimination." In Vincent Blasi, ed., *The Burger Court: The Counter-Revolution That Wasn't.* New Haven: Yale University Press, 1983.

Gladstone, Leslie W. *Equal Rights Amendments: State Provisions.* Washington, D.C.: Congressional Research Service, 2004.

Godzeno, Robert M. "The Role of Ultrasound Imaging in Informed Consent Legislation Post–*Gonzales v. Carhart.*" *Quinnipiac Law Review* 27 (2009): 285–325.

Goggin, Malcolm L. "Understanding the New Politics of Abortion." *American Politics Quarterly* 21 (1993): 4–30.

Goldvaser, Amalia. "Inflating Goodyear's Bottom Line: Paying Women Less and Getting Away with It." *Cardozo Journal of Law and Gender* 15 (2008): 99–116.

Goodman, Janice. "Comparable Worth: Time May Be Now." *New York Law Journal* (June 28, 1999).

Graber, Mark A. *Rethinking Abortion: Equal Choice, the Constitution, and Reproductive Politics.* Princeton: Princeton University Press, 1996.

Grady, Matthew. "Extortion May No Longer Mean Extortion After *Scheidler v. National Organization for Women, Inc.*" *North Dakota Law Review* 81 (2005): 33–73.

Green, Tristin K. "Insular Individualism: Employment Discrimination Law After *Ledbetter v. Goodyear.*" *Harvard Civil Rights–Civil Liberties Law Review* 43 (2008): 353–383.

Greenberg, Ezra S. "Stray Remarks and Mixed-Motive Cases After *Desert Palace v. Costa:* A Proximity Test for Determining Minimal Causation." *Cardozo Law Review* 29 (2008): 1795–1836.

Grossman, Joanna L. "Pregnancy, Work, and the Promise of Equal Citizenship." *Georgetown Law Journal* 98 (2010): 567–628.

Gunther, Gerald. "Foreword: In Search of Evolving Doctrine on a Changing Court: A Model for a Newer Equal Protection." *Harvard Law Review* 86 (1972): 1–48.

Hamers, Jill. "Reeling in the Outlier: *Gonzales v. Carhart* and the End of Facial Challenges to Abortion Statutes." *Boston University Law Review* 89 (2009): 1069–1101.

Hamlet, Pendelton Elizabeth. "Fetal Protection Policies: A Statutory Proposal in the Wake of *International Union, UAW v. Johnson Controls, Inc.*" *Cornell Law Review* 75 (1990): 1110–1150.

Harrison, Cynthia. *On Account of Sex: The Politics of Women's Issues, 1945–1968.* Berkeley: University of California Press, 1988.

Hart, Kaylin Redman. "Employment Law—Title VII and the Anti-Retaliation Provision—Beyond Employment and the Workplace: The United States Supreme Court Resolves the Split and Shifts the Balance. *Burlington Northern & Santa Fe Railroad Co. v. White,* 126 S. Ct. 2405 (2006)." *University of Arkansas at Little Rock Law Review* 29 (2007): 569–595.

Hart, LeiLani J. "*Pennsylvania State Police v. Suders:* 124 S. Ct. 2342 (2004)." *American University Journal of Gender, Social Policy, and the Law* 13 (2005): 219–233.

Hartmann, Heidi I., and Stephanie Aaronson. "Pay Equity and Women's Wage Increases in the States: A Model for the Nation." *Duke Journal of Gender Law and Policy* 1 (1994): 69–87.

Hawley, Ashley. "Taking a Step Forward or Backward? The 2009 Revisions to the FMLA Regulations." *Wisconsin Journal of Law, Gender, and Society* 25 (2010): 137–159.

Henn, John, and Maria Del Monaco. "Civil Rights and RICO: Stopping Operation Rescue." *Harvard Women's Law Journal* 13 (1990): 251–277.

Herbst, Daniel Z. "Injunctive Relief and Civil RICO: After *Scheidler v. National Organization for Women, Inc.,* RICO's Scope and Remedies Require Reevaluation." *Catholic University Law Review* 53 (2004): 1125–1160.

Higginbotham, H. Irene. "Pregnancy Discrimination in Unemployment Benefits: Section 3304(a)(12) Merely an Antidiscrimination Provision." *Stetson Law Review* 17 (1987): 219–247.

Hill, Catherine, and Elena Silva. *Drawing the Line: Sexual Harassment on Campus.* Washington, D.C.: American Association of University Women Educational Foundation, 2005, available at http://www.aauw.org/research/upload/DTLFinal.pdf.

Hochstetler, Jeffrey. "A Father's Presence: *Flores-Villar v. United States.*" *Duke Journal of Constitutional Law & Public Policy Sidebar* 6 (2011): 142–159.

Hodes, W. William. "Women and the Constitution: Some Legal History and a New Approach to the Nineteenth Amendment." *Rutgers Law Review* 25 (1970): 26–53; reprinted in Kermit L. Hall, ed., *Women, the Law, and the Constitution.* New York: Garland Publishing, 1987.

Howard, Joshua C. "'No Set of Circumstances' v. 'Large Fraction of Cases': Debate Resolved—*Gonzales v. Carhart,* 127 S. Ct. 1610 (2007)." *Nebraska Law Review* 87 (2009): 759–792.

Huckle, Patricia. "The Womb Factor: Policy on Pregnancy and the Employment of Women." In Ellen Boneparth and Emily Stoper, eds., *Women, Power, and Policy.* 2d ed. New York: Pergamon Press, 1988.

Hudson, David L., Jr. "Court Surprises with Family Leave Act Ruling." *American Bar Association Journal eReport* 2 (May 30, 2003): 21–22.

Institute for Women's Policy Research. "The Gender Wage Ratio: Women's and Men's Earnings (February 2008)," available at http://www.iwpr.org/pdf/c350.pdf.

Isbell, B. Tobias. "Gender Inequality and Wage Differentials Between the Sexes: Is It Inevitable or Is There an Answer?" *Washington University Journal of Urban and Contemporary Law* 50 (1996): 369–400.

Jacobson, Marjorie. "Pregnancy and Employment: Three Approaches to Equal Opportunity." *Boston University Law Review* 68 (1988): 1019–1045.

Jaffe, Frederick S., Barbara L. Lindheim, and Philip R. Lee. *Abortion Politics: Private Morality and Public Policy.* New York: McGraw-Hill, 1981.

Jensen, June E. "Title IX and Intercollegiate Athletics: HEW Gets Serious About Equality in Sports." *New England Law Review* 15 (1980): 573–596.

Johnston, John D., Jr., and Charles L. Knapp. "Sex Discrimination by Law: A Study in Judicial Perspective." *New York University Law Review* 46 (1971): 675–747.

Jones, Rachel K., Lawrence B. Finer, and Susheela Singh. "Characteristics of U.S. Abortion Patients, 2008." New York: Alan Guttmacher Institute, May 2010, available at http://www.guttmacher.org/pubs/US-Abortion-Patients.pdf.

Jost, Kenneth. "Single-Sex Education." *CQ Researcher Online* 12, no. 25 (July 12, 2002): 569–592.

Juliano, Ann C. "Did She Ask for It? The 'Unwelcome' Requirement in Sexual Harassment Cases." *Cornell Law Review* 77 (1992): 1558–1592.

Juliano, Ann C., and Stewart J. Schwab. "The Sweep of Sexual Harassment Cases." *Cornell Law Review* 86 (2001): 548–600.

Jurewitz, Ross A. "Playing at Even Strength: Reforming Title IX Enforcement in Intercollegiate Athletics." *American University Journal of Gender, Social Policy, and the Law* 8 (2000): 283–351.

Kandel, William L. "Current Developments in Employment Litigation." *Employee Relations Law Journal* 15 (1989): 101–113.

Kanowitz, Leo. "'Benign' Sex Discrimination: Its Troubles and Their Cure." *Hastings Law Journal* 31 (1980): 1379–1431.

Karin, Marcy. "Time Off for Military Families: An Emerging Case Study in a Time of War . . . and the Tipping Point for Future Laws Supporting Work-Life Balance?" *Rutgers Law Record* 33 (2009): 46–64.

Kay, Herma Hill. "Equality and Difference: The Case of Pregnancy." *Berkeley Women's Law Journal* 1 (1985): 1–38.

Kimball, Nina Joan. "Not Just Any 'Factor Other Than Sex': An Analysis of the Fourth Affirmative Defense of the Equal Pay Act." *George Washington Law Review* 52 (1984): 318–336.

Kiselewich, Rebecca A. "In Defense of the 2006 Title IX Regulations for Single-Sex Public Education: How Separate Can Be Equal." *Boston College Law Review* 49 (2008): 217–261.

Knapp, Alexis C. "Driving Them Away—the Employee Who Quits in Response to Harassment: The Supreme Court *Suders* Decision—Constructive Discharge and the Affirmative Defense: Reviewing History to Find a Predictable Continuation of Sexual Harassment Jurisprudence and Employer Liability Under Title VII." *Houston Business and Tax Law Journal* 6 (2006): 280–328.

Kohrs, Sarah Danielle. "What's *Ayotte* Left for *Casey*? The Newest Supreme Court Precedent in the Area of Abortion." *Georgetown Journal of Law and Public Policy* 5 (2007): 725–766.

Koontz, Elizabeth Duncan. "Childbirth and Childrearing Leave: Job-Related Benefits." *New York University Law Forum* 17 (1971): 480–502.

Kosaki, Liane, and Susan Gluck Mezey. "Judicial Intervention in the Family: Interspousal Immunity and Civil Litigation." *Women and Politics* 8 (1988): 69–85.

Kraditor, Aileen S. *The Ideas of the Woman Suffrage Movement, 1890–1920.* Garden City: Anchor, 1971.

Krieger, Linda J., and Patricia N. Cooney. "The *Miller-Wohl* Controversy: Equal Treatment, Positive Action, and the Meaning of Women's Equality." *Golden Gate University Law Review* 13 (1983): 513–572.

Kutner, Joan Ruth. "Sex Discrimination in Athletics." *Villanova Law Review* 21 (1976): 876–936.

Kyvig, David E. "Historical Misunderstandings and the Defeat of the Equal Rights Amendment." *Public Historian* 18 (1996): 45–63.

Labor Project for Working Families. *Know Your Rights: Family Leave Laws in California,* 2009, available at http://www.working-families.org/learnmore/ ca_family_leave_guide.pdf.

Lee, Kathryn A. "Intermediate Review 'with Teeth' in Gender Discrimination Cases: The New Standard in *United States v. Virginia.*" *Temple Political and Civil Rights Law Review* 7 (1997): 221–244.

Lee, S. J., H. J. Ralston, E. A. Drey, J. C. Partridge, and M. A. Rosen. "Fetal Pain: A Systematic Multidisciplinary Review of the Evidence." *Journal of the American Medical Association* 294 (2005): 947–954.

LeGrand, Lauren. "Proving Retaliation After *Burlington v. White.*" *Saint Louis University Law Journal* 52 (2008): 1221–1247.

Lens, Vicki. "Supreme Court Narratives on Equality and Gender Discrimination in Employment: 1971–2002." *Cardozo Women's Law Journal* 10 (2004): 501–567.

Levine, Kay L. "The Intimacy Discount: Prosecutorial Discretion, Privacy, and Equality in the Statutory Rape Caseload." *Emory Law Journal* 55 (2006): 691–748.

Libeson, Sandra J. "Reviving the Comparable Worth Debate in the United States: A Look Toward the European Community." *Comparative Labor Law Journal* 16 (1995): 358–398.

Lidge, Ernest F. "What Types of Employer Actions Are Cognizable Under Title VII? The Ramifications of *Burlington Northern & Santa Fe Railroad Co. v. White.*" *Rutgers Law Review* 59 (2007): 497–531.

Lies, Mark A., II. "Current Trends in Pregnancy Benefits—1972 EEOC Guidelines Interpreted." *DePaul Law Review* 24 (1974): 127–142.

Long, Alex B. "Viva State Employment Law! State Law Retaliation Claims in a Post–*Crawford/Burlington Northern* World." *Tennessee Law Review* 77 (2010): 253–298.

Loudon, Joseph P., and Timothy D. Loudon. "Applying Disparate Impact to Title VII Comparable Worth Claims: An Incomparable Task." *Indiana Law Journal* 61 (1986): 165–187.

Lough, John B., Jr. "Employers Still Cannot Retaliate: *Crawford v. Metropolitan Government of Nashville.*" *Hawaii Bar Journal* 13 (2009): 4–8.

Luker, Kristen. *Abortion and the Politics of Motherhood.* Berkeley: University of California Press, 1984.

Lye, Linda. "Title VII's Tangled Tale: The Erosion and Confusion of Disparate Impact and the Business Necessity Defense." *Berkeley Journal of Employment and Labor Law* 19 (1998): 315–361.

MacConaill, Gabriel R. "*Nevada Department of Human Resources v. Hibbs:* Does Application of Section 5 Represent a Fundamental Change in the Immunity

Abrogation Rules of 'New Federalism,' or Have the Burdens Simply Shifted?" *Penn State Law Review* 109 (2005): 831–855.

MacKinnon, Catharine A. *Sexual Harassment of Working Women.* New Haven: Yale University Press, 1979.

Mansbridge, Jane. *Why We Lost the ERA.* Chicago: University of Chicago Press, 1986.

Marilley, Suzanne M. *Woman Suffrage and the Origins of Liberal Feminism in the United States, 1820–1920.* Cambridge: Harvard University Press, 1996.

Marshall, Ray, and Beth Paulin. "Employment and Earnings of Women: Historical Perspective." In Karen Shallcross Koziara, Michael H. Moskow, and Lucretia Dewey Tanner, eds., *Working Women: Past, Present, Future.* Washington, D.C.: Bureau of National Affairs, 1987.

Maschke, Karen. *Litigation, Courts, and Women Workers.* New York: Praeger Publishers, 1989.

Matejkovic, John E., and Margaret E. Matejkovic. "If It Ain't Broke . . . Changes to FMLA Regulations Are Not Needed; Employee Compliance and Employer Enforcement of Current Regulations Are." *Willamette Law Review* 42 (2006): 413–438.

Mayer, Jane, and Jill Abramson. *Strange Justice: The Selling of Clarence Thomas.* Boston: Houghton Mifflin, 1994.

McCarthy, Martha. "Students as Targets and Perpetrators of Sexual Harassment: Title IX and Beyond." *Hastings Women's Law Journal* 12 (2001): 177–214.

McCullough, David. *John Adams.* New York: Simon and Schuster, 2001.

McGlen, Nancy E., Karen O'Connor, Laura Van Assendelft, and Wendy Gunther-Canada. *Women, Politics, and American Society.* 4th ed. New York: Pearson Longman Publishing, 2005.

Medlin, Nell J. "Expanding the Law of Sexual Harassment to Include Workplace Pornography: *Robinson v. Jacksonville Shipyards, Inc.*" *Stetson Law Review* 21 (1992): 655–680.

Metzger, Gillian E. "Facial and As-Applied Challenges Under the Roberts Court." *Fordham Urban Law Journal* 36 (2009): 773–801.

Mezey, Susan Gluck. "Gender Equality in Education: A Study of Policymaking by the Burger Court." *Wake Forest Law Review* 20 (1984): 793–817.

———. "Judicial Interpretation of Legislative Intent: The Role of the Supreme Court in the Implication of Private Rights of Action." *Rutgers Law Review* 36 (1983): 53–89.

———. "The Persistence of Sex-Segregated Education in the South." *Southeastern Political Review* 22 (1994): 371–395.

———. "The U.S. Supreme Court's Federalism Jurisprudence: *Alden v. Maine* and the Enhancement of State Sovereignty." *Publius: The Journal of Federalism* 30 (2000): 21–38.

Miller, Janella. "The Future of Private Women's Colleges." *Harvard Women's Law Journal* 7 (1984): 153–187.

Mirakian, Christopher. "*Gonzales v. Carhart:* A New Paradigm for Abortion Legislation." *University of Missouri Kansas City Law Review* 77 (2008): 197–225.

Mohr, James C. *Abortion in America.* Oxford: Oxford University Press, 1978.

Mota, Sue Ann, and Erin Elisabeth Waldman. "Employers Beware: Retaliation Prohibited by the Court in *Crawford v. Metropolitan Government of Nashville, CBOCS West, Inc. v. Humphries,* and *Gomez-Perez v. Potter.*" *Hamline Law Review* 33 (2010): 1–18.

Mowrey, Megan E. "Discriminatory Retaliation: Title VII Protection for the Cooperating Employee." *Pace Law Review* 29 (2009): 689–737.

Murr, Heather S. "The Continuing Expansive Pressure to Hold Employers Strictly Liable for Supervisory Sexual Extortion: An Alternative Approach Based on Reasonableness." *U.C. Davis Law Review* 39 (2006): 529–636.

Murray, P. J. "Employer: Beware of 'Hostile Environment' Sexual Harassment." *Duquesne Law Review* 26 (1987): 461–484.

National Committee on Pay Equity. *Pay Equity: An Issue of Race, Ethnicity and Sex.* Washington, D.C.: National Committee on Pay Equity, 1987.

National Partnership for Women and Families. "The Pregnancy Discrimination Act: Where We Stand 30 Years Later," October 2008, available at http://www .nationalpartnership.org/site/DocServer/Pregnancy_Discrimination_Act_ -_Where_We_Stand_30_Years_L.pdf?docID=4281.

National Women's Law Center. "Investigation by NWLC Finds $6.5 Million Athletic Scholarship Gap for Women at 30 Colleges and Universities." Washington, D.C.: National Women's Law Center, June 18, 2002.

Niehaus, Lindsay. "The Title IX Problem: Is It Sufficiently Comprehensive to Preclude § 1983 Actions?" *Quinnipiac Law Review* 27 (2009): 499–529.

Norman, Angela Benzo. "*Beal v. Doe, Maher v. Roe,* and Non-Therapeutic Abortions: The State Does Not Have to Pay the Bill." *Loyola University Law Journal* 9 (1977): 288–311.

Norrick, Crystal L. "Eliminating the Intent Requirement in Constructive Discharge Cases: *Pennsylvania State Police v. Suders.*" *William and Mary Law Review* 47 (2006): 1813–1839.

Norton, Eleanor Holmes. "Equal Employment Law: Crisis in Interpretation—Survival Against the Odds." *Tulane Law Review* 62 (1988): 681–715.

Note. "Abortion, Medicaid, and the Constitution." *New York University Law Review* 54 (1979): 120–160.

Note. "Sex Discrimination and Intercollegiate Athletics: Putting Some Muscle on Title IX." *Yale Law Journal* 88 (1979): 1254–1279.

O'Brien, Christine Neylon, and Gerald A. Madek. "Pregnancy Discrimination and Maternity Leave Laws." *Dickinson Law Review* 93 (1989): 311–337.

Olsen, Frances. "The Family and the Market: A Study of Ideology and Legal Reform." *Harvard Law Review* 96 (1983): 1497–1578.

Osterman, Rachel. "Origins of a Myth: Why Courts, Scholars, and the Public Think Title VII's Ban on Sex Discrimination Was an Accident." *Yale Journal of Law and Feminism* 20 (2009): 409–439.

Perry, Michael. "The Abortion Funding Cases: A Comment on the Supreme Court's Role in American Government." *Georgetown Law Journal* 66 (1978): 1191–1245.

Peterson, Heather A. "The Daddy Track: Locating the Male Employee Within the Family and Medical Leave Act." *Washington University Journal of Law and Policy* 15 (2004): 253–284.

Peterson, Nancy. "*Lieberman v. University of Chicago:* Refusal to Imply a Damages Remedy Under Title IX of the Education Amendments of 1972." *Wisconsin Law Review* (1983): 181–210.

Pine, Rachel. "Abortion Counseling and the First Amendment: Open Questions After *Webster.*" *American Journal of Law and Medicine* 15 (1989): 189–197.

Plumly, Natasha. "The United States Supreme Court Could Have Been Stuck Between a Rock and a Hard Place: *Ayotte v. Planned Parenthood of Northern New England.*" *Florida Coastal Law Review Special Supplement* 7 (2006): 72–80.

Porto, Brian L. "Halfway Home: An Update on Title IX and College Sports." *Vermont Bar Journal and Law Digest* 34 (2008): 28–34.

Rabin-Margalioth, Sharon. "The Market Defense." *University of Pennsylvania Journal of Business Law* 12 (2010): 807–847.

Raflo, Amanda. "Evolving Protection for Transgender Employees Under Title VII's Sex Discrimination Prohibition: A New Era Where Gender Is More Than Chromosomes." *Charlotte Law Review* 2 (2010): 217–250.

Ray, Rebecca. *A Detailed Look at Parental Leave Policies in 21 OECD Countries.* Washington, D.C.: Center for Economic and Policy Research, September 2008, available at http://www.cepr.net/documents/publications/parental-app_2008_09.pdf.

Ray, Rebecca, Janet C. Gornick, and John Schmitt. *Parental Leave Policies in 21 Countries: Assessing Generosity and Gender Equality.* Washington, D.C.: Center for Economic and Policy Research, September 2008, revised June 2009, available at http://www.cepr.net/documents/publications/parental_2008 _09.pdf.

Reagan, Leslie J. "Rashes, Rights, and Wrongs in the Hospital and in the Courtroom: German Measles, Abortion, and Malpractice Before *Roe* and *Doe*." *University of Illinois Law and History Review* 27 (2009): 241–284.

Reid, Glenda E., Brenda T. Acken, and Elise G. Jancura. "An Historical Perspective on Women in Accounting." *Journal of Accountancy* 163 (1987): 338–355.

Reidinger, Paul. "Will *Roe v. Wade* Be Overruled?" *American Bar Association Journal* (July 1988): 66–70.

Reuscher, Christopher Paul. "Giving the Bat Back to Casey: Suggestions to Reform Title IX's Inequitable Application to Intercollegiate Athletics." *Akron Law Review* 35 (2001): 117–158.

Rhoden, Nancy K. "Trimesters and Technology: Revamping *Roe v. Wade*." *Yale Law Journal* 95 (1986): 639–697.

Rhoodie, Eschel M. *Discrimination Against Women: A Global Survey.* Jefferson, N.C.: McFarland, 1989.

Richardson, L. Anita. "Parsing *Roe v. Wade:* Will the Court Reaffirm the Right to Choose but Make It Easier for States to Regulate?" *American Bar Association Preview of United States Supreme Court Cases,* May 15, 1992.

Roberts, Barry S., and Richard A. Mann. "Sexual Harassment in the Workplace: A Primer." *Akron Law Review* 29 (1996): 269–289.

Robinson, Donald. "Two Movements in Pursuit of Equal Employment Opportunity." *Signs* 4 (1979): 413–433.

Rodman, Hyman, Betty Sarvis, and Joy Walker Bonar. *The Abortion Question.* New York: Columbia University Press, 1987.

Rubin, Eva. *Abortion, Politics, and the Courts.* Westport, Conn.: Greenwood Press, 1987.

Rutherglen, George. "Disparate Impact Under Title VII: An Objective Theory of Discrimination." *Virginia Law Review* 73 (1987): 1297–1345.

———. "The Gender Gap in Compensation: The Theory of Comparable Worth as a Remedy for Discrimination." *Georgetown Law Journal* 82 (1993): 135–146.

Sachs, Albie, and Joan Hoff Wilson. *Sexism and the Law.* New York: Free Press, 1978.

Safar, Nicole. "The Seventh Circuit's Step Toward Ending Domestic Terror: A Case Note on *NOW v. Scheidler*." *Wisconsin Women's Law Journal* 17 (2002): 371–387.

Safier, Kristen. "A Request for Congressional Action: Deconstructing the Supreme Court's (In)Activism in *Gebser v. Lago Vista Independent School District,* 118

S.Ct. 1989 (1988), and *Davis v. Monroe County Board of Education*, 119 S.Ct. 1661 (1991)." *University of Cincinnati Law Review* 68 (2000): 1309–1329.

Salomone, Rosemary. *Equal Education Under Law*. New York: St. Martin's Press, 1986.

———. "*North Haven* and *Dougherty:* Narrowing the Scope of Title IX." *Journal of Law and Education* 10 (1981): 191–206.

———. "Title IX and Employment Discrimination: A Wrong in Search of a Remedy." *Journal of Law and Education* 9 (1980): 433–447.

Samuels, Suzanne Uttaro. *Fetal Rights, Women's Rights: Gender Equality in the Workplace*. Madison: University of Wisconsin Press, 1995.

Samuelson, Joan I. "Employment Rights of Women in the Toxic Workplace." *California Law Review* 65 (1977): 1113–1142.

Sandler, Bernice Resnick. "Title IX: How We Got It and What a Difference It Made." *Cleveland State Law Review* 55 (2007): 473–489.

Sanger, Carol. "Seeing and Believing: Mandatory Ultrasound and the Path to a Protected Choice." *UCLA Law Review* 56 (2008): 351–408.

Satinoff, Debra L. "Sex-Based Discrimination in U.S. Immigration Law: The High Court's Lost Opportunity to Bridge the Gap Between What We Say and What We Do." *American University Law Review* 47 (1998): 1353–1392.

Savage, David. "Look the Other Way and Pay." *American Bar Association Journal* (July 1999): 34.

Scales, Ann. "Student Gladiators and Sexual Assault: A New Analysis of Liability for Injuries Inflicted by College Athletes." *Michigan Journal of Gender and Law* 15 (2009): 205–289.

———. "Towards a Feminist Jurisprudence." *Indiana Law Journal* 56 (1980–1981): 375–444.

Schneider, Elizabeth M. "A Postscript on *VMI*." *American University Journal of Gender and the Law* 6 (1997): 59–64.

Schwin, Kevin. "Toward a Plain Meaning Approach to Analyzing Title VII: Employment Discrimination Protection of Transsexuals." *Cleveland State Law Review* 57 (2009): 645–670.

Shimabukuro, Jon O. "Abortion and the House- and Senate-Passed Health Reform Measures." *Congressional Research Service*, January 15, 2010.

Shiu, Patricia A., and Stephanie M. Wildman. "Pregnancy Discrimination and Social Change: Evolving Consciousness About a Worker's Right to Job-Protected, Paid Leave." *Yale Journal of Law and Feminism* 21 (2009): 119–159.

Silbaugh, Katharine B. "*Miller v. Albright:* Problems of Constitutionalization in Family Law." *Boston University Law Review* 79 (1999): 1139–1160.

Slagle, Allison K. "*Nevada Department of Human Resources v. Hibbs:* Regulation or Simply Encouragement?" *Capital University Law Review* 33 (2005): 869–895.

Speiser, Tina L. "The Future of Comparable Worth: Looking in New Directions." *Syracuse Law Review* 37 (1987): 1189–1218.

Sponseller, Carrie Urrutia. "Peer Sexual Harassment in Light of *Davis v. Monroe County Board of Education:* A Successful Balance or Tipping the Scales?" *University of Toledo Law Review* 32 (2001): 271–291.

Stiehm, Judith Hicks. *Arms and the Enlisted Woman*. Philadelphia: Temple University Press, 1989.

Strum, Philippa. *Women in the Barracks: The VMI Case and Equal Rights.* Lawrence: University of Kansas Press, 2002.

Sullivan, Georgia M. "Protection of Constitutional Guarantees Under 42 U.S.C. Section 1985(3): Operation Rescue's 'Summer of Mercy.'" *Washington and Lee Law Review* 49 (1992): 237–262.

Taub, Nadine, and Elizabeth M. Schneider. "Perspectives on Women's Subordination and the Role of Law." In David Kairys, ed., *The Politics of Law: A Progressive Critique.* New York: Pantheon, 1982.

Thomas, Lindsay Conway. "*Burlington Northern & Santa Fe Railroad Co. v. White:* Getting on the Right Track." *Mississippi College Law Review* 27 (2007–2008): 477–500.

Thornton, Sherri. "Title VII: The Equalization of Spousal Benefits in View of the Pregnancy Discrimination Act of 1978 *Newport News Shipbuilding and Dry Dock Co. v. Equal Employment Opportunity Commission.*" *Howard Law Journal* 27 (1984): 653–680.

Tobin, Harper Jean. "Confronting Misinformation on Abortion: Informed Consent, Deference, and Fetal Pain Laws." *Columbia Journal of Gender and Law* 17 (2008): 111–152.

Tolchin, Susan. "The Impact of the Hyde Amendment on Congress: Effects of Single Issue Politics on Legislative Dysfunction, June 1977–June 1978." *Women and Politics* 5 (1985): 91–106.

Treiman, Donald, and Heidi Hartmann, eds. *Women, Work, and Wages: Equal Pay for Jobs of Equal Value.* Washington, D.C.: National Academy Press, 1981.

Tribe, Laurence. *Clash of Absolutes.* New York: Norton, 1992.

Tussman, Joseph, and Jacobus tenBroek. "The Equal Protection of the Laws." *California Law Review* 37 (1949): 341–381.

Twing, Shawn D., and Timothy C. Williams. "Title VII's Transgender Trajectory: An Analysis of Whether Transgender People Are a Protected Class Under the Term 'Sex' and Practical Implications of Inclusion." *Texas Journal on Civil Liberties and Civil Rights* 15 (2010): 173–203.

Twomey, Rosemarie Feuerbach, and Gwen E. Jones. "The Family and Medical Leave Act of 1993: A Longitudinal Study of Male and Female Perceptions." *Employee Rights and Employment Policy Journal* 3 (1999): 229–250.

Underwood, Montre. "*Gebser v. Lago Vista Independent School District:* The Supreme Court Adopts Actual Knowledge Standard as Basis for School District's Liability Under Title IX." *Tulane Law Review* 73 (1999): 2181–2193.

U.S. Bureau of the Census. "Historical Income Tables—People, Table P-40: Women's Earnings as a Percentage of Men's Earnings by Race and Hispanic Origin: 1960 to 2008," available at http://www.census.gov/hhes/www/income/data/historical/people/p40.xls.

U.S. Department of Education, *Open to All: Title IX at Thirty,* available at http://www.ed.gov/about/bdscomm/list/athletics/report.html.

U.S. Department of Education, Office for Civil Rights. "Clarification of Intercollegiate Athletic Policy Guidance: The Three-Part Test." January 16, 1996, available at http://www2.ed.gov/about/offices/list/ocr/docs/clarific.html#two.

U.S. Department of Labor, Bureau of Labor Statistics. "Highlights of Women's Earnings in 2009," available at http://www.bls.gov/cps/cpswom2009.pdf.

———. "Labor Force Participation of Women by Presence and Age of Youngest Child, March 1975–2008," available at http://www.bls.gov/opub/ted/2009/ted_20091009_data.htm#b.

————. "Labor Force Participation Rates Among Mothers by Age of Youngest Child, March 1975–March 2008," available at http://www.bls.gov/opub/ted/2010/ted_20100507.htm.

————. "Table 1: Median Usual Weekly Earnings of Full-Time Wage and Salary Workers, by Selected Characteristics, 2009 Annual Averages," available at http://www.bls.gov/cps/cpswom2009.pdf.

————. "Table 2: Employment Status of the Civilian Noninstitutional Population 16 Years and over by Sex, 1973 to Date," available at http://www.bls.gov/cps/cpswom2009.pdf.

————. "Table 3: Median Usual Weekly Earnings of Full-Time Wage and Salary Workers, by State and Sex, 2009 Annual Averages," available at http://www.bls.gov/cps/cpswom2009.pdf.

————. "Table 4: Families with Own Children: Employment Status of Parents by Age of Youngest Child and Family Type, 2008–09 Annual Averages," available at http://www.bls.gov/news.release/pdf/famee.pdf.

————. "Table 9: Percent Distribution of the Civilian Labor Force 25 to 64 Years of Age by Educational Attainment and Sex, 1970–2007 Annual Averages," available at http://www.bls.gov/cps/wlftable9-2008.pdf.

————. "Table 11: Employed Persons by Detailed Occupation, Sex, Race, and Hispanic or Latino Ethnicity," available at http://www.bls.gov/cps/cpsaat11.pdf.

————. "Table 12: Median Usual Weekly Earnings of Full-Time Wage and Salary Workers, in Current Dollars, by Sex and Age, 1979–2009 Annual Averages," available at http://www.bls.gov/cps/cpswom2009.pdf.

————. "Table 16: Median Usual Weekly Earnings of Full-Time Wage and Salary Workers, 25 Years and Older, in Current Dollars, by Sex and Educational Attainment, 1979–2009 Annual Averages," available at http://www.bls.gov/cps/cpswom2009.pdf.

————. "Women Still Underrepresented Among Highest Earners." March 2006, available at http://www.bls.gov/opub/ils/pdf/opbils55.pdf.

U.S. Department of Labor, Women's Bureau. "Nontraditional Occupations for Women in 2009." April 2010, available at http://www.dol.gov/wb/factsheets/nontra2009.htm.

————. "Quick Stats on Women Workers, 2009," available at http://www.dol.gov/wb/stats/main.htm.

————. "20 Leading Occupations of Employed Women, 2009 Annual Averages," available at http://www.dol.gov/wb/factsheets/20lead2009.htm.

U.S. Equal Employment Opportunity Commission. "Celebrating the 40th Anniversary of Title VII," available at http://www.eeoc.gov/eeoc/history/40th/panel/expanding.html.

————. "Charge Statistics FY 1997 Through FY 2009," available at http://www1.eeoc.gov//eeoc/statistics/enforcement/charges.cfm?.

————. "Early Enforcement Efforts," available at http://www.eeoc.gov/eeoc/history/35th/1965-71/early_enforcement.html.

————. "EEOC Issues Comprehensive Policy Guidance on Employer Liability for Harassment by Supervisors," available at http://www.eeoc.gov/eeoc/newsroom/release/archive/6-21-99.html.

————. "EEOC Updates Guidelines to Comply with Supreme Court Rulings on Employer Liability for Harassment by Supervisors," available at http://www.eeoc.gov/eeoc/newsroom/release/10-29-99.cfm.

———. "Employer Best Practices for Workers with Caregiving Responsibilities." 2009, available at http://www.eeoc.gov/policy/docs/caregiver-best-practices.html.

———. "Enforcement Guidance: Unlawful Disparate Treatment of Workers with Caregiving Responsibilities." 2007, available at http://www.eeoc.gov//policy/docs/caregiving.html.

———. "1965–1971: A Toothless Tiger Helps Shape the Law and Educate the Public," available at http://www.eeoc.gov/eeoc/history/35th/1965-71/index.html.

———. "Pregnancy Discrimination Charges EEOC and FEPAs Combined: FY 1997–FY 2009," available at http://www.eeoc.gov/eeoc/statistics/enforcement/pregnancy.cfm.

———. "Sex-Based Charges FY 1997–FY 2009," available at http://www1.eeoc.gov//eeoc/statistics/enforcement/sex.cfm?.

———. "Sexual Harassment Charges EEOC and FEPAs Combined: FY 1997–FY 2009," available at http://www.eeoc.gov//eeoc/statistics/enforcement/sexual_harassment.cfm?.

———. "Shaping Employment Discrimination Law," available at http://www.eeoc.gov/eeoc/history/35th/1965-71/shaping.html.

U.S. House of Representatives. "Federal Employees Parental Leave Act of 2009." Report accompanying H.R. 626, H. Rep. No. 111-116, Part I, 111th Cong., 1st. sess., May 18, 2009.

U.S. Merit Systems Protection Board. "Sexual Harassment in the Federal Workplace," available at http://www.mspb.gov/netsearch/viewdocs.aspx?docnumber=253661&version=253948&application=ACROBAT.

Vaas, Francis J. "Title VII: Legislative History." *Boston College Industrial and Commercial Law Review* 7 (1966): 431–458.

Vermuelen, Joan. "Sexual Harassment." In Carol Lefcourt, ed., *Women and the Law*. New York: Clark Boardman, 1987.

Weber, Julie. "Policy Briefing Series, Work-Family Information for State Legislators." Sloan Work and Family Research Network, 2009, available at http://wfnetwork.bc.edu/pdfs/policy_makers17.pdf.

Weisel, Kerri. "Title VII: Legal Protection Against Sexual Harassment." *Washington Law Review* 53 (1977): 123–144.

West, Clay M. "*Nguyen v. INS:* Is Sex Really More Important Now?" *Yale Law and Policy Review* 19 (2001): 525–537.

Whalen, Charles, and Barbara Whalen. *The Longest Debate: A Legislative History of the 1964 Civil Rights Act.* New York: Mentor Books, 1985.

Wharton, Linda J. "State Equal Rights Amendments Revisited: Evaluating Their Effectiveness in Advancing Protection Against Sex Discrimination." *Rutgers Law Journal* 36 (2005): 1201–1293.

Whitley, L. Tracee. "'Any Other Factor Other Than Sex': Forbidden Market Defenses and the Subversion of the Equal Pay Act of 1963." *Northeastern University Forum* 2 (1997): 51–81.

Wilcox, Clyde. "Why Was 1992 the 'Year of the Woman'? Explaining Women's Gains in 1992." In C. Wilcox, S. Thomas, and E. Cook, eds., *The Year of the Woman: Myth or Reality.* Boulder, Colo.: Westview Press, 1994.

Wildman, Stephanie M. "The Legitimation of Sex Discrimination: A Critical Response to Supreme Court Jurisprudence." *Oregon Law Review* 63 (1984) 278–279.

Williams, Joan C., and Nancy Segal. "Beyond the Maternal Wall: Relief for Family Caregivers Who Are Discriminated Against on the Job." *Harvard Women's Law Journal* 26 (2003): 77–162.

Williams, Wendy. "The Equality Crisis: Some Reflections on Culture, Courts, and Feminism." *Women's Rights Law Reporter* 7 (1982): 175–200.

———. "Equality's Riddle: Pregnancy and the Equal Treatment/Special Treatment Debate." *New York University Review of Law and Social Change* 13 (1984–1985): 325–380.

Wilson, Joan Hoff. "The Legal Status of Women in the Late Nineteenth and Early Twentieth Centuries." *Human Rights* 6 (1977): 125–134; reprinted in Kermit L. Hall, ed., *Women, the Law, and the Constitution*. New York: Garland Publishing, 1987.

Wolf-Devine, Celia. *Diversity and Community in the Academy: Affirmative Action in Faculty Appointments*. Lanham, Md.: Rowman and Littlefield, 1977.

Woliver, Katherine B. "Title IX and the 'E-mail Survey' Exception: Missing the Goal." *Southern California Interdisciplinary Law Journal* 18 (2009): 463–483.

Wright, Susan. "*Franklin v. Gwinnett County Public Schools:* The Supreme Court Implies a Damage Remedy for Title IX Sex Discrimination." *Vanderbilt Law Review* 45 (1992): 1367–1386.

Yonover, Geri. "Fighting Fire with Fire: Civil RICO and Anti-Abortion Activists." *Women's Rights Law Reporter* 12 (1990): 153–175.

Zimmerman, Diane L. "*Geduldig v. Aiello:* Pregnancy Classifications and the Definition of Sex Discrimination." *Columbia Law Review* 75 (1975): 441–482.

Index of Cases

Index

About the Book

Elusive Equality explores how government institutions—the executive branch, the federal courts, Congress, and state legislatures—affect the legal status of women.

In this fully revised and updated edition, Susan Gluck Mezey traces the evolving legal parameters of gender equality from early court rulings through the most recent legislation and judicial decisions. She also examines the broader political context within which critical judicial decisions have been made. Giving thorough attention to issues ranging from education, work, and family to sports, sexual harassment, and reproductive rights, she provides a comprehensive analysis of the relationships among women's rights, public policy, and the law.

Susan Gluck Mezey is professor of political science at Loyola University Chicago. Her publications include *Gay Families and the Courts: The Quest for Equal Rights* and *Disabling Interpretations: Judicial Implementation of the Americans with Disabilities Act.*